A Critical Handbook of Children's Literature

8th Edition

Rebecca J. Lukens
Professor Emerita, Miami University
Oxford, Ohio

PEARSON

Boston   New York   San Francisco
Mexico City   Montreal   Toronto   London   Madrid   Munich   Paris
Hong Kong   Singapore   Tokyo   Cape Town   Sydney

Executive Editor: Aurora Martínez Ramos
Series Editorial Assistant: Lynda Giles
Executive Marketing Manager: Krista Clark
Production Editor: Annette Joseph
Editorial Production Service: NK Graphics
Composition Buyer: Linda Cox
Manufacturing Buyer: Megan Cochran
Electronic Composition: NK Graphics
Cover Administrator: Linda Knowles
Cover Designer: Studio Nine

For related titles and support materials, visit our online catalog at
www.ablongman.com.

Between the time website information is gathered and then published, it is not
unusual for some sites to have closed. Also, the transcription of URLs can result
in typographical errors. The publisher would appreciate notification where these
errors occur so that they may be corrected in subsequent editions.

Library of Congress Cataloging-in-Publication Data
Lukens, Rebecca J.
  A critical handbook of children's literature/Rebecca J. Lukens.—8th ed.
    p. cm.
 Includes bibliographical references and index.
 ISBN 0-205-49218-5
 1.Children's literature—History and criticism. 2. Children—Books and reading.
I. Title.
  PN1009.A1L84 2007
  809'.89282—dc22

                                                                2006040700

Printed in the United States of America
10 9 8 7 6 5 4 3 2 1   RRD-VA 11 10 09 08 07 06

*For my children
and theirs.*

Contents

To the Instructor

A Critical Handbook of Children's Literature, now in its eighth edition, has grown out of my conviction that literature for children differs from literature for adults in degree, not in kind, and that writing for children should be judged by the same standards as writing for adults. Children, like adults, read to explore the world, to escape the confining present, to discover themselves, to become someone else. Since adults—in the roles of teachers, librarians, or parents—help children choose books, we hope to put into their hands the best literature for these purposes.

What Is *A Critical Handbook of Children's Literature* Designed to Do?

The *Critical Handbook* is directed toward the college classroom audience of mature students who expect to work with children—whether as parents, librarians, or teachers—but it does not stand alone as a classroom text. Like other handbooks, it accompanies another project, in this case the reading of a great many children's books. Only by reading thoughtfully a variety of stories, poems, biographies, and informational books for children does a student become acquainted with children's literature. And by applying critical criteria to these works, the student learns to evaluate them.

Loving children—important, surely—is not enough to make one an effective teacher of children. Being steeped in the literature written for them, however, reminds us of their natures and their concerns, and helps us to direct them toward pleasurable literary experiences, even to make of them lifetime readers. Setting standards for literature addressed to children and applying these standards to each selection sharpens students' critical skills at the same time as it familiarizes them with the current range of children's books.

What Does the Handbook *Not* Do?

This is not a teaching methods book, and it absolutely does *not* recommend this way of "teaching books" to children. It may, however, suggest ways to talk with them about literature.

The *Handbook* does not provide book lists, although recommended titles, not definitive lists, are cited at the ends of chapters. The thoughtful student reads some of these, along with others not listed, determines their quality, and may or may not recommend titles to classmates.

The *Handbook* does not classify books as targeted toward specific age groups, because all of us know the infinite variety of interests and reading capabilities of children.

The *Handbook* does not discuss the developmental patterns of the average child.

And the *Handbook* does not attempt to become an extensive anthology (of poetry, for example), but rather, once again, sets up criteria for readers to judge imaginative poetry and prose, biography, and informational books.

Reading the Classics of Children's Literature

One sure way for you, as an instructor in children's literature, to encourage argument is to tell an adult acquaintance that you teach children's literature, only to hear, "The classics, I hope!" Thinking you have found someone interested in your field, you go on to say something like: "Well . . . yes, but sometimes books once called 'classics' don't interest today's children. Not all the books I was told were must-read classics interested me. How about you?" If the reply is honest, it may be, "Well-l-l, no-o-o-o," and conversation may continue, but it often stops at dead silence, or becomes an unwinnable argument.

As Peter Hunt says so well in his article "Passing on the Past: The Problem of Books That Are for Children and That Were for Children" (*Children's Literature Quarterly*, Winter 1996–1997), some books *were* for children, and some of them *still are* for children. Yet many of the books we read, books by authors our parents did not know, spoke to us, and if they also speak to a later generation, our own children, they are on the way to becoming new classics. Using as examples the fairy tales, the Little House books, and *The Secret Garden*, Hunt notes that a number of onetime classics have been successfully dramatized, but only by making many significant changes in them, moving the story from one art to another, from book to film. Such changes were essential not only to make the new art form, but also to make them appeal to today's children whose lives and expectations are so different from those of past generations. Books that speak to children now are many and varied; some will become classics.

Focusing on History and Critical Theory

Hunt's article contains several additional insights. He suggests, for example, that "in order to survive academically, 'Children's Literature' . . . has played the adult [literature] game, valuing history above the new challenges of literary interaction." Hunt's statement seems valid. College instructors understandably may become engrossed in the goals of academic acceptance, tenure, and promotion. Where pressure is strong for research and publication, instructors may feel that acceptance by their colleagues is possible only through historical or more "scholarly" approaches, or projects in contemporary critical theories. As each new critical theory becomes popular, the understandable pursuit of salary dollars and collegial acceptance prompts instructors to move away from their primary focus: teaching potential teachers, librarians, and parents to make sound critical judgments about books, and to know and love the literature, old and new, that at this time speaks to children in their classrooms or their homes.

Consider, however, a responsibility to two audiences other than colleagues: college students who are teachers-in-training, and the children *they* will teach. We are teaching college students "Children's Literature" so that they may teach or recommend the best of that literature to children. In the college classroom we help potential teachers learn what makes a children's book good—good enough to read aloud to children in their classrooms, to spend classroom and library dollars on, to encourage reluctant readers to read, and to enlarge children's worlds so they will understand themselves and others.

The study of literary history and critical theory as they apply to literature for both adults and children belongs in a college classroom, to be sure. But that classroom syllabus is for an audience different from students who have a single classroom experience of children's literature and plan to work with children. The critical approach used in this text—which to some instructors may seem far too simple and intellectually undemanding—is the most basic one of all: formalist criticism, the study of the form literature takes. Furthermore, the text incorporates the techniques of the New Critic, who, in carefully examining literature, believes in its intrinsic worth. This approach, too, seems highly relevant. And, finally, reader-response theory, with its focus on the implied reader, is relevant here. Although all adults were once children, their responses may be so changed by the years that reading "like a child" is difficult, if not impossible. Observant adults, however, try out books with children and evoke their responses.

Other critical approaches are many. Applying psychological, mythological, and archetypal perspectives, or phenomenological, socialist-Marxist, feminist criticism, and structuralist approaches are interesting exercises relevant to the study of literary criticism as applied to all literature. But if we care about the audience that librarians and teachers-in-training will face in their careers—including nonreading children—then examining children's stories under these critical approaches is less relevant. These future teachers need to know how to judge a book for children as they keep in mind the responses of their young classroom charges. Including reader-response theory in our critical examination of children's literature seems the most relevant critical method.

Thinking "Multiculturally"

North America, particularly the United States, nowadays is less frequently called "a melting pot." Perhaps that term was inaccurate even in the late nineteenth and early twentieth centuries, because often immigrant groups did not melt into a great "pot of soup." As each immigrant group arrived, it frequently settled into its own geographic area, urban or rural, and then divided into those who wanted to be assimilated—advocates of a great "soup" of Americans—and a smaller number who wished to maintain their ethnicity through their language, folklore, religious services, and ethnic traditions. Maintenance of group identity has led to what has more recently been called the creation, not of a soup, but of a "salad" of ethnic groups. The recent focus on multiculturalism seems to be part of that "salad" idea. Children of newly arriving immigrants are caught in the ambiguity of their new North American identities. Maintaining the traditions of their origins is important for them and their parents, and reading literature about their origins is thus helpful. At the same time, children whose forebears have long been assimilated may be curious and wish to know about the traditions and beliefs of their new friends and classmates. New immigrants and those born here have two things in common: their respect for democratic institutions and their common language. Reading about other cultures broadens that common ground. With that in mind, the *Critical Handbook* in its eighth edition includes additional multicultural examples of literature for children.

Since we are in the midst of great societal change—perhaps moving toward a true melting-pot continent—it seems wise that young readers know something of the cultural origins of our many ethnic groups.

The Eighth Edition

It is tempting in this eighth edition of the *Handbook* to add a chapter on reading aloud, and for this reason, I have included the following section To the Student. But in the interest of keeping the book somewhat close to handbook size (it grows longer with each new edition), consider the many books and journal articles on reading aloud. For example, some years ago Jim Trelease fostered belief in the importance of reading aloud with his *Read Aloud Handbook. Children's Literature in the Classroom: Weaving Charlotte's Web*, edited by Janet Hickman and Bernice A. Cullinan, includes an article called "'Please Don't Stop There!': The Power of Reading Aloud." Barbara Friedberg and Elizabeth Strong present strong arguments for the cause, as do others.

This edition retains the form of the seventh edition, but includes many new titles; again the chapter on picture books comes early in the text. The chapter on major literary genres delineates the common elements of literature and demonstrates how each genre may emphasize or rely on one element more than others. Main points are provided in a chart to help readers more easily spot possible shortcomings of a story and point out particularly significant elements. Some readers may find the chart useful; others may find it too simplistic, a common problem when one tries to quantify or make an abstraction concrete. Use the chart with caution.

Other chapters focus on the elements common to all imaginative literature—character, plot, theme, setting, point of view, style, and tone. These terms are explained simply and clearly and are illustrated with new or lasting examples from all genres of children's literature. Although these terms are the critical tools and basic vocabulary we use to discuss and evaluate any piece of imaginative literature, writing for children presents some special concerns and problems; chapters that discuss an element of imaginary narrative literature conclude with a discussion of such matters.

The chapters on biography and informational books contain updated examples, but do not deal with periodicals or reference materials. As for reading levels, they are available in the reviewing media. Furthermore, no substitute exists for an awareness of individual differences in the interests and capabilities of children. As any "kidwatcher" knows, children are different at different ages, and their consuming interests one month may be succeeded by new fascinations in the next. The bored child considered uneducable by a third-grade teacher may be hiding *The Perfect Storm* behind a spelling book. And tales of illiterate high school graduates continue to surface.

The glossary, of course, defines literary terms. The updated appendices include lists of award-winning titles, children's magazines, and publications that review children's literature, as well as an appendix suggesting useful websites. You may wish to assign the following section, "To the Student," as an introduction to the course and to this textbook.

Finally, during the planning stages of this eighth edition, I have been grateful for numerous comments and suggestions offered by instructors who have used earlier editions. Some have suggested the addition of new chapters, while others have hoped the book would not become forbiddingly long or turn into a teaching methods text. Some have suggested changing and rearranging genre descriptions, while others have hoped that they would stay as they were. Unfortunately but obviously, not all such suggestions can be followed. Including more current titles as examples is important; however, keeping abreast of the very newest is not always possible when a manuscript is due many months before the book is available to instructors. It seems inevitable that changes will please some readers and disappoint others. I can only hope that I have reached a suitable compromise.

One further note: Instructors might wish to assign the reading of *Charlotte's Web* early in the term, perhaps even before assigning Chapter 4 where it first takes on its role as a touchstone book. Other books frequently mentioned throughout the text as examples might be assigned at appropriate times.

Each time I prepare a new edition of the *Handbook,* I immerse myself in literature for children and am thrilled and astonished to find that it gets better and better. When I first began working on the *Critical Handbook* thirty years ago, my search for the truly fine was far less rewarding. Now, because this handbook simply cannot mention all of the many works that have satisfied the criteria for excellence, I must confine myself to mentioning just a few of the multitude, and can only hope that those I have selected are representative of the best. Readers must add their own titles.

To the Student

A Critical Handbook of Children's Literature is committed to the idea expressed by the children's poet Walter de la Mare: "Nothing but the best in anything is good enough for the young." Within that guideline, learning to make critical judgments about what constitutes "the best" that is "good enough" is everything. Of the many ways to examine and judge literature, readers' responses to its forms and effects seem the most sensible, simple as it is. Throughout the book, the forms of literature and the elements called character, plot, theme, setting, point of view, style, and tone are explained and exemplified; criteria for judging fiction, poetry, biography, and informational books for child readers and listeners are suggested.

The *Handbook* responds to the recent emphasis placed on using children's literature in virtually all areas of the curriculum. This emphasis responds to the "whole language" philosophy, which Ken Goodman describes as freeing "the minds and creative energies of pupils for the greatest gains in their intellectual, physical and social development." Building on John Dewey's age-old reminder that we start "where the learner is in time, place, culture, and development," the philosophy suggests that once children are exposed to reading, the decoding process has more meaning for them if they find *what* they read to be attractive.

Louise Rosenblatt, a pioneer in insisting that the best literature should be the substance of reading, believes that reading is a transaction and that the aesthetic—thinking, feeling, and experiencing—of reading literature must be recognized. My own terms for this transaction or aesthetic experience can best be described as the experiences of pleasure and understanding. Thus, Rosenblatt and I agree. To this description of the reading experience, Rosenblatt adds another: "Efferent" refers to the acquisition of information through reading, a concept that reinforces my own thinking, particularly regarding nonfiction.

Despite our differing terms, we agree that reading takes readers where they are with what they have experienced, and thus agree that different readers have different transactions. For example, most students when reading

Charlotte's Web by E. B. White react pleasurably to the understanding gained about emotions, thoughts, and behavior. Other students—perhaps only a single student—might limit an interpretation of the same story to elucidation of what a general farm is like, even noting the science lesson in how the different parts of a spider's jointed leg enable it to spin a web. In Rosenblatt's terms, the group stresses the private aesthetic experience of understanding, while the single student focuses on the public element, the efferent or informative one. Whatever our terms, I am delighted that elementary teachers are giving children greater pleasure than ever by encouraging them to read literature that involves and pleases them.

But how can we choose "the rarest kind of best" (to quote Walter de la Mare) from the thousands of children's books published each year, as well as from the thousands that remain in print year after year? What are the standards we can confidently apply in evaluating writing for children? We may have felt amused and touched when we read *Charlotte's Web,* but how do we discuss it or decide its literary worth beyond these vague feelings?

Why learn to make critical judgments? Because, although the techniques of judgment may in themselves be ordinary, an increased awareness of them is valuable training. When we say a hearty "I like it!" we may be responding to believable and interesting characters or to something we know is true about people. When we are disappointed in a book—"I don't like it!"—we may be rejecting the story's action as too coincidental or its dialogue as too stilted. Learning to recognize such literary elements as character and plot and theme helps us understand the effects a writer achieves and appreciate the reasons for his or her choices. After all, Peter Rabbit in the Beatrix Potter tale and Rabbit in *Winnie-the-Pooh* are not the same, nor does the setting for *Alice in Wonderland* have the same effect on us as the setting for *Julie of the Wolves.* We could say fairly easily *how* they are different, but we need to go beyond that and say why they *must* be different. Why did the authors make the choices they made, and what are the effects of those choices on us as readers?

This knowledge helps us discover the reasons for our emotional responses. It sharpens our perceptions and increases our enjoyment of reading. To use a familiar analogy, do we go to the football game merely to find out who won, or also to enjoy the plays and ploys that determine the winning score? In the same way, do we read only to find out how the story comes out, or do we also take delight in the people, in the shifts and turns of events along the way, in the words that tingle our spines or quicken our pulses, and in discovering something about ourselves?

An older student in my children's literature class once proudly told me that her eight-year-old son was in a "high achiever" class and that he was now reading *Moby-Dick.* It seemed to me that both she and that classroom teacher were failing to make a distinction between the capacity to decode, sound out, or recognize words and the capacity to understand and take into oneself the significant ideas being "read." *Moby-Dick,* a classic, was never for children, but that able eight-year-old, when introduced to books that speak to today's children, might profit in ways other than having his accomplishments become honor badges for his mother. Rather than merely the pleasure of decoding, the first profit might even be newfound pleasure in ideas, and in characters who are his contemporaries. Once again, it's a matter of audience. Just as good books of the past, written for children *then,* may say nothing to children *now,* so adult classics may say nothing to children, "readable" though they may be.

Examining Literature Carefully

Why not just read books for children and skip the evaluative process? Because without criteria for excellence, instructors merely turn students who are training to be teachers loose in the library or bookstore to learn very little beyond "what's out there."

And why the frequent references to *The Tale of Peter Rabbit* and *Charlotte's Web*? Because it is easier to speak about criteria if all students in the classroom have in common at least two books they have read.

Failing to apply critical standards to children's literature implies that children's literature is inferior to adult literature and that children will not benefit from good literature. But if literature of poor or mediocre quality is all children meet, they may be persuaded that reading is both boring and useless. This handbook takes another view: With some small differences, literature for children should be judged by the same standards as literature for adults. Children can benefit by becoming lifetime readers when their earliest exposure is to literature of high quality.

Occasionally an instructor whose field is literature or the arts is told that "picking the work apart" destroys both the work and the audience's pleasure in it. The response I once heard from concert pianist Eleanore Vail, who was lecturing about music appreciation, seems to apply here: "You and I both love music, but I truly believe that what I know about it vastly increases my appreciation of it." The *Handbook,* as it helps to examine literature, increases appreciation. That appreciation travels from the college classroom to children.

Considering "Children's Favorites"

A final word about children's favorites: It is always useful to learn which books children truly love. Although sometimes stories tied in with the screen dramatizations seem to dominate such lists, we may also be pleased to discover that some favorites are truly fine books. No harm—just delight—in that discovery. The Babysitters, the Goosebumps and the Lemony Snicket series, as well as Nancy Drew, the Rover Boys, and Elsie Dinsmore of even earlier days, may have their day, and no doubt similar series will take their places. But meanwhile, learning to judge children's books will increase competence in buying, recommending, and reading aloud literature for children. As children thus discover literature that is even better than some of their recent favorites—like, for example, the Harry Potter books—pleasures of all kinds continue. When nothing but the best is good enough for the young, everyone wins.

Dealing with Censorship

Worried parents often approach school administrators, teachers, or librarians about "inappropriate" books. But there is much to be said for the freedom to read in a democratic society.

Where would we be if thinking were forbidden?

What if our only thoughts were things we've "always" known?

Consider the revolutionary nature of the Declaration of Independence, or the often-copied Constitution of the United States. What controversy, what lengthy testing, what discussion and clarification were necessary for their adoption, and are still needed to help citizens understand. Even now, the original ideas of those documents and others are being tested and interpreted.

A highly convincing argument against censorship is eloquently expressed in the American Library Association's document, "The Freedom to Read." As the ALA notes, creative thought is unfamiliar and different, and until an idea is clarified and tested, it may be hard to accept. We "need to know not only what we believe but why we believe it." A totalitarian system, unlike a democratic system, silences those who have ideas different from those of the controlling authorities. In a democratic society, as ideas are proposed, clarified, tested, or modified, the whole process becomes more understandable.

Every book published is not worthy of endorsement, but considering new ideas enlarges us, helps our minds to grow, and increases our understanding of possibilities. Under censorship someone outside ourselves decides what we may or may not read. Once the reader knows the principles used by the censor-of-books, the reader may be appalled. Because the democratic society we live in allows us to determine things for ourselves, the political views or private lives of writers should not determine for us what is acceptable.

Furthermore, on a more pragmatic note, history shows that "banning" a book may make the sales soar. Rather than pragmatism, however, intellectual freedom, freedom to think for ourselves, is the issue.

Inevitably children meet the diversity of our society when they leave home. They are best prepared for that diversity if they have had parental and classroom exposure to thinking for themselves, to hearing the ideas of others, talking freely about them and learning to evaluate them. As the ALA document says, "the answer to a 'bad' book is a good one, the answer to a 'bad' idea is a good one."

Opposing Censorship

The ALA publication, "Intellectual Freedom Brochure," lists several suggestions for combating censorship. Paraphrased, they are:

- Make intellectual freedom part of the library mission.
- Educate people about the importance of intellectual freedom.
- Become advocates for freedom to think independently.
- Respond to requests for support when controversy arises.
- Be aware of relevant legislation or court cases.
- Support organizations that believe in this freedom.
- Start a local group that publicizes the right to read.
- Report incidents of censorship to the ALA.

Read, discover, understand, grow. That's what makes life worth living.

Acknowledgments

For indefatigable assistance, I thank the librarians of the children's department of the Lane Public Library in Oxford, Ohio; the help of reference librarians at Miami University has also been invaluable.

For reviews and suggestions, I thank the following: Fran Bender, University of Tennessee, Chattanooga; Loretta Brister, Tarleton State University; Wendy Claussen, Southwest Minnesota State University; Meggin McIntosh, University of Nevada, Reno; Frances R. Speilhagen, Mount Saint Mary College; Amy Thornburg, University of North Carolina–Chapel Hill; Jinx S. Watson, University of Tennessee; and Terrel A. Young, Washington State University.

I am grateful, too, to my many colleagues who have used earlier editions of *A Critical Handbook of Children's Literature*.

A Lifetime of Reading

Why read? For loads of reasons.

Reading Aloud to Children
The Why of It

Consider first the earliest reading experience: being read to. Children learn language from hearing it spoken—by parents, siblings, friends, and teachers. And it stands to reason that if they hear only limited vocabulary spoken by people with limited experience of language, or little exposure to it, children's growing vocabularies will be just as limited. In fact, if they hear nothing but the words of television cartoon characters, they will know only those few words.

The capacity of children to absorb language, however, is almost infinite. Between the ages of three and five, the child adds more than six hundred words per year to his or her vocabulary, and far more thereafter.

Why not leave it to television to provide the child with an expanding world? Without commenting on the quality of most television, think about its passivity. Little happens to the watcher: no interacting, no conversing, no oral exploration of ideas, no verbal invention of new events.

We have all heard and read of studies that demonstrate how children *act out* rather than *talk about* what they see on television. Television may actually put limits on their ability to verbalize reaction. If their growth is left to the tube, children's vocabularies will be stuck in the world of sitcoms, violent action dramas, grunting wrestling matches, or cartoons with less-than-human characters.

If, very early, words come only by mimicry, children's vocabularies and therefore their imaginations may be limited to bare simplicity. Limited also to mimicry of facial expression or of body movements, these children fail to grow intellectually. The fact remains that many children hear nothing but words of reproof and disapproval, or the language of entertainment, whether for adults or children.

However, the greater the vocabulary, the greater the capacity not only to express oneself, but also to understand one's own emotions and express them in ways other than physical action. The greater the capacity for verbal expression, the greater the possibility for growth in intelligence, as well as in understanding of concepts and of other humans.

Humans developed language slowly, over eons of effort. Language continues to grow, new words appearing in each new edition of a dictionary. Without language we would all be gesticulating and grunting at one another. Someone once said facetiously that language developed out of a deeply felt need to complain. (Imagine a world where complaint is the limit of verbal expression!) Couple complaint with physical aggression, and the world closes in around us.

So much for the growth of language. But reading aloud? Where does that fit in? It's not just growth in vocabulary that matters here, but what those words convey about the nature of life, of hope, of crisis, of security, of love—and of despair and of family. If we add the experiences of others, in other lands, in other family configurations, in other times, to what we experience in our own limited lives, we have the world's wealth. The capacity to be human means to understand others, to satisfy curiosity, to recognize and express compassion, to see cause and effect, to wish for justice, to seek independence, to awaken empathy. All this, and much more, begins with ideas gained through being read to. Nothing a parent or teacher does for a child's intellectual and social growth is more important than talking to and—by extension—reading aloud to a child.

We all have several comfort levels of language: the words we read, those we use when we write, and those we use in conversation, for example. A parent who brings a small child to the library is doing a good thing. But telling the child, "You can read now. Choose your own books," shuts off from the child many of the advantages of a library. Consider, for example, the limitations of a story told in the three hundred or so words a child recognizes. Perhaps interest, enthusiasm, even excitement can be found in so few words, but for how long? How often? New meanings, new relationships, ideas too big or too subtle for words of two syllables but interesting and valuable nonetheless—these are often available only when an older person reads aloud. The reader enlarges the child's world by adding stories, even simple stories that are both more complex and more subtle.

Many other good effects come from reading aloud to children. The one-to-one closeness of reader and child, as together they focus on a story, has emotional benefits. The feeling of a secret bond—knowing that they alone know about this story—wraps a child in the arms of the reader both literally and figuratively. Once children meet words, ideas, and experiences that expand their awareness of the world and what's in it, they grow, and their growth can be almost infinite.

The Time and Place for It

How old should a child be when stories are first read aloud? Some parents read aloud to babies in utero, knowing that the sound of a mother's voice and the cadences of what is being read become familiar even then. As for the infant, what about counting fingers or toes? Going to the market, watering the flowers, breaking an egg, or seeing a haystack are activities mentioned in nursery rhymes. At our house, every flower garden was known as a "garden grow," planted no doubt by Mistress Mary.

Naptime is a good time: Nimble Jack jumps over the candlestick into the crib. Waking up is a good time: The four and twenty blackbirds baked in a pie awaken to sing of a dainty dish to set before a king. Read rhymes together, say them aloud any time. Any time at all.

Reading aloud is a quiet activity, and it stands to reason that a quiet time is appropriate: Parents will think of before naptime, or before bedtime, when children often need a settle-down period. Once the evening go-to-bed tasks are over, the pleasure of a shared story serves perfectly.

Years ago our family lived in a block of duplexes, each home filled with children. I would sit on the front step each evening, reading to my own four additions to the baby boom. The crowd of children surrounding us grew each day, all of them hungry for stories. Sitting on the floor in the church nursery surrounded by books had the same effect. Rocking a child whimpering from a "boo boo" is time for a story. Waiting for dinner to be ready, or for a parent to come home—time for a story.

Teachers take advantage of other occasions, some of them equally available to parents. When children are settling into the school day, there's nothing like anticipation of the story or poem, or the next chapter to bring the class to silence, or to settle them down again after recess, an assembly, or a family outing.

Before a big event, to lessen the impatience of waiting, a story works well. When a field trip is coming up, a story related to the occasion in even the remotest way sets imaginations moving. When class attention is riveted on the windows, watching falling leaves or swirling snow, it's time for an appropriate poem or story: fall and butchering time or the Christmas party in the Little House stories come to mind. A holiday approaching, a vacation day, a patriotic commemoration about to happen, all are appropriate times for reading aloud—in the classroom or at home. Ask your librarian, one of those wonderfully helpful and knowledgeable people, for ideas.

The time for reading aloud is almost any time. Read from books, newspapers, magazines, anything with words. Find excuses to read aloud and once children begin to enjoy it, *they* will find the excuses.

Reading aloud does not stop with elementary-grade children. A substitute teacher, finding that her ninth-grade charges were reading a much truncated version of *A Tale of Two Cities,* decided to show the class what they were missing. She read aloud one of Dickens's uncut chapters, with its caricatures, its vividly shown actions, its humorous comments on individual behaviors and social mores; the severely cut story was not the story itself, any more than an outline of a history chapter is the chapter itself. That substitute teacher's wish was that a few students would go on to discover the whole of the story. The benefits of reading aloud begin early and may continue throughout life.

Currently, leisure time is diminishing. Working parents have less time for the responsibilities of homemaking and involvement with family. The warm lap of a parent or other adult is not always available for bedtime reading.[1] Study after study, however, reinforces the importance of reading aloud to children. While organized sports for children proliferate—an important focus on physical health—educators remind the public that without the adult and young child reading together, society may be at risk of raising an illiterate generation.[2]

Decrying the motivations of education as achievement training for adulthood, Heather-Jane Robertson[3] notes that in some places "electronic career portfolios" are initiated in the first grade. Teamwork is valued for building résumés, music increases math skills, and children's play is not for fun but for teaching cooperation. "Using today to get somewhere tomorrow" ignores the values of reading aloud, which increase children's "receptive" or understanding vocabulary. Unfortunately, focusing on the future trumps the values of children's present time. Good fiction for children celebrates the present with its variety of challenges and its infinite possibilities—presenting infinite pleasures.

A Lifetime of Reading

In midsummer 2005 the sixth volume of the Harry Potter series hit bookstores, libraries, supermarkets, and private mailboxes. The country suddenly thought worries about the demise of reading were unnecessary. Four million copies were sold that first weekend, not all to children. News media made excited predictions about how the phenomenon called *Harry* would establish lifelong reading among children.

Hoping the sensational interest in the series meant a "literary renaissance," librarians and bookstores organized read-ins, and adults discovered they actually liked their children's taste; some predicted that the fantasies would build imagination and creativity for the benefit of all humankind. In the United Kingdom, 59 percent of kids said the books improved their reading skills, and 48 percent said Harry Potter was why they were reading more. Even children with low reading skills believed they were missing out on something—unless they joined the crowd and slogged on through the series. Meanwhile, technology for the young grows rapidly, creating ever new challenges for parents who hope for book-reading children, and for grandparents who might despair about reading going out of style. Many bloggers choose the name "Harry Potter"; at least one website—established by a twelve-year-old—is called by a Harry Potter name: mugglenet.com. It receives more than 15 million hits a month. No doubt about it, Harry Potter has helped make reading popular.[4]

Although it may be unduly optimistic to say that a new era is dawning,[5] it is apparent that in recent years enthusiasm for basal readers with limited vocabularies has waned. Storybooks, real stories with real characters doing interesting things, often with humor and optimism, are being published in increasing numbers and used for classroom reading. Awards for literary merit proliferate and publishers seek manuscripts that might bring such awards. Book covers that sport bright award emblems boost sales.

Other signs are optimistic, too. Dan Brown's page-turner, *The Da Vinci Code*, has spent more than two and a half years on the best-seller list. More adults gather in discussion groups to talk over books they've read. Some groups read only best sellers, some fantasy or science fiction, some crime novels or mysteries, others books by women authors, still others read one memoir after another—then pause to read David McCullough's *John Adams*, a Pulitzer Prize–winning biography. For these groups, bookstores often dedicate a section of shelves filled with multiple copies on "special order." And at the checkout counter, the buyer can pick up bookmarks or pamphlets with "Discussion questions for (title of book)."

It has been said that the first lesson reading teaches is how to be alone. As one writer says, "The person who DOES NOT READ is no better off than the person who CANNOT READ." Reading may be a solitary act, but recent behavior patterns demonstrate that human beings find the pleasures of solitary reading can become communal pleasures as well.

A phenomenal success exploded in bookstores when many once non-reading adults suddenly discovered that Oprah Winfrey's book club selections were good, a pleasure to read. The summer of 2005 became "A Faulkner Summer," and the Nobel Prize–winner's work flew off the shelves. Inevitably, there were Oprah book clubs. Oprah, who says she reads each of the chosen books, has said on her web page, "One of the most wonderful things about a book club is that it starts being about books and grows into more than that. Reading along with other people and creating a community of readers is really a fantastic thing."[6]

One study funded by the International Reading Association demonstrates another pleasurable benefit of reading. Many older people live quiet or isolated lives. As their lives become circumscribed by loss of income, inability to leave their homes or to enjoy social activity, along with the inevitable loss of spouses and contemporary friends, many find company in books. When asked about being alone and housebound, one eighty-six-year-old gestured toward her bookshelves and said, "I'm not alone. I have the whole world right here with me." Positive attitudes toward life and feelings of well-being were evident when individuals had a love for reading. Reading knows no time boundaries: any place, any time is perfect, even the middle of the night. A sense of control, unfortunately not always part of being old, is restored when a person can choose to read *whenever*—morning or midnight—and *whatever* he or she wants, whether it be biography, fiction, or self-help. Time duration means nothing during sustained reading pleasure.[7]

"Lifelong learning" is a current label for adult education. "Lifelong pleasure" is enhanced by reading, from earliest childhood through old age.[8]

Notes

1. Heather-Jane Robertson, "The Decline of Small Pleasures," *Phi Delta Kappan*, September, 2002, Volume 84 Issue 1, p. 93.
2. See also *Becoming a Nation of Readers: The Report of the Commission on Reading*, The National Academy of Education, and the Center for the Study of Reading, 1985. The text mentions research-based studies of human cognition, environmental influences, and classroom practices. The approach, however, is focused on the reading process rather than on the lifelong pleasures of reading.
3. Robertson, p. 94.
4. Vicki Hallett, "The Power of Potter," *U. S. News and World Report*, July 25, 2005, p. 46.
5. Ibid., p. 45.
6. www2.oprah.com/books/books, (accessed August 8, 2005).
7. Donna Rane-Szostak and Kaye Ann Herth, "Pleasure reading, other activities, and loneliness in later life," *Journal of Adolescent and Adult Literacy*, October, 1995, pp. 100–108.
8. Eighteen specific pleasures are enumerated by Perry Nodelman in his book, *The Pleasures of Children's Literature* (New York: Longman, 1992). The list includes such varied pleasures as finding ourselves mirrored, as well as understanding other people's differences, gaining glimpses of history, and finding structure in meaningful patterns.

A Critical Handbook of Children's Literature

Charlotte's Web

E. B. White

Illustrated by Garth Williams

Literature: What Is It?

"Literature" as the term is used here, does not include just any printed matter.

How does the literature we examine and evaluate here differ from all other printed matter?

We pick up *People* magazine at the drug store, *TV Guide* in the supermarket, and *National Geographic* in the doctor's office to give us information and vicarious experience, but they are not literature. Literature *may* give us information and vicarious experience, but it also gives us much more. What sets a chapter in *The Wind in the Willows* apart from a *National Geographic* article on the plant and animal life of the English countryside? Many things, and they are at the heart of our definition of literature. Literature, sometimes called *belles lettres,* is traditionally described as the body of writing that exists because of inherent imaginative and artistic qualities. The fine line drawn between literature and writing that is primarily scientific, intellectual, or philosophical—or, in Louise Rosenblatt's terms, aesthetic or efferent—often wavers.

Why do we adults pick up and read a novel or a collection of poetry? In the words of storyteller Italo Calvino, literature gives opportunity to "stretch out from the utmost limits of what can be said; what stirs literature is the call and attraction of what is not in the dictionary." We can applaud narrative discoveries that seem to make sense of our lives. We seek ***pleasure***—not to find a lesson in ecology, not to be taught about the natural habitat of the armadillo or about sailing the China Seas. We choose literature that promises entertainment and, sometimes, escape. If other discoveries come to us, too, we are pleased and doubly rewarded. However, our first motive for reading a novel or a poem is personal pleasure: it comes in many forms, from rollicking laughter to sheer delight to awe or even titillating shock. We may lay the book aside

We read for pleasure.

with mixed feelings, but if there is no enjoyment, we reject it completely or leave it unfinished. For adults who have had a variety of experiences, who have known success and failure, who have had to decide what is "good" and what is "bad," who have had to face their own shaky standards of morality, the nature of pleasure in literature may be different from that for children.

Because we are all different, the pleasures we seek as well as those we may encounter may be very personal, and, for that matter, even different on different days or even hours. But what is required of us as critical readers is that we examine the pleasure the work aspires to give, the real subject of literary criticism. To paraphrase critic Frank Kermode, it is the function of the writer to make sense out of life, and it is the function of the critic to evaluate the writer's efforts to make sense out of life. We may restate that argument to say that we as critical readers do not stop with our personal pleasure: "I like it, and that's so personal that it cannot be debated." We go on, instead, to find in the work the sources of that personal enjoyment. To our surprise, they may lie in a painful recognition of ourselves, a satisfying verification of our humanness, or in variations of the great questions of the philosopher Immanuel Kant: What must I know? What should I be? What can I hope? But some kind of pleasure is essential, whether the reader is eight or forty-eight years old.

> The function of the writer is to make sense out of life.

Literature provides a second reward: ***understanding.*** This understanding comes from the exploration of the "human condition," the revelation of human nature, the discovery of humankind. It is not explicitly the function of literature, either for children or for adults, to try to reform humans, or to set up guidelines for behavior; however, it is the province of literature to observe and to comment, to open individuals and their society for our observation and our understanding. If there is any question about what we are to understand, notice that our terms are "human" and "humankind," synonyms for "people."

> Literature is not expected to reform but to help us understand.

As for information, it may or may not contribute to understanding. We may know a person's height, weight, hair color, ethnic background, and occupation—this is information. But until we are aware of temperament, anxieties, joys, and ambitions, we do not *know* that person. Information is not a person; spirit is.

Information is part of the story, and when we see it, we expect it to be relevant. The following passage from *Roll of Thunder, Hear My Cry* by Mildred Taylor, for example, contains both summarized and detailed information. Here is Christmas morning:

> In addition to the books there was a sockful of once-a-year store-bought licorice, oranges, and bananas for each of us and from Uncle Hammer a dress and a sweater for me, and a sweater and a pair of pants each for Christopher John and Little Man. But nothing compared to the books. Little Man, who treasured clothes above all else, carefully laid his new pants and sweaters aside and dashed for a clean sheet of brown paper to make a cover for his book, and throughout the day as he lay upon the deerskin rug looking at the bright, shining pictures of faraway places, turning each page as if it were gold, he would suddenly squint down at

his hands, glance at the page he had just turned, then dash into the kitchen to wash again—just to make sure.

The effect of the paragraph, however, is not merely to tell about the Christmas presents, but also to reveal something about the characters and their lives. Here is a family devoted to reading, to education, to learning about the world beyond. Books are precious, so precious that they must be protected, and only clean hands may touch them. The home is furnished simply with a deerskin rug that must have been carefully skinned and cured for use. There may be a hunter in the family. This family values appearance and takes good care of their clothing, not taking it for granted; clothes are important as special Christmas gifts, as are fresh fruit and licorice. Information alone without its contributing to understanding is not, by our traditional definition, literature.

Then perhaps a narrative of people acting in a way we can understand is all that is necessary to make literature. No, that is not the case. We may have a short account with understandable action called "Kevin Visits the A&P," and yet it may not qualify as literature. While Kevin's visit might conceivably tell us something about the nature of childhood, it just as easily might not. The grocery store situation provides vivid details about prices and cuts of meat and varieties of vegetables, and the action may be credible because Mother chooses a ripe cantaloupe and pays at the checkout counter. However, the significance of the experience in terms of the characters' lives may be lacking—significance that helps us, whatever our age, to understand a little more about ourselves and others. In the most general terms, then, literature is reading that, by means of imaginative and artistic qualities, provides pleasure and understanding.

To return to the comparison of the *National Geographic* article and *The Wind in the Willows:* We can feel fairly certain that although we may enjoy the process, we read the *National Geographic* article primarily for information, and we can also be reasonably sure that we read *The Wind in the Willows* primarily for pleasure.

Literature has other more specific appeals for us as readers. Literature **shows human motives** for what they are, inviting the reader to identify with or react to a fictional character. We see into the mind of the character, or into the subconscious that even the character does not know. Through the writer's careful choice of details from the past, the current environment, and an imaginary world, we come to see clearly the motivation for action. If in these chosen details we see some similarity to our own lives, we nod our heads and identify with the character, feeling that we understand the motives and can justify the deeds. Or seeing the error in judgment that the character fails to see, we understand. Seeing motives we disapprove of we distrust, or seeing a reflection of our own mistakes, we forgive.

Our *touchstone*[1] book is E. B. White's *Charlotte's Web*, a story that will serve us as a critical standard and a frequent example. It shows one character, Wilbur, at one moment crying out in panic: "I don't want to die! Save me,

Literature offers many kinds of understanding.

somebody! Save me!" However, months later his motive for action is selfless concern:

> "Templeton, I will make you a solemn promise. Get Charlotte's egg sac for me, and from now on I will let you eat first, when Lurvy slops me. I will let you have your choice of everything in the trough and I won't touch a thing until you're through."

Charlotte's motives, however, are born of pure sympathy and a desire to help Wilbur's suffering. She says briskly that Wilbur will not die, and she weaves words into her web until late at night. Our identification with each response to Wilbur's life-and-death crises varies as our experience varies.

Literature may also *provide form for experience.* Aside from birth and death, real life has no beginnings or endings, but is instead a series of stories without order, each story merging with other stories. Fiction, however, makes order of randomness by organizing events and consequences, cause and effect, beginning and ending. When we look back on our lives, we notice the high spots: "the first time we met," or even "the day we sold the Buick station wagon." With the perspective given by distance in time, what once seemed trivial now seems important. When we look back, we may be unaware of sequence, since chronology is merely the random succession of life's disordered events. Literature, however, by placing the relevant episodes—"and the next time we met"—into coherent sequence, gives order and form to experience.

In *Charlotte's Web* White selects events that, among other things, demonstrate the purpose in Charlotte's life. When she says, "By helping you, perhaps I was trying to lift up my life a trifle," we see more clearly the pattern of Charlotte's behavior. While she accepts the inevitability of death, she does not accept the prospect of passive waiting. Charlotte chooses instead to fill her days with order and purpose. As White directs our thoughts and alters our feelings in a chosen course, he gives form to the experience of the ongoing cycle of life.

Literature also may *reveal life's fragmentation.* Not a day goes by without our being pulled in one direction after another by the demands of friendship—"Please help." Of obligation—"I promised I would." Of pressure—"It's due tomorrow." And of money—"I wish I could afford it." Life is fragmented, and our daily experience proves it. However, literature, while it may remind us of our own and society's fragmentation, does not leave us there. It sorts the world into disparate segments we can identify and examine; friendship, greed, family, sacrifice, childhood, love, advice, old age, treasures, snobbery, and compassion are set before us for close observation. Little, if anything, is outside the province of literature.

While literature may be saying or revealing that life is fragmented, it simultaneously *helps us focus on essentials.* May Sarton, a writer of adult fiction, says that her books are born of questions she needs to answer for her-

Fiction makes order from disparate events.

Literature helps us to identify and examine fragments of experience.

Literature helps us to see essentials—the meaning and unity of life.

self. "Art is order, but it is made out of the chaos of life." This chaos reordered, experience given form, permits us to experience with different intensity but with new understanding of the parts of life that we have known: "That's how it happened to me, too!" Or parts we have yet to meet: "Do you suppose I'll ever get my diploma?" Or experiences we may never have: "What must it be like to live in a camp for refugees? Or in the crowded inner city?" In the process of giving order to life, the writer sorts out the essential details from the nonessential. Undistracted by irrelevant experiences or minor anxieties, the reader focuses on the essentials of action, people, events, and tensions. In retrospect, we see that life does not distribute events in order of their mounting intensity or their accumulative effects on us. Because literature ignores the irrelevant and focuses on the essentials, significance becomes clear. As we read, our detachment helps us to see events and their possible influences. Challenged, we make choices, feel the excitement of suspense, and glow with the pride of accomplishment. Literature *says* that life is fragmented. What it *does* is something else: Literature provides a sense of life's unity and meaning.

Literature can ***reveal the institutions of society.*** Every week we are presented with a new regulation in our personal lives—the rising cost of gasoline, a no-left-turn sign where we have always turned left, or the disappearance of our favorite Tuesday night TV show. A group of people called an institution, something bigger than we are, makes a judgment, and a form of institutional control determines for us something we would like to determine for ourselves. The institutions of society—like government, family, church, and school, as well as forces that shape our jobs—urge and coerce us into conforming to standards. Occasionally institutions seem so threatening, in fact, that we fear they will close in on our lives, restricting us completely. Of course, some restrictions establish the order needed for a group to survive and necessary institutions are born and grow. Literature clarifies our reactions to institutions by showing appropriate circumstances where people give in to or struggle against them.

> Society's institutions may confuse as well as establish order.

In the institution called farming, for example, it is unprofitable to keep a runt pig, because fattening him will not pay a good return on the dollar. In *Charlotte's Web,* within Wilbur's conflict with an institution, we see what a life-and-death struggle does to an immature innocent. We may not literally identify with Wilbur—since it is highly unlikely we will ever be commodities on an exchange market—but his struggle for life is nonetheless somewhat similar to our own. Wilbur soon discovers who his friends are, how resourceful they can be, how hard they will work for another's safety, and even, in Templeton's case, what a person's price may be. Through Wilbur's struggle with profitable farming we discover in a small way the impersonal nature of society. In other stories we may discover that racism is institutionalized, or that although we individually hate war, it is ordered by a body larger than we are. The variety of such conflicts seems infinite.

Not only do institutions affect our lives, but nature does, too. Some litera-ture ***reveals nature as a force*** that influences us. Tornadoes on the summer plains, avalanches in the springtime Rockies, hurricanes in the tropical Caribbean, blizzards on the Dakota prairies—we read of them each year, sea-son by season, region by region. Nature constantly reminds us of its effects on our lives. People's natural environment influences them, whether it be the stress of wind that wearies nerves, intense heat that produces lethargy, or extreme cold and lack of sun that depress spirits. Literature, by presenting humans involved in conflict with such forces, makes us see forces' effects on human life.

The natural world may influence us in varied ways.

Gary Paulsen's *Dogsong* shows Russel running his dogs in a dangerous wilderness as he searches for his own song:

> Running in the dark, even in the tight dark of the north where there is no moon, it is possible to see out ahead a great distance. The snow-ice is white-blue in the dark and if there is no wind to blow the snow around, everything shows up against the white . . . Now, suddenly, there was a dark line ahead of the lead dog. A dark line followed by a black space on the snow, an opening of the ice. A lead of open water, so wide Russel could not see across.

Nature is a force affecting humans, sometimes demanding that they exert all their powers against it. Although struggling cannot conquer nature, humans may struggle heroically and yet not be conquered. In such a conflict, the reader can applaud the human will.

Literature provides vicarious experiences. It is impossible for us to live any life but our own, in any time but our own life span, or in any space or place but our own. But literature makes it possible for us to live in the time of the French Revolution, in the period of the Vikings, or during the days of the American colonies. Through a good story, we can live in a small river town on the Mississippi, in the hold of a slave ship, in the hills of Appalachia, or even in a castle turret. The possibilities for us to live lives other than our own are infinite, as numerous as the books on the library shelves.

Literature provides us with other lives.

Finally, the vicarious experience of literature forces us, leads us, entices, or woos us into ***meeting a writer-creator*** whose medium, words, we know; whose subject, human nature, we live with; whose vision, life's meaning, we hope to understand. We are the student-novice before the artist. In the hands of a gifted writer, we turn from being passive followers into passionate advo-cates calling new followers. The writer's skill with words gives us a pleasure we want to share, and an understanding we have an urge to spread.

We might say that literature, because it is not an accurate duplicate of life, is lies, all lies. But through "lying," a story may express great truth; by refusing to recount life as it is, the fiction transforms and transcends, adding something to life, remaking, embellishing, or opening it for examination. Events translated into words—life written, not lived—constitute a profound modification, and become a momentary substitute for life, an experience of life different from our own. As novelist Mario Vargas Llosa says, fiction, "by spurring the imagination, both temporarily assuages human dissatisfaction and simultaneously incites it."[2]

Literature for Children

Children are not little adults. They are different from adults in experience, but not in species, or to put it differently, in degree but not in kind. We can say then of literature for young readers that it differs from literature for adults in degree but not in kind. We sometimes forget that literature for children can and should provide the same enjoyment and understanding as does literature for adults. Children, too, seek pleasure from a story, but the sources of their pleasure are somewhat different. Since their experiences are more limited, children may not understand the same complexity of ideas. Since their understanding is more limited, the expression of ideas must be simpler—both in language and in form. Related to the necessity for simplicity in the expression of ideas are vocabulary and attention span. Stories are more directly told, with fewer digressions and more obvious relationships between characters and actions, or between characters themselves. Children are both more and less literal than adults. They may find discrepancies between two descriptions of a setting and hold the writer accountable for error. However, children may accept the fantastic more readily than many adults. As long as the world itself is so remarkably complex and incomprehensible, one more fantastic experience in story form does not present an impossible hurdle. Often, for example, the personified animals and toys of the child's world, by behaving like humans, may show what humans are like. Children are frequently more open to experimenting with a greater variety of literary forms than many adults will accept—from poetry to folktales, from adventure to fantasy.

Children find spontaneous pleasure in rhymes and jokes, in comics and cartoons, in the inside secrets of friends. They may find a series of books to read them to the end, a series that satisfies these yearnings for another neighborhood, another world, another time. The many discoveries that children can make through literature might be sought in other ways by adults. Adults might discover human motivation through a study of psychology, or the nature of society and its institutions through a study of sociology, or the impact of nature on human behavior through a study of anthropology. However, literature can do all these things for children—as well as for adults.[3] Literature is more than a piece of writing that clarifies or explains; at its best, it delights and reveals. Throughout the pages that follow we will refer to literature as "a significant truth expressed in appropriate elements and memorable language." As we shall discover, the ideas expressed in poetic form, the truths of theme and character explored through the elements of fiction, and the style of the artist with words constitute literature.

Literature for adults is both similar to and different from that for children.

Summary

... and back to pleasure and under- standing.

Literature at its best gives both pleasure and understanding. It explores the nature of humans, the condition of humankind. If these phrases seem too pompous and abstract for children's literature, rephrase them in children's terms:

> What are people like?
> Why are they like that?
> What do they need?
> What makes them do what they do?

The answers, or mere glimpses of answers to these questions, are made visible in poetry or in fiction by the elements of plot, character, point of view, setting, tone, and style of an imaginative work; together they constitute literature. Words are merely words, but literature for any age is words chosen with skill and artistry to give readers delight and to help them understand themselves and others.

Notes

1. A touchstone is a test criterion, or standard; the meaning is derived from the age-old use of a stone as a comparison to detect the purity of silver and gold. Matthew Arnold, using the term in literary criticism, wrote: "There can be no more useful help for discovering what poetry belongs to the class of the truly excellent . . . than to have always in one's mind lines and expressions of the great masters and to apply them as a touchstone to other poetry."
2. Mario Vargas Llosa, "Is Fiction the Art of Lying?" *New York Times Book Review,* October 7, 1984, p. 40.
3. In her book *Love's Knowledge,* Martha C. Nussbaum writes of the refusal on the part of modern philosophers to consider literature seriously as "a form of moral argument." She maintains that literature helps us to see life in human terms—rather than in logical or theoretical terms.

Recommended Books Cited in This Chapter

GRAHAME , KENNETH. *The Wind in the Willows.* 1908. Reprint. New York: Scribners, 1953.

PAULSEN, GARY. *Dogsong.* New York: Macmillan, 1983.

TAYLOR, MILDRED. *Roll of Thunder, Hear My Cry.* New York: Dial, 1976.

WHITE, E. B. *Charlotte's Web.* New York: Harper, 1952.

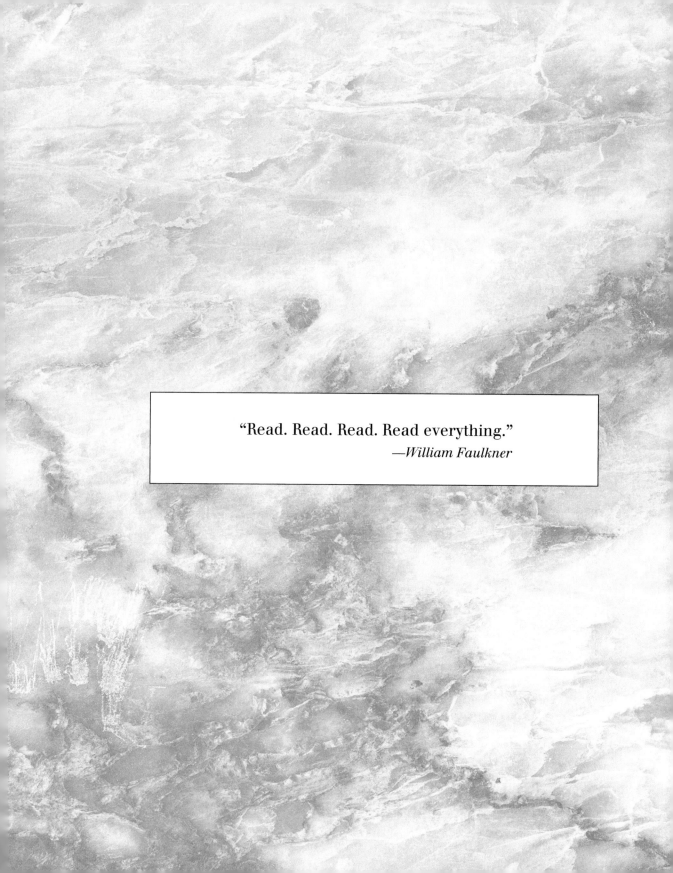

"Read. Read. Read. Read everything."

—*William Faulkner*

Wild Robert

Diana Wynne Jones

Illustrated by Mark Zug

Genre in Children's Literature

Why know about genres?

What does each of the genres contribute to the child reader? How?

Like adult literature, children's literature offers variety. It is not uniform, created with cookie-cutter sameness. We recognize rhymes and fairy tales, fantasies and lyrics, and realistic stories about other countries as well as our own. These and other kinds of literature we sometimes call "genres."

A discussion of genre in literature must begin with an effort to define the term—not a simple task. A **genre** is a kind or type of literature that has a common set of characteristics. As soon as we have said this, however, we face the fact that we can identify as many differences and variations among examples of a given genre as we can find similarities. Classification is easiest when each class or group possesses clear-cut, unchanging characteristics. The chemist's chart of the elements provides a helpful analogy. When an element is found that lacks the qualities to fit it precisely into any category, or that possesses additional qualities, a new class must be added. While this may work for classification in chemistry, it does not work so clearly in literature. If, for example, we divide literature into prose and poetry, where do we place rhythmic but nonmetrical writing spaced on the page in "poetic" line length? Is this kind of work poetic prose because it lacks meter or regular beat? Or is it prose-poetry because it is filled with sensory appeals and figurative language? Furthermore, if we decide that a work is poetry we might go one step further since, for example, both lyric and sonnet are themselves genres, yet both are poetry. Must we subdivide?[1] Genres are not always clear-cut and

"Genre" describes a group with similar characteristics.

13

easily distinguished; the terms are often used loosely. Today, genre distinctions, although helpful, are often seen as arbitrary.

Opinions differ about classifications, although each of us may have several reasons for our opinions. Some people may find it unnecessary even to mention genres; others like the sense of order that genre classification provides. For our purposes, the term "genre" can be useful in organizing our discussion of children's literature. First, it helps us to be aware that there is more literature for children than one finds in the familiar genres of stories and nursery rhymes. Second, the literary elements explored and explained in the following chapters—tone, setting, and others—function differently in different genres. And third, sensitivity to the broad and rich variety of literature available to children can help them to sample it.

For our purposes we will try to use "genre" in a way that is clear and useful, discussing here the kinds of literature that are most commonly written for or read to children and that are complete art forms when read. Since drama is complete only when staged and viewed, it is not discussed here. In Chapter 11, "From Rhyme to Poetry," kinds of poems from folk rhyme to lyric are noted, but in this chapter we look mostly at the kinds, types, or genres of fiction: realistic fiction, with subgenres of animal realism, historical realism, and sports stories; fantasy, with subgenres of fantastic stories, high fantasy, and science fiction; formula fiction and its variations, and traditional stories, with subgenres of fables, folktales, myths, legends, and folk epics.

Poetry, biography, and informational books are still other genres of literature for children.

All elements of literature are included in each of the major genres of fiction, but within each type one element may be more significant than another. In some cases the genre demands that a particular element be strong or well developed; without that strength, the credibility of the story may be in question. For example, animal realism requires an objective point of view, for it's impossible to know what an animal—a real animal, not a personified or imaginary one—is thinking. Historical fiction, to cite another example, relies for credibility on a clear sense of setting in a past time. And again, since folktales have been told orally from one generation to another, descriptions of setting or details of a character's past or a character's thoughts merely delay the telling. In a folktale, flat characters seem appropriate, because they are recognized immediately and the reader can move quickly into the action.

The genres, then, are both distinct and overlapping; they contain all elements but in varying combinations and degrees. Table 2.1 on pages 30–34 may be a helpful guide, showing how elements relate to the specific genres. Refer to it cautiously, however, aware that literature is not governed by rigid rules.

Genre makes us aware of literature other than simple stories.

Different genres may require emphases on different elements.

Realism

Realism means that a story is possible, although not necessarily probable. Effect follows cause without the intervention of the magical or supernatural. For example, in *Did You Carry the Flag Today, Charley?* by Rebecca Caudill, Charley is rewarded because he helped out in the library, not because a fairy godmother intervened. The outcome seems reasonable and plausible; the story is a representation of action that seems truthful. Realistic stories have in common several characteristics: they are fictional narratives with characters who are involved in some kind of action that holds our interest, set in some possible place and time. Once again, keep in mind that by dividing realistic fiction into subgenres, the divisions may at times seem to overlap.

Possible is not the same as probable.

Realistic Stories

Problem realism and social issues realism, which are similar in their focus on problems, were popular more than twenty-five years ago; their situations are realistic or possible. Their problems are not universal, like searching for friendship, but personal and particular, like being a foster child in *The Great Gilly Hopkins* by Katherine Paterson, or having a sibling with a mental disability as in *Summer of the Swans* by Betsy Byars. Novels about social issues showed the character—usually the **protagonist,** or central character—encountering a kind of problem engendered by society, like discrimination because of race, gender, or social position.

The protagonist's problem is the source of plot and conflict, and that conflict may be with self, society, or another person. In the best realistic fiction, character and conflict are both well developed and interrelated. In a poorly written novel, the character may either be stereotyped or may seem to be made up only of problems so overwhelming that they obliterate the credibility of the character as a whole human being made up of a mixture of feelings and thoughts, emotion and intellect.

In a well-written book, character and conflict are well developed and interrelated.

In poor fiction, the protagonist's problems may be solved in too pat a manner. Such fictional solutions are not only simplistic and sentimental, but also lack reality and justice. In real life, difficulties are not solved quickly or easily. Readers who identify with the characters may find false hope for solutions to their own problems; readers who observe the success of a problem-ridden character may become condescending. "What's bothering my friend? Look how easy it is in this book!" Such simplistic solutions may then result in false themes or ideas like, "Any problem is easily solved" or "Work hard and everything always comes out right." Difficulty, after all, is natural to a complex problem. *A Hero Ain't Nothin' but a Sandwich* by Alice Childress, in which Benjie struggles with drug addiction, provides an example of a more credible truth: "Despite love and care, a big problem is not easily solved." In *Lord of the Deep,* a suspenseful realistic story, writer Graham Salisbury develops a tense conflict depicting a moral struggle in which Mikey must confront ambivalence about right and wrong. Should Captain Bill, badly needing customers and their fees, compromise with truth and agree that his passenger did land the record-breaking fish all alone? The situation is thoroughly credible, the resolution controversial.

A Single Shard presents a particular problem for solution, and Linda Sue Park presents a credible resolution. Tree-ear, who wishes to become a ceramist, cannot because that honor is offered only to descendents of a potter. Tree-ear works hard at finding and supplying the potter with particular kinds of clay for fine work. He tends the kiln, searches for fuel, carries it in, and stokes the fire to the right temperature. His loyalty is exemplary. When he carries the potter's work for a long and dangerous distance to show the king, he is attacked by robbers and loses the bowls on the precipice edge; he scrambles down, seeking a perfect pot, but can find only a single shard. That, however, is sufficient to prove the artist's artistic excellence, earning him the honor of the king's patronage. The character, his struggle, and his successful work are particular to this story, a successful story.

Tone or attitude are also affected when the novel is poorly written. Works become sensational when, to hold readers' interest, the writer so loads the story with problems that the situation is incredible and the novel becomes sensational and unbelievable.

While all elements are important in realism, we notice particularly the elements of theme, character, and conflict. If such fiction is to help a reader understand self and others, soundly developed characters and believable conflicts are essential.

Animal Realism

Animal realism
remains true to
animal natures.

Nonfiction that evokes a thoroughly efferent response should deal accurately with animals, telling the details of their appearances, their habitats, and their life cycles. Animal realism as fiction adds another dimension by giving continuity and conflict or adventure to the story. The setting includes details of the seasons, the geographical regions, and the influence of the elements on the animals. Within the restrictions of scientific accuracy, the fictional portrayal of animals shows them in conflict of some kind. Some are the most important characters in the story, like the three pets of Sheila Burnford's *The Incredible Journey* that determinedly battle with nature to return to their masters through the wilds of Canada. While they are characters, they are not given human traits or anthropomorphized. Novels like *Charlotte's Web* by E. B. White, however, cannot be considered animal realism, because the animal characters behave, think, and talk not like animals, but like humans. Accuracy about animal life requires an objective point of view, but a human character who is telling the story, like Billy telling about owls in Farley Mowat's *Owls in the Family,* may offer interpretations of the animals' behavior. If the point of view falters and we "get into the mind" of the animal, the story may become not only unrealistic but also sentimental, as is Felix Salten's *Bambi*, where we know not only Bambi's thoughts but even those of the autumn leaves. In the course of an adventure in animal realism, our transaction is also aesthetic; we make some discovery about animals or about their relationships to humans.

Historical Realism

Historical fiction is placed in the past, and the time and place in the past determine setting. Details about vehicles, clothing, or food preparation, for example, must fit the time and place. Sometimes little is known of the period, and at other times much is known; it is possible to write historical fiction about the Vikings, like *Hakon of Rogen's Saga* by Erik Haugaard, as well as about the American colonies, like *The Witch of Blackbird Pond* by Elizabeth Speare. The integral setting demonstrates how the characters live and how families support themselves. Consider *Crispin, the Cross of Lead* set in the fourteenth century, the story of a peasant boy whose inscribed cross identifies him as the rightful heir to the throne. Juggler Bear, on a mission to rid his country of exploitative evil and promote freedom, gives Crispin the essential assistance. Since characters, and particularly the central character, are caught in the events of the time, setting influences plot. When the writer exaggerates the bad or the good of the times, the resulting historical fiction may suffer from sensational or sentimental tone. Although themes are often universal, they may relate clearly to a particular time; a story might easily show how in pioneer days the family unit was important to survival, as it is in the Little House stories of Laura Ingalls Wilder. Style may focus particularly on descriptions that draw for us time and place: the dress and homes, the work and recreation of the day. Because language should be appropriate to the time current slang would be out of place.

Historical fiction is placed in the past; details fit time and place.

History presents facts. To turn facts into fiction, the writer must combine imagination with fact, bringing about an integrated story with a fictional protagonist in a suspenseful plot. As the twentieth century ended, matters that not long ago were recent events became the materials of a historical period. Today, for example, writers are seeing with increased objectivity the events of World War II, as does Bette Greene in *Summer of My German Soldier*, and of the Great Depression, as does Mildred Taylor in *Roll of Thunder, Hear My Cry*. Such novels show the impact of the times on the people living in them.

To turn facts into fiction, the writer combines them with imagination.

Well-written historical fiction often rouses within the reader a question that begs to be answered: How much of this is true? Such is the case with Lois Lowry's *Number the Stars*. So convincing is the story that we feel a need to know what is truth and what is fiction. In an afterword, Lowry alludes to well-documented evidence of the personal deprivation and sacrifice made by courageous and honest Danish people who helped nearly seven thousand Jewish citizens escape the Nazis by fleeing to neutral Sweden. Destruction of the Danish navy, ordered by King Christian X and carried out by the Danes themselves, did keep the ships from the hands of the Nazis.

Sports Stories

Once a kind of formula fiction, sports stories have become increasingly individualized, with well-developed characters struggling with personal issues and discovering the forces and choices they must confront. Characters play, watch, or live on the fringes of all kinds of sports, although team sports such as baseball, football, and basketball are most common. Team play and sportsmanship are frequent themes, but in recent decades, with demand for more stories about integrated schools and nonracist themes, many stories involve acceptance of players of other races. Another shift has occurred with the appearance of sexually integrated sports.

Once a genre of undistinguished stories, sports fiction is much improved. Because children take gym classes, watch televised sports, and are involved in organized sports after school, sports are part of their lives; their reading interests may move naturally toward such stories. One sport story of excellent quality is Bruce Brooks's *The Moves Make the Man*, and writers of sport stories whose work is worth noting include Matt Christopher, Scott Corbett, Alfred Slote, R. R. Knudson, and Mel Cebulash, who writes of Ruth Marini's struggles to become a professional baseball player.

Sports stories need not be written to a formula.

Formula Fiction

Some kinds of stories follow distinct patterns and are therefore called **formula fiction.** Although following a formula does not necessarily eliminate the writer's originality, it may restrict it.

Mysteries and Thrillers

One popular type of formula fiction is the mystery story, in which mystery—and often terror—play controlling parts. But note that not *all* mysteries are formulaic. Mystery stories are set in any time, historical or futuristic or the present. They rely for suspense on unexplained events and actions that are sometimes, by story's end, resolved or explained by reasonable and carefully detected discoveries. Within the genre we include the detective story and novels of crime, suspense, and espionage. The Gothic novel, traditionally filled with magical or mysterious happenings, occasionally with chivalry, and frequently with horror and terror, perhaps rides the borderline between realism and fantasy.

Mystery stories rely for suspense on unexplained events that must be resolved by reasonable discoveries.

Plot carries most mysteries and thrillers, although those more carefully crafted also show strong characterization. The mood is almost inevitably suspenseful, and the setting may include such intriguing places as vacant houses or abandoned buildings. Mystery stories may also occur in the most ordinary of everyday settings. One of the traditional qualities of effective mystery stories is the clever planting of foreshadowing; those who read the genre over time acquire skill in putting together the bits of foreshadowing to predict outcome.

Once every schoolchild knew Nancy Drew and the Hardy Boys,[2] the most clearly representative of formula mysteries; the Babysitters Club series, the Goosebump stories, and Lemony Snicket's stories are more recent examples. A number of qualities make this type of fiction appealing. Easy to read and understand, these books move quickly with little description and much dialogue and come to satisfying conclusions. Although they present little challenge, their sameness provides comfort and reassuring predictability for young readers.[3] Not all mysteries are formula fiction. Many are carefully plotted and have strong themes, developed characters, and distinctive style.

> Not all mysteries are formulaic.

Mystery, a common element in many well-written stories for children, can hold readers in suspense related to character and theme as well as plot. Mystery novels that have been popular for some time include those of Scott Corbett and Robert Newman, and Donald J. Sobol's *Encyclopedia Brown* books. Sobol's *Angie's First Case* is the first in a series about a girl detective.

Romantic Stories

The romantic novel for young readers has seen a burst of popularity; millions have been sold since the 1960s. They have been around for generations; heroines in Victorian novels, for example, were often absorbed in them. Under the guise of realism, the romantic story may oversimplify and sentimentalize male/female relationships, often showing them as the sole focus of young lives. A thorough study of romances and their market suggests that these "fairy tales of desire" consistently show deeply feminine yet feisty females involved with the male paragon of tender–tough qualities, a combination that both verifies and contradicts the rise of feminism.[4] Romantic stories—since they follow highly similar patterns of plot development and their characters seem to differ in hair color or name rather than in personality—lead a perceptive reader to comment, "Read one, you've read them all"—an exaggeration, of course, but containing some degree of truth.

> Under the guise of realism, romantic stories oversimplify and sentimentalize male/female relationships.

The **romance** differs from formulaic romantic stories. The term is more often used today as describing a story that is freely imaginative, or as the *New English Dictionary* defines it, "a fictitious narrative in prose of which the scene and incidents are very remote from those of ordinary life." Under this definition, such stories might include Robert Louis Stevenson's *Treasure Island* or *Kidnapped*.

Series Books

Many stories are published as parts of a series, some of them with one uniting element and some with many elements. Gary D. Schmidt mentions several plans of organization, overlapping though they may seem to be.[5] "What ties the novels of a series together . . . is the structure of the novels." The first of these focuses, exemplified by series written by J. R. R. Tolkien, Ursula Le Guin, and J. K. Rowling, "documents character growth," with plots that are separated though similar in thematic point. The incredibly successful Harry Potter novels are prime examples. The second type is defined by "a strong central character" like Beverly Cleary's Ramona or Lois Lowry's Anastasia. Character focus means that the order of the novels in the series is unimportant, but each one suggests a slight change in the nature of the character.

Characters in a third type of series remain the focus, but the character is constant and does not change, as in, for example, the Tom Swift and Nancy Drew series, or like Klaus and Violet in *The Series of Unfortunate Events.* The constancy and predictability of the central characters offer no unsettling changes, but as Schmidt says, are "as permanent as Egyptian pyramids." Often called formulaic novels and denigrated by critics, these books are, however, reassuring to young readers whose reading speed increases over the series and who finally decide they have had enough and go on to other stories. Perhaps their greatest contribution to literature for children is the way they offer opportunity to share books, and help young readers discover pleasure in reading.

The fourth structure identified by Schmidt is defined by subject and constitutes primarily biography and informational books. The Childhood of Famous Americans series of the 1950s and early 1960s served to cut "the distance between the contemporary reader and the remote figures of the past." The natural history books of Jean Craighead George, *One Day in———,* offer another example.

Series books differ in organizational plan.

Fantasy

Fantasy requires the "willing suspension of disbelief," a phrase from Coleridge.

Fantasy, in Coleridge's terms, requires "the willing suspension of disbelief." The writer of **fantasy** (sometimes called "literary fantasy" of known authorship to distinguish it from folk fantasy, of unknown authorship) creates another world for characters and readers, asking that readers believe this other world could and does exist within the framework of the book. The acceptance of this other world requires of the writer an ability to make the imaginary universe so credible, "so solidly grounded in reality," as Madeleine L'Engle says, that we wish it were all true; for sheer pleasure, we believe. Fantastic stories, high fantasy, and science fiction are identifiable subgenres of fantasy; often they seem to overlap, and thus make clear distinctions irrelevant.

Fantastic Stories

We might call one subgenre of fantasy **fantastic stories,** stories realistic in most details but still requiring us to willingly suspend our disbelief. The lasting Borrowers books of Mary Norton, for example, show the daily lives of tiny people who face everyday problems like our own and make discoveries about fear of the unknown and about the disruption of family life through greed. In any of the subgenres of fantastic stories, we are drawn to willing suspension of disbelief primarily by character and theme.

Perhaps the fuzzy line between realistic and fantastic stories is best exemplified by Virginia Hamilton's *Sweet Whispers, Brother Rush,* in which everything seems realistic except the appearance of ghostlike Brother Rush. Tree is convinced he is the ghost of her uncle, and that he takes her into the past to reveal details about her father and mother. All else seems real—the mother's work, her denial of her mentally disabled son, Tree's responsibility for keeping the home—and we are prepared to believe in the ghost as fantasy, or to regard it as Tree's imagination.

Other fantastic stories are about characters that are not people but are represented as people because they talk or live in houses like ours, have feelings like our own, or lead lives like those of humans; these we might call fantastic stories of personification. In some, characters are personified animals, like Hans Christian Andersen's "The Ugly Duckling," E. B. White's *Charlotte's Web*, or George Orwell's *Animal Farm.* Their themes are about human life: Growing up is fraught with trauma; the humble are unappreciated; a community may disintegrate when individual jealousies arise. Another subgenre of personification is that of personified objects, like Andersen's "The Little Fir Tree" or his story about the darning needle.

Fantastic stories are written for every age, including the picture book group. For example, Chris Van Allsburg's story *The Widow's Broom* tells of a witch whose broom has lost its steam for transporting her and who is rescued by a widow. Now the broom does the widow's chores until frightened neighbors burn it, only to find that the ghost of the broom returns to the widow, and the frightened neighbors must flee to leave the widow cared for once again.

High Fantasy

The **high fantasy** genre is primarily characterized by its focus on the conflict between good and evil. If it is successful, it captures our belief in two major ways: first, by the internal consistency of the new world, like the categories or classes of small, nonhumans in *The Lord of the Rings* by J. R. R. Tolkien; and second, by the protagonist's belief in his or her experience.[6] High fantasy also portrays full and complete humans, like the hero Aerin in Robin McKinley's *The Hero and the Crown.* Point of view influences our acceptance of the character and the experience. Setting varies, but is most often integral because credibility may depend on a created world different from our own. Time becomes flexible; sometimes it "wrinkles" as in Madeleine L'Engle's *A Wrinkle in Time.* Sometimes it balloons out and returns, as it does in C. S. Lewis's Narnia books. At other times it may be globe-shaped—as Eleanor Cameron says, "holding in equilibrium all tenses" of past, present, and future.[7] Tone is serious, even awed. Themes encompass a broad concern for

Some stories mix the real with the fantasy world.

Characters need not be people, but may be personifications.

High fantasy is primarily characterized by its focus on the conflict between good and evil.

humanity, effectively objectifying and universalizing the greatest conflict of human life, that between good and evil.

Science Fiction

It has been said that while fantasy is the art of the impossible, science fiction is the art of the possible. **Science fiction** may be seen as a type of fantasy, and it is often difficult to decide whether a particular work is fantasy or science fiction. Perhaps when we realize that our enjoyment of *A Wrinkle in Time,* for example, is neither increased nor diminished by our decision to call it fantasy or science fiction, we may decide that such distinctions are unimportant. Yet, for the sake of order, when we think in genres, we might say that **science fiction,** or speculative fiction as it is sometimes called, stresses scientific laws and technological inventions—like gravity and the speed of light and the contrivances with which to deal with these forces and limitations.

Writers define science fiction differently.

Descriptions and criteria begin with definitions. Robert Heinlein, a well-known author of science fiction, calls it "speculative fictions in which the author takes as his first postulate the real world as we know it, including all established facts and natural laws." Don Moskowitz, a historian of science fiction, says that it utilizes "an atmosphere of scientific credibility for its imaginative speculations in physical science, space, time, social science, and philosophy." Kingsley Amis, critic and author, says that science fiction "is hypothesized on the basis of some innovation in science or technology, or pseudo-science, or pseudo-technology." Unlike fantasy, it must "achieve verisimilitude and win the 'willing suspension of disbelief' through scientific plausibility."

The best science fiction is built around humans.

Perhaps the definition that comes closest to our considerations is that proposed by writer of science fiction Theodore Sturgeon. He maintains that "a [good] science fiction story is a story built around human beings, with a human problem, and a human solution, which would not have happened at all without its scientific content."[8] In contrast, poor science fiction often shows characters committed to the scientific process of investigation and invention, and may therefore be governed solely by intellect. Their concerns are the products of their minds; they may expend their physical energies and mental powers mainly on inanimate objects and abstract theories. Intellect may also govern relationships between characters whose source of cooperation seems a union of intellects controlling or using a force either natural or mechanical.

The genre may often rely heavily on conflict rather than character to hold the reader's interest. Such conflicts are frequently with societies alien to us in form and in values, like the Tripods of John Christopher's *White Mountains* trilogy. When the conflict is person against nature, as it is in *The Time of the Great Freeze* by Robert Silverberg, the battle seems weighted on the side of the natural force. While early science fiction seemed to have few themes, recent work is more complex. Tone, like tone in any kind of writing, either for children or adults, may be, but is not necessarily didactic: "If we don't care for our environment . . ." Writers like H. M. Hoover, William Sleator, and Ray Bradbury, however, whose interest in humans is as keen as their interest in scientific speculation, write with subtlety and understanding of human motives. Traditionally science fiction has dealt with future worlds, but in a variation on that form, the time-lapse story takes a protagonist either forward into the future or backward into the past, and occasionally in both directions.

Time lapses occur into either the future or the past.

It has been suggested that science fiction's mechanical persons or robots may serve as the means by which today's children work out their psychological conflicts and fears, as Bruno Bettelheim believes folk and fairy tales have served to do for preceding generations.[9] From Frank Baum and his Oz stories on, anthropomorphized machines have explored relationships between persons and twentieth-century inventions, examining such questions as: Which is superior, human or machine? Does it matter how one is created? Are sophisticated robots truly alive? Might the computer, the thinking machine, pose serious threats to humans and their lives? Who is the smarter chess player—Russian Kasparov or robot Big Blue?

Young in comparison to many forms of literature, the best of the genre ultimately asks what it means to be related and connected and responsible for others. Such considerations are the substance and subject of imaginative and artistic writing. No other genre or subgenre, however, generates such a sharp division of readers into those who love it and those who do not care for it. Awareness of this division as well as of the evolution of the genre is bringing to readers increasingly complete characters and more varied themes.

Science fiction awakens both like and dislike.

Science fiction has changed and continues to change, attracting growing numbers of readers. British writer Richard K. Morgan maintains that "space operas" are things of the past, and that writers are beginning to "look inward rather than outward. There are exciting and scary things going to be happening to our bodies." Now the genre is less ultimately concerned with science, but "rather with a timeless vision of good and evil." Such comments suggest the merging of high fantasy and science fiction.

While, for the most part, British writers with their roots deep in the faerie stories and folklore of northern Europe once concentrated on fantasy, American writers created their specialty—fiction that depicts the conflicts between technology and the laws of nature. Such generalizations may no longer hold.

Traditional Literature

The term "traditional" (or "folk") literature implies that the form comes to us from the ordinary person, an anonymous storyteller, and exists orally rather than in writing—at least until some collector finds, records, and publishes the stories or rhymes, thus setting them into more permanent form. There is, then, no final and definitive version of a piece of folk literature. Folktales have been called the "spiritual history" of humankind, the "cement of society" binding a culture together. They seem to express the universality of human wishes

Folktales that once flourished where people did not read or write are now the property of all.

and needs. Hundreds of versions of the same story, such as "Cinderella," occur in countless cultures and show almost infinite variations, but are similar in their focus on human yearning for social acceptance and material comfort. We are now fortunate that because of scholarly collecting, folktales that once flourished only in communities where people did not read or write have become the property of all people.

Perhaps it is a need to maintain a sense of wonderment, to keep alive a hope that we can seize opportunities for transforming and improving our world, that sends us back to traditional literature.

Fables

The **fable** is a very brief story, usually with animal characters, that points clearly to a moral or lesson. The moral, an explicit and didactic or preachy theme, is usually given at the end of the story and is the reason for the existence of the fable. The fable makes visible and objective a lesson, like the one we see in "The Tortoise and the Hare": "Slow but steady wins the race." Brevity dictates that one or two characters each have a single trait. It also dictates that the conflict be sharp and clear, as it is in "The Dog in the Manger." The setting is a backdrop for the action, and the action has no interpretive narrator telling extra details of characters' thoughts or feelings. Style is crisp and straightforward. Everything in the fable exists to make an abstract point, to make a lesson clear—as clear as the moral in the story of the milkmaid who dreamily drops her basket of eggs on the way to market: "Don't count your chickens before they hatch." As more fables from various cultures appear, it seems that most contain morals.

Folktales

In form the **folktale** relies on flat characters, bad ones and good ones, easily recognized. Since folktales were heard by the teller and then retold in the teller's own words, there was hardly time for subtle character development. A brief phrase, which may be repeated often, serves to draw character, since the teller cannot risk losing the audience by departing from the fast-paced narration of action to describe thoughts and feelings.

Stock characters, like the fairy godmother and the wicked stepmother in "Cinderella," frequently appear. Conflicts are often between people or personified animals in person-versus-person conflict, like Jack and the ogre in "Jack and the Beanstalk." Plots are progressive, with the climax coming at the very end and the closing as brief as "They lived happily ever after." Action, fast and lively, is at the heart of the folktale. In European tales, incidents can occur singly, in threes as they do in "The Billy-Goats Gruff," or occasionally in more repetitions; in stories from Native American and other traditions, the numbers vary. The setting is usually a backdrop for the action, a background that creates universality by its vaguely recognizable appeal. Point of view is rarely first person, since the tales are told about flat characters in fantastic situations. Tone varies; it may be sentimental, as in "Beauty and the Beast"; objective, as in "The Little Red Hen"; or humorous, as in "The Squire's Bride." Themes also vary but comment on human needs and wishes, like the theme in "The Fisherman's Wife": "People are never satisfied."

For years people in the United States read and heard few tales other than those from Europe, although some read the Uncle Remus stories or saw them dramatized in animation. Now, with the collection, retelling, and publication of African tales by Harold Courlander, Ashley Bryan, and Verna Aardema, all children may meet them. Virginia Hamilton and Julius Lester effectively retell African American folk literature. Many of these stories are animal tales, showing how the weak defeat the strong, as does Br'er Rabbit, for example. A particularly attractive edition in very readable language is Hamilton's *The People Could Fly: American Black Folktales*. Native American tales are also published in collections and as single tales, like, for example, *Arrow to the Sun* by Gerald McDermott, who has published tales from several countries. As people from Asia, Africa, and Latin America come to the United States their tales are added to those of European origin. Now children can read Eric Kimmel's *Baba Yaga*, a Russian tale; Celia Barker Lottridge's *The Name of the Tree*, an African tale; or Susan Roth's **pourquoi**—a tale that responds to the question "why"—*Fire Came to the Earth People*.

Folk literature throughout the world is often quite similar. European tales and Asian tales may have identical themes, reinforcing what might be regarded as universal law. For example, the tales from ancient China retold by Linda Fang in *The Chi-lin Purse* sometimes conclude with morals stated as flatly as they are in Aesop's Western fables: "If you have a chance to do something good, be sure to do it." "Happiness will come back to you." "Everyone has a talent that will prove useful one time or another."

As the world grows smaller, tales from many cultures become available.

The style of the folktale relies on recurring images like "no bigger than my thumb" and often includes short rhymes like those in "Snow White": "Mirror, mirror, on the wall/Who is fairest of us all?" The cadenced prose fits the rhythm of oral telling. We recall, "No, by the hair of my chinny chin chin/I will not let you in." From the South American collection *Tales from Silver Lands* comes "A Tale of Three Tails," where "They sing and they play/For half of the day," and "I must do what I can/Is the thought of a man" are repeated. From "The Calabash Man" comes "From forest to hill/We come at your will./Call, Aura, call."

Sometimes folktales[10] are subdivided into tales of magic, romance, *pourquois*, cumulation, religion, sillies, talking beasts, tall tales, and realistic situations. These categories often overlap; the subgroups only emphasize the richness and variety of the genre,[11] all of them ideal media for the picture book. In *Why Mosquitoes Buzz in People's Ears*, for example, Verna Aardema boldly tells a **cumulative tale**—*Mosquitoes* reverses the cumulation (usually a series of additions like those in "The House That Jack Built") to unravel the question of how the owlet was killed.

Myths

Myths are stories that originate in the beliefs of nations and races and present episodes in which supernatural forces operate. Because they, too, are handed down by word of mouth, they have no right or wrong form. Myths, like that about the god Thor and his hammer of thunder, are stories that interpret natural phenomena. Some myths try to make visible and concrete the ways that humans see nature, like the division of the year into seasons: In the story of Ceres and her daughter Proserpine, the girl is abducted and kept for part of the year in the underworld of Pluto, an explanation for the disappearance of summer's warmth and growth. Myths may show people's relationships with one another, like the generosity demonstrated in the myth of Baucis and Philemon, in which hospitality is rewarded by an eternally filled oil cruse and an endless supply of meal.

Myths show the ways that humans see the forces that control them, like the separation of day and night caused by Apollo's crossing the sky in his sun chariot. Myths explain creation, religion, and divinities; they guess at the meaning of life and death, or at the cause for good and evil, as made clear in the myth of Pandora's box. As Virginia Hamilton says in an introductory note to *In the Beginning: Creation Stories from Around the World,* although "fairy tales take place *within* the time of human experience . . . myths take place before the 'once upon a time' . . . [and] go *back beyond anything that ever was,* and begin *before* anything has happened."

Past generations have had experience primarily with myths of European origin, but in today's multicultural society, we ideally meet myths from many lands. One of the benefits to readers of myths is the reinforcement of the truth that all peoples value similar human traits, and furthermore, that faraway countries, for example, can be warmly affectionate about human foolishness, as *Once the Hodja* by Alice Geer Kelsey shows in the stories about the simple country man who constantly gets into and out of trouble.

Each mythical character represents one or a very few qualities—for example, fertility—and therefore the supernatural or unexplainable issues of seasons and growth. Plots are often single incidents or a few incidents linked by characters. An opening phrase like "Long ago in ancient China" is sufficient for setting. Since the abstract issues or themes that myths explore are broad and universal, their tone is dignified and somewhat mystical. The effective telling of a myth has dignity and simplicity, for it tries to re-create the spirit and intention of the original. When myths are poorly told, as they are by Nathaniel Hawthorne in *A Wonder Book,* they condescend to or even insult the efforts of earlier societies to find meaning in life. When myths are well told, they appeal to something deep within us.

Legends and Hero Tales

Legends are similar to myths because both are traditional narratives of a people; sometimes the two subgenres are interwoven. Legends, however, often have more historical truth and less reliance on the supernatural. When, for example, we read the legends of the Trojan War, we are aware of the actual siege of the city as well as of legendary heroes and actions. Although there was a King Arthur, most stories about him are not historical truth but legend. The grandeur of the legend is maintained in *The Legend of King Arthur* as it is retold by Robin Lister, beginning with Arthur's pulling the sword from the stone and setting up the Round Table, to his love and loss of Guinevere, and his final departure for the magic isle of Avalon. Such figures as Abraham Lincoln, a national hero, accumulate legends rooted in the authenticity of the character but fictional in detail.

> Legends may combine historical truth with the supernatural.

Folk Epics

The **folk epic** is a long narrative poem of unknown authorship about an outstanding or royal character in a series of adventures related to that heroic central figure. Ezra Pound has called the epic "a poem including history." This character or hero is, like Beowulf, larger than life, grand in all proportions, and superhuman in physical and moral qualities. The action may involve journeys and quests, and it may show deeds of great courage and valor coupled with superhuman strength; the forces of the supernatural intervene from time to time. The setting is vast, including a nation, a continent, or even the universe. Point of view is objective, for the story is so grand that a protagonist of such remarkable accomplishments seems to need no interpretive narrator. The tone is dignified, and the style is therefore elevated. Often the story, which begins in the middle of things, includes long lists or catalogs of warriors, treasures, gifts, or ships. Extended comparisons called "epic similes" frequently occur. Like the best retellings of myth, those of epic do not condescend in any way; they show the values of the society and awe the reader with the possibility of great courage and moral strength. Few retellers are so masterful as Ian Serraillier in his retelling of Beowulf, or as Rosemary Sutcliff, who tells of Finn MacCool and of the Hound of Ulster.

> A hero is larger than life, superhuman in physical and moral qualities.

Poetry

Poetry, a kind of imaginative and artistic writing, can also be called a genre of literature. And, as with many genres, there are subgenres. For the sake of simplicity, we might identify them as ballads, narrative poetry, and lyric poetry, acknowledging, however, that these categories are not absolute any more than the genres of fiction are absolute. A lyric, or "personal poem" as some might call it, may have balladlike qualities—a refrain, for example—and a narrative may have lyric or songlike passages. Compactness is essential to poetry to make words say much more than literal or denotative meaning. Ballads, too, rely on compactness; they are elliptical in their phrasing, often forcing the reader or listener to leap from inference to inference. Perhaps the narrative poem at first glance does not seem to demand compactness. In all probability, however, the account of action and tension in a narrative poem uses far fewer words than a prose account of the same action and tension.

In poetry, words say more than their literal meaning.

We often make the mistake of calling any writing that has rhythm, rhyme, or short lines "poetry." Much of it, however, is rhyme or verse. Steeped as we are in the Mother Goose nursery rhymes, we identify them easily, and do not call the rhymes poetry. But when short lines are written in rhythm, or address a subject that lacks the familiarity of nursery rhymes, we think they might be poetry. A trace of uncertainty, however, may linger: Where does verse end and poetry begin? To answer that question we enter into one of the age-old literary controversies; we will not try to answer it here, although some effort to address the issue is made in Chapter 11.

Informational Books

Purists might find the title of this volume inaccurate, perhaps even blasphemous, because within a handbook of children's literature we have the temerity to include nonfiction. What is the rationale? Some nonfiction is written with high artistry; we think of Jean George's descriptions of the working of the natural world, or of the philosophical discourses of Plato's *Republic*—to juxtapose modern and ancient writings. Where to draw the line? Rather than draw any line whatsoever, we might instead express the wish that all nonfiction, informational books as well as biography, could be written with high artistry. Nonfiction is included here because it is written and read by children for their pleasure and understanding, evoking both aesthetic—or emotional and intellectual effects—and efferent transactions (to use Louise Rosenblatt's terms as mentioned in Chapter 1). We hope to discover how to recognize the best available.

Both efferent and aesthetic transactions, as well as pleasure, occur in nonfiction.

Nonfiction, too, can be subdivided, but with little likelihood of satisfying all readers. We might look at the librarian's classifications and decide that we must address each of the categories, from natural and physical sciences, social sciences, and history (if it is not seen as part of the social sciences) through the arts, then subdivide even further. In fact, we might go on and on with genres and subgenres. Once again, we must be practical. For that reason, we might subdivide nonfiction into informational books and biography, knowing full well that some would like finer distinctions. The standards for informational books of all kinds, however, are similar. And standards for biography, the account of the life of an individual, can be set with some degree of common sense.

Across Genre Lines

What is there left to consider? Some books are difficult to put neatly into categories because, although they have qualities in common, they cross genre lines. Some books are grouped together, not because of subject matter, but because they rely on pictures to extend the story—picture books, of course. (For a full discussion of picture books, see Chapter 3.) Other books are singled out for another reason; they are placed in a loose and overlapping group called "classics." These works come from all genres and are works that have lasted for some time.

Classics

Classics are books that have worn well, attracting readers from one generation to the next. They cross all genre lines; they are historical fiction, regional literature, and high fantasy. Although picture books have a short history, classics do exist among them, including *Madeline* and *Goodnight Moon*. Because its themes are parts of universal childhood, it is highly likely that *Where the Wild Things Are* will remain as a classic. Literature written for children has a brief history; books that interest two or three generations can be called classics, and we may thus regard the Little House and Pooh books as classics, for example. Some books have had a strong impact on generations of writers and readers; the recent arrival of many stories about the early United States may result from the popularity of Laura Ingalls Wilder's writing. Others, like *The Secret Garden* by Frances Hodgson Burnett, after a generation of being little read have returned to become regarded as classics. What seems to keep classics in continuous circulation may be the significance of theme, the credibility of character, the continuing reality of the conflict, or the engaging quality of style. Furthermore, they often serve as models; the success of the mischievous Tom Sawyer, for example, has resulted in periodic spates of books about mischievous boys.[12] What seems important, however, is that mischief is not what keeps *Tom Sawyer* alive. Instead, it is far more complex and universal matters such as Twain's perceptive portrayal of the adults in the community; his mixture of the experiences, emotions, rites, and yearnings of childhood; the significance of ideas like courage and sacrifice for the sake of other people; and his lively variety of tones and the aptness of his language.

A work may be popular for a time and then fade, as was the case with *A Dog of Flanders* and *Seventeen*. What seemed the height of ingenious wordplay at one time may at another time seem dull and trite; the wit in the once-popular *The Peterkin Papers*, for example, now seems heavy-handed. *Alice's Adventures in Wonderland*, however, remains an incomparable work of nonsense; readers have never outgrown Carroll's wit, and his playful inventiveness remains unsurpassed. Similarly, even if the diversified family farm becomes extinct, E. B. White's finest novel, *Charlotte's Web*, will last.

Classics last because of significant themes, credible characters, real conflict, or engaging style.

text continues on page 35

Table 2.1
Genre in Children's Literature

Realism

Genre	Character	Plot	Setting	Theme	Point of View	Style	Tone
REALISM EXAMPLES: *Roll of Thunder, Dicey's Song*	Best novels have round central characters. Poor ones load protagonist with problems, or have flat or stereotyped characters.	Any kind of conflict. If problem is solved too easily, story is flawed	Any	Any. Sentimentality, sensationalism, didacticism are flaws[1]	Any	Uses all devices	Any, but sentimentality or sensationalism are flaws[1]
ANIMAL REALISM EXAMPLES: *Incredible Journey, Owls in the Family*	Realistic portrayal of animals, without personification	Conflict is usually animal versus nature	Usually integral[1]	Usually related to some discovery about animals or their relationships to humans	Objective in respect to the animal character; human characters may be shown in other points of view[1]	Uses all devices	Any, but if point of view falters, tone may become sentimental[1]
HISTORICAL FICTION EXAMPLES: *The Witch of Blackbird Pond, Summer of My German Soldier*	Protagonist has universal human traits, but is a product of the time and place[1]	Any, but conflict more often person versus society or self, as well as another person	Integral setting with focus on particular time and place, usually time of stress or crisis, or of social change	Any universal theme	Any	Uses all devices. Relies for credibility on accurate descriptions of place–costumes, activities, etc.	Any, but flawed if past is re-created sentimentally or sensationally[1]
REGIONAL REALISM AND STORIES OF OTHER COUNTRIES EXAMPLE: *Where the Lilies Bloom*	Protagonist has universal human traits, but is a product of the time and place	Conflict often related to the region, whether topography, livelihood, or mores of the area[1]	Integral and essentially so[1]	Any universal theme	Any	Uses all devices	Any

[1]Represents elements that have special importance in a genre, or elements that are frequently sources of inadequacy in a work.

Genre	Character	Plot	Setting	Theme	Point of View	Style	Tone
MYSTERIES EXAMPLES: *Angie's First Case*	Well developed	Usually carries story, some coincidence	Any; often spooky	Any	Any	Uses all devices	Mysterious
SPORTS STORIES EXAMPLES: *The Moves Make the Man, The Baseball Bargain*	Realistic	Involves sports	Any	Often personal growth	Any	Uses all devices	Any

Formula Fiction

Genre	Character	Plot	Setting	Theme	Point of View	Style	Tone
ROMANTIC STORIES EXAMPLE: Sweetheart novels	Flat, stereotyped	Boy-meets-girl	Any, often exaggerated wealth	Often "Love conquers all"	Any	Trite[1]	Sentimental[1]
MYSTERIES EXAMPLES: Nancy Drew, Hardy Boys	Flat, stereotyped	Suspenseful	Any	Unimportant	Any	Often vernacular	Factual, or mysterious

Fantasy

Genre	Character	Plot	Setting	Theme	Point of View	Style	Tone
FANTASTIC STORIES EXAMPLES: *Sweet Whispers, Brother Rush, Charlotte's Web*	Like or unlike humans; magical qualities; personified toys, animals, objects	Any kind of conflict	Often realistic world with some fantastic qualities	Any	Any	Any	Any; often humorous
HIGH FANTASY EXAMPLES: *The Hero and the Crown, The Rats of NIMH, A Wrinkle in Time*	Realistically portrayed	Any, but underlying conflict is good versus evil	Often special world, an integral setting where time and place have qualities of expansion or limitation	Universal, important themes of good and evil in conflict	Any	Usually highly sensory	Serious, awed
SCIENCE FICTION EXAMPLES: *The House of Stairs, Future Forward*	Flawed stories often have inadequately developed central characters[1]	Any; often mechanical or natural forces are antagonists; plots usually progressive, suspenseful	Often distinguishes one story from another; set in future sometimes on unexplored planets	May be subtle, implicit, but flawed stories have didactic theme[1]	Any	All devices; often much description in concrete forms	Often objective, but flawed story may be heavily didactic

[1]Represents elements that have special importance in a genre, or elements that are frequently sources of inadequacy in a work .

(continued)

Traditional Tales

Genre	Character	Plot	Setting	Theme	Point of View	Style	Tone
FABLE EXAMPLES: "The Boy Who Cried Wolf," "The Fox and the Crow"	Flat and stock; often personified animals with single traits	Person-versus-person conflict; extremely brief; usually a single incident[1]	Backdrop	Explicit and didactic	Objective or dramatic	Terse, lacking imagery or connotative language	Straightforward, didactic, and moralizing
FOLKTALE EXAMPLES: "Cinderella," "Jack and the Beanstalk," A Story A, Story	Flat, even the protagonist; bad and good characters easily identified; stock characters like the wicked stepmother and the fairy godmother	Person-versus-person or person-versus-personified nature conflicts. Action moves rapidly to a climax and stock closing	Backdrop setting: "Long ago and far away . . ."	Either implicit or explicit. Often strongly focused on justice	Usually omniscient or limited omniscient	A few recurring images; often short verses; cadenced prose[1]	Varied. May be sentimental, humorous, objective, but is not often didactic
MYTH EXAMPLES: "Apollo's Sun Chariot," "How Fire Came to Earth People"	Gods and heroes with traits linked to supernatural powers	An incident or incidents linked by character	Backdrop: "Long ago in ancient China . . ."	Explanations of natural phenomena or human relationships	Usually objective	Significant symbols, abstract terms, little or no dialogue; brief descriptions of action	Dignified, perhaps mystical. Sentimentality is flaw
LEGEND or HERO TALE EXAMPLES: "King Arthur," "Robin Hood"	Historical figures with fictional traits and situations	Any conflict featuring protagonists	Backdrop: "When Arthur was King . . ."	Fictional glorification of historical figures	Usually objective	Significant symbols, abstract terms, little or no dialogue; brief descriptions of action	Often objective. Sentimentality is flaw
FOLK EPIC EXAMPLES: Beowulf, Finn MacCool	Protagonist is heroic, superhuman	Begins in the middle of things (in medias res); conflict is person versus person, society, or nature. Often three incidents showing hero victorious against supreme odds[1]	Undefined long-ago, but set in the vast world or universe	Good can be victorious over evil, but only after great struggle against superhuman odds and with assistance from gods[1]	Objective or dramatic	Long, cadenced lines of oral language; symbols and images; grandeur and simplicity; epic similes and elaborate comparisons; extended formal speeches	Dignified; grand; awesome

[1]Represents elements that have special importance in a genre, or elements that are frequently sources of inadequacy in a work.

32

Rhyme to Poetry

Genre	Form or Focus	Rhythm	Rhyme	Devices
NURSERY RHYMES	Topics open to young children; usually brief; any tone; folk in origin	Regular	Regular	Personification, simile, metaphor, and others
VERSE	Easily understood; for specific purpose; meaning less important than form; often trite, banal in form, subject, or phrasing[1]	Highly rhythmic; rhythm often more important than meaning	Usually regular in scheme; often forced, or more important than meaning	Often ordinary images, predictable; less emotion, imagination, intensity than poetry
NARRATIVE POETRY	Storytelling, long or short	Suited to story	Any form	Any, though fewer than in lyrics
BALLAD FOLK BALLAD: (author unknown) EXAMPLE: "John Henry" ART BALLAD: (author known) EXAMPLE: "Rime of the Ancient Mariner"	Narrative of physical courage; incidents in lives of common people; supernatural; largely dialogue; little characterization; great simplicity; refrains, often incremental; abrupt transitions; single dramatic episode	Great variation, but usually lines 1 and 3 having four accented syllables, lines 2 and 4, three unaccented syllables; variations in number of unstressed syllables	Refrain often used; usually *abcb* rhyme; approximate rhyme very common	Any (See "Form or Focus")
LYRIC or PERSONAL POETRY	Brief, subjective; personal emotional response; single unified impression; "An end in itself"; intense, compact	Suited to topic and emotion evoked	Rhymed or unrhymed	All figurative and sound devices used to produce compactness

[1]Represents elements that have special importance in a genre, or elements that are frequently sources of inadequacy in a work.

(continued)

Nonfiction

Genre	Essential Qualities	Organization and Scope	Style	Tone	Illustrations
INFORMATIONAL BOOKS EXAMPLE: *Building Big*	Gives information and facts; relates facts to concept; stimulates curiosity; "starter," not "stopper"	From simplest to most complex; from known to unknown; from familiar to unfamiliar; from early developments to later; chronological; may have slight narrative for younger reader	Imagery, figurative language, all devices; comparisons extremely useful; flawed if style is monotonous, repetitious, fragmented in statements[1]	Wonder, not mystery; respect; objectivity, occasional humor; fostering scientific attitude of inquiry. Flaws: condescension, anthropomorphism, oversimplification; facts not separated from opinions[1]	Diagrams and draw-ings often clearer than photographs
BIOGRAPHY	Gives accurate, verifi-able facts and authen-tic picture of period; subject worthy of attention; sources of information shown or listed	Assumes no omni-science; shows individ-ual, not stereotype; does not ignore nega-tive qualities of subject; focuses not only on events, but also on nature of person	Storytelling permis-sible for youngest readers; too much invention destroys credibility	Interest; enthusiasm; objectivity; didacticism and preaching to be avoided	Authentic

[1]Represents elements that have special importance in a genre, or elements that are frequently sources of inadequacy in a work.

White's thorough portrayal of character and his choice of life-and-death con-flict, his affectionately humorous tone, and his universal themes about friend-ship, satisfaction, and death are elements that identify classics. The classics of one generation may be supplanted by later works, but the appeal of other books may remain for a surprisingly long time. To paraphrase Ezra Pound, a classic is "news that stays news." It is not the Classics List graven in stone, but time, that will tell.

Summary

Awareness of the similarities and differences in the genres of children's liter-ature may or may not be useful. Perhaps the most obvious and most impor-tant thing to realize is that not all books or all genres appeal to all children. However, a child hooked on one genre—science fiction, for example—may find the craving for adventure is further satisfied through sports or other real-istic stories. Curiosity about imaginatively created worlds may lead the reader to find pleasure in another closely related genre—high fantasy, for example. Expansion of the young reader's world results as the reader finds new styles of writing, broader themes, and other motivations in characters with varied experiences. Greater appreciation of self and of other humans and their societies results as such vicarious experiences grow in number.

Table 2.1 on pages 30–34 summarizes similarities and differences in the genres. It may prove helpful, but only if we keep in mind the dangers of gen-eralizing. Literature, since it is not so easily classified as the chemical ele-ments, will often be elusive, refusing to fit neatly into a genre. The table may, however, serve as a reminder of the tremendous breadth of literature avail-able to children for their joy, pleasure, and increased understanding.

Notes

1. In Shakespeare's *Hamlet,* Polonius's speech praising the actors (Act II, Scene 2) makes fun of the genres of drama in such phrases as "pastoral-comical" and "tragical-comical-historical-pastoral."
2. Publishers of the seventy-five-year-old Hardy Boys books, which still sell over a million copies a year, are looking for new readers. Their search prompts them to turn to cell phones, computers, high-tech gadgets, and adventures that coincide with the news. Keeping them fresh is always a concern, but there are no plans to discontinue publication (*New York Times,* July 29, 2001).
3. Barbara Moran and Susan Steinfirst, "Why Johnny (and Jane) Read Whodunits in Series," *School Library Journal,* March 1985, p. 113.
4. Janice Radway, *Reading the Romance* (Chapel Hill: University of North Carolina Press, 1984).
5. Gary D. Schmidt, "'So here, my dears, is a new Oz story': The Deep Structure of a Series," *Children's Literature Association Quarterly 14,* Winter 1989, pp. 163–165.

6. For an enlightening discussion of the narrator and the reader-audience in fantasy, see "Some Presumptions about Fantasy" by Perry Nodelman, in *Children's Literature Quarterly,* Summer 1979.

7. Eleanor Cameron, *The Green and Burning Tree* (Boston: Little, Brown, 1969), p. 72.

8. These definitions are from *Alternate Worlds: The Illustrated History of Science Fiction,* by James Gunn (Englewood Cliffs, NJ.: Prentice-Hall/A&W Visual Library, 1975).

9. Margaret Esmonde, "From Little Buddy to Big Brother: The Icon of the Robot in Children's Science Fiction," in *The Mechanical God,* ed. Thomas P. Dunn and Richard D. Erlich (Westport, CT: Greenwood, 1982).

10. In an observation about folktales, Jack Zipes responds to Bruno Bettelheim's optimism regarding folktales, saying that "such focus on resolution and happiness only points to our tenacious capacity to avoid unpleasant insights into childhood experiences. . . . Perhaps the most therapeutic aspect of these stories is the reassurance they give *parents* that children survive the horrors they impose on them." "Child Abuse and Happy Endings," *New York Times Book Review,* November 13, 1988, pp. 39, 60.

11. Claire L. Malarte-Feldman, in her review of *Beauty, Beasts and Enchantment* by Jack Zipes, and *Beauty and the Beasts: Visions and Revisions of an Old Tale* by Betsy Hearne, says that fairy tales indicate "their strong vitality . . . as a genre that has survived because of its extraordinary ability to adapt to new forms of expression. This is the power of fairy tales: narratives without fixed texts, stories without authors, their origins are impossible to trace with precision. Their sources can be found in our strongest emotions: love and hate, violence and jealousy, fear and courage . . . a symbolic expression of our need for love and of our belief in the power of love." *Children's Literature,* Vol. 20 (New Haven, CT: Yale University Press, 1992), p. 240.

    By contrast, toymakers are interested in stories that feature their wares. Hasbro Inc., maker of Tonka®, has allied itself with Scholastic, Houghton Mifflin, and Golden Books to create books featuring twenty of the company's best products. Mattel is following suit for its Matchbox® cars and American Girl® dolls. Lego markets books featuring Legos® (*The Wall Street Journal,* July 7, 25, 2001).

12. While critics call *Huckleberry Finn* the better novel, *Tom Sawyer* seems more clearly a book for children.

Recommended Books Cited in This Chapter

ANDERSEN, HANS CHRISTIAN. *The Ugly Duckling; The Little Fir Tree.* New York: Macmillan, 1965.

AVI. *Crispin, the Cross of Lead.* New York: Hyperion, 2002.

BROOKS, BRUCE. *The Moves Make the Man.* New York: Harper & Row, 1984.

BURNETT, FRANCES HODGSON. *The Secret Garden.* 1911. Reprint. New York: Viking, 1989.

BURNFORD, SHEILA. *The Incredible Journey.* Boston: Little, Brown, 1961.

CARROLL, LEWIS. *Alice's Adventures in Wonderland.* Reprint. New York: Dutton, 1954.

FANG, LINDA. *The Chi-lin Purse.* New York: Farrar, Straus & Giroux, 1995.

KIMMEL, ERIC. *Baba Yaga.* New York: Holiday House, 1991.

HAMILTON, VIRGINIA. *Sweet Whispers, Brother Rush.* New York: Putnam, 1982.

L'ENGLE, MADELEINE. *A Wrinkle in Time.* New York: Farrar, 1962.

Lister, Robin. *The Legend of King Arthur.* New York: Doubleday, 1988.

Lowry, Lois. *Number the Stars.* Boston: Houghton Mifflin, 1989.

McKinley, Robin. *The Hero and the Crown.* New York: Greenwillow, 1981.

Norton, Mary. *The Borrowers.* New York: Harcourt, 1965.

Orwell, George. *Animal Farm.* 1945. Reprint. New York: Harcourt Brace, 1995.

Park, Linda Sue. *A Single Shard.* New York: Clarion, 2001.

Roth, Susan. *Fire Came to the Earth People.* New York: St. Martins, 1988.

Sobol, Donald. *Angie's First Case.* New York: Four Winds, 1984.

Speare, Elizabeth George. *The Witch of Blackbird Pond.* Boston: Houghton Mifflin, 1958.

Stevenson, Robert Louis. *Kidnapped.* 1886. Reprint. New York: Scribner's, 1913.

———. *Treasure Island.* 1883. Reprint. New York: Scribner's, 1911.

Sutcliff, Rosemary. *The High Deeds of Finn MacCool.* New York: Dutton, 1967.

———. *The Hound of Ulster.* New York: Dutton, 1963.

Taylor, Mildred. *Roll of Thunder, Hear My Cry.* New York: Dial, 1976.

Tolkien, J. R. R. *The Lord of the Rings.* Boston: Houghton Mifflin, 1974.

Twain, Mark. *The Adventures of Tom Sawyer.* 1866. Reprint. New York: Macmillan, 1966.

Van Allsburg, Chris. *The Widow's Broom.* Boston: Houghton Mifflin, 1992.

White, E. B. *Charlotte's Web.* New York: Harper, 1952.

Wilder, Laura Ingalls. The Little House Books. 1932–1943. Reprint. New York: Harper, 1953.

The Three Pigs

David Wiesner

Picture Books

Words or pictures:
Which are more important?

According to Bowker's *Children's Books in Print*, 2006, there are over 386,000 books for children in print. A glance at the many on library shelves shows clearly that illustration is growing in importance. We might call a book illustrated when it includes merely a pictorial dust jacket, a cover picture, a frontispiece, or three or four pictures throughout, but the profusely illustrated picture book is the genre most clearly dependent on illustration. Thanks to a more affluent society, to increased awareness of the importance of childhood, to courses in children's literature and its critical evaluation, and very importantly to the growing significance of awards given to children's books—as well as to publishers' profits accompanying such winning books and to the attractive packaging of many more—children seem to be continuously blessed with well-illustrated literature. This is not to say, of course, that poorly illustrated books do not abound, but that artistic excellence is increasingly apparent and appreciated.

Perhaps because illustration has historically been tied to text, it has often in the past been regarded as a lesser art. Although at one time Degas, Daumier, and Roualt all illustrated for the public, they are more appreciated now for their other art. Howard Pyle and N. C. Wyeth, who spent their professional lives making books beautiful, were not taken as seriously as other artists, but as printing processes improved and publishers employed art editors, successful artists such as Leo and Diane Dillon, Chris Van Allsburg, Ezra

Jack Keats, Maurice Sendak, and a multitude of others were attracted to illustrating children's books and collaborating on them.

Because illustration has the characteristics of an art form, however, it should be regarded as art. Illustrators use the techniques of representation, expressionism, impressionism, and surrealism, of cubism and pointillism, of native, folk, and collage styles as well as photography. Like other art forms, illustration uses symbolic language for communication. It has both meaning and content created from visual and usually verbal symbols as well. It creates its own illusions of reality often dissimilar to those of the practical world, and by use of figurative devices of all kinds, it opens for us an imaginary vision. Successful art takes us away from our current world to a level of understanding deeper and wider than our limited lives, maybe to a world more ugly or more beautiful, more humorous or more somber, more simple or more complex. And like the best of any art form, it forces us to confront the depths of our secret selves.[1] Unlike looking at the natural world to take it in and to appreciate it, looking at a picture book involves associational meaning, connecting picture with text, or in the wordless book relating what we see through the whole of the story.[2]

It is sometimes said that picture books for the younger child require simpler composition than those for older readers. But real artistry means that complexity may be appropriate for any age, as it is, for example, in *Anno's Journey* by Mitsumasa Anno or in any of Errol LeCain's or Susan Jeffers's pictures.

In any composite of verbal and pictorial storytelling, the picture's contents appear all at once, but the verbal story is revealed a little at a time in linear progression. Joseph Schwarcz comments that we remember, assemble, and associate the elements of the verbal story, keeping them in mind as we simultaneously acquire new information. In a similar but reverse way, we look at a picture to see it as a whole, then absorb the details little by little, noting how they compose the whole. Eyes wander over the picture, lingering here and skipping there, absorbing, assimilating, connecting details, colors, and shapes, until all the picture is absorbed. As Schwarcz says, "Following an illustrated text is, then, a complex activity." Despite complexities, however, and more likely because of them, children never weary of the intimately interwoven visual and verbal arts, demanding to see and hear new illustrated stories as well as being excited by continuing discoveries in the familiar ones.

Since finding the earliest records of pictorial art in cave drawings, people have assumed drawings are made to accompany verbal storytelling, that one complements the other. "Associates in a partnership" is one term used to describe the relationship of the writer and illustrator of a picture book. No matter what terms we use, it is clear that if two artists work separately and in differing media, together they create a whole. Pictures make the verbal visible and extend the textual meaning; they permit the artist to add personal interpretation while staying within the story, but they do not overwhelm the text. "Their responsibility is to reflect truly the imaginative tenor of the text (or, in the case of books without text, of the subject) and to create a sequence or

We seem to see a picture all at once, while text is revealed little by little.

A picture book is a partnership between writer and artist.

group of pictures which add up to a consistent whole," as B. W. Alderson says. He says further:

> Among the virtues of the traditional approach to book illustration is its care for the details of a picture's narrative content and design. This is not to say that there is always necessarily something going on in the illustrations, but that there is nearly always a nuance of detail for the eye to feed upon and one which in the best work will be in complete harmony (and may even be visually integrated) with the printed text.[3]

Decrying both artwork that is trite and artwork that distracts and seems to exist for the sake of showing off the artist's skill, Alderson reminds us of the technique, artistry, and versatility that have existed throughout the history of illustration, from Howard Pyle to present-day illustrators.

Partnership is somewhat different in pictures made of dolls and puppets in a photograph. There is an interdependence of several artists: the writer, the doll or puppet creator, the stage designer, and the director. Although one person may act in two or more capacities, the result is a compiled effort. Despite photographic techniques of long shots and close-ups, these illustrations convey a sense of still life and seem to be a moment from a play captured by the photographer.

The Illustrative Elements of the Picture Book
Designing the Book

Although illustration and other two-dimensional art have much in common, designing an entire picture book is not like designing other works. Publication requires that the illustrator's work be reproducible in mass, and that requirement determines the whole book design, including size, shape, endpapers, title page, cover, and dust jacket (choice of a wraparound illustration or separate pictures for front and back) as well as the use of single- or double-page pictures and the placement of the gutter. Some pages call for decoration, some are best left "silent"; other illustrations may be framed or unframed or may fill the page, edge to edge. All this requires decisions about placement of pictures and text, to create formality or informality, to suit the tone or pace of the story or poem.

Perry Nodelman, who has written extensively about picture books, believes that children who come to understand their conventions and structures can enjoy them with great enthusiasm and conscious appreciation, discovering how pictures and words work together.[4] He suggests that the two kinds of "texts" are read at different speeds, that one of their pleasures lies in grasping an element in one narrative that the other does not treat, and furthermore that a picture book presents these details at the proper time. "Reading [a picture book's] short text is a relatively speedy process, whereas reading the series of pictures that accompany the words is a lengthy one that

Trite pictures or those that seem to be "show-off" work add little.

Pictures may take longer to "read" than does the text.

involves the need for close attention, the search for clues, the putting together of apparently disparate pieces of information, the scanning, the remembering, projecting, predicting, discriminating."[5]

Pictures show what
the words tell—and
more.

The illustrator puts into visual form what the words say, or sometimes what they merely suggest. In *The Snowy Day*, Ezra Jack Keats uses many words to describe Peter's trek through the fresh snow, "with his toes pointing out, like this," dragging "his feet s-l-o-w-l-y" or dragging the "something" and making a third track. In *Fish Is Fish*, Leo Lionni, who like Keats is both author and illustrator, tells in pictures what would take a page of verbal description. When the frog returns to tell the fish of the wonders on land, they can picture only fish bodies: birds as fish with wings, people as fish in clothes, and fish-cows with horns, four legs, and "pink bags for milk." The illustrator has not only put into visual form what the words say, but he has also successfully added to the text, creating incongruous humor and commenting on how we see others in terms of ourselves.

Occasionally an illustrator will use *continuous narrative*, the technique seen frequently in comics, in which action is depicted through the repeated picturing of the character in different places or motions all within the same illustration. Using this technique in *A Whistle for Willie*, Keats shows two separate actions in one illustration. Willie, disappointed that he cannot whistle for his dog, tries to distract himself from his feeling of discouragement, first by walking the sidewalk cracks, then by trying to run away from his shadow.

A close look at an
old favorite can be
helpful.

Look next at a classic, Wanda Gág's *Millions of Cats*, first published in 1928. Gág is steeped in European folktales, and this original fantasy has the traits of such stories. Thumbnail characters (a very old woman and a very old man), the long cadenced lines of oral tradition, and a repeated rhythmic refrain—"Hundreds of cats, thousands of cats, millions and billions and trillions of cats"—are some of the folktale elements. The fantasy that all these cats could eat each other up and leave only one survivor is revealed at the brisk climax, and the refrain concludes with a happily-ever-after variation: "And not one was as pretty as this one."

The illustrations in sharp black-and-white lithographs are as straightforward and unadorned as the text; the design of each page produces emphatic rounded shapes and patterns that move the eye left to right across the spread. Shading and texture create three-dimensional hills, clouds, fields, trees—and cats, trillions of cats. Cats seen close up are individuals; the anonymous crowd stretches over the infinite hills.

On every page the illustration is adjacent to the substance of the relevant text. As the very old man chooses the first cat for his wife, the spread is balanced with a segment of a tree branch over his shoulder on the left margin and a similar picture on the far right. Centered beside the book's gutter and below the text are two views of him choosing cats, each one with a semicircular tree curving protectively around him and the chosen ones. The picture illustrating "And they began to quarrel" is chaotically filled with cats in all positions and contortions; it seems they may indeed eat each other up. In the final spread Gág uses continuous narrative illustration, beginning top left with the skinny survivor cat, picturing it greedily eating in eight additional poses that carry diagonally to the lower gutter and then move to the top right where the plump and contented cat sits. The little figures divide each page into two triangles; within the two upper triangles of each spread is the brief text. Of particular note is the way in which Gág has placed her hand-lettered text, often in centered lines, as part of the overall page design. Nothing is placed casually on the page. When we examine *Millions of Cats,* we understand the concept of *designing* a book.

A particularly satisfying marriage of text and pictures occurs in *The Name of the Tree,* a Bantu folktale retold by Celia Barker Lottridge and illustrated by Ian Wallace. Illustrations have a misty look that sharpens the feeling that this is a faraway land and a long-ago time when the jungle, the riverbank, and the parched plains yielded no food for starving animals, the lion was king of the jungle, and all the animals lived comfortably together. In quiet neutrals, the title and first pages show the vastness of the arid land and on the horizon silhouettes of the various animals trekking off in search of food. On the edge of the land is a bump that becomes a miraculously tall umbrella-like tree laden with every kind and color of fruit, but all so far up none can reach it. The tree itself, described in minimal words, is a colorful spread from margin to margin, with spidery branches topped by a mass of colorful fruit and foliage. The next page is particularly effective—an aerial view of the tree and its much larger shadow of fruited top and tracery branches. Next, a sober group of tearful animals confers with the central figure, a huge tortoise who tells them that to gain the fruit they must learn the name of the tree from the jungle king. The gazelle, fastest of all animals, offers to make the trip to ask the question; Wallace shows the confident gazelle leaping off, close to flight, knowing he will learn the name and return so quickly he cannot possibly forget it.

Now here is the lion, a drowsy-looking king roused from sleep on a jungle branch, who kindly says that Ungalli is the fruit tree's name but cautions that he will not tell it again. Bounding along now on the pride of his accomplishment, the gazelle carelessly steps in a rabbit hole and goes "head over hoofs over head over hoofs" and forgets the name. Wallace next shows only heads of eager waiting animals, their mouths open in anxious questioning, and includes only part of an elephant trunk, foreshadowing that that beast, known for its memory, may be the next messenger. On another misty page the questing elephant seems small compared to the vast land. His interview with the lion is quite different; the king's eyes blaze, and teeth show in a snarl as he angrily names Ungalli a second time. As the prideful elephant returns to the hungry animals, confident she cannot forget, she cockily recites the names of all the trees in the jungle and in the rest of the world, but in her arrogance steps in the rabbit hole, and forgets the name. Now, as Wallace shows her return, animal bodies show despondency, heads down in discouragement, among them a monkey cradling her hungry infant.

A lowly young tortoise, taught by his great-great-great-grandmother how to remember, next offers to save the starving group, and plods endlessly, "one short leg ahead of the other," across the cracked plains to the jungle, there to

The intimate relationship between words and pictures can be called a marriage.

Illustrations may create a frame for a picture book.

encounter a furious king crouched in snarling attack position and nose-to-nose with the humble tortoise. The polite tortoise recites the name over and over, and inches back across the land, creeping over rough rocks but faithfully remembering. As he says the name Ungalli, the tree branches, so spidery before, now bend to allow the animals to reach the luscious fruit. No longer hungry, they encircle the tree as they chant its name, and gratefully elevate the young tortoise. The final page shows an empty tree as an umbrella once again, silhouetted against the misty sky with the contented animals beneath it. Once again the animals, silhouetted against the vast sky, provide a frame for the story and a sense of contented closure for the reader.

Picturing Figurative Language

Figurative language is inherent in human speech. As children add new experiences and experiment with language, they speak figuratively, exploring how this and that are surprisingly like or unlike. Perhaps one of the most interesting ways in which an illustrator enlivens and complements the text is by picturing figurative language. The most common is the personification of animals, as in Robert McCloskey's *Make Way for Ducklings,* or of inanimate objects, as in Virginia Lee Burton's classic, *The Little House.* Sometimes, however, the illustrator may try a literal picturing of a metaphor, and the mood changes. For example, the moon's kiss on the face of a drowsy child awakens a sense of wonder at the luminous moon. But literally picturing the moon descending into the bedroom to touch the child's face would totally destroy the mood. In her illustrated version of Rudyard Kipling's tale *The Elephant's Child,* Lorinda Bryan Cauley avoids showing literally the elephant's nose as "no bigger than a boot"; the comparison is convincing as she pictures it but would be distracting if illustrated literally.

Amplifying the Text

The illustrator clarifies and amplifies text, extending it beyond the words or the reader's imagination. "Form," said Ben Shahn in a lecture at Harvard over forty years ago, "is the visible shape of content."[6] Even in books for older children, where illustrations are less frequent, the visual images enhance the text. In Robert McCloskey's *Homer Price,* for example, Uncle Telly's ball of string, "six feet across . . . biggest ball of string in the world," is funny to read about but vastly more humorous when we see Homer sprawled across the top, trying to add another yard of string. Pooh, tracking the Heffalump, is alarmed at the third set of tracks going around the tree; Ernest Shepard has made us laugh as the illustration solves Pooh's mystery. It is far easier to see the relative size of the Borrowers when Beth and Jo Krush picture them in their home beneath the floor, where postage stamps are hung as pictures, spools are used as stools, and stacked matchboxes serve as chests. The illustration creates a recognizable world and compels us to believe that Borrowers do indeed exist.

There's a joyful feeling of "crazy adventure to follow" created by the colorful pictures of *My Friend Rabbit* by Eric Rohmann. Against a sky blue background Rabbit controls Mouse's toy plane, and as often happens when a friend takes over a toy, the plane lands in a tree. Rabbit's not-to-worry response is amazing. He recruits Elephant, Rhino, Hippo, Ram, Monkey, and Crocodile to stand on one another's backs to build a writhing, tumbling tower high enough to reach the captured plane. And ironically, the top creature is the squirrel (who could have done the rescue alone). The simple spreads of illustration are strongly outlined in black to emphasize movement.

In another example, Keats uses somber tones when he paints with a dark palette the shadowy tenement of *Apt. 3*. Splotches of dark color give the impression of dinginess, dirty walls, lack of light, and a sense of mystery: What goes on behind these closed doors? This is not physical detail added to text but the mood of the whole. When Sam and Ben invite the blind man to take a walk the next day, his harmonica music becomes quiet and soft, and the double-page spreads change to happier, lighter tones. The final, lighter-colored spread says nothing about a walk, but silhouetted television antennas and a sky, smoky but blue, answer that question. Here illustrations do not merely extend the text, but the two also present a complete and inextricable combination, the creation of a new world. This is what Maurice Sendak, creator of *Where the Wild Things Are,* calls "seamlessness," or the perfect joining of text and pictures.

The colors in illustration may show mood.

Sendak calls the perfect joining of words and pictures "seamlessness."

David Wiesner in *The Three Pigs* has a new angle on what happened to the three little pigs. They all outwitted the Wolf. Houses blew down, but each one escaped and "Now we have room to move. Watch this—" From this point on the three have a ball. Each picture of each house becomes sheets of painted paper, perfect for making airplanes for flying off into the sky. Each illustration of their flight shows the three porkers from different perspectives, looking out over the triangular wings, or huddled at the rear end of the plane. A crash changes their plans, but now each paper airplane has become a wrinkled mess. One delight of the book is mentally reconstructing these flat, flying pieces of painted houses. "Let's see. Oh, this is part of the stick house . . . and that is the door of the straw one . . . " Small balloons in comic-strip fashion recite the pigs' reactions.

Changing the Story

The illustrator influences, and in some cases changes, the story—not the text, but the story. The greater the ratio of illustrations to text, the greater the influence the illustrations have in the creation of the composite. In some cases, text and pictures seem to provide two stories; the impact of Pat Hutchins's *Rosie's Walk,* for example, is dependent on recognizing this duality. The text tells us that Rosie walks innocently across the farm; the pictures tell us her life is threatened by the menacing fox. Holding these two stories in mind simultaneously constitutes the delight of the whole. In another example, objective narration combined with humorous illustration creates a two-dimensional story as pictures provide plot that is unspoken.

Occasionally pictures carry a second story.

Illustration may also give more exact information, create a mood and atmosphere by depicting a setting or action, or make us care about a character because the pictured dress and countenance reveal more of a person than does the text. Thus illustration not only clarifies and amplifies text, but extends it beyond our own imaginations. In A. A. Milne's *Winnie-the-Pooh,* Pooh's gluttony as he sits surrounded by water "on his branch, dangling his legs . . . beside him . . . ten pots of honey" is made vivid by Shepard's illustration. By contrast, notice how Gustav Tenngren's illustrations for *Snow White and the Seven Dwarfs* change the story. We assume from the title that this is Snow White's story, but that is not the case. Because the bland beauty of Tenngren's Snow White is no match for the personalities we read on the faces of the seven dwarfs and the wicked witch, this has become *their* story: *The Seven Dwarfs, the Witch (and Snow White).* The story has changed, and we do not face so clearly one of its major themes, that the forbidden is tempting.

The Man Who Walked between the Towers by Mordecai Gerstein is the true and remarkable story of Philippe Petit, street performer and juggler who strung a wire between the twin towers of the World Trade Center and walked across it. If Philippe "saw two towers, he had to walk! That's how it was." Without this setting, there would be no story. One picture shows a tiny figure walking a wire strung between the towers of Notre Dame Cathedral in Paris, and is followed by others showing police forbidding such behavior. Plans must be secret. With the help of friends who shoot an arrow with wire attached from the roof of one tower to the other, Philippe makes his first connection. Next they struggle to get a 440-pound reel of cable into the elevator, then up the 180 steps to the roof, and pulled across to the first tower. Each step of this process done in the dark of night is vividly illustrated. Then, in a three-part fold-out picture, Gerstein shows Philippe walking the cable as the city, a quarter of a mile beneath him, is bathed in golden sunlight. Another three-part vertical picture shows the tiny figure dancing back and forth in the air while, below him, New Yorkers gasp. In another spread, the artist shows Philippe from the vantage point of a soaring bird. Can there be any doubt that pictures tell this story far better than any words could? Finally, and sadly, the last picture shows the New York skyline, now empty without its familiar towers

When illustrated by different artists, a story becomes many quite different tales, each influenced by the vision of the artist, the episodes selected for picturing, the chosen palette, the rhythm and movement of line, the meticulous detail or the bold sweep of pen or brush. Look, for example, at different versions of the Cinderella story. Despite knowing well the texts of Charles Perrault and others, the reader still gains very different impressions from the various versions. In Shirley Hughes's retelling with twenty-five pictures, Cinderella herself, whose story this is, appears eighteen times, often in less than central focus, while her wicked stepsisters appear eleven times, and often as the major focus. We see Cinderella being scorned by her stepmother, dressing her stepsisters' hair, scrubbing the floor while the sisters preen, watching wistfully in the doorway while in the foreground they dress for the

Illustrations that subordinate the major character may affect theme.

ball, abjectly weeping while we focus on the fairy godmother, and, in a rear view, watching as the splendid coach appears. Then, at long last, on a full page we see her dressed in her magical finery. In the next picture, she does not appear at all, and in still others, she shares equal billing with the prince, the townspeople, the fairy godmother, the chamberlain. In ratio of two pictures of the stepsisters for every three of Cinderella, stepsisters echo their mother's sneer on the frontispiece, and kneel in supplication for mercy in the twenty-fourth picture. Because of the strong focus on the stepsisters, the impact of the story is that Cinderella is the victim of their envy but is magically saved.

In Paul Galdone's version, Cinderella appears not as beautiful and good, but as pathetic, as Goldone seizes the opportunity to paint wonderful lizards, mice, horses, town criers, coach, and cartoon-like stepsisters. Plot details seem to carry illustrations; Cinderella herself, though important, still does not illuminate the theme of the good person who yearns for and receives acceptance and appreciation.

In still another version, Errol LeCain's highly stylized illustrations distance us from all the characters. In a palette of low color intensity and in pictures swirling with stylized motion, all characters are strictly fairy-tale-never-happened figures. The illustrator seems to have been carried away with the infinite possibilities for creating elaborate coaches, footmen, ball guests, and an evil-looking witch never mentioned in the text. Since in this book pictures are often unrelated to the accompanying text, they serve more as decorations than as illustrations for the story.

Poor illustrations may distort a story.

The way in which the pictures portray or add to the textual information creates the information itself, as we might note from Nonny Hogrogian's version of Cinderella. She uses soft pastels in illustrations bathed in a mist of fantasy that enhance the fairy-tale qualities. Cinderella, herself a lovely girl not unlike lovely girls we might know, convinces by her humility and devotion that she is indeed as good as she is beautiful and deserves therefore to live happily ever after.

Look next at another contrast. Two picture book versions of Hiawatha's childhood provide an interesting comparison. Both books record the Longfellow text about the legendary Native American, but the two are very different. As Errol LeCain often does, here he creates a sense of mystery with his dark colors and intricately framed action. Young Hiawatha is a wide-eyed child with a round face and round eyes. This is Hiawatha's story, but the double-spread title page features in tiny profile his ancient and wrinkled grandmother Nokomis. Hiawatha's bent knee, normally indicative of running movement, does little to animate a picture, nor do the animals from whom he learns have any but stationary form. LeCain's illustrations have a static quality, as though a camera had taken pictures. No one and nothing is animated. Susan Jeffers's title page, however, pictures the forest environment, and opens the story by showing Nokomis grieving for her dying daughter Wenonah who lies beside her newborn, Hiawatha. The story has already begun. Using a subdued palette, Jeffers depicts in heavenly shadow the warrior ghosts as Nokomis teaches

Hiawatha the lore known to Native Americans. Wide-eyed Hiawatha grows older from page to page as he learns more and still more of human relationships with the natural world of animals, flowers, sun, and moon. By the endpaper, the boy is close to manhood, a young brave at home in the forest and carrying bow and quiver. LeCain's book is a group of pictures; Jeffers's is a story with illustrations that extend the text.

The Literary Elements of the Picture Book

We are often deceived into thinking that because the text for picture books is brief, the text need not be judged by the standards of literary excellence. However, it is possible to develop surprisingly full characters, like Beatrix Potter's Peter Rabbit; to create an engaging plot, as Maurice Sendak so skillfully does in *Where the Wild Things Are;* and to show with words as well as pictures an integral setting like that in *Just a Dream* by Chris Van Allsburg. A good picture book is not as simple as it looks. Appreciation grows as words make comparisons and sound resembles meaning. Style is important. As Perry Nodelman comments: "The excitement of a good picture book is the constant tension between the moments isolated by the pictures and the flow of words that join these moments together. The jumpy rhythm of picture books is quite different from the gradually intensifying flow of stories told by words themselves."[7]

Thus, words as well as pictures—fresh comparisons, vivid sensory appeals, and the writer's intelligence and wit—make the most successful story. Some slight tension holds our interest, and the simplest of thematic ideas, such as "We need food for the spirit as well as for the body" from *Frederick* by Leo Lionni, ties it all together. The elements of literature, then, are important here, too. By pinning pictures to words and words to ideas, the best text can enlarge the child's world in ways that even the most careful observation of pictures cannot do.

The elements of literature are important to text.

How Raven Brought Light to People, retold by Ann Dixon in the long phrasing of an oral *pourquoi* tale, begins traditionally: "Long ago when the earth was new" and there was no light, the Raven used his magical powers to become first a pine needle, then a willful child beloved by his adoring grandfather, who gives the crying child the boxes that hold sun, moon, and stars. The familiar three—doting grandparent, mischievous child, magical changeling raven—and traditional ending, implying that now the world will be blessed with light, constitute a familiar form for this tale from southeastern Alaska. Illustrations are as convincing as text. The chief's age and power, the Native American dress and totem poles all convince the reader that this is a true tale.

By contrast, *Dreamplace* is a place for tourists to speculate about the Pueblos. Tourists and Native Americans appear in the same pictures, as travelers attempt to picture the life lived by the former dwellers. Text and pictures confuse rather than clarify.

Character

One of the surprising discoveries about **character** in fiction is that a round character can emerge from a brief story for a young child. Contrast *Peter Rabbit* with *Cowboy Small*. What does any child remember from *Cowboy Small?* It might be called "a ho-hum book—soonest read, soonest forgotten."[8]

Cowboy Small saddles, mounts, rides, dismounts, cooks, eats, sleeps under the stars, rides again, rounds up cattle, eats again, ropes a calf, helps in branding, plays a guitar and sings, sleeps, rides a bronco, falls off, and rides again. Cowboy Small is just his name, and even that is no name. The story is merely a message, the job description of the mythical American cowboy.

Would Cowboy Small have stuffed himself as Peter Rabbit did? We understand and care about Peter Rabbit; we remember him. In a text shorter than that about Cowboy Small, Ezra Jack Keats shows another Peter in *The Snowy Day* as a real boy who is delighted at the snowfall, happy with his angel-making, sad at his snowball's melting, and wistful about joining the snowball fight; in short, Keats's Peter is a character we know and like.

Perhaps at this point it is necessary to digress, since in Beatrix Potter's *Peter Rabbit* some adults may find rabbits and people difficult to interchange. What matters here is not that Peter, like a rabbit, moves on four legs and lives in a sandbank under the roots of a fir tree, nor for that matter that, like a child, he wears a little blue jacket with gold buttons. What makes Peter a little boy is his childlike personality and behavior.

While adults may find it difficult to attribute to animals the traits of humans, this is not difficult for most children. The child listening to *Peter Rabbit* has no difficulty seeing Peter as a child, because he is a developed, or round, character. When an animal in a children's story is a believable human being, the **anthropomorphism** creates fantasy. If the fantastic but believable character is involved in action related to character, children feel very much at home with the whole idea.

Character and incident in *Peter Rabbit* are so closely tied to each other that there is no separation. Peter is mischievous from the start; throughout the story he believes he knows better than he actually does. He is adventuresome, since he crawls under the gate despite his father's accident—his being eaten in a rabbit pie. He is greedy: he gorges himself on lettuces, French beans, and radishes. He is frightened and frantic in his flight and, woebegone, he cries. This is the second lost jacket and shoes in a fortnight, so Peter's behavior is consistent. Uncomplaining, Peter accepts the kind nursing of his loving mother; he is a secure child, not a cardboard, two-dimensional rabbit but a round and believable central character.

Maria of *Too Many Tamales* by Gary Soto yields to temptation while kneading tamale dough and tries on her mother's diamond ring. The extended family enjoys the tamales, but Maria suddenly discovers she has lost the ring in the dough, and her cousins must join her in eating all the

Even the briefest of picture book texts can show fully developed characters.

Young children have no problems with talking animals or objects.

tamales to find the ring. Illustrations by Ed Martinez demolish stereotypes of Mexican Americans as poor, dependent migrants.

In *Armien's Fishing Trip* by Catherine Stock, a truly multicultural society lives peacefully on the southern tip of Africa. Filipinos, Europeans, and freed slaves from Malaya and Java are all part of the fishing enterprise. The story follows a boy who is taunted for having lost his skills when he moved to the city. To prove himself, he stows away on his uncle's boat, sees an old sailor swept into the sea, and becomes a hero through his cries and quick thinking. The issue is not only that many cultures can live together peacefully; Armien is also challenged and responds, a strong character.

In *The Patchwork Quilt,* Valerie Flournoy and illustrator Jerry Pinkney show character clearly as they tell of Tanya's beloved grandmother in the midst of making her masterpiece quilt, one that includes, among many others, scraps from a brother's old jeans and her mother's holiday dress. Tanya's diligence in finishing the quilt entices her family into joining in the project, and its completion coincides with the grandmother's recovery.

Do children want to hear their favorites again and again because of curiosity about the outcome of the story? Hardly, since the first reading satisfies both parents and children on that score. There must be other considerations. While Beatrix Potter's detailed, delicately colored illustrations and suspenseful action give pleasure to the reader and the listener, the character of Peter Rabbit as the universal child is the magnet that pulls us back to read and reread the book. Peter's actions are inherent in his personality, or as F. Scott Fitzgerald says, "Action is character." The one produces the other, true to Henry James's views on the interrelatedness of character and action.

> Character pulls us back to familiar stories.

Plot

The brevity of text in picture books does not eliminate the necessity for some kind of **plot,** some action or tension, the quality most likely to keep us reading. Peter Rabbit's curiosity and waywardness create the tension in his story; Max's wild behavior in *Where the Wild Things Are* opens the action, and the exciting roars and threats followed by his taming them all continue the tension. Even the story *The Snowy Day* has its quiet surprises, the simplest kind of plot.

In *The Bravest Flute: A Story of Courage in the Mayan Tradition* by Ann Grifalconi, a young, hungry boy chosen to play his flute and lead the procession on New Year's Day barely has the strength to walk the long way to the assembled elders and shamans at the cathedral. He must also carry the big drum strapped to his back while the bigger drummer bangs away on it. Fortified by a rainbow and a glass of water, he bravely makes the long walk and is rewarded by the widow of the former flutist. The boy finishes the walk with new energy and the silver-and-black gift, the flutist's instrument. His courage is rewarded by the elders; his family will have food and seed corn for the next year. The handsome child and the gentle, peace-loving Mayans are vividly pictured as they celebrate.

Another bilingual picture book, *Calling the Doves*—by Mexican poet Juan Felipe Herrera—shows what life must be for a migrant worker. Juan was born on the road, his mother tells him. The narrator recalls in simple but evocative language the pleasures of sitting under the starry night sky; hearing his father's stories of his immigration from Chihuahua and his imitated bird calls; eating his breakfast in the open air; and moving from farm to farm while laborers pick broccoli, melons, and lettuce and leave the grapes to dry in the sun to make raisins. Juan's memories are all pleasant—of his father playing his harmonica and his mother healing migrants' painful legs and feet. Finally, when it is time for Juan to stay in one place and go to school, the family lives in a little house his father has made on the chassis of an abandoned car. Now the father works as a gardener. Despite their itinerant lifestyle, the family is stable and happy. The quiet title about doves, symbols of peace, reflects the story's tone, a serene appreciation—of family, of the wonders of nature, and of growing and working. Illustrations in bright colors, "happy colors," show stylized fabric design, rolling hills, brightly colored birds, and contented families.

Occasionally a picture book may have an **open ending**, such as that in *The Garden of Abdul Gasazi* by Chris Van Allsburg, which leaves a question: Has Fritz the dog actually been turned into a duck—temporarily?

Picture books without tension or conflict are less successful. Look at *Hold My Hand*, described on the jacket as "a moment of intensity," yet there is no tension, no intensity. Another example is *Willie Goes to the Seashore*, a picture-story book with little excitement. The family has a small cottage at the beach. In a total of seventy-five printed lines, they unpack, roll in the sand, swim, hunt shells, build a sand castle, rebuild the sand castle, and splash in the water. They hang seaweed around their necks and go to bed. Next day Willie finds an old boat, explores the rocks, sees a crab dart off, collects firewood, and puts wieners on roasting sticks. Willie "never had such fun." Willie does everything—and nothing.

Suppose, instead, that Willie had built an elaborate sand castle, planning it, admiring it, embellishing it, and patting it into shape. Then, during the wiener roast, the waves in their regular tidal shifts destroyed the castle! Result: tension. Or suppose Willie had explored the old boat, found it had oarlocks and a hollow bow, and made an imaginary fishing expedition beyond the point. Now the seashore truly becomes a place to have fun; tension or conflict is the cause.

Even in a simple plot each character has a part to play; in fact, the simpler the story, the more confusing it is to have irrelevant characters. In *The Tub People*, seven small wooden dolls are lined up on the edge of the tub: father, mother, child, grandmother, doctor, police officer, and dog. The child disappears down the drain, the drain slows, the plumber pulls him out, and he is reunited with his father and mother. Now they all stand on the bedroom windowsill. At no time are the grandmother, the doctor, the police officer, or the dog part of the plot; they are merely pictured. The author chose to write about seven specific toys, but without a point in including them all, the story is poorly planned.

Some kind of tension is necessary to hold a reader's interest.

Straightforward chronology is easily understood in two picture books that trace a family through generations of change. In *Island Boy* by Barbara Cooney, a father buys an island, builds a house, raises a family, and sees twelve children leave; one returns, cares for the father's grandchild there, and is finally lost at sea.

By contrast, *Soon-Hee in America* lacks any organization and is merely a collection of photographs of a Korean child in school, at the zoo, in New York or Washington. Without a recognizable logic in the sequence the static pictures seem the sole reason for the book.

Look, too, at *Nessa's Fish,* a story of Arctic dwellers identified only by their depiction in the clothing of the Far North. Nessa and her grandmother ice fish, "jigging" all day. But what is "jigging"? Grandmother falls sick, and Nessa protects her from freezing, as well as from foxes, wolves, and bears. How does Nessa know what to do? Are there traditions, legends, or charms that help? Are intergenerational fishing trips common? The story lacks suspense or action, and just stops: Nessa walks home with her parents and her grandmother.

Plenty of excitement accompanies the fanciful (and bilingual) *My Aunt Otilia's Spirits* by Richard Garcia. Aunt Otilia's visit brings mysterious wall knocking, kitchen crashes, and shaking beds. But when Aunt Otilia's bones leave her body and fly out the closed window, that's truly remarkable. Demonio puts the body parts back together all wrong, suspenseful action that Robin Cherin and Roger L. Reyes picture wonderfully. Garcia says in an afterword that Latin Americans often believe in the supernatural.

Birthday parties are favorites for children. In Valiska Gregory's *Happy Burpday, Maggie McDougal,* Maggie, who has spent all her money, cannot buy a gift for her best friend, Bonkers. But Grandma turns up the first Green Lizardman comic book ever printed, Bonkers's absolute favorite of all time. Problem solved. Meanwhile, in the classroom, a frustrated teacher tries to explain a "family tree" with its branches, which do *not* include puppies and goldfish; she has no better luck with heirlooms that have been "handed down"—through a group of relatives, each one taller than the last. Families and friendships are the substance of the story, which is interspersed with "the grosses," like big burping binges and jealousy. Plot moves as casually as life itself.

The brief text of Sherry Garland's *The Lotus Seed* tells the story of a seed taken from the garden of the Vietnamese emperor, who is forced by war to leave his throne. To the grandmother, the lotus seed represents her country and its traditions. When a child steals the seed and plants it, the blooming lotus brings joy: its seeds will preserve the immigrants' culture in their new homeland.

Yang the Youngest and His Terrible Ear by Lensey Namioka is another story of integration into the U.S. way of life. In a progressive plot, Chinese Yang loves baseball, and his American friend Matt loves the violin. At the obligatory music recital, Yang bow-syncs, and from behind the screen Matt plays the violin for the Yang family's quartet. Matt's huge success leads his surprised father to allow him to take violin lessons and Yang's father to let Yang forget the violin and learn to play baseball. To the boys, customs and language are baffling. Matt, staying for dinner at Yang's house, asks to go to the bathroom to wash his hands; he finds live carp in the bathtub because Chinese never buy dead fish. When Matt's father is "laid off," Yang wonders whether he fell and got hurt. Furthermore, how does one sit a baby?

In *The Drinking Gourd* by F. N. Monjo, the handle of the Big Dipper, the gourd of the title, points toward the North Star. Slaves, working and singing, refer to the "Drinking Gourd" as the way to freedom on the Underground Railroad. Tommy discovers that his father is a conductor who hides slaves in his barn and guides them to the next station. When Tommy finds a hidden slave family of four, he fakes a story for the marshal about his own flight from punishment by driving off in the sanctuary hay wagon. Bond between father and son is strengthened as they assist families in defying the unjust Fugitive Slave Act. Plot is revealed in chronological order.

Quiet suspense is carried throughout *The Wednesday Surprise* by Eve Bunting, illustrated by Donald Carrick, as we wonder about the birthday gift being prepared for Papa. Only at the end is it clear that the narrator, seven-year-old Anna, has secretly taught Grandma to read. The story concludes with a **closed ending.** A similar triumph occurs in *The Day of Ahmed's Secret,* as told by Florence Parry Heide and Judith Heide Gilliland. Ahmed—who, judging from the lush and detailed illustrations by Ted Lewin, seems to live in the Middle East—is proud that he can contribute to his family by earning money delivering bottles of fuel to city dwellers. He holds his secret close until he is at home in the evening: He has learned to write his name.

Even the simplest stories for children can have conflict or tension. Will Goldilocks be caught? Will the Three Little Pigs survive by the hair of their chinny-chin-chins? Will the troll who lives under the bridge get the Billy-Goats Gruff? Suspense builds in each of these stories as a threat is repeated three times, and conflict is climaxed by defeat of the threatener. Goldilocks gets away, the wolf falls into boiling water, and the troll is crushed to bits, body and bones.

Theme

Some stories for young children are both humor-filled and rich with a variety of **themes,** but check the shelf of children's fare in any bookstore and notice how often action or situation humor is its only element. The popularity of books such as Hans Rey's *Curious George,* with its exciting action and variety—the monkey's balloon flight, which coincidentally ends on top of the traffic light, and his play with the telephone, which calls in a fire alarm—seems to suggest that a child can appreciate only coincidence and situation humor. But children love George for a different reason: his curiosity matches theirs.

There is additional satisfaction in a story with a theme. The South African children of Rachel Isadora's book *At the Crossroads* greet the reader with great smiles. They are gathered to await the return of their fathers, who work for ten months at a stretch in the mines. In the heat, the families sing and dance as they await the trucks bringing fathers and husbands. One by one, family by family, they leave until only six children are left at the crossroads in the moonlight. The final picture shows the children, hugging their fathers and marching home in joyful song. As the fathers carry little ones on their shoulders, they demonstrate the theme: Families are loving units in all cultures.

The simplest story can illustrate a significant point. The jacket blurb of *Billy the Great* by Rosa Guy, illustrated by Caroline Binchy, says that parents cannot determine a child's future, but the story's implied theme is that racial prejudice may work in both directions. Billy's best friend is White and the son of a tattooed truck driver, not good enough for Billy's Black parents, who want him to grow up to be a doctor. Billy just wants to play baseball with Rod. Fun is fun.

From the first words in *Mama, Do You Love Me?* by Barbara Joosse, the theme is apparent. As the little girl who lives in the Arctic repeats her question, she posits several scenarios: Even if I break ptarmigan eggs, or turn into a musk-ox or moose, will you love me? Nothing, not even misbehavior or transformation, limits a mother's love.

In Maurice Sendak's *Where the Wild Things Are*, we have a character, Max, whom we care about, acting out a conflict that interests us—and all united by an implicit theme that can be stated in several ways. The story is more than a situation with wonderfully effective illustrations, more than the pleasure of its rhythmic style. The story also has a strong theme.

Many kinds of stories have their place for young children: some offer the listening child laughter from a narrative with physical or situation humor, or the reassurance found in pure day-to-day routine, the unexciting commonplace. Other stories, like Miska Miles's *Annie and the Old One,* combine freshness in language, imagination in plot, and significance in theme, as well as distinctive illustrations.

Once again look at *The Tale of Peter Rabbit,* which has its own implicit theme. Based in reality, action and suspense race to the point of Peter's flopping down on the sandy floor of the rabbit home, where he shuts his eyes. Mother, who is busy cooking, wonders what he has done with his new clothes, but she does not lecture, or spank, or compare naughty Peter to good Flopsy, Mopsy, and Cotton-tail. Although Peter didn't feel very well that evening, there is no hint of "It serves him right. He was naughty." Peter's mother puts him to bed and gives him a dose of camomile tea. Potter does not call the tea punitive medicine, nor does she describe it as tasting bad. Nor does she call Flopsy, Mopsy, and Cotton-tail's bread, milk, and blackberries reward for goodness.

Is the story didactic? Although we adults see clearly that disobedience and curiosity can get you into trouble, *Peter Rabbit* is, after all, for a young child. The theme is implied, but not didactic or patronizing. *Peter Rabbit* becomes didactic, however, if a reteller adds a single phrase to Potter's final paragraph, saying that Flopsy, Mopsy, and Cotton-tail, "who were good little bunnies," ate bread and milk and blackberries at suppertime. Or when we see another illustrator's picture showing an admonitory plaque hanging on the kitchen wall, saying, "Good bunnies obey," or preaching a more positive lesson, "Obedience is rewarded." It seems likely that an implied theme—

Even a simple story can make a significant point.

Theme is not a preachment.

"Even when you're naughty, Mother loves and accepts you"—has kept *Peter Rabbit* a much-loved story.

Lucille Clifton writes picture book texts clearly focused on theme. Her book *My Brother Fine with Me* is a simple story of Baggy, the little brother who wants to leave home with his minibike cards and a toothbrush to be independent, to be a Black warrior without parents to make rules. Johnetta, who says she likes it fine at home except for him, doesn't wish to join him. But Johnny finds it lonely without Baggy to bother her, to watch over at the park, to eat the peanut butter and jelly sandwiches she fixes. Thus the theme: My brother's fine with me.

When Africa Was Home by Karen Lynn Williams portrays an interracial friendship; this one blooms when Peter lives in Africa and plays with Yekha, eating balls of corn paste from the same bowl and dipping them in the African sauce. When Peter's father must leave for a job in the United States, Peter is afraid he won't know what to do. He knows no other way of eating or playing, or of being mannerly. When the family's stay in the United States is over, Peter is delighted to return to Africa and his friends. The theme is that acceptance is easy in childhood

A controversial picture book published in 1990 is Michael Willhoite's *Daddy's Roommate,* a matter-of-fact picture of gay family life in which Daddy's friend comes to live with him. The speaker is a boy who tells us that Daddy and his friend work, and eat, and shave, and fight and make up, and sleep in the same bed. They also read to him, catch bugs, play ball, picnic, and shop with him. The boy's mother explains that this is one more kind of love and that love is a good thing. The boy is happy, and that is that.[9]

> Themes may address current issues.

An increasing number of books for all ages explore the theme of conservation and the restoration of the earth. Two such picture books are *The Land of Gray Wolf* by Thomas Locker and the wordless *Window,* written and illustrated in collage by Jeannie Baker. In the first, land taken from Native Americans is cleared and farmed until the soil is exhausted and returns to wilderness. In the second, the family sees their country lot gradually surrounded by development and tract housing, and the next generation moves to the country, looking for the landscape of childhood. Chris Van Allsburg, frequent prizewinner for his picture books, has produced another beauty with *Just a Dream.* Unenlightened Walter is too lazy to recycle—until his dream takes him into a future time when trash submerges homes, neon-lit hotels rest on mountaintops, fishermen finally celebrate the first fish of the week, and forests become factory land. Walter thus realizes that protecting the environment is important.

Themes of all kinds occur in picture books. Kevin Henkes's *Chrysanthemum* explores the idea that having one's name ridiculed makes one miserable, but approval can change self-image. Names are our identity. Your name is you.

In a stunning combination of words and photographs, Toni Morrison has given children an account of the failures of "separate but equal" education for African American children, as well as hopeful pictures of change. *Remember: The Journey to School Integration* opens with three full pages of narrative recounting the devastation wrought by Jim Crow laws, then follows the Supreme Court decision and the slow progress of integration. Introductory information is illustrated by portraits of children and adults displaying both innocence and hatred. Then begins the three-part account, each one opening with a single page of text. Pages that follow show brief text on the left, and a poignant picture on the right. The first section, called "The Narrow Path," pictures the sad state of African American schools. Section two, "The Open Gate," needs little text because the ugly faces of hatred and the angry taunts on placards say it all. Pictures and text in "The Wide Road" section are honest about the slow and painful progress, showing bus boycotts, peaceful protests, jailed children, lunch counter sit-ins, Martin Luther King—and little by little the changes wrought. Finally, children of both races smile tentatively at one another, study together, play together, and clasp hands in friendship. The final page proclaims, "Anything can happen. Anything at all. See?" The book is aptly named: *Remember.* The hopeful theme of the book makes it impossible to forget.

In Margaree King Mitchell's picture book *Uncle Jed's Barber Shop,* the implicit theme is "despite setbacks, hold on to your dream." Uncle Jed, too poor to open his own shop, walks across the county cutting hair. Sarah Jean's operation and the Great Depression took his savings, but Uncle Jed manages to save enough so that at the age of seventy-nine, he can open his own shop complete with four chairs, a shining floor, and a barber pole. Throughout the story, the reader glimpses discrimination against African Americans, who must wait in rooms separate from White patients to see a doctor when they are sick, must wait until all White patients have been seen, and must pay before treatment. Separate water fountains, restrooms, and schools are also mentioned. The strong theme, however, depicts pride and determination rather than self-pity.

In a more traditional tale, Native American women trade with humility and gratitude. *Heetunka's Harvest* by Jennifer Berry Jones, illustrated by Shannon Keegan, is filled with naturalistic drawings of the tiny mouse and her environment, fitted into framed pages. The moral tale of greed is about a woman who fails to trade her own corn for the white beans she discovers and steals from a mouse's shallow nest; greed is punished with disaster.

Readers discover similar values in quite different cultures.

Setting

Picture books can and often must be extremely effective in depicting setting. The brief text of Cynthia Rylant's *When I Was Young in the Mountains* describes primarily the actions of the child narrator, but the pictured swimming hole, the cabin kitchen, the general store, the backyard pump, and the porch swing are all extensions of the text. Pictured setting more than words reveals why the child never wanted to go anywhere else.

Contemporary society, as we are reminded by the battering of advertisements, is relying less on words for communication and more on pictures. The trend toward nonverbal communication is reflected in some picture-story books that depend entirely on illustration to create setting. Arnold Lobel's pictures in *Ming Lo Moves the Mountain* show the important Asian setting. In literature for children, however, word pictures give a child an opportunity to create setting in his or her own mind, a special kind of experience that is one of the delights of literature.

We "see" setting through words as well as pictures.

The Tale of Peter Rabbit is a classic example of **integral setting.** As both author and illustrator, Beatrix Potter integrates visual and word pictures; setting is closely interwoven with character, action, and theme. On the first page, the family home appears with its soft, sandy floor—the bank under the roots of a large fir tree. Inside the gate is the cucumber frame. In this garden, cabbages and potatoes as well as French beans and lettuces grow not far from the net-covered gooseberry bush and the toolshed, with its watering can and its three flowerpots on the windowsill. The stone wall has a gate and a stone step; close by are a pond and a wheelbarrow. There is the garden sound of the "scritching, scratching" hoe. This setting is not a suburban front yard. What happens to Peter is influenced by elements in the garden: the gate, the cucumber frame, the gooseberry bush, the pond, and the toolshed with its three flowerpots. Although Potter mentions each item in the setting, nowhere does she stop the action to describe it, and yet at no point is setting unimportant. In this perfectly integrated picture book, illustration and text work together to create setting.

Point of View

Point of view, or the mind through which the writer chooses to tell the story, varies in picture books, as it does in all literature. Beatrix Potter wishes to tell a story about a rabbit whose mischievous nature gets him into trouble in a vegetable garden. How should she tell the story? Potter has several choices of point of view. She can be objective, telling just what happens and saying nothing about the effect of events on Peter's feelings. If Mother Rabbit tells the story, she might be weary of Peter's regular disobedience and of buying new jackets and shoes, but loves Peter just the same. If Flopsy, one of the good little bunnies, tells the story, we might see a prim little sister who, because she is always good, thinks Peter really ought to know better. Cotton-tail might tell the story enviously: "If I had any courage, I'd have some excitement, too." But Potter chooses to tell her tale from a point inside Peter's feelings and thoughts. We know Peter's curiosity, his appetite as he munches on, his worry as he asks directions, and his panic as he upsets the flowerpots. We are as relieved as Peter when he finds his way home and is not scolded for his adventure. Every element in the story has been affected by Potter's choice of point of view. He is the protagonist and Mr. McGregor the antagonist. We know the character of Peter; his conflict is determined by the setting. Because of Peter's adventure and his mother's kind care, we understand the thematic point—that although a child is naughty, he or she is still loved.

Two different characters tell two different stories.

There are first-person stories among picture books for the youngest child, such as Dr. Seuss's *If I Ran the Zoo*. The "I" narrator of these stories, however, is of minor significance, since the focus is on the sheer nonsense of the doggerel and the pleasure of the sounds and rhythms, to say nothing of the stories' greatest assets, the inventive illustrations. *And to Think That I Saw It on Mulberry Street* uses first-person point of view effectively; it is not only skillful nonsense, but it also shows a child's imagination creating a fantastic parade. In writer Diane Siebert and illustrator Wendell Minor's collaborative *Heartland,* the heartland of America is the first person speaker, telling of all it sees and is, what it grows, the blessings of nature, the trials it endures, and how it changes with the seasons. A serious book, it praises the farms, the farmer, and all that the heartland contributes.

The Polar Express by Chris Van Allsburg, published in 1985, has taken its place as a Christmas classic. It, too, is written in first-person point of view, one that perfectly fits the story itself. The boy did not wish to believe there was no Santa Claus, and his experience disproves his friends' skepticism. He boards the Polar Express train when it stops in his front yard at midnight to take him and the trainload of children to the North Pole to meet Santa and his elves. Given a single sleigh bell by Santa, he is delighted—but loses it through the hole in his pajama pocket. Yet under the tree next morning is the bell, wrapped and accompanied by Santa's note. No one can hear the bell but the boy and his sister Sarah—because no one else believes. We must hear this story from the believer himself; it requires the first-person narrator.

Successful objective point-of-view narration at picture book level occurs in Ludwig Bemelmans's *Madeline,* where minimal omniscience is present. Ezra Jack Keats's *The Snowy Day* seems at first glance to be objective. We know that Peter has a happy time in the snow because we see all his fun, and we remember our own similar pleasures. But an omniscient writer also comments that Peter *thinks* it might be fun to play with the big boys, and he *knows* he isn't old enough. When Peter cannot find the vanished snowball he had tucked into his jacket pocket the night before, he *feels* sad. Even this simple and short story makes brief use of an interpretive omniscience. First person or "I" stories are increasingly common for picture book age, but either of the omniscient points of view may be successful in stories for the young child.

Style

Picture books, too, need style that awakens the interest of the young child in the nuances of possible meanings and the pleasures of language. The Blackfoot tribe of the Plains have a traditional belief that the buffalo herd springs from a misty lake in the west. *Where the Buffaloes Begin* by Olaf Baker is a beautiful book in black and white, impressive in its evocation of the infinite plains and their awesome buffaloes. Little Wolf is caught in a stampeding herd: A "heaving mass of buffaloes billowed like the sea." His "blood stirs along his scalp," and to his cry the animals reply, "bellowing a wild answer that rolls" above the plains like thunder. Contrast these phrases with the halting style of *Mika's Apple*

Style can introduce us to the pleasures of language.

Tree: "They dressed and went into the house. Supper was ready. They had cabbage soup with rye bread and butter. They had pancakes with jam." Even combining short sentences would create more vitality in style, and yet, if the early reader were reading alone, it would add no more difficulty to the language.

Look again at *Peter Rabbit,* the imagery describing setting, the blue jacket with brass buttons, the five currant buns. Notice the understatement of Father's getting into trouble there, the mock-serious tone of "implored him to exert himself," the onomatopoeia of "scritch-scratch" and "lippety, lippety," the assonance and consonance of "Flopsy, Mopsy, Cotton-tail," and the surprise of the name "Peter." *Peter Rabbit* has style.

One of the pleasures of Jamake Highwater's *Moonsong Lullaby* is the figurative language. The moon sings a sweet lullaby to the people beside the campfire, while the rabbit and the fox dream, the hawk praises the moonlight, and the roots burrow into the depths of the earth. The night is a shelter for troubled souls, and the moon caresses them. All of nature is personified, and each image connotes contentment and security.

Successful stories use many stylistic devices.

Owl Moon, Jane Yolen's very successful picture book, achieves a soft silence by her phrasing. Stillness pervades the snowy landscapes painted by John Schoenherr, and stillness is everywhere in the text. The woods are "quiet as a dream," the snow more white "than the milk in a cereal bowl." The child narrator is going owling with Pa. "But I never said a word./If you go owling/you have to be quiet/and make your own heat." When they do sight an owl, they watch silently "with heat in our mouths,/the heat of all those words/we had not spoken." The text and pictures are in quiet, beautiful synchrony.

A very different style is apparent in Judith Viorst's *Alexander, Who Used to Be Rich Last Sunday,* illustrated by Ray Cruz. Alexander is the first-person narrator, telling in a child's diction how little by little, four cents by thirteen, he has spent his grandparents' gift dollar. "Anthony told me to use the dollar to go downtown to a store and buy a new face. Anthony stinks." But instead, Alexander buys fifteen cents' worth of gum, bets away another fifteen, rents a snake for twelve, and is fined ten for "certain words" a boy can't ever say, "no matter how ratty and mean his brothers are being."

Rhythm often appears in picture book narration, as in a story about a boy whose name is too long, *Tikki-Tikki-Tembo* by Arlene Mosel, illustrated by Blair Lent. Recite the name "Rikki-Tikki-Tembo-no sa rembo-chari bari rucki-pip peeri pembo" and the pleasure begins. And in Maurice Sendak's *Where the Wild Things Are* as well: "And when he came to the place where the wild things are they roared their terrible roars and gnashed their terrible teeth and rolled their terrible eyes and showed their terrible claws."

Tone

Tone may vary in picture books, just as it does in books of other genres. The thoughtful tone of Norma Farber's *How Does It Feel to Be Old?* or the serious tone of Virginia Lee Burton's *The Little House* is as appropriate as the mock-serious tone of *The Elephant's Child* or the joyous one of *Frog Went A-Courtin'.*

Tone, the attitude of writer and artist toward reader and story, is often humorous.

Like character and point of view, tone too is the choice of the author or author-illustrator. Humor—that important quality that helps us develop a perspective on life's ups and downs and keeps us sane—is essential in the life of a young child. Many writers and illustrators respond to that need, or perhaps they respond to their own need to see things through the sound of laughter.

Years ago, a biography series about the lives of the presidents stressed the accomplishments of each president. Occasionally, a writer would use a touch of humor to bring the important figure to life, to become a recognizable normal human being complete with quirks and whims. But Judith St. George in *So You Want to Be President* has deliberately identified funny traits or distinctive statements of many presidents. These unusual details demonstrate a president's individuality; personality quirks make honored men come alive. St. George cites the first President Bush's attitude toward broccoli, football scrimmages with his children on the White House lawn, comparing conversation to "talking to a hitching post." She enumerates the presidents who have been named "John," and comments on a president whose goat pulled his grandchildren about on the White House lawn. Nor does she omit the shetland pony's trip upstairs in the White House. In each case, illustrator David Small matches the humor of his cartoonlike illustrations to the humor of the text.

The train ride from New Jersey to Cottondale to spend the summer with the narrator's grandmother opens *Big Mama's* by Donald Crews. Unlike the urban coast, Big Mama's country has bumpy, narrow roads leading to the big house and farmyard, where the children fill the bucket at the well and drink from a dipper. They wash up on the back porch, hunt for eggs under the tractor, and marvel at the big pot for making cane syrup. The final page shows the grown-up narrator hoping to wake up and find himself down on Big Mama's farm. The simple story shows the historical change in the move from rural to urban living, and despite its nostalgic tone—which does not always appeal to children—it is an interesting return to other days.

By helping to carry a book's text, illustrations become a large part of the book's humor. John Langstaff's *Frog Went A-Courtin'* is filled with personification, cover to cover. Feodor Rojankovsky, whose drawings are convincingly both animal and human, increases the humor by dressing them in suitable garb for their roles in the verses. Beetles of different kinds wearing aprons and chef's caps and carrying spoons and forks, a table-setting moth sporting a fuzzy domestic hairpiece, an insect trio performing atop the wedding cake, a bonneted snake who looks benign rather than fearsome—all of these are part of the pictured humor.

Ray Cruz, who illustrated Judith Viorst's *Alexander, Who Used to Be Rich Last Sunday,* chooses to amplify the humor of Alexander's frittering away his dollar by showing the gleeful antics of his two older brothers. The text itself is effectively understated ("And even when I told my friend Donald I'd sell him all the gum in my mouth for a nickel, he still wouldn't buy it."), while Alexander's cheeks bulge with three packs of gum. The final two illustrations show Alexander, his hand on his chin, squashing his face, contemplating

A nostalgic tone rarely appeals to children.

what he has to show for his ventures; on the last page, he is alone and looking away, holding two bus tokens, back where he started.

The mock-serious tone of Rudyard Kipling's *The Elephant's Child* is humor of its own delicious kind, and Lorinda Bryan Cauley's black-and-white illustrations add to it in a harmonious way. Seeing a family of four elephants marching across the title spread, each one with a nose no bigger than a boot, is a startling verification of Kipling's *pourquoi* tale: This is the way it was—before. Off goes the Elephant's Child to find out what the crocodile has for dinner, wearing big pouchy saddlebags filled with long purple sugar cane, short red bananas, and green crackly melons. His tracks are littered with rind, "because he could not pick it up." When we come to the crocodile who "winked one eye—like this" and "wept crocodile tears" to show his sincerity, we are delighted with his deceptiveness. The breathless Elephant's Child, kneeling on the bank, his round eyes and open mouth eager for the answer to his question, is truly innocent. Each page has its own textual humor; humorous illustration contributes to an inspired story.

Humor is common in picture books. Ogden Nash, long known for nonsense verse, is author of the picture book text for *The Adventures of Isabel,* illustrated by James Marshall; in the brief story Isabel banishes every known bugaboo, and the cartoonlike hyperbole of her successes rouses our laughter. A tone of high gaiety runs all through Grandpa's reenactment of his old role as *Song and Dance Man* by Karen Ackerman, illustrated by Stephen Gammell. A satisfying combination of humor and tenderness characterizes Mem Fox and Julie Vivas's efforts in *Wilfred Gordon McDonald Partridge.* Old Miss Nancy, Wilfred hears, has lost her memory. In his search for the word's meaning, he is told that "memory" is sad, funny, and precious; he then finds things that are dear to him, and gives them to Miss Nancy. Each one awakens a memory for her.

We may all dream of turning the tables on one who has exploited us, but the mother of *The Boy of the Three-Year Nap* by Dianne Snyder accomplishes this. Her lazy son Taro plots to marry the daughter of the wealthy rice merchant next door, and Taro's mother tells the merchant that his daughter cannot live simply—their house must be enlarged and improved, and Taro must find a job to support the girl. Lazy Taro goes to work as the merchant's storehouse manager. Humor makes the point for the story.

Exaggeration is part of childhood play as well as adult humor. Patricia C. McKissack has written a story filled with hyperbole, *A Million Fish . . . More or Less.* Hugh Thomas has heard the tall tales of Papa-Daddy and Elder Abbajon, but in his own tale he has caught a million fish in the bayou, then has had to forfeit them to the talking alligator, raccoons, crows, and Chantilly the talking cat, leaving him with just three tiny fish. Dena Schutzer's pictures are as filled with hyperbole as brilliantly colored as the tale. In order for Pauline of *The Easter Egg Farm* by Mary Jane Auch to lay eggs, she has to concentrate; then whatever she sees is reflected in the colored egg she lays—the sky or Mona Lisa's smile, for example. Of course, Easter eggs are the result. Although the imaginative text has humor, Auch's vivid pictures double our amusement.

The quiet verbal humor of Russell Hoban's picture books has merit, too, and yet it is quite unlike the humor of Maurice Sendak's *Pierre, a Cautionary Tale,* which is, in fact, a spoof of didacticism. Arnold Lobel's *Frog and Toad Together* is funny not only because of situation—they are odd animals for stepladder climbing—but also because of understated verbal humor, a surprise in basic vocabulary. Lobel uses a series of limericks for *The Book of Pigericks,* which is illustrated with pigs in all positions. Whenever his rhythms falter, departing from the required meters of the limerick, the humor stalls. When his rhythms work, his humor works. In Eric Kimmel's *Hershel and the Hanukkah Goblins*—illustrated by Trina Schart Hyman in her usual rich and imaginative manner—the humor results from Hershel's tricky defeat of the goblins, who don't want the candles lit for the festival. One is frightened away by Hershel's ability to break a stone (really a boiled egg) in his hands; another gets his hand stuck in the pickle jar and cannot snuff out the candle; another loses his gold in the dreidel game; and the biggest of all is just not visible to Hershel, who insists that the goblin light all the candles so that he can be seen. When the goblin lights the Hanukkah candles himself, they will never again be snuffed out by goblins at festival time. The lowly outwit the powerful once again.

Lasting Favorites

Words and pictures may fill in for each other.

We cannot speak of picture books without looking to Maurice Sendak, his view of the illustrator's function, and his best-known and most-loved book, *Where the Wild Things Are,* the book that Selma Lanes calls "the most suspenseful and satisfying nursery tale of our time."[10] In describing the role of the illustrator, Sendak speaks of the "seamlessness" of the perfectly integrated picture book, distinguishing between the direct approach that puts the facts of the story into clear and simple images and the "illumination" of a text, in which just as the musical composer interprets the words of a poem, the pictures interpret the text, "serving the words" by enlarging and interpreting. He goes on to say that the illustrator does not picture exactly the words that are written, but he or she finds a space where pictures can go further than words. In fact, "they each tell two stories at the same time . . . Words are left out and the picture says it. Pictures are left out and the words say it." Pictures "quicken" text; they are "not something just glued onto the page" beside the words. Liveliness, conviction, vitality, "the touch and smell and *hold* of a book," the "zing" and the animation of the whole—these are Sendak's descriptive terms. As he praises Randolph Caldecott's illustrations, Sendak says that words take "on unobvious meanings, colors, and dramatic qualities. He *reads* into things, and this, of course, is what the illustrator's job is really all about," interpreting text as a conductor interprets a musical score.[11]

Sendak's *Wild Things* was published in 1963. For many adults, it focused their difficulty in acknowledging the anxieties and preoccupations of childhood, their desire for children to be happy-happy-happy, to deny all unpleasantness and uncertainty. In addressing this issue, Sendak takes a different view. He marvels "that children manage to grow up," to get through childhood, defeating "boredom, fear, pain, and anxiety." He says that he remembers "sounds, feelings, and images" or the emotional quality of significant childhood moments. He successfully pictures many of these feelings and images in his books.

Sendak's Caldecott Award–winning *Wild Things* exemplifies a perfect marriage of text and pictures. The first pictures show Max as angry and naughty as he pounds a huge nail into the wall for a clothesline made of knotted clothing. He bounds down the steps, jabbing at his dog with an enormous fork, making "mischief of one kind or another," and threatens in boldface capitals to eat his mother up as he stands scowling, defiant, a wolf claw on his hip. The text tells us that a forest grew inside his room, and now Max is content, giggling, even smug, about the new turn of events, exotic foliage the setting for his dancing. As the first six pictures grow from $4 \times 5\frac{1}{2}$ inches to a full 9×10-inch page, the story's suspenseful pace accelerates. In his private boat named *Max,* his body is confident, then uncertain before the wild things, then more assertive as he waves his arms like a magician and with a stare tames the ferocious creatures, so that in fear they soon cover their faces and ears. "The most wild thing of all" has tamed them, and they line up to give obeisance to the crowned "king of all wild things." In total command, Max orders the rumpus to start and for three double-page spreads they rampage—until he sends them off to bed. Now Max is lonely for those who love him "best of all," and departs in his boat while the wild things roar, roll their eyes, show their claws, and reach out to him. Quietly pleased with himself, Max returns through time and space to his room, no longer a wild thing but a boy in his loving home. Sendak's ideal of seamlessness in words and pictures is perfectly realized.

Another favorite is *The Tale of Peter Rabbit,* first published in 1902 when it sold for seven cents in today's currency. Its popularity endures among children all over the world. Potter once said that many stories for children are "condescending, self-conscious inventions," but Potter herself was never condescending or self-conscious in either pictures or text. First, Potter insisted on the $4 \times 5\frac{1}{2}$-inch illustrations, reminding us of Sendak's comment on the importance of "the touch and *hold*" in a picture book. Pictures alternate with text and are consistently in vignette form, irregular ovals surrounded by white space. But perhaps the little gem has had enough examination here. Each rereading may uncover new pleasure.

"It's a good feeling to be able to put down a line and know it is right." Robert McCloskey has said this helps to explain why *Make Way for Ducklings* is still a great favorite with children, and one adults seem not to weary of either. The pages can be examined again and again, each time yielding new details. In a perfect union of text and pictures, the uniqueness of the ducklings and their parents, realistic yet individualized, is never lost. The pictures give excitement and vitality to the text, resulting in a new composite whole.

Aside from accuracy in picturing the mallard family, the book has a number of assets, including humor. The balanced first pages are an effective bird's-eye

As Sendak demonstrates, a great variety of feelings can be found in picture books.

view of the world as with Mr. and Mrs. Mallard we look down in perfect perspective for the right spot to build a nest. Size, placement on the page, depth of
tone, and force of line show that this is the mallards' story. Below, in distant and
softly shaded areas and incomplete lines, are houses, water, and woods. Turn
the page and we are still in the air with the ducks, but now the scene below is
clearer, more particular; obviously we are coming closer to the earth and perhaps to the perfect homesite. Now the page is balanced by the two mallards
and a tree strikingly bare in early spring on the left, opposite the diagonal
bridge and the little island in the Public Garden on the right side. Noting tiny
details, we can count eight children walking with parents along the water's
edge, and when we turn the page to see the swan boat's passengers, we count
again: seven children and their parents. Along the water's edge five more
children play, an emphasis that carries throughout: This is a family story.

Turning to the spread of the bicyclist speeding past the ducks, tie and
shirttail flying behind him and his action filling the whole right-hand page,
Mr. and Mrs. Mallard's fear and shock are apparent. Mr. Mallard is knocked
off his feet and Mrs. Mallard is tilted off-balance with one foot raised. Placing
the text at the top of the left-hand page and using a large triangle of white
space to duplicate the triangle formed by the startled birds gives emphasis to
their terror. Shadowing horizontal lines show the bicycle's rapid movement,
and diagonals echo the sudden movement of the startled ducks. The gutter
dividing the pages is the right division for the action. Three more spreads
show from the air the mallards' search until at ground view, children's height,
we look at stones and weeds and bushes and nest, a domestic scene in a quiet
island setting. A new figure now enters in the person of Michael, the police
officer, benign, hospitable, his kindness and roundness reassuring us about
safety. Next page, the balance is reversed: the focus at left in "power position"
is Mrs. Mallard counting her eggs—and we must count them, too. The following page is filled with parental pride revealed on the left by the imposingly
dark and vertical father, and on the right by the horizontal line of Mrs.
Mallard's back echoing the quiet horizontal of the text block. If there is any
disappointment, it is the hiding of one duckling in the gutter of the spread.
Here, as in all other pictures, the parents are confident, dignified adults. Like
children, each duckling is different from the others; the identical puffball
ducklings of mass-produced picture books are boring by comparison.

In a "perfect marriage," effectively designed pictures enhance text. Each
spread is different; each page is an addition to the text; each one begs us to
count the ducklings, to notice their differences. Within each picture one or
two are mavericks, watching a butterfly, hurrying to catch up, following in
proper single file but looking the other way. As they approach the traffic,
McCloskey incorporates into the pictures the raucous sounds of cars, ducks,
and a police whistle. At the point of Michael's run to save the mallard family,
he again dominates the picture. His heavy dark boots, and the diagonal of his
outstretched leg continued in the diagonal of his meaty hand raised to stop
the traffic, are the focus, yet we never lose track of the mallard family. In the

next pages the city takes over, but the ducklings are always there, strutting down the walk as mere dots in one picture, tiny individuals noticed and marveled at by passersby in another. Finally they are isolated in a big empty space in the midst of traffic stopped in four directions. The ducklings might easily have been lost in the city fray, but McCloskey keeps focus on them through skillful composition using white space, dark and light tones, and thin, fat, or shaded lines for solid forms—and of course through the placement of pictures close to relevant text. The last few spreads, devoted again to family and security, show the setting in detail, with the family all settling into a serene routine, following the swan boats and the peanut-throwing passengers and returning at night to their island home.

Virginia Lee Burton's *The Little House* has been popular since it won the Caldecott Award in 1943. The frontispiece condenses and simplifies the story, the title page is illustrated, the dedication is encircled by a wreath of daisies, and even the page numbers are carefully placed for the sake of design. Text is placed rather consistently on the left-hand page, with pictures on the right. Clouds circle across the first page, the sun, with varying expressions, arches across the next spread, while stars light a swirl of navy blue sky in a third. As seasons change, the hills take on different colors, moving from light to deep green to autumn rust to winter white. In spring a group of robins flies from top left around the shaped text to lower center; in summer daisies follow a similar pattern; in fall leaves drift from top left to lower right; and winter snowflakes follow a similar route.

As the little house is surrounded by encroaching roads, then by other houses, and by apartment and tenement houses, the colors become somber browns and grays, on to deep charcoal gray lit by inadequate circles of city street lamps. Cars, trucks, buses, trolleys, and subway and elevated trains surround the drab little house, and by now the rolling, tranquil country landscape has changed into a series of dark and darker buildings surrounded by a frenetic visual clamor. Here Burton's pictures are drab grays of all shades, the only color that of the trucks and train cars, the tiny hurrying pedestrians, and a faded little house. Once the little house begins the move back to the country, the colors become lively again; the sun, moon, stars, leaves, daisies, and snowflakes reappear, and the expression on the face of the house is again cheerful. Throughout the book, the cyclical history of the little house has been illustrated with the circular flow of seasonal images and the swirling lines of the pictured settings.

Perhaps the final picture of the house at night, placed on the left facing a blank page, is unnecessary. As we have just read, "Once again she was lived in and taken care of," and that seems sufficient; we need not hear the "never agains" to know that the little house will thrive and be happy. All in all, this is a most satisfactory picture book. The change in time of day, in seasons, in the takeover by city life, and in the little house that remains the same yet changes with its changing surroundings—all these elements are there for endless detailed examination.

Color, white space, dark and light tones, thin or fat lines, text and picture placement all contribute to success.

Wordless Picture Books

When pictures tell it all, words are sometimes unnecessary.

Like works in any genre or subgenre, wordless picture books vary in quality. What seems important is that they have a focus and a unity created by the pictures themselves and by the format in which they are presented. Unlike wordless object and number books, picture books have some thread of story, but because pictures tell it all, words are unnecessary.

Wordless books provide complexity and detail, as well as continuity and consistency. For example, look at the many qualities in Mitsumasa Anno's book *Anno's Journey*. The intricacy of the pictures offers enduring pleasure, each complex double-page spread filled with detail shown from above. The shore, woods, farm, village, town, park, city, cathedral square, and festival all show people in characteristic actions. Hours of looking could occupy a child taking in each of the people, each of their varied actions, the architecture, the foliage, the vehicles—it goes on and on. In addition to the consistency of aerial views, as the journey moves from simple country life to complex city and back to country life, all pictures are spreads; tiny Anno returns to the shore to complete the circle of his journey. The result is a totally successful wordless book.

Similar continuity and consistency characterize *The Secret in the Dungeon* by Fernando Krahn, in which each picture is framed with white space and shows a separate action. Marked by her red dress, a spot of color in the shaded line drawings of the castle, the pony-tailed little girl is always the focus. Lost from the tour group, she wanders through the castle, falls down the water chute, and lands on top of a sleeping dragon whose smoky breath next catapults her through the chimney flue back into the midst of the group. The adults, who of course know better because they have listened to the guide, laugh and won't believe her story about the dragon in the dungeon. The final left-hand picture shows her gazing sadly out the back window of the car as the family leaves the castle. The story is successful in the clarity of its thematic content: Though it is common for adults not to believe children, children quite naturally find it hard to accept. The story line is clear, the humorous tone is consistent, and even without verbal description or comment, the protagonist is still a believable little girl.

Even without words, protagonist and action can be believable.

In another successful wordless picture book, *Sunshine* by Jan Ormerod, sunshine awakens a little girl who then awakens her father. They breakfast together, prepare a tray for her mother, and linger in bed for a while. The little girl then gets up to dress for school, leaving her parents to drop back to sleep. When she is dressed and ready to go, she appears in her parents' room with the alarm clock. The ensuing pictures show the parents in various actions—hasty dressing, showering, father leaving—and then the little girl is off to school. Here the pictures vary in size, but with reason and continuity. A series of twelve narrow pictures in one spread, for example, shows the girl removing her nightclothes and putting on one item of clothing after another. The story is simply about getting up and getting out in the morning, but the additional interest lies in the child's relationship with her father, and in her taking responsibility not only for her own readiness but also for that of her parents.

In *First Snow* Emily Arnold McCully also tells a simple story without words. None of the mouse characters has a name, but it is easy to focus on the one with the pink scarf (obviously a girl from the color she wears) who is afraid to slide down the hills on her sled. Support from her grandparents (the ones with the glasses who drive the truck) and the fun she has with her friends (cousins, perhaps) are not sufficient encouragement. But when she discovers the great fun for herself, she cannot be stopped. She's off, her sled tracks running up and down the hill, and everyone must wait for her when they reload the truck. The action for the most part is clear, although one of the last pictures shows her seemingly terrified, flying downhill on the overturned sled, while the connecting page shows her delighted with her success. The illustrations, which are usually double-page spreads, are humorous. Having developed the expectation that these illustrations are spreads, mild puzzlement occurs when two pictures that each bleed into the gutter occasionally show different actions.

As in all books of a given category, variety in subject matter as well as in quality is infinite. A wordless picture book with little significance, *Time Flies,* is built around a natural history museum as setting. A bird enters and flies as time is supposed to do, going in and out among the skeletal reconstructions of dinosaurs, and is surprised by a skeleton that snaps. The bird flies on, however, in and out of jaws and rib cages. A more intriguing wordless book is Istvan Banyai's *Zoom,* which reverses the device of accumulation. Beginning with a close-up of a rooster's comb, zoom camera action works in reverse, taking the reader back and back as the pictures include more and more information. Children watch the rooster through the window; then one sees the whole house, a toy town, a child building the town, that picture on the cover of a toy catalog held by a boy, the boy sleeping by a pool, and so on until the pilot of a plane looks down at the town, then the country, and then flies off into the atmosphere. The world revolves in space and becomes finally a speck in the universe. Each provocative picture shows proportion and position in space.

A book with far more story is Jeannie Baker's *Window,* illustrated in collage pictures and easily followed as the pictures grow increasingly complex. At the window is a mother with an infant boy looking out at the wooded lot in the country. As the child grows, the view from the window changes, first to show a single house in the distance, then a small town, and finally a city. Now grown to manhood, the child sees through the window the too-close houses, billboards, traffic, litter, and stores; he loads a van with his possessions and moves away to a country lot, where he finds a country house and plans to raise his family in an environment like that of his own childhood. As he stands in the window with his own infant, he sees the city in the distance, and the river before him—but beyond is a sign advertising lots for sale. The cycle will repeat itself. The story makes a point about the changing country as urbanization takes over, and about what seems the inevitability of such change. The story moves and has a point, its increasingly intricate pictures a source of both curiosity and familiarity. The tone is regret that this is what happens, and the theme hints at the sad truth of the loss of country and a simple bucolic life.

Not all wordless picture books are successful. The Waldo books, for example, are closer to puzzles than picture books. Others seem to have little reason to exist, and may be merely a way to get a series of pictures published. There is little story to hold our interest in *Oink*, for example. A sow with eight piglets naps, feeds her young, walks across the field to a puddle, and there they all get in and get wet. They nap, she sleeps, but the piglets awaken and wander off, find an apple tree, and throw themselves at the tree, where they get stuck in the branches searching for apples. The sow's loud "Oink" brings them down, and they march off behind her. In *The Birthday Trombone*, the arrangement of pictures presents a major problem. Most pictures are a single page, but they are without frames of any kind around the separate actions. Once accustomed to the lack of white space—even in the gutter, which might tell us that each page is separate—a full spread surprises the reader. Now we must count the tigers, hippos, rhinos, giraffes, lions, and monkeys before deciding that this double page represents one action, one picture. The monkey's birthday trombone startles each of the animals: the zebra hanging up striped socks and shirts, the rhinoceros riding a bicycle, the giraffe rocking her young giraffe, and the lion doing a jigsaw puzzle. When a huge snake suddenly appears, threatening to surround all of these large animals, the monkey uses his trombone for snake-charming, and all is well. The story lacks a point; instead, it seems to be an opportunity for the artist to draw animal pictures.

Wordless picture books, like those with text, require consistency. While the conventional "art" of the mass-produced book does not hold our interest, a personal vision can. Mere cleverness and facility are not sufficient here, any more than in other children's books.[12]

A highly imaginative wordless picture book is Molly Bang's vividly colorful *The Grey Lady and the Strawberry Snatcher*. Silently pursued by the blue-skinned Snatcher, the Grey Lady evades him through town, into the country, and through the woods, until, distracted by blackberries, the Snatcher gives up. The last spread shows the Grey Lady sharing berries with a happy family in a colorful house complete with baby, cat, and parrot. The story rests on the suspense of pursuit and the intriguing way in which the Grey Lady disappears into the background.

Ed Young's two books—*Up a Tree* about a cat, and *The Other Bone* about a dog—have more to interest us. In shadowy black and white, the cat plays, leaping at a butterfly, its body in typically beautiful cat configurations. When it is chased by a dog, it climbs a tree, and there we see its many expressions. When a group of turbaned men try to rescue it with a ladder, the cat resists with fearful grimaces. Only when it smells a fish does it decide to climb down on its own and, cocky and secure, it walks away. *The Other Bone* shows a napping dog dreaming of a bone, stretching, wriggling, lying on its back, pawing the air, and generally relishing its possession. When it awakens, it knows the bone to have been a dream. Its disappointment is soon over when it smells a bone in the garbage can. Attacking, then dumping the can to retrieve the bone, the dog once again is happy as it prances off. Walking beside the pond, it sees the bone reflected. Like Aesop's dog, greedy for another bone, it drops the bone for the reflected one, then unsuccessfully dives in after it. The dog shakes vigorously, looks puzzled, and again daydreams about the bone. In both brief stories the animals are distinctive and yet characteristic in their poses. Pages are uncluttered so that focus is strong and the story clear. Both amuse and allow the reader to speculate.

Summary

Picture books are dependent on illustration; some contain text and others are wordless. The design of the whole—the entire book, including size, shape, whether there are single pictures or double-page spreads, endpapers, title page, cover, dust jacket, and the placement of the gutter—all are important. The illustrator puts into visual form what the words say, and yet, in amplifying the text, conveys more than what the words say. When put into pictures, figurative language can be enhanced. By picturing one element or incident rather than another, illustrations can also change the story so that identical text—a folktale, for example—with different pictures creates different stories. Like other stories for children, the text of a picture book is judged by standards of literary excellence in plot, character, theme, setting, point of view, style, and tone. Wordless picture books require focus and unity, created by pictures and the format of presentation. Complexity and detail may accompany continuity, consistency, and a unique personal vision.

Words and pictures work seamlessly and in tandem.

    Children's taste, like that of most adults, is dependent largely on exposure. While it is important to learn what children like or dislike, we remember that children have had only limited exposure to literature and art. Their taste cannot be the most important criterion for judging which illustrations are acceptable, suitable, or desirable. As more than one critic has said, the popular taste is not untrained, but wrongly trained. The training is the responsibility of parents and educators in the arts as well as in literature. Exposure to trite, cliché-ridden illustrations, like exposure to trite, cliché-ridden language, does little to move the child along.[13] As we contemplate illustration in leisurely enjoyment, as children do, we attend to it as an extension of experience, an additional source of pleasure.

Notes

1. Joseph H. Schwarcz, *Ways of the Illustrator: Visual Communication in Children's Literature* (Chicago: American Library Association, 1982), p. 169.
2. Donald Weisman, *The Visual Arts as Human Experience* (Englewood Cliffs, NJ: Prentice-Hall, n.d.), pp. 18–21.
3. B. W. Alderson, *Looking at Picture Books* (New York: Children's Book Council, 1973), p. 6.

4. Perry Nodelman, *Words about Pictures: The Narrative Art of Children's Picture Books* (Athens: University of Georgia, 1988). On visual perception, Nodelman refers to Rudolf Arnheim, Norman Bryson, and E. H. Gombrich, sources well worth study.

5. See the excellent review of Nodelman's book by Jane Doonan in *Children's Literature,* vol. 20 (New Haven, CT: Yale University Press, 1992), pp. 204–210.

6. Ben Shahn, *The Shape of Contents* (New York: Vintage Books, 1957), p. 124.

7. See Perry Nodelman, "How a Picture Book Works," in *Image and Maker,* ed. Harold Darling and Peter Neumeyer (New York: Greenwillow, 1984).

8. See Sheila Egoff, *The Republic of Childhood* (New York: Oxford University Press, 1967).

9. Perry Nodelman, in "The Other: Orientalism, Colonialism, and Children's Literature" (*Children's Literature Association Quarterly 17,* Spring 1992, pp. 29–35) suggests that childhood may never have been "as innocent, as creative, as spontaneous as adults like to imagine. Perhaps children are always more like adults than adults are ever able to see." Addressing innocence, he maintains that by literature's silence on sexuality, we suggest their lives are devoid of sexuality and "make it difficult for children to speak to us about their sexual concerns: Our silence on the subject clearly asserts that we have no wish to hear about it, that we think children with such concerns are abnormal." And we become "unable to hear what children are saying even if they do attempt to speak about such matters," a convincing argument for openness on all issues concerning sexuality. Publishers are currently stocking bookstores with a spate of new gay titles; stories deal with the anxiety of "coming out," or finding the right partner. Three of the ALA's 2004 list of "Ten Most Challenged Books" contain gay themes.

10. Selma G. Lanes, *The Art of Maurice Sendak* (New York: Harry N. Abrams, 1980), p. 87. Much has been written about Sendak's work; this is just one of many sources.

11. See the interview with Maurice Sendak in *Victorian Color Picture Books,* ed. Jonathan Cott (New York: Chelsea House, 1983).

12. Pop-up books and other novelties are regarded by many as toys masquerading as books, but they may have their place. Although Selma Lanes suggests that it "is wise to look with suspicion on books . . . that can be scratched and sniffed, that float in bathtubs or burst into song . . . an evanescent genre," some author-illustrators are creating them.

13. The move to simplify language recurs throughout publishing history, although it is known that language skills decline for lack of stimulation. In one case, Beatrix Potter's "It would have been a beautiful thing to hide in, if it hadn't had so much water in it" becomes "Peter hid in the watering can but the watering can had water in it, and suddenly Peter felt a sneeze coming on." The humor of the understated punch line is gone. Illustrations are stuffed animals with plastic eyes. See also Susan Ohanian, "Ruffles and Flourishes," *Atlantic Monthly,* September 1987, pp. 20–22.

Recommended Books Cited in This Chapter

ADAMS, ERIC AND KATHLEEN. *On the Day His Daddy Left.* Illustrated by Layne Johnson. Morton Grove, IL: Whitman, 2000.

ANNO, MITSUMASA. *Anno's Journey.* New York: Putnam, 1977.

AUCH, MARY JANE. *The Easter Egg Farm.* New York: Holliday House, 1992.

BAKER, JEANNIE. *Window.* New York: Greenwillow, 1991.

BANG, MOLLY. *The Grey Lady and the Strawberry Snatcher.* New York: Four Winds, 1980.

BANYAI, ISTVAN. *Zoom.* New York: Viking, 1995.

BEMELMANS, LUDWIG. *Madeline.* New York: Dutton, 1937.

BUNTING, EVE. *The Wednesday Surprise.* New York: Clarion, 1989.

BURTON, VIRGINIA LEE. *The Little House.* Boston: Houghton Mifflin, 1942.

CLIFTON, LUCILLE. *My Brother Fine with Me.* New York: Holt Rinehart and Winston, 1975.

COONEY, BARBARA. *Island Boy.* New York: Viking Kestrel, 1988.

CREWS, DONALD. *Big Mama's.* New York: Morrow, 1991.

DIXON, ANN. *How Raven Brought Light to People.* Illustrated by James Watts. New York: Macmillan, 1992.

FARBER, NORMA. *How Does It Feel to Be Old?* New York: Dutton, 1988.

FLOURNOY, VALERIE. *The Patchwork Quilt.* Illustrated by Jerry Pinckney. New York: Little, Brown, 1992.

FOX, MEM. *Wilfrid Gordon McDonald Partridge.* Illustrated by Julie Vivas. New York: Kane Miller, 1989.

GÁG, WANDA. *Millions of Cats.* New York: Coward McCann, 1928.

GARCIA, RICHARD. *My Aunt Otilia's Spirits.* Illustrated by Robin Cherin and Roger Reyes. New York: Children's Book Press, n.d.

GARLAND, SHERRY, *The Lotus Seed.* San Diego: Harcourt Brace Jovanovich, 1993.

GERSTEIN, MORDICAI. *The Man Who Walked between the Towers.* Brookfield, CT: Roaring Brook Press, 2003.

GREGORY, VALISKA. *Happy Burpday, Maggie McDougal.* Illustrated by Pat Porter. Boston: Little, Brown, 1992.

GRIFALCONI, ANN. *The Bravest Flute.* Boston: Little, Brown, 1994.

GUY, ROSA. *Billy the Great.* Illustrated by Caroline Binch. New York: DelaCorte, 1991.

HEIDE, FLORENCE PARRY, and JUDITH HEIDE GILILLAND. *The Day of Ahmed's Secret.* Illustrated by Ted Lewin. New York: Lothrop, Lee & Shepard, 1990.

HENKES, KEVIN. *Chrysanthemum.* New York: Greenwillow, 1991.

HERRERA, JUAN FELIPE. *Calling the Doves.* Illustrated by Elly Simmons. New York: Children's Book Press, 1995.

HIGHWATER, JAMAKE. *Moonsong Lullaby.* New York: Lothrop, Lee & Shepard, 1981.

HOGROGIAN, NONNY. *Cinderella.* New York: Greenwillow, 1981.

HUTCHINS, PAT. *Rosie's Walk.* New York: Macmillan, 1968.

ISADORA, RACHEL. *At the Crossroads.* New York: Greenwillow, 1991.

JONES, JENNIFER BARRY. *Heetunka's Harvest.* Niwot, CO: Council on Indian Education, 1994.

JOOSSE, BARBARA. *Mama, Do You Love Me?* Illustrated by Barbara Lavallee. New York: Chronicle, 1991.

KEATS, EZRA JACK. *Apt. 3.* New York: Macmillan, 1971.

———. *A Whistle for Willie.* New York: Viking, 1962.

———. *The Snowy Day.* New York: Viking, 1962.

KIMMEL, ERIC. *Hershel and the Hanukkah Goblins.* Illustrated by Trina Schart Hyman. New York: Holiday House, 1989.

KIPLING, RUDYARD. *The Elephant's Child.* Illustrated by Lorinda Bryan Cauley. New York: Harcourt Brace Jovanovich, 1983.

KRAHN, FERNANDO. *The Secret in the Dungeon.* Boston: Houghton Mifflin, 1983.

LANGSTAFF, JOHN. *Frog Went A-Courtin'.* Illustrated by Feodor Rojankovsky. New York: Harcourt, Brace & World, 1955.

LIONNI, LEO. *Fish Is Fish.* New York: Random House, 1970.

———. *Frederick.* New York: Pantheon, 1966.

LOBEL, ARNOLD. *Frog and Toad Together.* New York: Harper & Row, 1972.

———. *Ming Lo Moves the Mountain.* New York: Greenwillow, 1982.

———. *The Book of Pigericks.* New York: Harper & Row, 1983.

LOCKER, THOMAS. *The Land of Gray Wolf.* New York: Dial, 1991.

LONGFELLOW, HENRY WADSWORTH. *Hiawatha.* Illustrated by Susan Jeffers. New York: Dial, 1983.

LOTTRIDGE, CELIA BARKER. *The Name of the Tree.* Illustrated by Ian Wallace. New York: Macmillan, 1990.

McCLOSKEY, ROBERT. *Homer Price.* New York: Viking, 1943.

———. *Make Way for Ducklings.* New York: Viking, 1969.

McCULLY, EMILY ARNOLD. *First Snow.* New York: Harper & Row, 1985.

McKISSACK, PATRICIA. *A Million Fish . . . More or Less.* Illustrated by Dena Schutzer. New York: Knopf, 1992.

MILES, MISKA. *Annie and the Old One.* Boston: Little, Brown, 1971.

MILNE, A. A. *Winnie-the-Pooh.* New York: Dutton, 1926.

MITCHELL, MARGAREE KING. *Uncle Jed's Barber Shop.* New York: Simon & Schuster, 1993.

MONJO, F. N. *The Drinking Gourd.* Illustrated by Fred Brenner. New York: Harper Trophy, 1993.

MORRISON, TONI. *Remember: The Journey to School Integration.* Boston: Houghton Mifflin, 2004.

MOSEL, ARLENE. *Tikki-Tikki Tembo.* Illustrated by Blair Lent. New York: Holt, 1968.

NAMIOKA, LENSEY. *Yang the Youngest and His Terrible Ear.* Canada: Little, Brown, 1992.

NASH, OGDEN. *The Adventures of Isabel.* Illustrated by James Marshall. Boston: Little, Brown, 1991.

ORMEROD, JAN. *Sunshine.* New York: Lothrop, Shepard & Lee, 1981.

POTTER, BEATRIX. *The Tale of Peter Rabbit.* New York: Warne, 1902.

ROHMANN, ERIC. *My Friend Rabbit.* Brookfield, CT: Roaring Brook Press, 2002.

RYLANT, CYNTHIA. *When I Was Young in the Mountains.* Illustrated by Diane Goode. New York: Dutton, 1982.

ST. GEORGE, JUDITH. *So You Want to Be President.* David Small, illustrator. New York: Philomel, 2000.

SENDAK, MAURICE. *Pierre, a Cautionary Tale.* New York: Knopf, 1962.

———. *Where the Wild Things Are.* New York: Harper & Row, 1963.

SEUSS, DR. *And to Think That I Saw It on Mulberry Street.* New York: Hale, 1937.

———. *If I Ran the Zoo.* New York: Random House, 1950.

SIEBERT, DIANE. *Heartland.* Illustrated by Wendell Minor. New York: Crowell, 1989; New York: Golden Books, 1999.

SOTO, GARY. *Too Many Tamales.* Illustrated by Ed Martinez. New York: Putnam, 1993.

STOCK, CATHERINE. *Armien's Fishing Trip.* New York: Morrow, 1990.

VAN ALLSBURG, CHRIS. *The Garden of Abdul Gasazi.* Boston: Houghton Mifflin, 1979.

———. *Just a Dream.* Boston: Houghton Mifflin, 1990.

VIORST, JUDITH. *Alexander, Who Used to Be Rich Last Sunday.* Illustrated by Ray Cruz. New York: Atheneum, 1978.

Wiesner, David. *The Three Pigs.* New York: Clarion, 2001.

Willhoite, Michael. *Daddy's Roommate.* Boston: Alyson, 1990.

Williams, Karen Lynn. *When Africa Was Home.* Illustrated by Floyd Cooper. New York: Orchard Books, 1991.

Yolen, Jane. *Owl Moon.* Illustrated by John Schoenherr. New York: Philomel, 1987.

Young, Ed. *The Other Bone.* New York: HarperCollins, 1984.

———. *Up a Tree.* New York: HarperCollins, 1983.

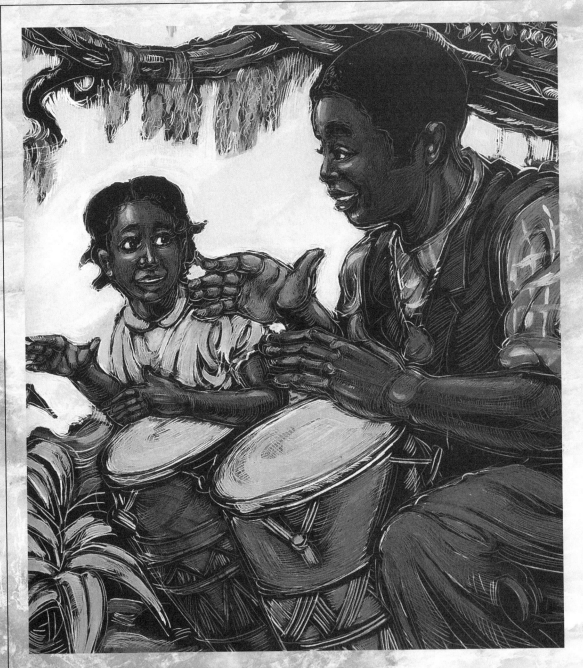

In the Time of the Drums

Kim L. Siegelson

Illustrated by Brian Pinkney

Character

Why begin with character? Suppose there are no characters in a story. What happens? Or no characters that you know very well?

Children sometimes say: "I like stories where the people are one way at the beginning of the book, and different at the end."

Some time ago, theory suggested that children at birth were "blank slates" and that parental responsibility was to shape them into proper adults. Fortunately, that idea has been largely, but not completely, rejected. In recent years society has learned a great deal about children and their development. Research, plus wisdom and observed experience, have awakened people to the complexity of young minds. Children are shortchanged when they are offered nothing but stories that are intent on forming or reforming them, that describe their ordinary daily routine, or that rely for interest entirely on excitement and suspense. Such reading fare may make of children a nation of nonreaders.

Children can catch many of human nature's subtleties. They care about humans and are sensitive to them. Even an infant responds to differences in people, hiding in a protective shoulder to avoid a noisy stranger, leaning out of a crib to be snuggled by a familiar friend. The youngest child, furthermore, recognizes and expects consistency in people. Try to persuade a child that the usually brusque and irritable Aunt Amy is—this time—loving and kind. By turning away from what he or she regards as Aunt Amy's fakery, the child clearly demonstrates not only sensitivity to personality but also an expectation of consistency.

It seems to follow that if even the youngest children are aware of personality in the people around them and can detect their differences, they are able

The child who responds to real people will respond to characters in books.

then to recognize personality in stories they read. It also seems natural that the child who responds to real people will respond to people in a story and will be sensitive to consistency in their actions. If the functions of literature include pleasure, plus the discovery and understanding of ideas and of other humans, then character development in literature makes its own contribution to these ends.

Character, as the term is generally used, means the aggregate of mental, emotional, and social qualities that distinguish a person. In literature, however, the term **character** is used to mean a person, or in the case of children's literature, sometimes a personified animal or object. Each of the living beings in a story, play, or poem is a character.

When we add the word *development,* we have a literary term, **character development,** which also has a special meaning. In life the development of a person's character or personality is a matter of growth and change. In literature, however, character development means showing the character—whether a person or animal or object—with the complexity of a living being. Each of us in real life is three-dimensional; that is, we are a mixture of qualities. None of us is completely generous; we have our limits. None of us is completely selfish; we have other traits. We all like to laugh; some of us like to provoke laughter. In the full development of character in the literary sense, the writer shows the whole, composed of a variety of traits like those of real humans.

The importance of a character determines how fully the character is developed and understood.

The writer has both privileges and responsibilities in this matter of character development. Since the reader follows a central character in a story, it is the writer's obligation to make this person's thoughts and actions believable. However, if the character is less important, the writer has the privilege of making the character two-dimensional or even representative of a class— for example, the bossy older sister or the impish little brother. The importance of a character in a story—primary, secondary, minor, or background importance—determines how fully the character is developed and understood. The closer the character comes to the center of the conflict—and therefore the more important the character is—the greater is our need to know the complexity of the character's personality. Conversely, the more the character functions merely as background, the less likelihood that the character needs to be developed.

Revelation of Character

We come to know character by several means.

In life we become acquainted with people in many ways. We see our new neighbors from a distance and draw tentative conclusions about age, occupation, and social status. We hear the accent of the Cockney, the twang of the Texan; even the precision or the explosiveness of short sentences indicates something about temperament. From their public actions we decide that the neighbors seem to be assets, since they prune their shrubs and walk their dog in the proper places. Finally, if the new neighbors are known to our friends, we listen to their opinions. We have come to know these neighbors by how they look, what and how they speak, how they act, and what others say about them.

In literature the process of coming to know a character is comparable. In literature, however, the writer has an additional alternative: the author may choose to tell what the characters are thinking. In this case, the writer may fill in details about the characters' innermost anxieties and dreams, the patterns of childhood behavior, and early home life.

By Actions

Templeton in *Charlotte's Web* is an example of a character whose actions help to define his nature. After Wilbur moves to the barn, we meet Templeton, who creeps up cautiously to the goslings, keeping close to the wall. Templeton's furtive manner arouses our curiosity; we are as suspicious as the barn animals. Twice in the story Templeton grins, first when Wilbur lands with a thud, hurt, crushed, and tearful after his unsuccessful web-spinning efforts. Templeton grins a second time as he takes Wilbur's tail and bites it as hard as he possibly can. Gleefully savage, Templeton delights in slinking about and nipping at his friend; he is surly, sneaky, and ill-tempered, pleased at others' discomfort. He is self-centered and gluttonous, going to the fair only to scavenge in the garbage and litter. Templeton's actions create a picture of Templeton's character.

By Speech

Accompanying Templeton's actions are his predictable sarcasm and ill-tempered outbursts as he gripes to Wilbur in sneering tones. He crawls into Wilbur's crate as a stowaway and grumbles:

> "Kindly remember that I am hiding down here in this crate and I don't want to be stepped on, or kicked in the face, or pummeled, or crushed in any way, or squashed, or buffeted about, or bruised, or lacerated, or scarred, or biffed. Just watch what you're doing, Mr. Radiant."

At the Fair, when Wilbur is optimistic that he may avoid becoming bacon, Templeton cannot resist commenting that when Zuckerman hankers for smoked ham, he will take the butcher knife to Wilbur. Templeton boasts about every grudging action and every carefully bought favor; he even pretends his motives are kind when he bites Wilbur's tail or saves the rotten egg. Complaining, "What do you think I am, anyway, a rat-of-all-work?" Templeton resentfully orders the directors' meeting to break up because meetings bore him. He grumbles at his commission, finding words for the web; he is not spending all his time rushing over to the dump after "advertising material." Templeton characterizes himself by what he says, showing himself to be cynical and selfish, resenting any intrusion on his own pursuits.

By Appearance

Gluttony is one of Templeton's most obvious traits, and his appearance shows it. He returns after his night of gorging at the fair, swollen to double his usual size. Only an appeal to appetite will tempt Templeton to fetch the egg sac, and as he eats first at Wilbur's trough every day, he grows fatter and bigger than any other known rat. Templeton's appearance verifies and supplements what we know of his character: gluttony and self-interest are the essence of Templeton.

By Others' Comments

Templeton is characterized by what he does, what he says, and by the way he looks. However, there is more to be learned from the comments of others about him. The animals carefully watch his furtive actions, since they neither like nor trust Templeton. The old sheep enlists Templeton's help in finding words, and reports that the rat can be persuaded only by appeals to "his baser instincts, of which he has plenty." Since the sheep is on our side, the side of saving Wilbur, we trust his judgments. And we distrust those characters who are on the wrong side of our sympathies. We are less accepting of their judgments, just as we would doubt Templeton's opinions on any character because we know how deceitful he is. The comments of the other characters, like the comment of the old sheep, help to show character.

By Author's Comments

White's comments also add to the picture we have of Templeton's character. He calls Templeton a crafty rat who does as he pleases; even his tunnel shows his cunning. White's thoroughly negative description of Templeton verifies the goose's and gander's feelings about the rat who "had no morals, no conscience, no scruples, no consideration, no decency, no milk of rodent kindness, no compunctions, no higher feeling, no friendliness, no anything. He would kill a gosling if he could get away with it." Templeton becomes a character we know so well that we know what to expect of him in almost any situation; he is consistent.

Unity of Character and Action

The writer creates the whole cast of characters for the story—some important, some minor, some complex, some relatively simple—through the use of these techniques. As we come to know these characters, we respond to them.

Most of us respond to others as we see similarity to ourselves, or if not similarity, recognizable traits and responses. We may say we "identify with" someone, and that someone is credible. While reading a story, we make the same demands of character—not that every character be exactly like our-selves, but that a character be credible.

In real life we know that change occurs in ourselves and in those we know well. We recognize that change only if we see a person before and after. We say that a child has grown, but even that statement implies a comparison between what was his or her height and what is now that height. If we must know both the *was* and the *is* to see growth, so it is with a character's change. If the impact of the events shapes or reshapes the personality of the character, the author is obligated to show how that change has come about.

Implicit within the acceptance of change is, of course, the idea of cause, and cause involves the story—its action. Given this complex character and adding these events, the combination may result in change. In life we say, "Just what you'd expect of her" or "It could happen only to him," and by these words admit that character and action are inseparable. The phrase "unity of character and action" may not mean much at first glance, but it expresses an important idea, one of the most important in understanding any fiction. In the best fiction, according to writer Henry James, "What is character but the determination of incident? What is incident but the illustration of charac-ter?"[1] *This character* because of *this personality* provokes *this action:* this action by its nature demonstrates this character. In literature the skillful writer shows characters by means of actions and speeches so that character, incident, and outcome seem interwoven—and, at the end, inevitable. Think of Brian Robeson in Gary Paulsen's *Hatchet* or *The River,* or Laura from the Little House books. Can you think of these characters apart from the actions in which they take part? (When we say "actions," we are also talking about plot, of course, the subject of the following chapter.)

Look at Hans Christian Andersen's "The Ugly Duckling" as an example of James's view on the unity of character and action. Notice how we come to know the central character. The Duckling's *appearance* seems of primary importance, since that is the basis for his being excluded. He is big and ugly, clumsy and grayish black throughout the story. However, at the end of the story his strong wings, white ruffled feathers, and slender neck have replaced his earlier awkwardness with beauty and grace. As for the dejected Duckling's *actions,* he does not look up when he is bitten and ridiculed in the duckyard. In the old woman's cottage, his panic sends him into the milk dish, the butter trough, and the flour barrel. But at the end of the story he floats gracefully on the water, his head tucked modestly under his wing. What the Duckling *says* is equally revealing of his character; several times he says sadly, "I'm so ugly," or "Even the dogs won't bite me." The Duckling is sure that he is an inferior nothing, and he never resists his enemies. At the end of the story, the Duckling shows by his speech that he is still modest when he says joyously, "I never dreamed of so much happiness when I was the ugly duckling."

As for what *others say* about the Ugly Duckling, his mother says he is not pretty, his brothers and sisters that they will not put up with him, for he is

"What is character but the determination of incident? What is incident but the illus-tration of character?"

Henry James

too big, and some wish that the cat would get him. The old woman's hen calls him a fool and finds him no fun. However, at the end of the story, the children call him the prettiest, "so young and lovely!" Finally, Andersen the writer has kept us informed about the Duckling not only by describing appearance and actions and reporting speeches, but also by his writer's comments, the result of his knowing everything. Andersen, *the author,* calls him a poor duckling and tells us he is miserable, exhausted, unhappy, terrified, a laughingstock. He calls the Duckling "poor thing!" and informs us of the Duckling's strange desire to float on the water, of his mysterious yearning to join the migrating swans. Finally, at the end of the story, Andersen tells us of the Ugly Duckling's beauty, which combines with his shyness, his happiness without pride as the Duckling speaks "from the depths of his heart."

Through all the means at his disposal, Andersen has shown us the character of the Ugly Duckling. The result is that we know this character well, and know that the story is the result of the character's traits combined with the actions that occur. The two are inextricably intertwined; together they demonstrate the unity of character and action. The character of the Ugly Duckling lives because the trials and harassments he goes through in the course of growing up determine his personal change and are his character; the story identifies the reality of maturing. Family rivalry, rejection, fear of failure, inability to find friends or to relate to others, even the feeling of ugliness and wishing one were dead are included in Andersen's story of the self-doubt of childhood.

Koly is the central character in Gloria Whalen's *Homeless Bird,* a story set in India, where Hinduism, a principle religion, has certain customs of marriage and family as well as those surrounding funerals, and the role of widows and daughters-in-law. Koly, an impoverished child of thirteen, must be married off for the sake of the family's survival. Without funds for a dowry, Koly's father must make the best marriage arrangement he can, and Koly is soon the bride of a young man she has never met—and who soon dies, leaving Koly a widow. A docile daughter-in-law, she is thus enslaved, and must work endlessly. "I also knew that I could not crawl about like a beaten dog. I had heard about families that had murdered the widows of their sons to get rid of them." As Koly's resentment grows, she becomes mischievous, like the god Krishna. Meanwhile her quiet resistance and her meticulous artistry in embroidery save her spirit, and ultimately her life. The change in Koly shows her to be a dynamic character; her change is credible.

In the early chapters of *The Watsons Go to Birmingham* by Christopher Paul Curtis, Byron is a troublesome boy who grows steadily more defiant of parents and teachers. His parents, thinking he needs to see what may be ahead for an African American in this country, take him to Birmingham, Alabama. There, younger brother Kenny takes a risk and is almost drowned in a whirlpool. To Kenny's surprise, Byron rescues him, but is angry that

Kenny has been so foolish. Little by little, Byron pays more attention to his family, and when someone sets fire to the church where little sister Joetta is attending Sunday School, he, like Kenny, is deeply concerned. By's next behavior is significant evidence of change: persuading Kenny—depressed at such acts of hatred—that he has not been negligent. By manages to bring Kenny out of his deep depression and help him to see his strengths. Byron has changed from a self-destructive adolescent to a caring brother. Just as people change slowly, this change develops slowly.

Buddy is a diminutive name, and Bud of another book by Curtis, *Bud, Not Buddy*, wants it known that he is self-reliant, resourceful, and able as well as determined to find his father. Bud consoles younger Jerry about the foster home he's to be placed in, is wary about revealing himself, protective of his cardboard suitcase that holds all he knows of his past, awestruck about restaurants and their varieties of food, intrigued by a flush toilet, worried about Mr. Calloway's health, and delighted with his gift from the band—a recorder soon replaced by a saxophone. Bud is whole, interesting, convincing—a boy we care about.

In *The Thief,* which can be called high fantasy, Megan Turner writes of rude, impudent Gen, who brags that he "can steal anything" and is "a lot more important than anyone else" in prison. Bitter and rebellious, Gen angers everyone. His captor, Sophos the magus who has saved Gen from a prisoner's death, is an admirable character, and his example has impact on Gen. By the end of the suspenseful search for an engraved ruby, Gen is thoughtful and honest, his cockiness turned to concern for the royal family—who, he finds, are his own family.

Not all writers are successful in integrating or unifying character and action. Judy Blume is highly successful in choosing situations common to children and with great skill holds their interest. Perhaps one of the biggest disappointments to a perceptive reader of Blume's novels, however, is inadequate portrayal of characters. Even the main characters in such novels as *Then Again, Maybe I Won't* seem shallow and unbelievable. Speaking in clichés, possessing little self-understanding, and acting in stereotypical fashion, the young people and the adults contribute little to our understanding of human motivation or to the integral nature of humans and their actions.

The writing of Norma Fox Mazer also addresses issues common to children. In *Babyface,* for example, Julie and Toni begin as best friends, but experience a separation as their experiences differ—a situation that frequently occurs in real life. Toni's relationship with her older sister is far from close, as such sister relationships sometimes are, and their rapprochement is neither simple nor instantaneous. But by building full characters for whom miracles in relationships do not occur, Mazer manages to keep the reader interested in her characters' natures, and in conflict that is both believable and interesting.

One of the biggest disappointments for a perceptive reader may be inadequate character portrayal.

Types of Characters

There are terms that describe the degree of character development and that refer to change or lack of it in a character in the course of a story. Briefly, a **round character** is one that we know well, who has a variety of traits that make him or her believable. A **flat character** is less well developed and has fewer traits. A **dynamic character** is a round character who changes, while a **static character,** despite credibility, does not change in the course of the story.

Flat Characters

Flat or little-known characters are the least important to plot.

Begin with the less important characters. They are essential to the action, but since they are not fully developed, we call them flat. In most stories, these flat characters help carry the action, show how the central character behaves or relates to others, and make the setting a believable place because in this setting live these people. Flat characters are quickly made known to the reader, and they quickly assume their necessary places in the narrative so that the story can then focus on the central characters.

For example, in *Charlotte's Web*, Fern is a relatively flat character, a child with an intense interest that absorbs her for a time. She treats Wilbur like a doll, and listens to the animals' conversations and reports them to her incredulous parents. She plays and quarrels, and she loves the Ferris wheel and the freedom of the Fair. However, Fern has few traits that distinguish her from other little girls; she remains a believable little girl but not a special one. Wilbur's relationships and worries are the focus of the story, and the conflict goes on without Fern's being totally aware of all that spiders and pigs mean to each other. Because this is Wilbur's story, not Fern's, she needs no greater development. Dr. Dorian and Mr. Arable are more obviously flat characters.

Often children get hooked on a particular series of books. In many cases, characters in such stories as Nancy Drew, the Hardy Boys, the Babysitters or Goosebumps are flat; plot carries the story. Characters are undeveloped, as they are in the recent Lemony Snicket books. Fun, a quick read, but the characters in *A Series of Unfortunate Events* are essentially flat, with few character traits. Violet is an inventor who gets the three out of danger, often with the help of Klaus, the reader who knows where to find necessary information. Sunny is little, a tagalong who needs interpretation; the plot carries the story but without new understanding. However, who can argue with the pleasure of mystery and suspense?

When a character has very few individual traits, the character does not seem to exist as an individual human being. When the character seems to have only the few traits of a class or of a group of people, the character is called a **stereotype.** Each of us has a few mental stereotypes—of politicians, mothers, athletes, or poets. When we examine these mental pictures and compare them to individuals we know well, we find that each stereotype is inaccurate and unjust. In literature, however, the stereotype, like the stock character who appears in many folktales, is useful, since he or she quickly settles into a background position and performs there in an easily understood role.

In *Charlotte's Web,* Lurvy is an example of a *stereotype*—in this case of a hired man. Lurvy has only the expected traits and does only the expected things. He nails down the loose board on Wilbur's pen, he slops Wilbur, he discovers the exploded dud. Lurvy is neither eloquent nor imaginative:

> "You notice how solid he is around the shoulders, Lurvy?"
> "Sure. Sure I do," said Lurvy. "I've always noticed that pig. He's quite a pig."
> "He's long, and he's smooth," said Zuckerman.
> "That's right," agreed Lurvy. "He's as smooth as they come. He's some pig."

As Lurvy's speech shows, stereotypes describe themselves by what they say as well as how they say it.

Occasionally the writer may use a **foil,** a minor character whose traits are in direct contrast to those of a principal character, and thus highlight the principal. The snobbish lamb is as young and naive as Wilbur, but she is smug instead of humble. Pigs are little or nothing to her. Since the lamb is consistently disdainful, her behavior contrasts sharply with Wilbur's humility, thus acting as a foil.

Stereotyping, or compressing people into flat caricatures that eliminate individual differences, is useful in literature for particular background figures that fill narrow roles. Flat and stereotyped characters, however, are not suitable protagonists; we should be particularly watchful for stereotypes of people from cultures other than the dominant ones, because stereotypes do great injustice. (The flat characters of folk literature will be discussed later in this chapter.) We have noted the necessity for character and action to be unified. However, flat and stereotyped characters do not truly grow out of action, and action cannot grow out of their less-than-full human natures. It seems more descriptive of flat characters and action to say that they coexist; flat characters and stereotypes move over the surface of the action, rather than being integrated with the action. Flat characters, furthermore, make little contribution to our understanding of human nature. In fact, if we read only about stereotypes, our perceptions about people may be narrowed rather than expanded. While stories for adults do occasionally make their points by careful stereotyping, these protagonists are reaching a more sophisticated readership, one that is capable of seeing a point by contrast to what is already known of the complexity of human nature.

Laurence Yep does not resort to stereotypes of Chinese Americans in *Child of the Owl.* Casey, the protagonist, struggles to find a connection between her footloose life with her father and her new life, living first with her wealthy Uncle Phil, then with her grandmother in Chinatown. As she lives the ways of the transplanted Chinese society, she is aware of her failure to understand them or to speak their language, and struggles to discover who and what she is.

Flat or stereotyped protagonists do not contribute to understanding.

Stereotypes in literature about cultures other than the dominant one are unfair and misleading.

Round Characters

A **round character** is one that is fully developed; we know this character well, because the many traits are demonstrated in the action of the story. We know appearance and actions, speeches and opinions, what others say and think about the character, and oftentimes what the writer thinks about him or her. The character is so fully developed that we may even be able to predict actions and reactions. Yet, like a real person, the character may surprise us or respond impetuously on occasion. It is as though we know the character so well that the character has become a real person, one we wish we could meet or might enjoy knowing.

Children's literature has a great many round characters that we may feel we know. However, in order to see clearly what is meant by a round character, compare the many traits of Wilbur, for example, to the few traits of Mr. Arable, or the stereotype Lurvy. From the first words of the first page, when Fern asks where her father is going with the ax, we are anxious about Wilbur's fate. We soon discover that Wilbur's struggle is the conflict, and that he is therefore the **protagonist,** or central character. Tiny, dependent Wilbur has almost no life of his own at the opening of the story, except to amuse himself like a toddler, finding the mud moist and warm and pleasantly oozy. When he goes to live in the barn, he is bored, unable to dream up anything exciting to do. Friends must introduce themselves to him. When he squeezes through the fence and is pursued, he has no idea what to do with freedom, and his appetite makes him captive again. Since Lurvy's pail of slops is irresistible, Wilbur plans his day around his body: sleeping, eating, scratching, digging, eating, watching flies, eating, napping, standing still, eating.

On the day that Wilbur wants love more than comfort and food, he has grown. But now he wonders uncertainly about friendship, which seems such a gamble. After Wilbur makes a friend, life becomes more exciting and he becomes confident enough to try spinning a web. Cheerfully, he tries and fails; he humbly admits that Charlotte is brighter and more clever. Wilbur's innocence and dependence are clear when he pleads for a story or a song, for a last bedtime bite, a last drink of milk, and calls out the series of quiet goodnights to Charlotte. Panic is Wilbur's reaction to news of his destiny—the Arables' dinner table. But once he is assured that Charlotte can perform miracles, he calms down, becoming patient, trusting, and humble. The congratulatory words in Charlotte's web make Wilbur an exemplary pig; he decides that if he is called "radiant," he must act radiant, and in his way he becomes radiant. Despite all the admiration Wilbur attracts, he remains modest. Happy and confident, he honestly admires Charlotte's peach-colored egg sac and gazes lovingly into the faces of the crowd. He looks both grateful and humble. Wilbur has enough traits to classify him as a round character and a suitable protagonist.

Change in Character

If there is a unity of character and action such as James speaks of, then the character is not only affected by events, but his or her nature may also bring about various events. Frequently, the events of the story may change a character.

A character is not affected only by events, but the character's nature may cause the events.

When the word *dynamic* is used in ordinary conversation, it may mean forceful, or perhaps exciting. However, in the context of literature, the word has special meaning: a **dynamic character** is one who changes in the course of the action. He or she may change from being shy to being poised or even domineering, or from cowardly to brave, from selfless to selfish. The character may demonstrate a new realization about himself or herself, or about his or her personal values. He may show that he is now able to take care of himself, or she may show that she has become able to care for others as well as herself. Somehow, the events of the story and qualities of the character have effected some basic character change. The variety of possibilities for change is huge.

The character, of course, may grow older by an hour or by a decade in the course of the novel's action. However, the mere passage of time is not sufficient evidence of character change. Some people are as immature at thirty-five as they were at fifteen. However, we know some people who have been changed by a single event—a traumatic experience or a simple and joyous one that has brought a realization of some kind. It is not then the passage of time that is important in character change, but the impact of events on the character—the unity of character and action—creating new traits to supplant or alter the old. The character may not necessarily be aware of his or her own change, just as in looking back we may see that we are different from what we once were, but cannot necessarily account for the where or when of our change. The essential matter is that we are different.

Wilbur changes. He is a believable character early in the story, although he is young and immature. The experience of receiving selfless friendship makes him able to give selfless friendship. Slowly, as we watch this change occurring, Wilbur is altered by his part in the action, by his receiving so much. Now he is the same Wilbur, and yet not the same. To his early qualities of humility and naiveté are added dependability and steadfastness, sacrifice and purpose. Even Wilbur's vocabulary matures. When first he hears the bad news, he is a panicky child:

> "I can't be quiet," screamed Wilbur, racing up and down. "I don't want to die. Is it true . . . Charlotte? Is it true they are going to kill me when the cold weather comes?"

By the end of a summer of maturing, Wilbur responds to news that his dearest friend will die, and knows that he must save the egg sac. Notice how his vocabulary has changed to adult words, and his tone has changed to reasonable persuasion:

"Listen to me! . . . Charlotte . . . has only a short time to live. She cannot accompany us home, because of her condition. Therefore, it is absolutely necessary that I take her egg sac with me. I can't reach it, and I can't climb. You [Templeton] are the only one that can get it. There's not a second to be lost. . . . Please, please, please, Templeton, climb up and get the egg sac."

Wilbur does not scream; he uses "please" liberally. His desperation does not arise from his own need, but from the need of another. Charlotte had once said to the screaming Wilbur that he was carrying on childishly; the new Wilbur tells Templeton to "stop acting like a spoiled child." Wilbur—who once planned his day around his slops—can now, out of deep concern for Charlotte, promise solemnly that Templeton may eat first and take his choice of all the goodies in the trough.

During winter Wilbur warms the egg sac with his breath in the cold barn. By the end of the story, it is Wilbur who offers the first mature greeting, a cheerful "Hello!" to the baby spiders. The change is significant, and it occurs slowly. It is convincing. Little by little, events have molded a self-centered child into responsible maturity; we believe in Wilbur's maturity just as we believed in his childishness.

Jake, in *Surviving the Applewhites* by Stephanie Tolan, is a dynamic character, changing throughout the story from a belligerent cynic who has been in trouble with the law to a caring family member. When, at the Applewhite's, he meets kindness, he changes, a change that occurs as Winston the Bassett hound adopts him, as little Destiny adores him, as Jake helps E.D. with her butterfly science project, then discovers he can sing as the goatherd in the musical *Sound of Music*. Character and action are intricately entwined in a believable character change.

For still another example of a dynamic character, look next at *A Girl Named Disaster*, Nancy Farmer's story of an African girl from Mozambique. An old man's fourth wife at the age of eleven, docile Nhamo is a drudge, a virtual slave to her new mother-in-law, who treats her brutally and accuses her of bringing the disaster of cholera to the village. Her resignation and passivity change when her grandmother advises her to flee to her father's people. With new physical strength and determination she survives wild animals and wilderness travel, struggles on, then finds herself in a research community where she is appreciated. Physical stress might have left her spirit cowed; that is not the case. Each period of difficulty has brought change, and Nhamo is now an independent young woman in both body and mind.

The struggle to find out who we are is paramount to growing up; it may resemble a dialogue between our two views of ourselves. Such a technique is central to *The Ashwater Experiment* as Amy Goldman Koss tells the story. Hillary's parents are free spirits, moving from one flea market to another, selling their "gizmos" in one city after another. Hillary thinks that's fine—always being on the outside watching a new group of people around her, keeping a journal about their strange behavior. But when the threesome settles in Ashwater for a full nine months, Hillary discovers that being on the outside is less fun than excelling, coming to understand others' lives, being helpful, having friends who congratulate and approve, seeing the problems of others and becoming part of their lives. In nine months, Hillary changes from Watcher to Participant.

Since less important characters are not so closely focused on, and may remain on the fringes of action, their change is unlikely to be important or to grow out of the events of the plot. Furthermore, their changing could even be distracting.

> Characters on the fringe of action are unlikely to change.

A **static character** is one who does not change in the course of the story. The conflict does not influence the character by making any impact on personality or outlook. Flat characters—including stereotypes and foils—will not change; they are not known well enough for us to recognize changes or to care, but a round character, too, may be unchanged by the conflict, and, in fact, even the protagonist may be unchanged by the action.

Although Charlotte is not the center of Wilbur's story, we know her consistent nature very well. Charlotte is not only motherly, but hardworking as well, and her web words prove it. She is the same wise and selfless character at the end of the story that she was at the beginning, and we therefore call her a static character.

It is not necessary that a story have a dynamic or changing character. In one story the round central character may change, and in another the round central character may not. The change or lack of it does not constitute a judgment about the quality of characterization. However, the static or dynamic nature of the protagonist does help the reader to see the action and to understand the idea behind it.

> Change is not necessary.

In life a person rarely changes overnight, and in literature we find such a change unbelievable. In Victor Barnouw's *Dream of the Blue Heron,* Wabus, a Native American boy, must choose between his own culture and the White man's. Wabus sees brutality, rigidity, depersonalization, and the substitution of material goals for spiritual ones, all epitomized in the character of Mr. Wickham, the disciplinarian in the government school, who hustles Wabus roughly, rips and tears his clothing, seizes him by the hair to jam a hat on his cropped skull. When Mr. Wickham finds the tribe ceremonially burying Wabus's grandfather, however, he changes. In minutes he flashes a smile, makes an offering, reassures Wabus, springs to carry the body, seizes a shovel and leaps into the grave to dig furiously. Then, although he is convinced of the innocence of Wabus's father, he turns him in to the law. In the final pages of the story, he offers books to the father in prison and promises to help Wabus become a lawyer. Wabus's choice to follow the culture of the White man is unbelievable and insufficiently motivated. Nothing in the White society he has experienced is appealing. The source of our dissatisfaction is the sudden and unconvincing change in Mr. Wickham's character.

In another story contrasting Native American and European cultures, note the experience of Matt in Elizabeth Speare's *The Sign of the Beaver* compared to that of Wabus. Left to keep the new cabin in Maine when his father leaves to bring the family north, Matt must survive by means of fishing line, rifle, and garden, experience enriched by his friendship with the Native American boy Attean. During the seven months of waiting, Matt matures, learning to live in solitude, to find his way through the forest, to adapt to the Native American culture, and to triumph in his independence.

One of the delights of children's stories is the frequent introduction of funny people, sometimes the protagonist, but often a minor character, one whose sole function seems to be to provide comedy. Polly Horvath creates such comics. Although children probably miss the humor in her name, Miss Perfidy in *Everything on a Waffle* does not know where Primrose's sweaters are, but says, "Let me assure you, Primrose . . . I always know what I know for a reason and I always know the reason that I know what I know. And that is how I keep an orderly life." But Miss Perfidy adds proudly that she "even remembers things that never happened." Primrose's recipe (one of several included) for Miss Perfidy's tea biscuits: "double the baking soda and leave out the vanilla. Then age for ten days in a drawer full of mothballs. They won't be tasty but they'll be authentic." Primrose has lost a fingertip in a fishing accident, so Miss Honeycut, school counselor, preaches to Primrose by way of anecdotes, like the one about the "cat who kept having accidents. In the end there was so little left of her that the mouse was stalking her. *The mouse was stalking her.*"

A particularly successful book for sports enthusiasts is Scott Johnson's *Safe at Second,* but there is far more than baseball to hold the reader. Paulie admires Todd, the sensational pitcher who is courted by scouts and colleges—until Todd is blinded in a game. Paulie practices with Todd, refusing to acknowledge Todd's failures and insisting on a comeback. Paulie, no longer a mere shadow of Todd, becomes a success in his own right. With the encouragement of the editor of the school newspaper, Paulie becomes a good sports reporter. Sometimes strength consists of acknowledging one's failed dreams.

Jennalee in *Me and Rupert Goody,* by Barbara O'Conner, finds Uncle Beau's general store a refuge from a chaotic home. There she helps Uncle Beau by shelving cans, sorting vegetables, and "buttoning up the door" at night. When Rupert Goody, a mentally disabled man, shows up claiming to be Uncle Beau's son, Jennalee is angry. She cannot believe that dark-skinned Rupert is Uncle Beau's son, until a crumpled birth certificate proves his claim. Little by little Jennalee sees the devoted bond between the two and reluctantly admits Rupert's claim, giving up her favored position. Now Jennalee says, "Button the door, Rupert." She has come around. Change is gradual and credible.

A totally credible character change occurs almost overnight for Harriet Hemings in the historical novel *Wolf by the Ears* by Ann Rinaldi. Secure Harriet, daughter of Thomas Jefferson and his slave Sally Hemings, is the victim of an attempted rape by Jefferson's son-in-law. Shattered by the experience, she sleeps for two full days, until her mother insists that she rise and dress.

> Get up, she says. I told her I didn't want to get up. Want to stay here, I told her. The days, they just bleed right into each other, and that suits me just fine.
>   Then she tells me I have to get up. . . . She's purring it, the way she does when she wants something out of me. So I said I would. I ought to know better than to trust Mama when she purrs like that, but somehow I just never learn.

A few pages later, Jefferson tells Harriet that she should leave Monticello at twenty-one and from then on "pass for white." Now, in the language of a grown woman, she says,

> I was a child no longer. What had happened the other night had ended my child-hood forever. It had put me face to face with a brick wall and nowhere to go. And this dear, kind, misunderstood man [Jefferson] was forging a hole in that wall for me and attempting to lead me through it.

The number of round characters depends on the complexity of the plot, and thus there can hardly be a firm rule about number. Certainly it is not feasible that every character be round. It seems evident, furthermore, that a large number of fully developed characters becomes highly distracting in a story for children. Even *Charlotte's Web*, which has three round characters, focuses more fully on Charlotte and Wilbur than on Templeton, important as he is. Some writers, in speaking of the writing process, say that a too fully developed minor character can get out of hand and become so round as to lose his or her place as subordinate and take over, thus changing the plot. For the sake of unity in the story, it then becomes the writer's choice between flattening out the character once again, or giving him or her new importance in what must now be an altered plot. This seems to happen with television spin-off programs: characters have begun to take over and change the plot. So get rid of them. Make a new story.

A complex plot may require more round characters.

✪ Special Issues of Character in Children's Literature

While character study alone may be enough for some adults, it is not enough for most children, and for several reasons. First, the younger the child, the more limited his or her awareness of alternatives. Young children are often prevented by their elders from making discoveries about "what happens if"; they often hear instead "Do this, so that may happen," or "Don't do this, or that might happen." Chances for exploring outcomes and discovering alternatives on their own are often denied them. A related problem for the young reader is a limited understanding of motivation. Children rarely see motives for behavior beyond what they would like to see happen. Furthermore, to the young, choices are black and white, yes and no; unaware of their own mixed motives, they rarely see those of others. With maturity—which the experience of literature increases—children become aware of unselfish motives like Wilbur's, or of subtle and self-serving motives disguised as unselfish, like Templeton's.

Although children may have keen interest in character, most want character involved in action and making decisions. Children, like adults, are intent on the peace or uproar that results from the action. Children, too, like to follow characters and their motives through their emotions and their reasoning as they face decisions and make choices. Children are also excited by the possibility of the accidental, and perhaps even more by the inevitable. The likelihood of success or the change of defeat keeps readers of any age involved in a story's action. While character, then, is essential, there are other considerations.

A discussion of character in children's literature is incomplete without reference to various kinds of protagonists, since characters are not only people or animals, but may also be inanimate objects. Winnie-the-Pooh and Piglet may once have been stuffed toys, but now they are believable characters. Hans Christian Andersen shows skill in characterizing the inanimate—from tiny toy soldiers to willow trees, from shirts to darning needles—endowing them with few or many traits, depending on the length of his story and the theme he is exploring. He can give to the old lantern willpower and intelligence, to the starched collar pride, to the teapot arrogance, and to the silver shilling imagination. The tin soldier in *The Steadfast Tin Soldier*, although an inanimate object, is a convincing character. In the many tales Andersen told and that are still frequently read, it is the unity of character and action that makes each story live.

We cannot ignore the characterization provided by picture-book illustrations. The limited text of *Wilfrid Gordon McDonald Partridge* by Mem Fox is enhanced by Julie Vivas's pictured portrayal of the little boy: a child in constant motion on skateboard, trapeze bar, and blocks, upside down on the floor, feet up the back of the sofa, collecting his possessions, looking eye to eye with the hen, sharing his personal finds with Miss Nancy. This is one busy, happy child, always pleased to visit with the old people in the house next door. In Karen Ackerman's *Song and Dance Man,* no Grandpa was ever more delighted to be back in the past. He gleefully dons his hat and grabs his cane to be the vaudeville dancer he once was. Stephen Gammell's illustrations show a loving and demonstrative older man who might look a bit out of shape, but who surely can dance and still loves to.

Traditional Literature

Traditional literature has been handed down orally from generation to generation and finally been set into print. Perhaps because of the necessity to keep the spoken story moving with suspense, the folktale relies on *stock characters.* The jealous fairy, the foolish youngest son, and the girl as good as she is beautiful are all useful stock characters. "A beautiful daughter" calls from the

---

Character alone is not enough in children's stories; action is also important.

Stock characters behave predictably.

listener of any culture the same set of responses each time the phrase is used. Since suspense and action carry the folktales and the usually optimistic ending makes its comment on life, characters need only be mentioned by a class name to be known. In a sense, this is one of the pleasures of traditional literature; we enjoy meeting characters we have met before, and whose actions are thoroughly predictable. Free then to concentrate on action and idea, it all moves along quickly. Discovery of human nature comes, then, from the relationship of theme to action, often a discovery about universal human yearnings.

Stock characters, or character types like the wicked stepmother or the charming prince, often appear in folk literature. Baba Yaga the Russian witch, for example, is capable of acts both cruel and kind, both of which she performs in *Baba Yaga* as retold by Eric Kimmel. The trickster is another such character; in stories from the Plains Indians, Iktomi the trickster is often tricked himself, as in Paul Goble's *Iktomi and the Ducks*. Br'er Rabbit tricks the Fox, who is a less accomplished trickster in the Uncle Remus tales.

Ruskin Bond tells a story, *Binya's Blue Umbrella*, that has many of the qualities of a folktale, and yet develops major characters fully. Binya, who is so taken with a blue silk umbrella that she trades her lucky leopard's claw for it, is the envy of the village. The umbrella protects her from a snake and from the monsoon, but a greedy tradesman steals it. Because Binya knows how the tradesman longs for the umbrella, she leaves it in his shop, and even accepts his gift of a lucky bear's claw. Short as the story is, Binya is convincingly generous and sympathetic, a proud girl and a lover of beauty.

It is interesting to note that stories from many cultures focus on the lazy but tricky person, usually a boy or a man. Not only do Andersen, the Grimms, and Perrault have such stock characters, but we find them in stories from other countries as well. Dianne Snyder's retelling of the traditional Japanese tale, *The Boy of the Three-Year Nap*, uses as the central character the clever but lazy boy who nonetheless marries the wealthy merchant's daughter and settles into a job. *The Magic Leaf*, a Chinese story retold in folktale tradition by Winifred Morris, is about Lee Foo, who believes himself highly intelligent because he reads big books. One of these books tells him that hiding behind the leaf, under which the praying mantis hides before attacking the cicadae, will make him invisible. Arrested when he believes himself invisible, he hoodwinks the judge with that same leaf. The Irish tale, *Jamie O'Rourke and the Big Potato*, retold and illustrated by Tomie DePaola, is about a husband who will starve when his wife is sick unless he gets out of bed and works. He, too, comes out on top as he manages to make the whole village his food supplier.

Lazy but tricky characters often appear in folktales.

Animal Realism

In fantasy like *Charlotte's Web*, the animals are people, but in a realistic story we expect animal characters to behave like real animals, to be true to their

Realistic animals must be true to breed.

natures. Sheila Burnford, in her award-winning novel *The Incredible Journey*, knows the qualities of her animal characters and depicts them as true to family and breed. In a story filled with suspense and conflict, she makes us care what happens to her three central characters as they struggle for survival against the Canadian wilderness.

First, there is Luath the Labrador retriever. A one-man hunting dog, Luath is at home in the wilderness. Though his soft, protective mouth is not good for fighting, he can ford a river and encourage the cat and the terrier to swim. The two followers are the Siamese cat, an independent loner, and the English bull terrier, a sociable clown. The feline aristocrat is also true to family and breed: she races straight at her friends and then darts away, and opens doors with a leaping twist. While shy Luath seeks the trail, the bull terrier seeks human habitation along the way. The English bull, always the pet, smiles at a hermit, expecting like any pet that the hermit's dinner time is his dinner time, too.

As noted in Chapter 8, animal realism is at its best when the animals act like animals. The temptation for the writer is to imagine and to report what thoughts and feelings the animals are having. However, the writer, who does not really know what animals think or feel, must draw conclusions from observing appearance and behavior. And, of course, when the writer permits the animals to talk with one another in human speech, realism is destroyed and fantasy created. Burnford, however, has developed the characters of her animals primarily through observation, and the reader therefore believes in their reality.

Writers of animal stories may be tempted to guess thoughts and feelings.

Science Fiction

Examining literature by genre sets up a collective set of expectations derived from our experiences with the particular genre. Science fiction has been called the fiction of change, "future history." Although some historians of the genre credit Heraclitus and Aristophanes with the seeds of it all, others credit H. G. Wells and Jules Verne with its beginnings. Wells and Verne are still much read, but more frequently readers use the term science fiction to cover the work of more recent authors. Historian James Gunn notes that it springs from naturalism, or the view of humankind as animal, but a dominant animal that must be tough and aggressive while using innate human qualities to temper animal qualities with love, self-sacrifice, and creativity, combined with a concern for the race. In the changing of science fiction from naturalism toward more mainstream contemporary literature, science fiction now has greater concern for character, for a subjective reality, and for subtlety in language; it is now reaching a larger audience. As critic Kingsley Amis says in verse, "These cardboard spacemen aren't enough,/Nor alien monsters, sketched in rough, /Character's the essential stuff." Although such broadening of concern to encompass character as well as problems may extend sci-

Fully developed science fiction characters are becoming more common.

ence fiction's audience, it also causes regret among some writers and critics because they see science fiction as growing virtually indistinguishable from mainstream fiction.

Early science fiction focused on plot and action, but *Space Race,* by Sylvia Waugh, which is filled with an empathic exploration of character, is the story of a father and son sent from the planet Ormingant to observe and chronicle the nature of Earth's inhabitants. Five years ago they had arrived on Earth in a space ship the size of a golf ball, and soon must shrink again to resume their lives on their own planet. The two are reluctant to leave, because on Earth they have been loved and cared for. The thread of their emotional contact never fails.

However, note for contrast the stereotyped scientists in Ben Bova's *The Flight of Exiles.* By page 45 the reader has met thirteen characters of almost equal development, names rather than people. Unable to identify the protagonist, the reader can scarcely be expected to identify the murderer. Specialists—psychotechs, cryogenists, molecular geneticists, and one astronaut—are all known only by their technical jobs. In Henry James's terms, characters and action are not fused but described only from the outside.

A more satisfying work is William Sleator's *Interstellar Pig,* the account of Barney's involvement with three mysterious neighbors who draw him into a new board game in which a player draws pieces and instruction cards that change the player into the monster described: lichen, giant spider, or gill-breathing waterman, for example. The goal of the game is to find The Piggy, the source of power. Through fearful transformations of nightmare proportions, Barney battles the three stranger/monsters and finds that The Piggy, the prize, is really powerless. The novel abounds in themes, the most significant being that power merely for its own sake corrupts. Caught up with a very real Barney, a reader cares. Another of Sleator's novels, *The House of Stairs,* in which the power of human love conquers the inhuman machine (as it does in Madeline L'Engle's *A Wrinkle in Time*), carries our concern for the outcome because the believable human qualities of the characters give the action significance.

The characters of *The Ear, the Eye, and the Arm* by Nancy Farmer are futuristic fantasies themselves. The title lists names of characters in a detective agency, men who grew up near a nuclear reactor: Arm can outreach anyone; Ear can fold his ears in "like morning glories"; and Eyes has no whites, only pupils. By 2194, toxic waste threatens the "family," many species are extinct, and most characters are mutants of some kind: gardener robots, house robots, an automatic Doberman, and a walking communicator whose feelings can be hurt, for example. Praise from the Mellower makes everyone feel good, and the three children respond. Even Father, who is harshly military, relaxes under the Mellower's praises. Children who are trapped in the house for security reasons even "go to Scouts" by holophone, although they'd like to attend a Scout meeting without bodyguards. The frightening world

outside the house is filled with genetically engineered monkeys and rats—
Fist, Knife, and the Sea Elephant, for example. Even mounds of trash stand up
and approach the three children. Characters in this society are strange to us
and seem to have few recognizable qualities; perhaps that is what makes
such stories unappealing to many readers.

If we apply the axioms of character development, we realize that believing in the reality of character makes us believe in the experience. If the experience is fantastic, as it is in science fiction, a believable character can make
us feel that the discoveries within the story have significance. Shallow character delineation limits our discovery about ourselves. When action does
not grow out of the nature of character, the plot seems contrived and unimportant. The failure of such a story is often one of failure in character development.

Clearly some science fiction suffers from inadequate character development, but such inadequacy is not inevitable in this genre and is becoming less
frequent.

Classics

A classic is a book that lasts, not because it is continually enshrined on lists,
but because it continues to be read. The most memorable stories—those like
Tom Sawyer that we take with us from childhood to adulthood—create solid
and believable characters. Frequently, what characters did—or what the plot
was—has faded from memory, but we recall with vividness the characters
themselves.

Look at two classics now classified as historical fiction, read perhaps by
more girls and boys than any other two. They are two very different novels.
Louisa May Alcott's *Little Women,* which has very little action or plot, is primarily a thematic story of daily, even routine, activity, and the thinking and
doing of five females. Mark Twain's *The Adventures of Tom Sawyer* has many
chapters of seemingly unrelated episodes, but it still has action and suspense
leading to an exciting climax and discovery.

The character of Jo March carries *Little Women* and has made it one of
girlhood's favorites.[2] In her family, composed of vain Amy, saintly Beth,
proper Meg, and worn but cheerful Marmee, Jo is the center. Jo is alive—
aggressive and tomboyish, awkward and clumsy. She invents, acts, directs,
complains and teases, sings off-key, and resents any restriction that would
turn her into a stereotypical girl. She makes up games, dreams of heroism in
active roles, and without guilt or gloom drops her bread on the carpet, butter
side down.

Tom Sawyer is a second classic example of memorable character—as
innumerable imitators tend to prove. Tom, seeking freedom, goes off pirating;
observes a murder; ingeniously hunts treasure; smugly attends his own
funeral; levelheadedly finds the way out of a cave; contritely does favors for

---

Unless plot grows out
of character, it seems
contrived.

Muff Potter; and courageously gives evidence in court. Tom is memorable for his variety of character traits, each demonstrated in episodes of action throughout a long and absorbing story.

Not all characters. are as memorable as Tom Sawyer or Jo March, but there are others. The Ugly Duckling and Peter Rabbit have been tested and have endured. Perhaps Wilbur will live as long as Tom and Jo. However, other characters are so real to us that we feel we would recognize them on the street—characters like Laura of the Little House books. Our pleasure in our earliest introduction to the characters is renewed each time an event is recalled from the plots involving them. Because we have known these characters, we have not only experienced vicariously their exciting adventures, but have come to understand something about ourselves and others. Furthermore, one generation is pleased to find that the next enjoys the same stories, but is sometimes disappointed to learn that a favorite does not speak now with the significance it once did. In a sense, the characters of true classics are a social cement, joining one generation to another by common exploration of humans, plus great pleasure, of course

Real characters from classics join one generation to another.

Summary

In life and in books, children can sense differences in humans and are capable of recognizing and responding to well-developed characters. Even in the simplest stories it is possible to find characters that verify truths about human nature. We meet these characters in action that seems part of their natures, and know them—whether they be personified objects, real or personified animals, or humans—by their appearance, words, actions, and thoughts, and the opinions of others about them. Round characters have many traits, while flat characters have limited development. Two kinds of characters that serve as background figures or contrasts are stereotypes and foils. Central characters in the action are round, so that by believing in their reality we are led to discover something about humanity, and we are thereby convinced that the conflict in the story, like conflict in life, is significant. The round characters may or may not change, but if they do, we expect such change to be convincing.

Great pleasure comes in reading about people like ourselves or people we know, beings both wise and foolish, brave and cowardly, frightened and confident, lonely and secure. It is this pleasure of recognition that leads to understanding. Children, as much as adults—or perhaps even more than adults—need the discovery of themselves as part of humanity. Conversely, they need the pleasure of discovering that humanity exists in themselves. If literature is to help children understand the nature of humans, we need reality in the portrayal of character. Nothing—not style, or conflict, or adventure,

"What I do in writing of my character is try to enter into the mind, heart, and skin of a human being who is not myself."

Eudora Welty

or suspense, or vivid setting, or even laughter or tears—nothing can substitute for solid character development in creating pleasurable and lasting literature for children as well as adults.

Notes

1. Henry James, *The Art of Fiction and Other Essays* (New York: Oxford University Press, 1948), p. 13.
2. As we will note in the chapter on theme, the strengths of *Little Women* lie in theme as well as character.

Recommended Books Cited in This Chapter

ACKERMAN, KAREN. *Song and Dance Man.* Illustrated by Stephen Gammell. New York: Knopf, 1988.

ALCOTT, LOUISA MAY. *Little Women.* 1868–1869. Reprint. New York: Dutton, 1948.

ANDERSEN, HANS CHRISTIAN. *The Steadfast Tin Soldier.* New York: Atheneum, 1971.

———. *The Ugly Duckling.* New York: Macmillan, 1967.

BOND, RUSKIN. *Binya's Blue Umbrella.* Honesdale, PA: Boyd's Mills Press, 1995.

BURNFORD, SHEILA. *The Incredible Journey.* Boston: Little, Brown, 1961.

CURTIS, CHRISTOPHER PAUL. *Bud, Not Buddy.* New York: Delacorte, 1999.

———. *The Watsons Go to Birmingham.* New York: Delacorte, 1995.

DEPAOLA, TOMIE. *Jamie O'Rourke and the Big Potato.* New York: Putnam, 1992.

FARMER, NANCY. *A Girl Named Disaster.* New York: Orchard Books, 1996.

———. *The Ear, the Eye and the Arm.* New York: Orchard Books, 1994.

FOX, MEM. *Wilfrid Gordon McDonald Partridge.* Illustrated by Julie Vivas. New York: Kane/Miller, 1990.

GOBLE, PAUL. *Iktomi and the Ducks.* New York: Orchard Books, 1990.

HORVATH, POLLY. *Everything on a Waffle.* New York: Farrar, Straus & Giroux, 2001.

JOHNSON, SCOTT. *Safe at Second.* New York: Putnam, 1999.

KIMMEL, ERIC. *Baba Yaga.* Illustrated by Megan Lloyd. New York: Holiday House, 1991.

KOSS, AMY GOLDEN. *The Ashwater Experiment.* New York: Dial, 1999.

L'ENGLE, MADELEINE. *A Wrinkle in Time.* New York: Farrar, Straus & Giroux, 1962.

MAZER, NORMA FOX. *Babyface.* New York: William Morrow, 1990.

MORRIS, WINIFRED. *The Magic Leaf.* New York: Atheneum, 1987.

O'CONNER, BARBARA. *Me and Rupert Goody.* New York: Farrar, Straus & Giroux, 1999.

PAULSON, GARY. *Hatchet.* New York: Bradbury, 1987.

———. *The River.* New York: Delacorte, 1991.

RINALDI, ANN. *Wolf by the Ears.* New York: Scholastic Hardcover, 1991.

SLEATOR, WILLIAM. *The House of Stairs.* New York: Dutton, 1974.

———. *Interstellar Pig.* New York: Dutton, 1984.

SNYDER, DIANNE. *The Boy of the Three-Year Nap.* Boston: Houghton Mifflin, 1988.

SPEARE, ELIZABETH. *The Sign of the Beaver.* Boston: Houghton Mifflin, 1983.

TOLAN, STEPHANIE S. *Surviving the Applewhites.* New York: Harper Collins, 2002.

TURNER, MEGAN WHALEN. *The Thief.* New York: Greenwillow, 1996.

TWAIN, MARK. *The Adventures of Tom Sawyer.* 1876. Reprint. New York: Macmillan, 1966.

WAUGH, SYLVIA. *Space Race.* New York: Random House, 2000.

WHALEN, GLORIA. *Homeless Bird.* New York: Harper Collins, 2000.

WHITE, E. B. *Charlotte's Web.* Illustrated by Garth Williams. New York: Harper & Row, 1952.

WILDER, LAURA INGALLS. *The Little House Books.* 1932–1943. Reprint. New York: Harper & Row, 1953.

YEP, LAURENCE. *Child of the Owl.* New York: Harper & Row, 1977.

Salsa Stories
Lulu Delacre

Plot

Without some plot in a story, what may happen to the reader?

While some adult readers may be more interested in character than in any other element in the story, most of us—and most children—cannot get involved with stories that are only character studies. We want things to move and things to happen; we call this order **plot.** Plot is the sequence of events showing characters in action. This sequence is not accidental but is chosen by the author as the best way of telling his or her story. If the writer has chosen well, the plot will produce conflict, tension, and action that will arouse and hold our interest.

The child wants what most adults want in literature: action, happenings, questions that need answers, answers that fit questions, glimpses of happy and unhappy outcomes, discovery of how events grow and turn. The very young child finds pleasure in recognizing daily routine within the pages of a book, but many people think that *all* a child needs in a narrative is the recognition in printed words of an everyday happening they call action—an action as prosaic as going to bed at night or waking up in the morning. It is surprising that adults who would never find pleasure in a literal, hour-by-hour account of their own daily routines expect such accounts of children's daily lives to satisfy them. No matter how content the young are with daily order, children very soon expect that they should find life more exciting in a story than in their own experience. Here, in a book, children and adults alike can lose themselves in possibility as they pose the big question of all literature: What if? This element of possibility, of possible action and reaction that confronts character, builds the plot.

> Plot is the sequence of events showing characters in conflict.

Types of Narrative Order

One of the writer's privileges is to reorder existence, to rearrange events, or, in other words, to create plot. The writer may focus on one moment of a day and ignore all others, or he or she may charge one hour with significance and portent that influences months or years of a life. The writer may either ignore the segments of time that have little significance or simply summarize those moments. The writer makes alterations and deletions that our memories are unable to make for us in our own lives. The writer's selectivity and purposeful reordering and highlighting create plot.

Children learn about narrative order very early in their lives, as C. W. Sullivan III reminds us.[1] Earliest play with babies in "This Little Piggy" and "Patty Cake" follows simple narrative form; nursery rhymes use narrative a bit more complex in "Mary Had a Little Lamb" and "Jack and Jill." Soon children hear "Little Red Riding Hood" and "The Three Little Pigs." As they listen to and tell for themselves ghost stories, folk jokes, and jump rope rhymes, they learn about situation and sequence and come to expect the "beginning, middle, and end" of Aristotle's "Poetics." **Narrative order** in fiction, the order in which events are related, may follow several patterns, but the most common pattern in young children's literature is the chronological arrangement.

Chronological Order

As we all know, our lives are one twenty-four-hour period followed by another. This time order is simple chronology. If a story relates events in the order of their happening, the story is in **chronological order,** perhaps moving with the characters from one place of action to another and yet chronological. The writer may make the story line more complex by showing action that occurs with one character in one place, then turning to action that occurs to another simultaneously, but in another place: "Meanwhile, back at the ranch . . . " The accounts of simultaneous action follow one another in the story, but the events have occupied the same point in time; therefore, the action is still chronological.

Variations in Narrative Order

Angela Johnson employs an unusual narrative order in her gripping novel, *The First Part Last.* Bobby, a sixteen-year-old African American, learns that his girlfriend is pregnant and struggles to do the right thing—to be a father. The novel opens with Bobby's memory. In alternating chapters, noted as "then" and "now," the reader follows Bobby's loving relationship with Nia in the "then" sections, and the results of their sexual intimacy in the "now" chapters. Past time explores the ordinary lives of the teenagers, their mischief, hanging out, dances, close friendships, as well as the couple's discovery of pregnancy, and the tearfully angry disappointment of both sets of parents.

Told to take responsibility for their actions, the couple explores with a social worker the idea of adoption. In the "now" sections, the new father tells of his exhaustion, his disappointments, loss of time with friends, a mediocre school record, and his frequent despair. Bobby's new life as a teenage father is filled with effects of guilt and baby or babysitter problems, but beneath it all is his loving commitment to the tiny baby he calls Feather.

> NOW
>   MY MOM SAYS that I didn't sleep through the night until I was eight years old. It didn't make any difference to her 'cause she was up too, listening to the city. She says she used to come into my room, sit cross-legged on the floor by my bed, and play with my Game Boy in the dark.
>   We never talked.
>   I guess I thought she needed to be there. And she must have thought her being there made everything all better for me.
>   Yeah.
>   I get it now. I really get it.
>   We didn't need to say it. . . .

In one section called THEN, Bobby describes fondly his "before fatherhood" life.

> SO HERE'S A GOOD DAY.
>   We'll call it a fairy tale day.
>   Once upon a timer, really right now, there was this hero (I always wanted to be one) who lived in the city. He was born in the city, loved the city, and never wanted to be anywhere else but the city. . . .
>   He loved the feel of it. The way you got juiced when you walked down the sidewalk an' everybody was out.
>   He loved the smell of it. Pizza on one corner, falafel and French pastries on the next. . . .
>   He loved the sounds that woke him in the morning and put him to sleep at night. . . .

Despite the changes in his life, Bobby is determined to "be there" for Feather, but his life will be different. The ending leaves questions: Will Bobby get to college, his parents' dream? Will he remain a committed father?

Pictures of Hollis Wood by Patricia Reilly Giff uses a similar narrative form, moving from the past to the present in alternating chapters. Hollis, a foster child who thinks of herself only as "trouble," has lived in several foster homes, feeling sure each one is the wrong place for her. In some she resents rigidity or condescension, and in others feels unwanted, not part of a "real family." When the Old Man Regan, his wife, Izzy, and their son Steven take her in for the summer, everyone is happy with the arrangement—until Holly is lost on a dangerous hike in the mountains. Steven, underage, takes his father's truck, finds her, and is hurt in an accident. Holly, who has done a bad thing, feels she must leave this home, too. Her next placement is with a forgetful old woman named Josie, an artist who encourages Holly's artistic talent and whom Holly cares for lovingly. Chapters are alternating memories of her love for the Regan family, where she felt like a daughter, and her life with Josie.

In the form of a diary, Karen Hesse in *Stowaway* provides a fictional daily journal of Captain Cook's voyage around the world, describing not only crises of the voyage, but also friendships and animosities on shipboard. The journal form may seem less immediate, but it shows effects of events on the young journalist. The *Endeavor* sailed for three years, between 1768 and 1801, and endured being becalmed for days and weeks at a time and losing most of the seamen to unknown fevers. Nicolas begins by scrubbing decks, scraping the hull, standing watch, and imitating bird calls. He concludes his voyage as an essential seaman who helps collect specimens, nurses the sick, discovers unknown insects and animals, and meets cannibals while fighting the force of a hostile sea.

The View from Saturday, by E. L. Konigsburg, shows a foursome of sixth graders chosen by their paraplegic teacher, Mrs. Olinski, to represent the school in the Academic Bowl contest. In brief italicized sections Mrs. Olinski ponders the reasons for having chosen the successful foursome—Ethan, Nadia, Julian, and Noah. Each one has a story to tell about him or herself. Each one feels in some way different from everyone else. Nadia Diamondstein, for example, feels different because she splits the year between her mother, her father, and even her grandfather. One Saturday Julian recruits the others for a mystery meeting. They name themselves "The Souls," and meet to drill and practice for the Academic Bowl. Through their growing closeness, each one develops strong feelings of kindness, service, and kinship.

Flashbacks

A flashback may juggle time to show how things began.

In fiction for mature readers, narrative order may involve a **flashback.** Many readers can recall their first experience with a flashback: it was puzzling. "What happened? How come?" The writer disrupts normal time sequence to recount some episode out of the character's past, showing how that event influences the character's response to an event in the present. Or the writer shows in flashback a past event that has brought on the present one. In either case, the writer chooses to juggle time to make a point about the character and the character's story. The young child, however, may find it difficult to follow such movement back and forth in time.[2]

As children mature, they understand time in its infinite variations.

The child relies on his or her own experience of time to understand when and how events occur. Since the child knows from experience, for instance, that one falls asleep and dreams, he or she understands Maurice Sendak's *Where the Wild Things Are.* The child knows that such a marvelous adventure could happen to Max while he sleeps or daydreams, since the child has had dreams. As the child grows in sophistication, he or she comes to comprehend the possibility in literature of mixing memory, imagination, dream, day-dream, and flashback. Television probably increases children's exposure to flashback and dream techniques, and this experience could help them to recognize them in literature.

Types of Conflict

Plot is a more inclusive concept than narrative order or its synonym, story line, since it involves not only sequence of events, but also **conflict.** In this discussion of books for the young, tension, friction, force, alternatives, excitement, suspense, discovery, and resolution are parts of conflict. Conflict occurs when the protagonist struggles against an **antagonist,** or opposing force. In short, it is conflict that, added to narrative order, makes plot.

A conflict is struggle against opposing forces.

The following subsections discuss four kinds of conflict in literature: person-against-self, person-against-person, person-against-society, and person-against-nature.

Person-Against-Self

Consider, for example, the classic *Tom Sawyer*—not Twain's best, but his most popular work for children—which has a plot of such complexity that we can discover several types of conflict. Mark Twain shows Tom as he faces an internal conflict, a tension within Tom that pulls him toward either of two courses of action. Tom happens to see Injun Joe—a pejorative name that would be unacceptable today—murder the doctor. He makes a pact with Huck not to reveal what he has seen, and signs it with his blood, but Tom cannot forget that the town has condemned innocent Muff Potter while Joe goes free. Tom takes tobacco and matches to Muff in jail. He often speculates about how to free him. Afraid of Joe's revenge, but guilty about keeping Muff's innocence secret, Tom cannot sleep. When he does, he talks in his sleep. Fearful lest he tell what troubles him, Tom ties his mouth shut. Such an internal struggle is between Tom's fear and his conscience, and there is no mistaking its intensity. When Tom's conscience—his keen awareness of his moral responsibility even in the face of danger—wins the battle, he goes to the judge to tell the truth about the murder. Such an internal conflict of feelings within the protagonist is called **person-against-self.**

A particularly good example of internal conflict occurs in the high fantasy *A Wizard of Earthsea* by Ursula K. Le Guin, written for an older reader. In the struggle between good and evil within himself, Ged must first recognize his own flawed nature, represented by the shadow:

> Aloud and clearly, breaking that old silence, Ged spoke the shadow's name, and in the same moment the shadow spoke without lips or tongue, saying the same word: "Ged." And the two voices were one voice.
>
> Ged reached out his hands, dropping his staff, and took hold of his shadow, of the black self that reached out to him. Light and darkness met, and joined, and were one.

Ged neither wins nor loses the battle, but by seeing that the shadow and he are one, he makes himself whole: "a man: who, knowing his whole true self cannot be used or possessed by any power other than himself." He will from now on live his life for its own sake, not for hatred, pain, ruin, or the darkness of evil.

Internal conflict is the core of Katherine Paterson's *Lyddie*, a story set in New England in the mid-nineteenth century. When a bear enters the family's tiny house, Lyddie, determined to save her family, stares him down, and he turns tail and runs. Although Lyddie would like to go on to college, she leaves for Lowell, Massachusetts, to earn money working eighteen-hour days at the cotton mills to pay off a loan made to the family earlier. Ignoring the recruiting union members pushing for shorter work days, and better pay and working conditions, she suffers instead with the long hours and constant airborne lint with its inevitable effect on health. When a young woman she has coached and guided is victimized by the supervisor, Lyddie confronts him—just as she had confronted the bear. She will sign the petition and take charge of her life. "'I'm off . . . ' she said, and knew as she spoke what it was she was off to. To stare down the bear! The bear she had thought all these years was outside herself, but now, truly, knew was in her own narrow spirit. She would stare down all the bears." And she goes off to Ohio to be a student at the only college that admits women. Lyddie's conflict is internal, person-against-self.

Many other examples exist. In *On My Honor* by Marion Dane Bauer, Joel's internal conflict arises from his guilt. He is afraid to tell anyone that he has disobeyed and gone into the polluted and dangerous river, and he is afraid to admit that after he dared Tony to swim to the sandbar, Tony drowned. The guilt is so strong that he wishes he could sleep, run away, or even die. Only when his father understands Joel's anguish is Joel in any way able to deal with his internal conflict.

Hillary in *The Ashwater Experiment*, by Amy Goldman Koss, is struggling with her two views of herself. As the family moves from one school, temporary home, and flea market to another, she has always felt like an outsider, watching and commenting in her journal. Staying a full school year pulls her into involvement with classmates as tutor, student, mathematics contestant, and friend to very different classmates, one a mall shopper, another a gardener. Hillary asks, "Who am I? A Watcher? Or a regular kid with friends and fun."

These days children's stories confront death head-on, as does Sally Warner's *Sort of Forever*, in which Cady's friend Nana is increasingly unavailable to help Cady out of difficulties. Cady's pleasure in everyday events like new school supplies and a new friend is dulled by knowing Nana's cancer is progressing. Trying to laugh and have fun as always helps.

A protagonist may face two possible choices, thus causing an internal conflict.

Internal conflict may mistakenly be called "idea-against-idea," but such a term omits the protagonist who is the one "of two minds." Tensions and conflicts in stories vary; some seem more likely to occur in the lives of children and may, therefore, seem more real, but others may give readers glimpses of important moral issues.

Stories about divorce proliferate. *The Top-Secret Journal of Fiona Claire*

Jardin by Robin Cruise is one. Others about homelessness are becoming equally common. Situations differ somewhat, but the best among them involve the protagonist's internal struggle to come to terms with a life-changing experience. Most seem to be set in contemporary society, but others, like *Found* by June Oldham, are set in the latter twenty-first century where society has undergone great change.

Latin American life is spread before the reader in *Salsa Stories* by Lulu Delacre. The gift of a blank book for a journal prompts Carmen's friends and family to suggest what she should record. One by one she hears stories from Guatemala, Cuba, Puerto Rico, Buenos Aires, Mexico, and Peru. In lively, distinctive and colorful stories, each storyteller reveals something of daily or festival life in the place of origin. The characters are universally recognizable. An added section of the book includes characteristic recipes.

Other problems are the background for *When Zachary Beaver Came to Town* by Kimberly Willis Holt. Toby's mother leaves to seek her fortune as a country singer at the same time Toby's friend Cal loses his brother in the Vietnam War. The arrival of Zachary, the fattest boy in the world, is a distraction to the small town. Lost in their own agonies, the two boys befriend Zachary, and townspeople one by one find ways to help Zachary, who seems to have been abandoned by his manager. Here the issues of obesity, war, and loss of a parent are all treated with sensitivity; difficulties are neither solved easily nor glossed over.

Life is not perfect, and today's stories don't try to pretend that it is. The plot of *Spindrift* by Colby Rodowsky faces the fact of disappointment in marriage, and the need for divorce. When Cassie the narrator sees her much-loved brother-in-law wrapping his arms around a red-head at a beach party, even while sister Cindy is in the hospital with new baby Erin, the world seems to end. Fix-it Cassie struggles with this problem and must face the reality of a new family arrangement with her mother, Cindy, and baby Erin. The story ends with the marriage of two more mature adults, Cassie's grandmother and Will, her longtime friend. Rodowsky does not show an easy change for anyone, but concludes with optimism.

Still another personal problem, muteness, is explored in *Bird Boy* by Elizabeth Starr Hill. The story concerns a boy who lives on a river houseboat who, with the squawks and caws of the birds, can "talk" with them, instructing the cormorants that fish for his father. Entrusted with a cormorant egg to care for, and upset when the hatchling is stolen, Chang rescues it and trains the tiny cormorant, which becomes a healthy addition to his father's fish-catching birds.

Person-Against-Person

Tom Sawyer must face an additional conflict. Muff Potter is freed only because Tom has the courage to testify—in court and in Joe's presence—that Joe is the murderer. From the moment of his testimony, Tom's life is in danger. Joe disappears and then, disguised as a deaf-and-dumb Spaniard, he comes back to prey on the town and to steal the buried treasure. Once again Joe is a very real threat to Tom's life. As the boys hide breathlessly in the haunted house, they know that Joe will turn on them viciously if he finds them there. Later, lost in the cave with Becky, Tom catches a glimpse of Joe and knows that his murderous enemy is close by, hiding from the law. This is a **person-against-person** conflict.

The terms used to describe the conflict are not so important. What does matter is that we see clearly the protagonist and the antagonist. The strain between the two forces is what holds our continuing interest and our intense curiosity about the outcome. Tom's internal conflict, his growing awareness of justice opposing his fear for his life, forces him to take action in a person-versus-person conflict that causes him to face the vengeance of a villainous man. Children's literature is filled with suspenseful examples of person-against-person conflict. In *Peter Rabbit,* Peter evades Mr. McGregor; in *The Hundred Penny Box* by Sharon Bell Mathis, Michael and his mother are in conflict about letting his grandmother keep her precious box; and in Madeleine L'Engle's *A Wrinkle in Time,* Meg defeats IT, the disembodied brain.

In folktales, where protagonists are stereotypes or stock characters, person-against-person conflict is very common. Jack climbs the beanstalk and defeats the giant. Hansel and Gretel shove the wicked witch into the oven and all is well. Both Red Riding Hood and the Three Little Pigs face a wolf. In some folktales, the person-against-person conflict moves quickly and vigorously to conclusion. In others, conflict travels with gentle humor to an equally satisfactory resolution, as it does in "The Squire's Bride" or "The Old Woman and Her Pig." Virginia Hamilton's stories *The Time Ago Tales of Jahdu* and *Time Ago Lost: More Tales of Jahdu,* with their traditional motifs of African and African American folklore, show Jahdu running, in conflict with Trouble, as he helps Trouble's victims and shows the creatures how to manage against adversity and puzzlement.

Television cartoons, too, are filled with examples; Coyote frantically battles to overcome Roadrunner, while Tom the cat is in constant conflict with Jerry the mouse.

Person-Against-Society

Conflict and an unknown outcome keep us reading *Charlotte's Web*. Wilbur's struggle is serious: life and death. Although we may define the struggle as a **person-against-society** conflict, the child knows it simply as "Will Wilbur live? Will Charlotte save him from being made into bacon?" In this case we may regard society as the farming business, which, after all, is based on profit. A runt pig is not worth keeping. Although the child reading *Charlotte's Web* gets involved in the conflict of Wilbur-versus-dinner-table, the conflict is actually Wilbur against good business. The conflict begins immediately, page 1, line one: "Where's Papa going with the ax?" Whether Wilbur will be saved from death commands our interest. This conflict of Wilbur against the business of farming keeps our interest from start to finish.

Person-versus-person conflict is common in folktales.

Person-versus-society may be hard for a child to identify or explain.

Person-against-society conflict is much more easily understood by adults than by children. When we read, for example, of Hester Prynne's conflict with the Puritan society in *The Scarlet Letter*, we see society's instrument of degradation—the stocks. We know the society by bits of dialogue as the crowd shouts its taunts at Hester's back, or plots to take Pearl from Hester. To children, however, society as antagonist is clearer if a person is representative of society.

Southern society of the 1960s is the antagonist in *The Watsons Go to Birmingham* by Christopher Curtis. Chicagoans Kenny and Byron find that to them as Northerners, Birmingham seems like another world. They are surprised at segregated facilities, violence against Blacks ignored by authorities, vicious comments overheard, and lawless actions barely concealed. At the burning of the Black church, they see clearly the nature of the powerful antagonist—Southern society.

The historical novel by the master storyteller Avi, *Crispin: The Cross of Lead,* is set in the fourteenth century. Falsely accused of theft and murder, Crispin, a fatherless peasant boy whose only possession is a leaden cross, must flee. His encounter with Bear the juggler, who takes Crispin on as an apprentice, is his salvation. The soldiers of the widowed queen are determined to eliminate anyone opposed to her reign, but Bear's mission is to rid his country of exploitative evil and promote freedom for the kingdom. The inscription on the leaden cross identifies Crispin as the rightful heir to the throne. Suspense runs high throughout the novel as Bear and Crispin evade the queen's soldiers. Spies, swords, daggers, torture, ambush, flight, captivity, a dungeon, and ultimate escape hold attention.

The 1960s saw a rise in what were then called "problem novels"; often the plots focused more on social problems than on their effects on individuals. Such problems have not gone away, but today other varieties of social problems have come to our attention. Although there is nothing new about bullying behavior, recent acts of violence among young people are often traced to feelings of being an "outsider." A certain amount of feeling that one is different from others is part of the growth of self-awareness, as the continuing popularity of J. D. Salinger's book *Catcher in the Rye* attests. Recent acts of violent retaliation against those who seem to control the social group suggest that feelings of ostracism lead to violence.

Such a topic has rarely been addressed in literature for children. Vicki Grove in *Reaching Dustin* maintains high suspense as she creates credibly complex characters. Dustin Groat lives in a family compound in the swamps, where he is isolated, abused, and hungry; at school he is also the object of derision and ostracism. His very difference seems to be a threat. To fulfill an interview assignment, Carly must talk with Dustin. As she tries to reach him, she recognizes the sources of his behavior, but also sees in him tenderness and kindness. When gunshots erupt from Dustin's walled vigilante community, Carly sees how her taunts have played a part in his behavior, and recognizes that the rest of the community has made outsiders of the swamp dwellers. An additional issue Grove touches on is the matter of how home-schooling can be abused in a secretive community that keeps a child outside of ordinary society. The absorbing novel is somewhat similar to S. E. Hinton's earlier story, *The Outsiders;* it, too, faces the complex role that schools play in the creation of outsiders, carrying that theme further to show a whole social group of outsiders.

Person-Against-Nature

In *The Talking Earth*, by Jean George, young Billie Wind, a Seminole alone in the Everglades, wants to learn the Native American lore of reliance upon nature, and is trapped in a cave by a raging fire. George describes a cave at the bottom of a sinkhole, Billie's refuge as the fire roars and crackles:

> After a long while she looked up. The island was a firebox. Green limbs came to a boil and exploded like bullets. Flames ran up and around the trees like slithering serpents: millions and millions of them. A burning limb fell into the pit, struck the water, hissed like a snake and went out.

Lizards fall from trees; turtles and snakes creep into the pool of cool water. Billie Wind realizes that she will be confined to her cave for a long time—until rain has cooled the earth sufficiently for her to walk on it.

Master of suspense Gary Paulsen has written several books with a conflict of person-against-nature, *Hatchet* and its sequel, *The River,* among them. Brian Robeson, whose plane goes down in the northern wilderness while he is on his way to see his father, struggles and survives for fifty-four days because he has one tool—a small hatchet. Breathlessly we follow his defeat of the natural forces that seem insurmountable. In *The River,* the government wants Brian to repeat the survival process so that a watchful representative can follow and record his experiences and thus be able to train others. Thinking it could be helpful, Brian reluctantly agrees. Once in the wilds, however, Brian sees that this trip will not be a true test because he is provided with life-sustaining supplies. Without a real struggle nothing will be proven and his senses will be dulled to what must be done in crisis after crisis. He sends back the entire load of equipment, and he and Derek have only a radio. When lightning strikes Derek, leaving him unconscious, the radio is useless. With nothing but his own wits, this experience is totally different: he has nothing, and is not only responsible for his own survival but also for the unconscious Derek. Without tools, Brian must build a raft, move Derek and tie him to it. Then he must maneuver the unwieldy raft down the winding river, survive the rapids, and, when thrown into the turbulent water, swim until he finds the rapids-tossed raft with its inert body. Can Brian's strength last? Seeing him tempted, in an internal conflict, to lose Derek's body in the wild river so that he can move more easily, we wonder if he has the courage to continue in his rescue. Person-against-nature is not the only tension holding us to the final page.

Another story with a combination of conflicts is Avi's *The True Confessions of Charlotte Doyle.* In a keenly suspenseful historical novel, Charlotte tells of

A variety of conflicts may exist in a single story.

her 1832 Atlantic crossing as the only passenger on a trading ship commanded by a cruel captain, who on the surface seems to be as kind and genteel as her own father, the shipowner. Charlotte, a well-brought-up thirteen-year-old, knows she must obey, and yet cannot do as she is told when it means accepting the captain's vicious and vengeful behavior. Her conflict between accepting her father's instructions to place herself in the captain's care and her rejection of his immorality provokes internal struggle. But to free herself from his power, she must defy the captain himself; in a person-against-person conflict she aligns herself with the rebellious crew and works as hard as any sailor, dressing as a boy and climbing 130 feet of mast to the main royal yard. The story arouses breathless attention to what happens: Whom can Charlotte trust? What were the murderer's motives? Who is the murderer? Does the crew think Charlotte is guilty? How can she prove her innocence?

Conflict of any kind grows out of character. Peter Rabbit's character—his mischievous nature, combining curiosity with greed—brings him to Mr. McGregor's garden and keeps him eating long enough to be discovered. In some stories with minimally developed characters, conflict carries all of the reader's interest; some are mysteries like the Nancy Drew series while others depict everyday events like the Babysitters Club. Plots for the Goosebumps are often so predictable or coincidental that children are finally bored. However, the traditional stories from folk origins do not depict fully developed protagonists, and do not lack conflict; rather, they rely on universal human traits and dreams expressed in their themes. These themes seem to take the place of character as the origin of conflict.

> Conflict grows out of character.

Intent upon conflict, poor television often neglects to create a fully drawn protagonist; as a result children do not learn to see the relationship between conflict and character. Plot incidents seem merely to happen *to* protagonists, rather than to be brought about by the protagonist's personal traits; the result is a dramatic story that makes little contribution to the viewer's understanding of humans.

Patterns of Action

Plot is more than the sequence of actions or conflict. It is also the pattern of those actions. If we oversimplify plot patterns by diagrams, we might describe three of them as a line slanting upward, a straight horizontal line, and an upward slanting line followed by a peak and a downward slide.

1   2   3

In pattern 1, the story
ends at the peak of
action.

The first of these patterns moves from one incident to another related incident, building on discoveries and changes toward a final climax that brings the action to its peak—and ends there! Such a pattern is clearly demonstrated in Mary Norton's *The Borrowers*, a story with a **frame,** since it begins and ends with Mrs. May relating the events to Kate. Within the frame enclosing the developing plot occur the events that involve the Clock family. The Borrowers change from people with simple needs to a family ruled by their possessions. Homily's materialistic grab for more and more leads to discovery, to the rat-catchers, the fumigators, and the high suspense surrounding the family's escape. In the final chapter, when the focus returns to Mrs. May and Kate, we know only that the Borrowers might have established a new home by the hawthorn hedge, or perhaps that the family might have been a figment of a young boy's imagination. The plot line of development has moved steadily up to leave us in uncertainty, an open ending.

In pattern 2, suspense
is minimal.

The second of these patterns of action, a straight horizontal line, is demonstrated by Sharon Creech's story *Walk Two Moons*. Tension does not mount to a breaking point, but keeps us interested in the friendship between Phoebe and Salamanca—misnamed for the Seneca tribe of her ancestry. Despite minimal suspense, there is a conflict consisting of concern, curiosity, and pleasure in knowing narrator Sal and in watching her unravel the story of the disappearance of her own mother, as well as the disappearance of Phoebe. In *Little House in the Big Woods*, Laura Ingalls Wilder shows Laura's life as eventful and filled with pleasure; the security of Laura's home keeps the reader interested in day-to-day happenings, but without building anxiety.

In pattern 3, climax
is the high point,
followed by
resolution.

Exposition tells what
happened before the
story opens.

The third pattern of action is more complex. The story rises to a peak or climax and then clearly concludes. **Rising action** begins with a situation that must be shown and explained. What has happened before the story opens, what has created the current situation? This explanation of the situation and the characters' condition is called **exposition.** In most stories for children, it is woven into early action so that attention is caught immediately and held. When, for example, on page 8 of Mildred Taylor's *Roll of Thunder, Hear My Cry,* Little Man is nearly run down by the school bus loaded with White children, we are aware of the situation, of the feelings between Blacks and Whites.

Returning to the historical novel *The True Confessions of Charlotte Doyle,* exposition is essential; even in the earliest action, writer Avi fills the reader in. The first page begins:

> Just before dusk on the late afternoon of June 16, 1832, I found myself walking along the crowded docks of Liverpool, England, following a man by the name of Grummage. Though a business associate of my father, Mr. Grummage was, like my father, a gentleman. It was he my father had delegated to make the final arrangements for my passage to America. He was also to meet me when I came down from school on the coach, then see me safely stowed aboard the ship that my father had previously selected.

Writers of series books may make each one independent of the other except for the characters, or may build on events in preceding novels with the same characters. Phyllis Reynolds Naylor, in her five books about Lynn, Mouse, and Mrs. Toggle the witch, chooses to connect them by tying the events of a previous story to those of the new one. *Witch's Sister, Witch Water, The Witch Herself,* and *The Witch's Eye* are followed by *Witch Weed.* As the story opens, through Lynn's responses to the questions of the psychologist, Naylor gives exposition or background that will make the new story understandable. The school psychologist is seeing Lynn about her "fantastic, imaginary" stories about Mrs. Toggle; the nine crows that followed Lynn; Mrs. Toggle's eye with mysterious powers; the control she had over Lynn's mother, sister, and little brother; and how Mouse saved Lynn by throwing the glass eye into Cowden's Creek. When in *Weed's* first few chapters we read of the flock of crows and of the strange smell that makes them feel "woozy," we have enough information to move into the story, and can see that we are back in the realm of Mrs. Toggle's influence.

Kate DiCamillo's *Because of Winn-Dixie,* a story of a girl and a dog, is understandable when the reader knows Opal Buloni's background. The exposition comes quickly in the second and third chapters.

> That summer I found Winn-Dixie was also the summer me and the preacher moved to Naomi, Florida, so he could be the new preacher at the Open Arms Baptist Church of Naomi. My daddy is a good preacher and a nice man, but sometimes it's hard for me to think about him as my daddy, because he spends so much time preaching or thinking about preaching or getting ready to preach.

While Opal is grooming Winn-Dixie, her stray-dog friend, she tells him about herself, making their similarity a bond between them.

> I told him how we were alike. "See," I said, "you don't have any family and neither do I. . . . But I don't have a mama. I mean I have one, but I don't know where she is. She left when I was three years old. I can't hardly remember her."

Since children's stories are usually short and must move quickly, **complications** begin very soon. The elements of a story that deal with rising action are suspense, the cliff-hanger, foreshadowing, sensationalism, the climax, denouement, and inevitability. Each of these terms will be treated separately in the following subsections.

Suspense

From the first line in the first chapter of *Charlotte's Web*—"Where's Papa going with the ax?"—we know that Wilbur's fate is uncertain, and from that initial moment White holds us in **suspense,** a state that makes us read on. By tears, sobs, cries, and yells, Fern wins temporary reprieve for Wilbur, who becomes Fern's baby. Wilbur's brothers and sisters are all sold, and it is Wilbur's turn. But see if Uncle Homer Zuckerman will buy Wilbur so Fern can visit him at the nearby farm. Wilbur is lonely, finding his life boring without Fern as constant companion. When he finds a friend, loneliness vanishes.

Suspense is the emotional pull that keeps us reading.

Then, electrifying news comes: An old sheep spitefully tells Wilbur he is being fattened for Christmas slaughter. Charlotte to the rescue. She weaves the words "Some Pig" into her web; people come from miles around to see Wilbur. Mr. Zuckerman now admires him, and no celebrity has ever been made into sausage.

As the excitement wears off, our worries revive. Charlotte, however, sends Templeton to the dump for more words. When each of the woven words miraculously appears, we have new hope. Then Wilbur's protector announces regretfully that she cannot accompany Wilbur to the fair. Catastrophe looms again, but a ray of hope glimmers: "We'll leave it this way: I'll come to the Fair if I possibly can." Our security lasts only until we overhear Arable and Zuckerman talking about the fine ham and bacon he'll make. A huge pig called Uncle is stiff competition: "He's going to be a hard pig to beat." Wilbur's doom is sealed. Suddenly, an unprecedented award, but Wilbur faints and "We can't give a prize to a *dead* pig. . . . It's never been done before." No prize. Then Templeton bites Wilbur's tail, and Wilbur revives and wins the prize.

But Charlotte is languishing. Can Wilbur survive without Charlotte? Charlotte spins her final magnum opus and dies, and Wilbur, now mature, takes responsibility for Charlotte's egg sac. When spring comes, Wilbur is still alive and hearty, and life continues.

Suspense, the emotional pull that keeps us wanting to read on, involves us in conflict up to the climax in the final pages. These moments of suspense, however, are not panic points in the story, nor at any time do we know the outcome with certainty. White controls the suspense to keep it peaking and leveling. At every point we remain not only curious but concerned for the outcome, because either success or failure looms, and we cannot be completely certain which will prevail.[3]

Suspense has kept us reading, but White has carefully led us with optimism, never despair. The author skillfully builds the story so that nowhere is the ending too predictable, lest we lose interest, or too frightful, lest we give up. At the end of the book, the reader feels that the ups and downs of "perhaps he'll win, perhaps he'll lose" are finally settled. Suspense does not go beyond the story's ending. White, as he pulls us to the satisfactory end of the story, makes us heave a final, relieved sigh. The feeling that all will be well, even after the final page, results from White's skill in handling suspense. Our optimism has been justified.

Suspense is held throughout *A Single Shard* by Linda Sue Park, a Korean story of Tree-ear, orphan helper to the skilled potter Min. Tree-ear, who admires Min's skills, waits patiently and works long days, hoping that the master potter will teach him to throw pots. Tradition and law, however, demand that an apprentice be the potter's son. Nonetheless, devoted Tree-ear carries and cuts wood for the kiln, and digs and prepares special clays for innovative inlaid vases. When the king's emissary admires Min's beautiful work, Tree-ear offers to walk for weeks through the mountains, carrying the best of Min's vases to the king for his approval. When he is threatened by two

Interest flags if the ending is too apparent.

Suspense holds readers in both realism and fantasy.

robbers, in a nearly fatal fight, Tree-ear struggles at the canyon edge to save the vases, but the robbers throw them into the abyss. Tree-ear searches frantically but finds only a single shard to carry to the capital. That single colorful shard, inlaid with chrysanthemums, is so stunning, that at the story's **climax** Min is awarded the commission. During Tree-ear's eighteen months with Min, he has been learning only to mold the clay. Now a grateful Min calls him "son" and will teach him to throw pots. These final events provide **resolution** for the story.

An example of the increasing numbers of stories about slavery, Colliers' *Jump Ship to Freedom* is fairly throbbing with suspense. The first line is: "I crept up the cellar stairs in the dark, with the bundle of hay in my arms, going as quiet as I could." The slave Daniel Arabus has a plan to recover payment from his master's wife for his father's service in the Civil War, money that she has taken "for safekeeping," money to buy Daniel and his mother's freedom. Daniel hides the bank notes, is accused of theft, and is shipped off to be sold in the West Indies. Perilous work in the ship's rigging, near death in a hurricane, a desperate swim to land in New York Harbor, hiding again, then flight with a Quaker and more—all just ahead of the ship's captain and his handbills describing the fugitive slave. The central facts of the story are established in the author's note.

The most interesting books for early readers also have suspenseful plots, and their mystery format seems most intriguing. For example, Marjorie Weinman Sharmat's *Nate the Great and the Fishy Prize* tells, in simple vocabulary, how Nate's dog Sludge solves the puzzle of the missing prize. Nate checks out all the possibilities, going from one master and pet to the next, all of them entering the Smartest Pet Contest. The thread line of Nate's biking to the store for ingredients to make pancakes, his stop at each entrant's house, and Sludge's curious sniffs at the grocery bag lead to the missing trophy—a tuna fish can lettered "Smartest" in gold. Of course, Sludge is the winner. The brief story has all the elements of a progressive plot, from exposition to final climax and denouement.

There is no shortage of suspense in Gary Paulsen's *Hatchet* as Brian, the protagonist, avoids a black bear, an attacking moose, and an invasion by a porcupine.

Early readers, too, like the suspense of "What's going to happen?"

> . . . slithering. A brushing sound, a slithering brushing sound near his feet—and he kicked out as hard as he could, kicked out and threw the hatchet at the sound, a noise coming from his throat. But the hatchet missed . . . and his leg was instantly torn with pain, as if a hundred needles had been driven into it.
>
> Now he screamed, with the pain and fear, and skittered on his backside up into the corner of the shelter, breathing through his mouth, straining to see, to hear.
>
> The slithering moved again, he thought toward him at first, and terror took him, stopping his breath. He felt he could see a low dark form, a bulk in the darkness, a shadow that lived, but now it moved away, slithering and scraping it moved away and he saw . . .

The Cliff-hanger

A form of suspense that White does not use is the **cliff-hanger,** the exciting chapter ending that makes it hard to lay the book aside. Unlike the chapters in *Charlotte's Web,* wherein each contributes to the central conflict in the total plot, each moving to its own peak and yet managing to end quietly, the cliff-hanging chapter ends with such suspense that a listening child's plea, "Please, just one more chapter!" is irresistible. The cliff-hanger is most obvious in the old series novels like Nancy Drew and the Hardy Boys, and in today's soap operas, as well as in newspaper, magazine, and Saturday movie serials of the past. Each child left the darkened theater for the afternoon sunlight, worried about the hero, left, perhaps literally, hanging by the fingernails from a sheer cliff. The hero was in mortal danger and might not survive until the following Saturday matinee.

The cliff-hanger is also used by John Bellairs in his time-lapse novel *The Trolley to Yesterday,* a story in which Fergie and Johnny travel by decrepit trolley back to 1453 C.E., when the Turks seized Constantinople. Three of the first five chapters, for example, end in these words:

> "I should have *known.* You're going to ruin everything!"

> "This was not a movie set or a dream or a Viewmaster slide. It was real, and he was there."

> "But Johnny was still worried about the professor."

Suspense is particularly essential in a mystery story; one device often used effectively is the cliff-hanger. Notice how Wendelin Van Draanen closes the chapters of *Sammy Keyes and the Hotel Thief* with hints of what is coming.

> And scribbled across the napkin are the letters HH. And underneath them, the number 423.

> Next thing you know, he's going to decide *I'm* the one who stole Gina's money.

> Trouble is, I didn't have a clue now.

> I know who the hotel thief is.

Cliff-hangers enhance the suspense of *Harry Potter and the Sorcerer's Stone,* the first book of J. K. Rowling's enormously successful series. One chapter concludes with gigantic Hagrid knocking on the castle door, suggesting ominous possibilities. A second ends with a question about who knows what: Hagrid and Snape. And a third suggests disaster because the cloak that makes Harry invisible has been left behind. Another moment of high suspense leaves us hanging: Why is Hagrid looking so furious?

Foreshadowing

The writer for children must decide how much suspense the child can sustain and how much reassurance is necessary to balance suspense. To relieve the reader's anxiety and to produce a satisfying sense of the inevitable, the writer must drop clues about the outcome—without destroying suspense. These clues are called **foreshadowing.** Such clues must be planted artfully and unobtrusively within the action. Not all readers will be alert to all dropped hints, it is true, but White in *Charlotte's Web* uses them to hint at Wilbur's ultimate safety and Charlotte's death, and to reassure us that finally all will be well.

In Wilbur's first conversation with Charlotte, he learns that gentle Charlotte lives by eating living things; friendship looks questionable. Seeing a need to reassure, White adds that "she had a kind heart, and she was to prove loyal and true to the very end." The first clue suggests friendship; the second, "to the very end," has a prophetic ring.

Foreshadowing and suspense balance throughout the narrative. When in the chapter "Bad News" Wilbur hears he is being fattened for slaughter, he wails. However, his safety is foreshadowed when Charlotte says calmly, "I am going to save you."

Another event for which we must be prepared is Charlotte's death. If her death had been unforeseen, we might accuse White of playing with our emotions. But Charlotte's acceptance of her life span foreshadows her approaching death and prepares Wilbur and the readers. The song of the crickets foreshadows death of all kinds. "Summer is over and gone. . . . Over and gone. . . . Summer is dying, dying," they sing. Charlotte, whose life, like the crickets and the seasons, has a predictable cycle, "heard it and knew that she hadn't much time left." Of the word "humble," she says, "It is the last word I shall ever write." When she says that she is "languishing," she is peaceful and contented, and we are as resigned as she. *Charlotte's Web* concludes with a sense of inevitability, and, because of the 514 baby spiders, with optimism.

Clear examples of foreshadowing occur throughout good children's stories. For example, in William Armstrong's *Sounder*, an African American father has been sent to prison for stealing food for his family. When at long last a figure appears in the red dust of the road, Sounder the coonhound revives. Once near death from the sheriff's gunshots, now, before the approaching figure is identifiable, Sounder pants, whines, wags his tail, and paces the dooryard. His agitation foreshadows the father's limping return.

Very early in *Space Race*, Sylvia Waugh prepares the reader for mysterious happenings. Deep in the night, a siren shatters the peace in Belthorp, but Thomas is the only child to sleep through it. Thomas's father tells him to observe carefully and report, saying that it is *very* important, although Thomas doesn't know why. "Some day I'll make it up to you," hints at reasons. Thomas "felt suddenly afraid, as if his father knew something and was not telling." Patrick tucks Thomas in, thinking, "It will all come back to him." Thomas is warned, and so are we.

Even in a suspenseful story with a well-developed protagonist, however, plotting problems can occur. In *Jasmin*, for example, adequate foreshadowing of events is lacking, like a violent storm as well as the arrival of the social workers to take Leroy, who is mentally disabled, away to a special home and school. Without foreshadowing, the outcome seems coincidental.

Sensationalism

If the reader is to feel satisfaction as the story unfolds, the author must drop reassuring hints about what is ahead. In the strong life-and-death conflict of *Charlotte's Web,* unrelieved suspense might be too much for the young child. The skill of the writer lies in balancing two elements—suspense over the action and hints at the outcome.

Unrelieved suspense, however, makes a story *sensational;* it plays us like instruments, keeping us holding our breaths in crescendos of anxiety. The writer for adults has greater latitude in the creation of anxiety, since adults can tolerate it; with persistent enthusiasm, some adults read **sensationalism:** mystery stories, murder thrillers, spy stories, and survival adventures. The suspense absorbs them; they breathe horror and terror with the protagonist. However, they are never deceived, since they never forget that it's just a story. Other adults are bored with the unrelieved suspense because they, too, know that it's just a story, and wanting more than sensationalism, seek some discovery of real people in suspenseful action. They demand the significance of well-developed character in a conflict that reveals something about humans.

A situation of unrelieved suspense, however, may be more than a child can bear. Take, for example, the folktale "Snow White and the Seven Dwarfs." The storyteller, watching the expressive faces of the listeners, relieves the suspense with reassuring hints about the outcome. In making the movie, however, Walt Disney turned suspense to sensationalism, and many children were upset by it. The ugly witch with clawlike hands and viciously evil features roused sheer terror. Many children hid their faces and suffered nightmares long after they had seen—as the ad described it—"the great children's story come alive on the screen."

Any action may be made sensational, but important and even violent events can be described with accuracy and sensitivity, yet without sensationalism. Sensationalism results when the writer focuses on the thrilling or startling at the expense of character and idea. For example, the Colliers's description of Sam's execution before a firing squad at the end of *My Brother Sam Is Dead* is realistic without being sensational.

The Climax

The peak and turning point of the conflict, the point at which we know the outcome of the action, is called the **climax.** Throughout the development of plot, from initial recognition of the conflict through the critical turns and irregular progress, past reversals and discoveries, up to the point where we know who wins the conflict, we follow the plot to the climax. While we speak of the climax as the turning point in the conflict, children call it "the most exciting part," or "where I knew how the book would end." No matter which term is used, the climax is inextricably related to conflict.

A Day at the Beach and *Willie Goes to the Seashore* lack climax because they lack conflict. Instead of plot being resolved, it merely peters out. Instead of coming to a decisive conclusion, the narrative just quits. The result is disappointment.

Climax of some kind exists in any story with conflict (Hooray! Peter Rabbit made it through the gate!), although the climax may come with varying degrees of intensity or varying closeness to the end of the story. For example, in the three parts of the epic *Beowulf,* there are dramatic confrontations and triumphant battles between Beowulf and Grendel, Beowulf and Grendel's mother, and, finally, between Beowulf and the dragon.

> Intense or quiet, the climax comes when we know the outcome of the conflict.

However, look at the quiet climax of *Charlotte's Web.* Here, in the conflict of person-against-society, Wilbur is in a life-and-death struggle. The climax logically comes when we know that he will live. Checking on suspense, we find that the high point, brought on by frequent minor crises and excitement peaks, finally comes when Wilbur revives and wins the prize—the handsome bronze medal for "attracting so many visitors to our great County Fair." The runt pig has defeated good business, since Wilbur has taken the final round of the contest. By his additional award—the special prize of twenty-five dollars—Zuckerman is rewarded with money and Wilbur is a good business investment after all; this is the climax. From here on Wilbur has nothing to worry about; the conflict is resolved.

In *The Borrowers,* where the conflict pits the family of tiny people against Mrs. Driver the housekeeper, the climax comes within a few exciting pages of the end. Mrs. Driver's discovery of "the little varmints," living amid their borrowed luxuries below the floorboards, brings on the rat-catchers. They board up the gratings and seal the space below the floor. Then they start the gas and the fumigating bellows, hoping to kill the creatures, whatever they are. But the Borrowers, whom we have worried about since Chapter 1, have a friend in the Boy, who sets out to give them ventilation:

> Pick-ax in hand [he] ran out of the door. . . . Already, when he reached it, a thin filament of smoke was eddying out of the grating . . . a flicker of movement against the darkness between the bars . . . behind him the crunch of wheels on the gravel and the sound of horse's hoofs. . . . With two great blows on the brickwork, he dislodged . . . the grating. It fell.

Although we do not see the Borrowers fleeing from the gas, we think they may have escaped. With the airtight grating gone, their path to fresh air and freedom is open.

Sid Fleischman brings his story *Jim Ugly* to a strong climax when Jake's dog, inherited from his father, finds evidence of murder in the place where an accident was assumed to have taken the father's life. Jim Ugly's finding the evidence means that the mystery of an accident now opens a search for murderers.

The Witch of Blackbird Pond poses a conflict for a young woman who emigrates from Barbados to the witch-hunting Puritan society of New England.

Elizabeth Speare shows us how Kit's independence, her compassion, her defiance of rules, even her luxurious wardrobe and her swimming ability, work against her to suggest to the Puritans that she is a witch. Accusation and trial bring us to the climax. The accuser, faced with evidence that Kit has not bewitched his child but has taught her to read, drops charges, and Kit is now free. Throughout the story Kit has been different: she is willful and will not conform. We have seen the frowning and suspicious community and concluded that witchcraft charges will be brought. But it has not all been so pat. Will Prudence be brave enough to prove that Kit was teaching and not bewitching her? Will Nat's ship be in port? Forbidden to enter the town, how can he help? Will he be able to convince the villagers of the truth? When all these questions have been answered, the climax occurs.

The final chapter of *A Wrinkle in Time* is filled with Meg's thoughts, and yet Madeleine L'Engle maintains suspense to the climax. When Meg, the protagonist, finally gathers her courage to return to Camazotz and to confront the monster brain that holds her brother prisoner, we know that the climax approaches. Meg discovers that she has love and IT has not; she adds all the love of those who surround her with all she feels for them, and love and will together defeat evil and bring joy. Only when Meg's battle with IT frees the last hostage are we satisfied about the final outcome. Conflict and suspense have been intense until the last two pages.

When we look back over these examples of climax, we note that each involves the final battle of the protagonist with an antagonist. Each results in victory for the protagonist, and this victory seems right in children's literature. Antiheroes, or badly flawed protagonists, and defeated protagonists are for adults only, or more accurately, for some adults only. The child has been involved in the life of a protagonist and wants the protagonist to win. However, the winning has not happened without a struggle. There is a difference between the climax that says with sticky sweetness, "The world is good, since right always wins," and one that says, "The forces of evil are powerful, but courage and justice together can defeat them." A conflict brought to a climax makes the idea of the story clear through plot that has tension and resolution.

Denouement

Denouement is called either the unknotting of ends, or the tying up of loose ends.

Children who are following an exciting story may have trouble pinning down what for them is the climax. Agreeing on that, however, is not as important to the success of the story as agreeing that the story ends with a sense of completeness, or **resolution.**

The **denouement** begins at the climax, at the point where we feel that the protagonist's fate is known. From here the action of the plot is also called the **falling action.** In the denouement of *Charlotte's Web*, Templeton and Wilbur, the two survivors of the original trio, reach a bargain about who eats first at Wilbur's trough. Wilbur returns the egg sac to the barn, and its presence sustains the feeling that Charlotte is still there. Finally, warmed and protected by Wilbur's breath, the eggs hatch. Joy, Aranea, and Nellie, three of Charlotte's tiny progeny, stay on in the barn to keep Wilbur company, and to learn from him the ways of barn life. The seasonal cycle continues; everything is resolved. There is no question left unanswered. There is a resolution.

The unknotting of the plot is highly satisfactory in Janet Lunn's *The Shadow in Hawthorn Bay*. In the final pages Mary rids herself of the ghost of her cousin Duncan (to whom she has felt tied since birth), fearlessly walks into the alien forest, and claims it as her new land, acknowledging both her love for Luke and her wish to mother his younger brother, Henry. She takes responsibility for making her own decisions.

When the reader is assured that all is well and will continue to be, we say that the denouement is closed, or that the plot has a **closed ending.** In this case, the tying of the loose ends is thoroughly optimistic and satisfactory, a good conclusion for a young child's story. There is no anxiety for reader or listener on the last page of *Charlotte's Web*. The sigh is not a breath of anxiety, but one of regret that so good a story is over.

> Young children seem to prefer the reassurance of closed endings.

With a highly suspenseful plot filled with intricacies and turnabouts. Carl Hiaasen's *Hoot* holds the reader to the denouement. Roy, new in his Florida school, is victimized by Curt, an aggressive troublemaker who rides the bus with him. Meanwhile Curly, construction supervisor for a building project, is infuriated by nightly vandalism. Stakes that define the territory to be cleared are pulled and the holes filled so the bulldozer crew cannot clear the area. Alligators appear in the portable toilets; vicious guard dogs are routed by snakes; and Curly may soon lose his supervisory job. Police are baffled. False names, strangers hiding in odd places, various injuries—there is no let-up in destructive actions. The solution to the mystery finally rests on Roy, the fearless environmentalist whose suspicions of Curt prove correct.

In an **open ending,** an occasional device of fiction, we are left to draw our own conclusions about final plot resolution. Among enduring examples of children's literature, there seem to be few with open endings, although stories do appear from time to time. The realistic stories of the 1970s, particularly those for the older child, occasionally leave the end open. At the end of Alice Childress's *A Hero Ain't Nothin' but a Sandwich,* for example, we are left with an urgent question: Will Benjie show up for the drug counseling session?

> Open endings force readers to think, to consider options.

Just as some adults find the open-ended story unsatisfactory, many more children are left dissatisfied and frustrated by unsolved mystery. Depending on the gravity of the conflict and the maturity of the readers, they may even be left frightened. Without the experience and perspective needed to supply their own endings, some children may turn away from the story with a disturbing sense of anxiety. If tension has been high and the possible outcome serious, the unresolved plot and the open ending seem far less suitable for a children's story.

Inevitability

Through White's use of the device called foreshadowing, we are well prepared for Wilbur's salvation and Charlotte's death. Her life is complete, and her mission is accomplished. She has saved her dearest friend and produced her egg sac to carry on another spider generation. There is no other way for the story to end. Although there may be a shadow of sadness, there is a more profound sense of the quality called **inevitability,** or "it had to be." "It was inevitable" is high praise for a writer's skill in bringing plot to conclusion.

Properly motivated action that grows out of character provides inevitability, just as Peter Rabbit's curiosity and greed bring about his inevitable squeezing into Mr. McGregor's garden, his flight, and his stomachache. At the other end of the literary spectrum, Beowulf, "mightiest yet mildest of men," is the organizer and leader of the band that sails to Hrothgar's country to liberate it from Grendel's scourge. Since Beowulf is pure valor, unsullied by any past defeat or any selfish motive, and since his motive is love for his fellow beings, he cannot lose his battle with personified evil. Despite the suspense of the epic story, we are sure that such goodness will conquer evil. The battle must be to the death, since too easy a victory demeans the godlike hero. The struggle is satisfying in its intensity, and the outcome is inevitable.

The plot that depends on sudden and incredible changes in character for resolution of conflict fails because it lacks inevitability. Without foreshadowing, Mr. Wickham, the cruel disciplinarian in the school for Native Americans in *Dream of the Blue Heron,* becomes kind and sympathetic to Wabus. Wabus's becoming a lawyer because he can count on the assistance of the reformed Wickham depends on unbelievable character change; the plot lacks inevitability.

Types of Plots

The plots of *Charlotte's Web* and *A Wrinkle in Time,* with their central climaxes followed quickly by denouement, are called **progressive plots.** Apparently people have always liked suspense and climax because the progressive plot is common in traditional European tales. In "The Shoemaker and the Elves," for example, we move directly into the action from a few short phrases—"once upon a time," and "the couple was very poor." The first short paragraph also includes the elves' first visit and the work they leave behind. By the end of the second paragraph, the shoemaker is rich and we are halfway through the story. The couple hides to watch; their grateful gift of clothes for the elves brings on the climax—the dance of the delighted elves, who then disappear. In "The Wolf and the Kids" the climax comes three lines from the end; filled with stones, the wolf falls into the well and drowns. The Bremen Town Musicians raise a furor that frightens the robbers away; the musicians stay forever. When the Fisherman tells the fish that his greedy wife wishes to be God, they are returned to their vinegar jug. The teller of oral tales knows that once the climax comes, he may lose his audience; he must end the story quickly and conclusively.

It is natural that as groups of people arrive in the Western world from around the globe, their tales should be added to the wealth of folk literature available to us. Because these tales speak of countries and ways of life different from the new land, the folk stories may vary in many ways. We know the Uncle Remus tales were brought here by slaves, stories in which the underdogs outwit their masters, a theme also common to the folk literature of some Western European groups. Elsewhere social structures may vary, and stock characters may be different. Victims and perpetrators come from anywhere in the social structure. Form, too, may differ from the European tales of the Brothers Grimm or Hans Christian Andersen, which usually follow a progressive plot.

The Chinese tales so ably retold by Laurence Yep seem to meander, ignoring what by the Grimms' standards might seem discursive. They comment, nonetheless, on human behavior and values, as do the tales of other ethnic groups. Yep says in the introduction to *The Rainbow People* that "trying to understand Chinese Americans from these tales is like trying to comprehend Mississippian ancestors by reading a collection of Vermont folktales. Some tales come from a common heritage; but others are specific to the region." One thinks of the Captain Stormalong tales of New England and those of Big John from the mining regions, as well as Pecos Bill from the Southwest. Just as the people enrich our society, all these stories enrich their readers.

Some book-length stories for children have another type of plot, an **episodic plot,** in which one incident or short episode is linked to another by common characters or by a unified theme. A clear contrast to the progressive plot of *Charlotte's Web,* already discussed in some detail, is the episodic one of *The Wind in the Willows.* Like White, Kenneth Grahame uses personified animals as characters in his fantasy. In the twelve short chapters, each a separate story and each a part of the whole, Mole meets Rat, they picnic, and they meet Toad, who can think only of motor cars. Mole, lost in the Wild Wood, is found by Rat and they visit Mole's home. Toad "borrows" a car and is jailed, but he escapes and returns to Toad Hall. Each chapter is an episode in the life of an idyllic community of kindly animals whose lives are intertwined by loyalty and mutual concern. Any suspense in a chapter is usually resolved within it. Instead of a central conflict, our interest is held by the relationships of the group of developed characters. Rat is consistently kind and reliable; Toad is consistently inconsistent; and Mole, as his self-confidence increases, changes from follower to leader. The idyllic community life of these diverse beings, living their leisurely and unselfish lives, is the discovery of *The Wind in the Willows.* We are further warmed by discovering among other things that one loves the home where one's belongings are, and that even the most contented find faraway places alluring.

Despite cultural differences in form, "traditional Western values" are often found in tales from all cultures.

Episodic plots may consist of a series of incidents related by a central character.

Winnie-the-Pooh supplies another example of episodic plot, and its form is well suited to its young listeners. One episode follows another, each with its own high point and resolution, and with a natural stopping place at the end of chapter and episode. To keep readers reading and listeners listening, the episodic plot relies on characters, theme, and tension within each chapter. Books with episodic plots make excellent bedtime stories.

Robert McCloskey's *Homer Price* amuses children with the story of the runaway doughnut machine, or Miss Terwilliger's huge ball of string that she unwinds in a county fair competition. Each chapter is a story, and many of the same characters appear throughout—Uncle Ulysses and the Sheriff, for example. Other books, like Beverly Cleary's Henry Huggins and Ramona books, show their mischief in a series of episodes. New stories in episodic form, both fantasy and realism, are continually written for children, stories that rely on character, theme, humor, or nonsense to sustain the reader's interest.

There is great possibility for variation and combination in plot structure. *Alice in Wonderland* combines progressive with episodic plot. The underground setting, Alice's growing and shrinking, and her increasing self-confidence provide unity and progress. We recall the many ingenuities—the pool of tears, the caucus race, the caterpillar's advice, the mad tea party, and the croquet game—without being sure of their order. However, the story concludes in a flurry of excitement and a whirl of angry cards as Alice sees the ineffectual adults at the trial and finally asserts herself. *Tom Sawyer*, too, combines elements of episodic structure with progressive plot and climactic focus. Although the book includes a strong conflict and a final climax, many chapters are merely episodes in the life of a small-town boy, and those, though enjoyable in themselves, make little contribution to the central conflict.

❂ *Special Issues of Plot in Children's Literature*

Most of what has been said about plot up to this point applies to plot in adult literature as well as in children's literature. The remainder of the chapter discusses some of the special problems in stories for children.

Earlier discussion of patterns of action mentions the dangers of sensationalism. While adults may choose such stories, children may find sensationalism is more than they can bear. Sensational suspense, furthermore, places the focus on tension rather than on humans and ideas. If the functions of literature are pleasure and understanding, the latter is slighted by sensationalism.

Coincidence

The concurrence of events apparently by mere chance is **coincidence.** In real life, we know that coincidence does occur. In literature, however, where the truths of human nature and human existence are explored, reliance on coincidence to resolve conflict weakens plot. One example in which excellence is flawed by coincidence is *The Incredible Journey* by Sheila Burnford. As the three pets find their way through the Canadian wilderness, three chance happenings without foreshadowing are puzzling to readers, perhaps causing doubt about the larger plot. A handwritten note blows into the fireplace and leaves the housekeeper baffled. Later, by a "twist of fate," a crumbling beaver dam gives way at just the right moment to sweep the frightened cat downstream. Third, a boy, hunting for the first time with his own rifle, saves the Siamese cat from a lynx by one remarkably accurate shot. Fortunately, however, the story of the pets' struggle against the wilderness is so strong in many other ways, from character to style, that the coincidence can be overlooked.

Such fictional strength is not always the case, however, since inadequate foreshadowing leads the reader to doubt the credibility of an event. The test of coincidence, therefore, is foreshadowing. We are prepared to accept the concurrence of events if the incident does not seem to be mere chance, but a previously threatened or foreseen possibility.

Coincidence is tested by foreshadowing.

White might easily have fallen into the coincidence trap in *Charlotte's Web*. If, for example, the enormous and healthy Uncle, the obvious choice for first prize, had happened to take sick at the fair, that would have been coincidence. However, had Wilbur won the blue ribbon by mere default, our pleasure in the outcome would then have been a mixed pleasure over a far less satisfying victory. Furthermore, if Charlotte had by incredible coincidence eventually lived as long as Wilbur, she would have defied the natural laws of a spider's life cycle. Charlotte may talk and write words in her web, but she is a spider leading a spider life. White, by using foreshadowing and by rejecting coincidence, has given *Charlotte's Web* an inevitable and satisfying conclusion.

Sentimentality

Nor should another negative element, called **sentimentality,** mar a well-constructed plot. We term **sentiment** a natural concern or emotion for another person. When, for instance, our parents are hurt in a painful accident, our natural sentiment, called love, causes an emotional response. We are hurt with those we love. However, when our sentiments are used, or played on as they are in soap opera, we have what we call a tearjerker situation, or sentimentality.

Sentimentality evokes disproportionate emotional response.

We have all at some time left a movie theater surreptitiously wiping our eyes, knowing the movie wasn't worth tears. At other times we have been unashamed of our tears, perhaps even proud. It is the legitimacy of our emotional reaction that makes us feel honest. When we are honestly moved by art, we may weep because we suffer with the character empathically, taking his or her sorrow upon ourselves. But sometimes the writer may cause us to weep or to exult and we are uncomfortable because we are asked for an emotional response in excess of what the situation requires.

Sentimentality takes varied forms. Character may be sentimentally drawn. For instance, a saintly, sweet woman who never raises her voice, who is patient, kind, loyal, and true, and who keeps a full cookie jar and a spotless kitchen is no reality. She is a cardboard, two-dimensional figure, a highly sentimentalized picture of Mother. Sentimentality may also occur in a plot. Sydney Taylor's *All-of-a-Kind Family* pictures growing up poor in an Orthodox Jewish family. However, the writer not only creates a sentimental picture of Mother, but also sees family life as a continually joyful chain of events, or perhaps nonevents. Five identically dressed little girls go happily to the library in a group, live frictionless lives in a large family, accept and make the best of poverty; the sentimentalized pictures challenge our knowledge of the reality of family life. Because we are dubious of Taylor's sentimentalized view we may reject the far more important discoveries about the practice of Jewish orthodoxy.

A typical story and a great favorite among children of the late nineteenth century was a supposedly realistic horse story called *Black Beauty*, Anna Sewell's novel told in first person by Black Beauty himself. The book made an influential appeal to Victorian society about cruelty to animals, but as we look at it now, heavy sentimentality strikes us. The pathos of Beauty's own life is comparable to that of "Poor Ginger," as one chapter is titled. Ginger tells Black Beauty her story, and the short chapter concludes with Black Beauty's observations:

> A short time after this a cart with a dead horse in it passed our cabstand. The head hung out of the cart-tail, the lifeless tongue was slowly dropping with blood; and the sunken eyes! but I can't speak of them, the sight was too dreadful. It was a chestnut horse with a long, thin neck. . . . I believe it was Ginger; I hoped it was, for then her troubles would be over. O! if men were more merciful they would shoot us before we came to such misery.

A steady diet of sentimentality may cause emotional shallowness.

While none of us would argue that people have a right to be cruel to animals, Sewell's sentimentality is apparent in the graphic description of a lolling, bloody tongue, the frequent exclamation points, and even the basic idea of a realistic story of a horse being told in first person by the horse—all are tear-jerkers. Because of the sentimentality, the reader may sob more soulfully over Ginger's death than over that of a human being—although there is little confusion in our minds as to which misused creature is more deserving of grief.[4]

Rarely do we have sensationalism in folktales, and rarely does the story-teller stop to rouse our tears by false sentiment. The wicked wolf whose stomach is full of rocks falls into the well and is drowned; we waste no sighs. The unkind girl whose punishment is to spout toads creeps into the corner and dies. The rapid pace of the folktale plot seems to prohibit pauses for tears. We appreciate the celebration of a marriage "the very next day," and are not anguished over the fate of Rumpelstiltskin, who stamped his feet so hard that he split in two and "that was an end of him." Instead of being sentimental, the tale-teller resorts to humor. Some of Hans Christian Andersen's stories, however, are sentimental, including one of his personal favorites, "The Little Match Girl." Those of his tales told in the folktale manner do not lapse into sentimentality.

Charlotte's Web does not resort to sentimentality. Lingering sobs and whimpers from Charlotte at her own death would have destroyed credibility. Charlotte is a spider and knows it. Her spider-defined life prepares Wilbur and readers for her dignified and inevitable death. Or again, Wilbur's fainting might easily have become sentimental panic, but is instead humorous. Or Templeton might have broken down, become a reformed rat, and committed some unselfish or heroic act. Such an incredible change would have been sentimentality. Our response to each situation in White's story is legitimately roused, never exaggerated or superficial, and therefore unsentimental.

What is wrong with sentimentality? A good cry never hurt anyone. Perhaps not. However, there are dangers inherent in a steady diet of forced emotion. We have all had our turns at sneering at soap operas, but perhaps we have not really considered why we sneer. Again and again, dramatic occurrences, crises, and tragedies push one another out of our memories. We are pumps primed to spout tears and then, just as we have settled down, primed again.

The most destructive element in the overuse of sentiment is not boredom, but the fact that the young reader, faced with continual sentimentality, will not develop the sensitivity essential to recognize what is truly moving and what is merely a play on feelings. The use of judgment and the sense of proportion grow and mature when we see honest emotion, whether it be joy or sorrow. If, after all, we regard the death of a pet mouse with the same degree of emotional intensity as the death of a brother, we have no sense of emotional proportion.

By contrast to *Black Beauty*, notice in Katherine Paterson's story, *Bridge to Terabithia*, the wide range of emotions that readers wrestle with. They follow Jess from his shyness with other children to his rivalry with his sister, Brenda, from pleasure over the secret bridge to the hideaway island, to numbness and grief at his friend Leslie's drowning. Or chart the genuine sentiment that a young child, reading or being read to, experiences over the relationship with Charlotte and Wilbur. Here he or she comes to know loneliness, friendship, sacrifice, tact, patience, loyalty, and maternity—as well as death and continuity; the child meets such negative human traits as selfishness, avarice, and gluttony. Furthermore, among the more surprising discoveries is the way in which such significant human traits and experiences are explored in both books—not with bathos or sentimentality, but with seriousness and deft humor. The total impact of White's book embodies respect for animals, yes, but more important, respect for people, as Wilbur and Charlotte personify humans.

The child fed only on such surface sentimentality as soap opera with its sterile and stereotyped pictures of humans and its distorted sensationalism

Sentiment, yes. But sentimentality inhibits the growth of emotional honesty.

with simplistic solutions—this child risks developing emotional shallowness.[5] The child nourished through real literature in the breadth and depth and range of true emotion grows in understanding of human nature.

Lack of Conflict

Many of today's mass-produced storybooks, like those often found on racks in supermarkets and drugstores, lack conflict. Events follow one another in chronological narrative. Without any struggle, the story lacks suspense, any hint of alternative outcomes, a sense that it had to happen, and therefore satisfaction. All the reader can say at the conclusion of such a story is, "So what does that prove?" Conflict, the tension that keeps a story interesting, has never appeared.

Inadequately developed conflict, like flat characterization, leaves us unconcerned about the outcome of a story. Conflict holds our attention if it presents some semblance of a fair fight, and if the question of outcome is open. Inadequate conflict occurs in poor science fiction, when the protagonist combats an irresistible natural force, or, in person-against-person conflict, the ingenuity of two intellects without emotions becomes a dry, academic struggle. When pure intellect does battle with itself in person-against-self conflict, the struggle is merely a problem with a rational answer. The reader who is uninvolved in either characters or conflict becomes apathetic; "I cannot conceive of it; I therefore cannot care."

Once again, however, take the example of *A Wrinkle in Time,* where conflict is person-against-person. Meg battles against a disembodied brain that controls the citizens of Camazotz, whose people are programmed to be identical. Meg and Calvin struggle against IT's magnetic persuasion, but Charles Wallace, whose allegiance to mind is stronger than it is to spirit, arrogantly gives in. Pure mind, however, cannot conquer stubborn Meg, whose believable flaws make her human enough for us to care about. When Meg sees that her strength lies in her power to love, she overcomes IT and frees Charles Wallace. These human responses of will, dependence, and love oppose the antagonist IT. We are concerned about the outcome, and yearning to help Meg in a fantastic plot based on the possible reality of opposing forces in conflict.

Without conflict, the reader may shrug and say, "Who cares?"

Summary

Character study alone rarely carries the child's interest, but character becomes inextricably woven into plot by the very nature of the protagonist and the antagonist in the conflict. Order is easier for the child to follow if it is within his or her experience; chronological order is therefore more frequent, while flashback is more common in stories for older children. In a progressive plot, suspense pulls the reader through the rising action to the central climax, where conflict is resolved in a manner foreshadowed and thus inevitable; the last questions are usually answered in a denouement, with its closed ending.

By contrast, each chapter in an episodic plot may have its own small tensions and be joined to the others by theme and character. Finally, a well-plotted story relies on neither sentimentality nor coincidence for action and resolution.

There is no right plot structure in a story for children. There are only variations of the principal forms. The understanding of the child—reader or listener—may determine the length or structure of the story, whether that story is a single progressively arranged unit or an episode in a longer work. However, what does matter is that the piece of literature sustain interest and give pleasure.

In considering the plot development, we are most aware that without sufficient conflict or tension, accompanied by suspense, foreshadowing, and inevitability, a story is just plain dull. Few adults want to read a dull story, and certainly no children will.

Pleasure comes in all kinds of ways. A good story can provide them all.

Notes

1. C. W. Sullivan III, "Narrative Expectations: The Folklore Connection," *Children's Literature Quarterly 15,* Summer 1990, pp. 52–55.
2. For a discussion of time in time fantasy, a subject in itself, see Eleanor Cameron, *The Green and Burning Tree.*
3. Perry Nodelman writing of tension in "Pleasure and Genre" notes perfectly: "I want to know, I need to know, I don't know quite . . ."
4. Readers take opposite views on *Black Beauty.* Perhaps it is not the personification in a realistic story, but the injustice of the horse's treatment and the justice of his feelings that prompt their legitimately positive responses.
5. Walt Disney's early films for children, his retelling of folk and fairy tales, have been criticized for their graphic portrayal of frightening characters and episodes. Imagined scenes and characters in a storybook can be as scary as the child wishes, but can be absolutely terrifying when seen in vivid color.

Recommended Books Cited in This Chapter

ARMSTRONG, WILLIAM. *Sounder.* New York: Harper & Row, 1969.
AVI. *Crispin: The Cross of Lead.* New York: Hyperion, 2002.
———. *The True Confessions of Charlotte Doyle.* New York: Orchard Books, 1990.
BELLAIRS, JOHN. *The Trolley to Yesterday.* New York: Dial, 1989.
BURNFORD, SHEILA. *The Incredible Journey.* Boston: Little, Brown, 1961.
CARROLL, LEWIS. *Alice's Adventures in Wonderland.* 1865. Reprint. New York: Dutton, 1954.
CHILDRESS, ALICE. *A Hero Ain't Nothin' but a Sandwich.* New York: Coward, 1973.

CLEARY, BEVERLY. *Henry Huggins.* New York: Morrow, 1950.

COLLIER, JAMES LINCOLN, AND CHRISTOPHER COLLIER. *My Brother Sam Is Dead.* New York: Four Winds, 1974.

CREECH, SHARON. *Walk Two Moons.* New York: Harper, 1992.

CURTIS, CHRISTOPHER. *The Watsons Go to Birmingham.* New York: Delacorte, 1995.

DELACRE, LULU. *Salsa Stories.* Scholastic Inc., 2000.

DICAMILLO, KATE. *Because of Winn-Dixie.* Boston: Candlewick, 2000.

FLEISCHMAN, SID. *Jim Ugly.* New York: Green Willow, 1992.

GEORGE, JEAN. *The Talking Earth.* New York: Harper & Row, 1983.

GIFF, PATRICIA REILLY. *Pictures of Hollis Wood.* New York: Random House, 2002.

GRAHAME, KENNETH. *The Wind in the Willows.* 1908. Reprint. New York: Scribner's, 1953.

GROVE, VICKI. *Reaching Dustin.* New York: Putnam, 1998.

HAMILTON, VIRGINIA. *Time Ago Lost: More Tales of Jahdu.* New York: Macmillan, 1973.

———. *The Time Ago Tales of Jahdu.* New York: Macmillan, 1962.

HESSE, KAREN. *Stowaway.* New York: Simon and Schuster, 2000.

HIAASEN, CARL. *Hoot.* New York: Knopf, 2002.

HILL, ELIZABETH STARR. *Bird Boy.* Illustrated by Lesley Liu. New York: Farrar, Straus & Giroux, 1999.

HOLT, KIMBERLY WILLIS. *When Zachary Beaver Came to Town.* New York: Holt, 1999.

JOHNSON, ANGELA. *The First Part Last.* New York: Simon and Schuster, 2003.

KONIGSBERG, E. L. *The View from Saturday.* New York: Atheneum, 1996.

KOSS, AMY GOLDMAN. *The Ashwater Experiment.* New York: Dial Books, 1999.

L'ENGLE, MADELEINE. *A Wrinkle in Time.* New York: Farrar, Straus & Giroux, 1962.

LE GUIN, URSULA K. *A Wizard of Earthsea.* Berkeley, CA: Parnassus, 1968.

LUNN, JANET. *The Shadow in Hawthorn Bay.* New York: Scribner's, 1986.

MCCLOSKEY, ROBERT. *Homer Price.* New York: Viking, 1943.

MILNE, A. A. *Winnie-the-Pooh.* New York: Dutton, 1926.

NAYLOR, PHYLLIS REYNOLDS. The Witch Books. New York: Delacorte, 1991.

NORTON, MARY. *The Borrowers.* New York: Harcourt, 1965.

PARK, LINDA SUE. *A Single Shard.* New York: Clarion Books. 2001.

PATERSON, KATHERINE. *Bridge to Terabithia.* New York: Harper & Row, 1980.

———. *Lyddie.* New York: Dutton, 1991.

PAULSEN, GARY. *Hatchet.* New York: Bradbury, 1987.

———. *The River.* New York: Delacorte, 1991.

POTTER, BEATRIX. *The Tale of Peter Rabbit.* London: Warne, 1902.

RODOWSKY, COLBY. *Spindrift.* New York: Farrar, Straus & Giroux, 2000.

ROWLING, J. K. *Harry Potter and the Sorcerer's Stone.* New York: Arthur A. Levine, 1997.

SENDAK, MAURICE. *Where the Wild Things Are.* New York: Harper, 1963.

SERRAILLIER, IAN. *Beowulf the Warrior.* New York: Walck, 1961.

SHARMAT, MARJORIE WEINMAN. *Nate the Great and the Fishy Prize.* New York: Coward McCann, 1985.

SPEARE, ELIZABETH. *The Witch of Blackbird Pond.* Boston: Houghton Mifflin, 1958.

TAYLOR, MILDRED. *Roll of Thunder, Hear My Cry.* New York: Dial, 1976.

TWAIN, MARK. *The Adventures of Tom Sawyer.* 1876. Reprint. New York: Macmillan, 1962; Random House, 2002.

VAN DRAANEN, WENDELIN. *Sammy Keyes and the Hotel Thief.* New York: Knopf, 1998.

WARNER, SALLY. *Sort of Forever.* New York: Knopf, 1998.

WAUGH, SYLVIA. *Space Race.* New York: Random House, 2000.

WHITE, E. B. *Charlotte's Web.* New York: Harper, 1952.

WILDER, LAURA INGALLS. *Little House in the Big Woods.* 1932. Reprint. New York: Harper & Row, 1953.

YEP, LAURENCE. *The Rainbow People.* New York: Harper & Row, 1989.

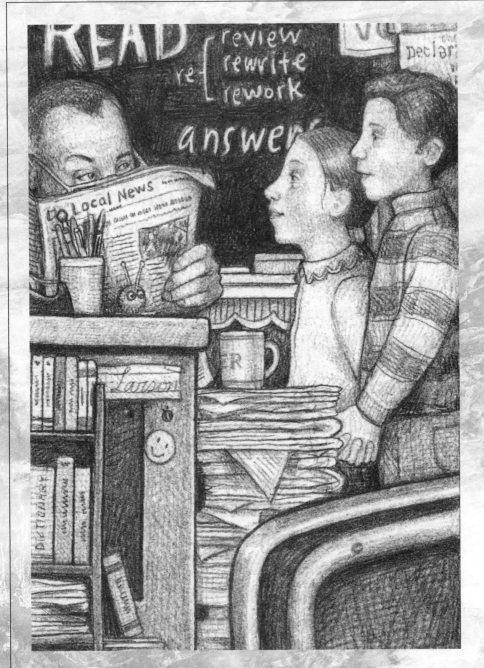

The Landry News

Andrew Clements

Illustrated by Brian Selznick

Theme

"What happens" and
"Whom it happens to"
—is that all there is?

We each have at least one friend who tells a story by linking one anecdote to another, using slender threads of association as continuity: "And the next night . . . " or "And then we . . . " We have heard a more artful storyteller whose stories are involved and who keeps us in suspense: "You'll never believe what she said then" or "And what should happen next . . . !" The first of these narrators can bore us quickly; the second can hold our interest longer. However, the storyteller we especially value is someone whose stories awaken us to awareness of new meaning—of the inconsistency of people, or the mixed joys of family living, or the pain of social exclusion, for example. This storyteller is aware of meaning and has reached for idea, or theme.

In storytelling, "What happened next?" is a question about chronology and narrative order. "Why did it happen?" is a question about character and conflict. But when we ask, "What does it all mean?" we begin to discover theme.

Theme or Unifying Truth

Theme in literature is the idea that holds the story together, such as a comment about society, human nature, or the human condition. It is the main idea or central meaning of a piece of writing.

Ask a woman about the plot of *Little Women*, the story she loved as a child, and she looks baffled and perhaps chagrined that she cannot remember it. Setting, too, has faded from memory to become merely "in the past." Character, however, is still with her, because restless Jo, who has difficulty fitting into traditional female roles, seems to be Everywoman—or at least Manywomen. And chances are the adult's memory of the idea or theme of the novel is still strong; she can confidently say, "It's about a close family of varied but accepting people." The characters of Louisa May Alcott's story convince us of one of its themes—the love of family members for one another is real and enduring.[1] Theme comes alive and becomes memorable as the characters act out the plot.

Look back at the definition of literature: it is "a significant truth expressed in appropriate elements and memorable language." The "significant truth" is an essential element to turn a simple narrative into literature. This truth goes beyond the story and comments on humans. The discovery holds the story together so that long after details of plot are forgotten, the theme remains.

This significant truth unifies and illuminates a story, as it gives the reader enjoyment. The reader gains one pleasure from the discovery of the simplest of truths, and another from the discovery that truth is not simple.[2] Theme provides this discovery, this understanding, this pleasure in recognizing, "Yes, that's the way it is!"

Types of Themes

Explicit Theme

Stating theme in a sentence clarifies its focus.

Sometimes the writer states theme openly and clearly—an **explicit theme.** Once again look at *Charlotte's Web* for examples. The devotion between Charlotte and Wilbur suggests many ideas that make the reader say, "It's true"; their relationship reveals and defines friendship and other themes.

Charlotte has encouraged, protected, and mothered Wilbur, bargained and sacrificed for him, and Wilbur, the grateful receiver, realizes that "friendship is one of the most satisfying things in the world." And Charlotte says later, "By helping you perhaps I was trying to lift my life a little. Anyone's life can stand a little of that." Because these quoted sentences are exact statements from the text, they are called explicit themes.

The theme in *Miracle's Boys* by Jacqueline Woodson is stated explicitly. This is the story of inner-city boys, each of whom feels responsible for a death. Despite being completely innocent, each one feels guilty for failing to intervene successfully. Ty'ree, seeing a dog drowning in a frozen pond, begs his dad to save the dog, and feels responsible for his father's death from hypothermia; Lafayette, who finds his mother in a diabetic coma, somehow feels guilty for not having revived her; and Charles holds himself responsible for the death of a dog hit by a car. When each reveals his feeling of guilt, the others insist that he could not have saved the victim. Freed of guilt, each is able to free the other. The function of freedom may be to free someone else.

As immigration and population numbers alter the makeup of U.S. and Canadian society, the trend toward multicultural stories is justifiably common in today's books for children. In *Class President*, Johanna Hurwitz states an explicit point about ethnic pride when the new teacher, Mr. Flores, gives Julio's name its proper Spanish pronunciation: *Hulio.* "It's a good Spanish name and you should be proud of it. . . . Your name is a very important part of you." He tells the class that electing a president should not be a popularity contest. "A good leader is . . . fair and . . . stands up for what he or she thinks is right." Julio begins to stand up for what he believes in, first of all his ethnic heritage.

Circle of Fire, like Mildred Taylor's *Roll of Thunder,* shows the impact on society of the Ku Klux Klan's hatred and cross burning. In an explicit thematic statement, author William H. Hooks replies to Harrison's question "Why?" by having Pa explain human frailty:

> "Your Grandma would tell you that they're just poor white trash and that quality folks would never resort to such meanness. . . . But there's more to it than that. There's something in all of us that wants to be top dog, that wants to keep *our kind* in control. Human decency doesn't seem to be a God-given gift. It's a precious thing you have to learn early and keep working at."

Hooks does not leave it at that, but in a comment following the story, a concluding author's note reminds readers of the KKK's prevalence everywhere, and warns, "These same events could happen today." Hooks avoids didacticism when he keeps this comment out of the story itself. Its truth is sufficiently clear in Pa's statement. Such explicit themes are common in children's literature because the writer may wish to be sure the reader finds the unifying truth.

Throughout Karen Cushman's *The Midwife's Apprentice,* Alyce's life changes. At first she must sleep in a warm dung heap; then she is praised for delivering twin calves. Later she delivers a healthy infant for the bailiff's wife. After a failure, she goes away to become an "inn girl" and there her curiosity about the Magister's writing helps her learn to read. Her "miraculous" delivery of the young squire's infant follows. With successes behind her and a strong will to learn all she can, Alyce returns to become the midwife's apprentice. In the last lines of the story, Alyce states an explicit theme concerning the real source of success: "I know how to try and risk and fail and try again and not give up."

Explicit themes are easily understood.

Implicit Theme

Underlying *Charlotte's Web* are certain implied or **implicit themes,** as important and almost as apparent as explicit themes. If two such different characters as a runt pig and a carnivorous spider can find friendship, others can; even a self-centered rat can be a friend of sorts. White thereby implies that friendship can be found in unexpected places.

Charlotte's selflessness—working late at night to finish a new word, expending her last energies for her friend—is evidence that friendship is giving of oneself. Wilbur's protection of Charlotte's egg sac, his sacrifice of first turn at the slops, and his devotion to Charlotte's babies—giving without any need to stay even or to pay back—leads us to another theme: True friendship is naturally reciprocal. As the two become fond of each other, still another theme emerges: One's best friend can do no wrong. In fact, a best friend is sensational! Both Charlotte and Wilbur believe in these ideas; their experiences verify them. These themes are all developed through the characters, their actions, and their thoughts as we see them throughout the story's conflict.

Thinking of theme as "a moral" or "a lesson," or even "a message," provokes the idea that we must learn how or how not to behave. But a good story is not meant to instruct. Its purpose is to entertain by its action and characters; at the same time, it gives us insight into people—how they think and feel—and enlarges our understanding. However, when thinking of theme as the unifying idea that holds the other elements of a good story together, it's a satisfying pleasure to find not only entertainment but a discovery of some kind.

The theme of Ruth White's novel *Belle Pater's Boy* is that appearances are less important than what one is inside. Arbutus, called Beauty by her father, dislikes the focus on her appearance, and calls herself Gypsy instead. When Cousin Woodrow, who hates his crossed eyes, moves in next door, Gypsy comes to love him dearly. She learns that his mother was a loving but unattractive woman, and that her own gentle father killed himself because, following his heroic rescue of a child in a fire, he could not accept his disfigurement. Gypsy's mother says that "appearances were too important to your father" and he became deeply depressed. The outside doesn't matter; inside, each was worthy of love.

Virginia Hamilton's *Cousins* is a story in which the protagonist dreads the death of her aged Gram Tut and is haunted by the memory of seeing her cousin Patty Ann drown. Absorbed in both her grief at Patty's death and her own guilt at being jealous of her pretty cousin, Cammy cannot face death but buries it, then chews it over and over until she is helped by Gram Tut to recognize that death happens to us all. Some wait for it, like Gram; for others it comes too early, as it does for Patty. Because this theme is suggested but not stated precisely at any point, it is implicit.

Implicit themes, such as "friendship knows no ethnic barriers," also underlie *Circle of Fire*. Harrison values his African American friends and adds another friend, Liam Cafferty, from among the migrant Irish gypsies traveling the East Coast. Harrison's fear that his father might be a Klan member dissolves when he learns that Pa is responsible for the eviction of the Klan from the area. The implicit theme remains: "When we don't know the facts, we may doubt even those we love."

It may seem unnecessary or even unwise to state theme in sentence form. Why not say, "The theme of Charlotte's Web is friendship"? Notice what happens if we do state the theme this simply. Friendship is too broad a term. "Friendship is fraudulent" or "Friendship is a useless luxury" or "Friendship is all giving and no receiving"—any of these statements concerns friendship and might reasonably be explored and proven in literature, but none is the truth of E. B. White's story. Forcing ourselves to make a specific statement based on the facts of the story defines the theme more carefully.

Theme is a unifying idea that holds a story together.

Multiple and Secondary Themes

Each reader brings to a story a personal past, a present, and plans for the future. These elements shape our *responses* to the story. It seems absurd, then, to expect that diverse humans must agree that exactly the same ideas are most important, and must take from the story exactly the same themes. The story speaks to us out of our own individual and varying experiences. It speaks a universal truth to us, but our own universal truth, a personal transaction

Several themes are often linked.

Although complexity and variety in themes may be one of the strongest proofs of a work's excellence, most literature for children seems to center upon a **primary theme.** When a story contains a variety of themes, however, they are often linked.

Consistent with high fantasy's focus on good-versus-evil conflict, Ursula K. Le Guin's *A Wizard of Earthsea* explores the greatest of all struggles: that within one's self. Ged, in his flight from the shadow, heeds the advice of his mentor: "You must choose. You must seek what seeks you. You must hunt the hunter." When, after sailing for days, Ged confronts the thing that has sloughed off all human form, and recognizes it as the evil within himself, he is strong enough to win the battle. Internal conflict has illuminated theme. Other less personal themes abound. "Need alone is not enough to set power free; there must be knowledge." "To hear, one must be silent." "Danger surrounds power." "As a man's real power grows and his knowledge widens . . . he chooses nothing, but does only and wholly what he must do." "The wise man is one who never sets himself apart from other living things." The novel is rich in thematic ideas.

If a story has multiple themes, some seem less important than the primary one. These we call **secondary themes.**

In *Charlotte's Web*, almost as important as the themes about the nature of friendship is a secondary one about death. It is the possibility of Wilbur's death that disturbs us; we would feel different if he were an old boar who had lived long and well. We recognize, just the same, that "death is inevitable and not to be feared." Charlotte, knowing her life cycle, foresees her own death, but neither dreads it nor asks for pity. Others accept death, too. Seasons die when they have run their terms. Maple trees, crickets, lilacs, baby spiders, and the Harvest Fair all celebrate the inevitable cycle of birth, life, and death. There is no grief, only acceptance.

A wealth of minor themes also emerges in *Charlotte's Web*: "People are gullible"; "People don't give credit where credit is due"; "The meek may inherit the earth"; "Youth and innocence have unique value." Each character accepts and maintains the simplicity of his or her own particular style of living, so "Be what you are." As for nature, "Beauty and wonder exist in all things, even the simplest," "Life in nature is constant and continuous," and finally, "Nature is a miracle," from the silver forest of asparagus to the waterproof egg sac.

In *Cousins* the return of Cammy's divorced father when she is suffering with grief and shock suggests an optimistic secondary theme about change: "Even in difficult times, things may change and good things happen." In her brief novel *Journey*, Patricia MacLachlan suggests related themes. Journey and Cat are left to live with their grandparents when their mother, grieving over a husband who has abandoned the family, in turn abandons her two children. "Try though we may, we cannot always understand the behavior of others" comes through. "A family need not be the traditional parents and children, but may be a different form" is a second theme.

In one story, value lies in the explicit yet nondidactic statement of theme. In another, the fact that the theme is implied and must be stated by the reader for him- or herself is value of another kind. The only general rule that can be made is that a theme should be there. On first reading a good story, we usually see one or a few thematic ideas, both explicit and implicit. We see more perhaps on second reading. However, thematic wealth in a book for children often creates continuous discovery.

James Lincoln Collier and Christopher Collier, writers of *Jump Ship to Freedom,* show how Daniel Arabus grows in character and strength by confronting crises and solving problems. Early in the story he calls himself a "nigger," a "stupid darky," "not as smart as white folks." "I knew that black folks were supposed to be more stupid than white folks; that was God's way, the minister said. . . . If God had made black folks smart, they'd have got restless about doing the hard work." But by the time he has saved himself from apprehension under the Fugitive Slave Act, worked like a seasoned seaman in the rigging of the square-rigger, and managed to save his father's Civil War soldier's pay, he is told that he is a smart and resourceful young man. But Daniel disagrees. "If I'd been really smart I'd have figured out a way to get those soldiers' notes [long ago]." By the story's end, he calls himself by his given name, thinking to himself, "When you figured you was one kind of person all your life, it's hard to start thinking of yourself as another kind." Once we accept a negative view of ourselves, accepting another is not easy. As Eleanor Roosevelt once said, "No one can make you feel inferior without your consent."

Children differ, and the variety of their capacities for discovery, as well as for phrasing that discovery, is almost infinite. The younger the child, the less likelihood of a coherent statement. We realize, however, that although a young child cannot define "home" or "mother," even the youngest knows what each concept is. Security and love, comfort and constancy, warmth and protection are abstractions they know, but abstractions beyond articulation. For children, knowing and saying need not be—and rarely are—the same.

The best stories have a thematic idea or point.

Children may know concepts they are unable to express in words.

✪ *Special Issues of Theme in Children's Literature*

Traditional Literature

Folktales have similar themes even though they originate in different cultures. Their presence in traditional literature passed on from one generation to another seems to be evidence that people everywhere create and respond to similar ideas about life and human nature. By noting just a few of these themes, we become aware that a simple, optimistic core of truth like "Good can conquer evil" is explored in a great many tales, Asian, African, and South American as well as European. Some leave the theme as simple as that, but others explore ideas a bit more complex, clarifying the kind of good or the kind of evil. "The Goosegirl," a German tale, explicitly identifies the conquered evil as deception: the servant girl who threatens and impersonates the princess is punished. "Snow White," another German tale, defines the defeated evil more clearly as jealousy; the witch-queen tries ceaselessly to kill the one more beautiful than she. "Drakestail," from the French, identifies the particular good as humility; the modest hero calls on the Fox, the Ladder, and the River to save him from a tyrant king.

Other folktales, like the Norwegian "The Three Billy-Goats Gruff," prove that keeping your wits about you can save you from danger. In the German tale "The Twelve Dancing Princesses," the soldier outwits the princesses and wins one for his bride. The Scandinavian "Boots and His Brothers" shows that if you have the wit to see its potential, curiosity can pay off. Both the Russian "The Little Humpbacked Horse" and the Norse "The Princess on the Glass Hill" praise the capacity of cleverness to bring success. Both "The Bremen-Town Musicians" from Germany and "The Ram and the Pig Who Went into the Woods" from Scandinavia offer proof that each creature can use its gifts to contribute to common success. Tales told over and over, tales told in one land or another, tales complex in structure for older readers or simple in outline for younger readers—most have themes that state a universal truth.

Folktales about outwitting the powerful, for example, occur in many cultures. In *Fire Came to the Earth People*, a West African tale from Dahomey retold and illustrated by Susan L. Roth, earth people had no fire because Mawu, the selfish Moon-god, kept it to himself. Even the strongest could not steal fire, but returned saying, "Fire is not meant for earth people." The chameleon and the tortoise became sacred to the people because only these lowly ones had the wit to steal coals, set fire to straw, and hide the fire beneath the shell of the tortoise. The story has the familiar form of the pourquoi, or "how/why?" tale. The three tasks set for Ananse the Spider Man by the Sky God of Gail Haley's Caribbean African *A Story, A Story* are completed by a simple man who ties the leopard in a net of vines, catches the hornets in a calabash, and captures the fairy-whom-no-man-sees by means of a latex-covered wooden doll reminiscent of Joel Chandler Harris's Tar Baby. Now the Spider Man carries the Sky God's stories to the world. In the Native American story "How the Bear Got His Stumpy Tail," the bear is outwitted by the fox, who tells him he can catch fish by leaving his tail to freeze in the ice. And in *The Name of the Tree*, a Bantu tale retold by Celia Barker Lottridge, neither the fleet gazelle nor the elephant with the long memory can remember the name of the tree; only the youngest tortoise manages.

Like the conflicts in folk literature that so obviously set protagonist against antagonist, the themes are straightforward and easily seen. Although themes are often implicit, the conflict and the characters make them so evident

Similar themes from all cultures seem to surface.

that explicit statements are unnecessary. Hard work can bring success; intelligence is more valuable than physical strength; kindness brings rewards—these are basic issues that the vigorous action of the folktale makes clear. Their prominence in traditional stories seems to verify the human wish to know not only what happened, and how it happened, but also *why* it happened and what it means. According to critic Wayne Booth, one of the strongest of human interests is the "desire for causal completion." "Not only do we believe that certain causes do in life produce certain effects; in literature we believe that they should." This interest is distinct from the "pleasure of learning, of satisfaction of intellectual curiosity."[3]

The Myths of the Orient, retold and illustrated by Barbara Chestesen, are perhaps as old as any told. In each of them, virtuous behavior is rewarded. The son's wish to pay for his father's funeral is so strong that he sells himself as a slave. The daughter whose royal father cannot have the right combination of metals for a beautiful bell throws herself into the boiling metal; her death melds the metals for a perfect, sweet-toned bell. The kindhearted Ming Li, who cannot kill the tortoise for food, finds that wealth and a king's daughter are his.

Not all folktale themes are optimistic. *Heetunka's Harvest,* a picture book by Jennifer Berry Jones, illustrates how greed is rewarded by disaster in Indian society. Among the tribes, women trade with humility and gratitude, but Heetunka, who takes white beans from the mouse's nest, fails to make a trade and is punished.

Humans are not totally good or completely successful; good does not always conquer evil. Hans Christian Andersen, although he uses the traditional forms of folktales, makes no effort either to be constantly optimistic or to preach about what people ought to be. He is too busy showing what people are. Many of his stories of humble people, animals, and inanimate objects demonstrate one of his most personal and optimistic themes, that of the Ugly Duckling: "Humble beginnings and painful trials can end in happiness." But Andersen's themes also frequently remind us that people are foolish; they value the artificial and the trivial more than the real, as "The Swineherd," "The Nightingale," and "The Princess and the Pea" tell us. People will do anything for vanity, as we see in "The Emperor's New Clothes." Whether we like it or not, the rogue sometimes wins the prize, as he does in "The Tinder Box." Andersen[4] honestly admits that death is sometimes sudden and may leave children bereft; he explores serious themes and develops them into individualized and realistic comments on humankind. His stories prove that literature for children as well as for adults can make sad or even negative comments and still give both pleasure and discovery.

Didacticism

We often wish to help children by telling them what they ought or ought not to do. We give them little mottoes and short, preachy verses to hang on their bedroom walls. From our own past experience we tell them stories that really are instruction disguised as reminiscence. The result may be the child's com-

One of the strongest of human interests is "the desire for causal completion."
Wayne Booth

"Sad but true" themes are often only implied.

ment, "I'm sick of hearing how my dad *loved* to walk to school every day. And according to him, it was uphill both ways." No one is fooled.

Or we admire the welcome hyacinths in the springtime flower bed, but instead of comparing their varied colors, smelling their fragrance, or touching their curled, waxy petals, we turn our admiration into a botany lesson on stamen, pistil, and corolla. The science lesson has its place, of course, but not every flower bed must stimulate it. A growing awareness of startling beauty and perfection in nature may sometimes be stifled by a lesson from Botany 101.

Didacticism, or instruction, is the function of textbooks. Some literature gives a great deal of information without letting it take over from suspenseful and exciting plot, or from well-developed characters. Other narratives are so filled with teaching details about a historical period, a geographical area, a social inequity, or a physical disability that conflict, character, and theme are lost in "what the reader *ought* to know." If the information displaces the understanding, then didacticism has won out. Literature, however, does not teach; it helps us understand.

Nor does literature preach. "Eat it; it's good for you" never persuaded anyone. Adults who choose stories for children that force a moral on them think that a story is good only if it contains obvious lessons. However, knowing our own adult dislike for "do this, but don't do that," we can scarcely expect children to enjoy such preaching, and we may be preventing the child from making personal discoveries. Perhaps growth is impeded rather than fostered. Furthermore, sugar-coating a moral by surrounding it with a shallow story deficient in plot, character portrayal, and style does injustice to children. They come to a story excited by the promise of some fun, only to discover they have been tricked into a sermon. The preached-at child may come to reject all reading and thus close off the great joys and vast discoveries about society available to them.

The obvious purpose of some narratives, like *I Want to Be a Homemaker*, shows little imagination on the part of the writer and awakens little response from the reader; it may even stimulate resistance.[5] Because everything in this narrative is commonplace, the narrative itself is commonplace. We have a sexist view of what a homemaker does: She bakes and sews and tends the baby. Why? Because that is her job. But there is no word of what a mother *is*. A real mother loves her children and finds satisfaction in providing for them—like the mothers of Peter Rabbit and the Moffats, or the mother of the troubled children in *Roll of Thunder, Hear My Cry*. In a story exploring motivation in a real parent, we might come to see the dimensions of motherhood as part of homemaking and make it more than a list of chores.

A selfish, tit-for-tat approach to friendship that says, "Be nice to your friends and they will be nice to you" or "Make everyday occurrences into fun" would be preachy. This is hardly the story Charlotte and Wilbur enact. Throughout a story, understanding of friendship may grow and ordinary experience may be joyful, but the stories need not be reduced to neat little mottoes suitable for framing.

Didacticism is the function of textbooks; pleasure and understanding those of literature.

Inevitably, young people question their parents' views. Avi, author of *Crispin: The Cross of Lead*, touches on several concerns of young readers, principal among them youthful questioning of parents' religion. Instead of telling the reader that this is right and that is wrong, the writer acquaints us with Jason Bock, the narrator. He speculates about religious convictions, and decides that if there is no proof that God doesn't exist, then no one can prove that another kind of god doesn't exist. For the sheer pleasure of invention, he and his friend Henry decide that the water tower, the "ten-legged one," is God. They concoct a complicated theology called Chutengodian, and a number of officials—the Head Kahuna, the High Priest, a Keeper of the Sacred Text. The religion gets away from its inventors; Henry makes the new religion dangerous and exciting, and gets them into trouble with the law as they make a terrifying ascent up to and into the Ten-Legged-God; they break into the tower itself, and swim in the city's drinking water. The suspenseful novel explores group cohesion, adolescent stereotyping, playing with danger, and the responsibilities of leadership, among other thematic ideas.

Early science fiction was intent on reform.

Although the setting of science fiction is commonly future time and alternative worlds, science fiction of the past often seemed to have a "missionary" bent. It often urged on readers a new set of morals and ethics, of religious views, of thinking patterns—a new way of living life, in fact. Science fiction has been called "the last refuge of the morality tale." Over the years, plots have moved from exploration to colonization of the solar system. In order to colonize successfully, however, humans must learn to conquer war, pollution, and overpopulation, and to conserve natural resources. If our children are to inherit a world worth anything, we must be careful conservators. To accomplish these goals, humans must learn to control themselves. And to achieve such overwhelmingly difficult transformations, writers often take their characters to new and alien worlds. Moving from concern for survival of humankind to a sense of futility about changing human behavior, writers create successors to humans, new species that are less corrupt. Given their missionary concerns, science-fiction writers may be dedicated to proving that prejudice and sentimental or romantic views of reality make no sense; the universe is indifferent and has concern for neither human life nor death. It is this indifference that in the past distanced many readers from the genre. Some advocates of distance and objectivity regret the movement away from the common sense of logical outcome toward regarding human emotions as more "real."[6] Didacticism in science fiction seems, if not inevitable, at least difficult to avoid. Recently, however, didacticism has been less prevalent.

Going backward and forward in time is a variation on science-fiction themes. Time travel is the fantasy element in Jane Fresh Thomas's *The Princess in the Pigpen*. Arriving in the twentieth century from her life in the seventeenth, Elizabeth marvels at disease cured by pills, at electricity, clothing, women doctors, horseless carriages, and gasoline power. The point of the story seems to be that inventions cannot take the place of family; Elizabeth longs to return to her own.

Matt, in *The House of the Scorpion* by Nancy Farmer, is a clone of the Master of a country called Opium; he is to be the source of eternal life for El Patron. Regarded by others in the country as nothing but a beast, Matt is sneered at, isolated, abused, ignored and treated like an animal. His treatment makes him resentful and, at times, cruel. Matt sees automatons who, because of an implanted chip, have lost all human emotion. Opium workers die of dehydration beside clear water, and bodyguard Tam Lin tells him that if fresh water were known to authorities, it, too, like the opium farmers, would be exploited. Only because of a loving caretaker/nurse, a thoughtful girl, and an understanding bodyguard, can Matt become remotely human, a person with intelligence and creativity. Being truly human results from being treated humanely.

Even the slightest stories in the I Can Read series may have themes. Katherine Paterson in her first book for new readers, *The Smallest Cow in the World*, suggests that an active imagination is a good thing to have. Marvin misses Rosie, the cow that has been sold: in her place an imaginary Rosie lives in Marvin's little bottle. Ridiculed in school, he is saved by Jenny, who proclaims loudly that the other kids have no imagination, but Marvin does! *Harry's Mom* by Barbara Ann Porte manages, despite the narrative simplicity, to convey an important idea. To Harry, "orphan" means anyone who has lost father or mother and so tells his father he knows nothing about his mother. When he sees his Aunt Rose, he hears loving stories about his mother. More stories about her from his affectionate grandparents make his mother a real part of his now complete family.

> *Simple stories for early readers also have themes.*

Nonsense

Such nonsense-fantasy stories as Kipling's *Just So Stories* or *Pippi Longstocking*, and even *Alice in Wonderland*, seem to lack theme, but each has as its core the idea of wonder and delight at the order and disorder of life. We marvel as the *Just So Stories* tell why whales have tiny throats and leopards have spots. *Winnie-the-Pooh* seems to say that people do strange and exciting things—and with such solemnity. Although adults find satire and social comment in *Alice*, Carroll in his opening poem speaks of a child's discovery of the wonders of life:

> *Even nonsense may have a theme.*

The dream-child moving through a land
Of wonders wild and new . . .
And half believe it true.

Nonsense as a whole seems to say, "The world and all its inhabitants—thank heaven—are illogical and inconsistent." Nonsense, in its own way, may develop such a theme as "Life is easier and more enjoyable if we don't take ourselves too seriously." If it doesn't, it finally palls.

Mature Themes in Children's Stories

As we look back on our own lives, themes occasionally emerge. In literature, however, the writer can look at and recount the events of a life and show that they add up to a pattern that becomes a theme. Such is the case in Ann Rinaldi's historical novel set during the American Revolution, *A Ride into Morning: The Story of Tempe Wick.* In a single paragraph Rinaldi says explicitly and in several different ways that "everyone . . . is just part and parcel of the whole of their life experiences. Everything we do in life, every transaction we have with another human being, is overshadowed by the events that make us what we are. We carry with us always the burdens and joys of the past, like so much baggage." The central characters of her novel demonstrate this theme. Tempe, a young woman of twenty-two, is left to care for a sick and aged mother. She also has the farm to run, a farm on which her father before his death permitted the Rebels to camp. Her unfamiliar management role and other responsibilities beyond her experience temper her behavior; she is always willing to compromise for safety's sake. Mary, sent to join her Rebel cousin Tempe, refuses to give in to demands other than those of the Rebels; her life with her Tory family has convinced her that the Rebel cause must go forward—without compromise. Tempe's brother Henry feels he has been a coward, and to avoid ridicule feigns madness while he acts as a spy for the Rebels. Sergeant Bowzer, British turncoat, chooses duplicity once again when he organizes a Rebel mutiny against General Wayne. Each has been influenced by the differing burdens and joys of a different past. A secondary theme emerges as Mary, the narrator, finds that, after all, people are not perfect. "And if this is what growing up means . . . then I don't like it." "We all live with the choices we make," says Tempe to Henry; this is another secondary theme. In keeping with earlier discussion about reader response, one theme may speak especially to one reader, and another to a second.

Stories like those from Hans Christian Andersen may introduce children to ideas far more mature than we would expect them to grasp, ideas we find difficult to explain in other ways. Fear, for example, is very much a part of childhood. However, what one is afraid of is often hard to pin down. Child psychologist Bruno Bettelheim writes of the capacity of folk and fairy tales to help the child "externalize" the fears that go on in the child's mind. Folktales confront and thus legitimize universal fears like that of the death of a parent in "Hansel and Gretel," the attractiveness of evil in "Snow White and the Seven Dwarfs," and the fear of going out into the world in "Dick Whittington and His Cat."

The Borrowers can carry the child through a variety of fears that may haunt the reader in real life and yet are rarely clarified. We fear the unknown: Homily fears what will happen to Pod on his cup-borrowing expedition. Both parents keep Arrietty at home lest she be seen by a human. They fear the fate of Uncle Hendreary, and what the Boy will do; they fear Mrs. Driver, her friend Mr. Crampfurl, and the exterminators. Most of all, Homily fears mov-

Stories can clarify where explanations fail.

Big ideas may appear in stories for the young.

ing, emigration to the unknown world beyond the floorboards. Moreover, there is in *The Borrowers* another idea that adults find easy to understand but hard to put into words for children: Materialism is a destructive force. Homily admits, "My mother's family never had nothing but a little bone thimble which they shared around. But it's once you've *had* a tea cup . . . " Homily nags Pod for new blotting-paper carpet, and sends him off for things to store away. Even when she is screaming with fright at the Boy's appearance, she wants more possessions. Homily's materialism sends Pod to his "club" upstairs, and brings on the exterminators. Materialism has disrupted the family and brought it to disaster—a big discovery for readers too young to know the word "materialism."

In a highly suspenseful story about deep-sea fishing, Graham Salisbury addresses a difficult theme in *Lord of the Deep*. Mikey's soon-to-be stepfather Bill is a captain of a deep-sea charter boat, and it has been a slow season. Two unpleasantly demanding passengers are willing to spend any amount of money to catch a fish of prize-winning size, and have no concern for honest reporting. According to the rules, the catch must have been played and landed, start to finish, by the fisherman who claims victory. Captain Bill, however, helped and knows that Ernie does not qualify; he at first refuses to attest to Ernie and Cal's claim.

> "Ernie's right," Cal said . . . "this is our charter, we paid for it, it's our fish to do with what we like. When we get in there and this turns out to be some kind of record fish, then Ernie caught it, and he caught it alone. That's the end of it. This picture coming into focus?"

When Bill, whose reputation for honesty is at stake, refuses once again, the two men offer Mikey a bribe to keep silent, and Bill a triple fee and a promise to throw more business his way. Mikey, who loves and admires Bill, is shocked to hear Bill agree and rejects him. A reluctant truce occurs finally when Bill says, "'Believe it or not, Mikey, I was thirteen years old myself once. I believed something was either right or it was wrong, and there was no in-between.' Bill paused, then looked down and said, 'Well, there is an in-between, Mikey.'" Such themes were once unusual for children's literature.

True Believer, by Virginia Euwer Wolff, is concerned with another significant issue; this time it's "What should I believe?" When LaVaughn's childhood friend Jody returns to the neighborhood, her heart is "too loud for comfort and [her] brain not so level either." Sadly, Jody is not interested in her old friend LaVaughn but in a boy at school. LaVaughn's two best friends are attracted to the Jesus Club and try hard to recruit her, but when she hears that the people she knows and loves are "hell-bound," she resists, longing for the day when little girls "weren't troubled by what was a sin and what wasn't." Feeling like an outsider, she stops at a church near her job at Children's Hospital, and asks the minister about whom his church would exclude. "God doesn't turn anybody away, and neither do we," he says. LaVaughn is invited to a tutorial called Grammar Build-Up, meets kids like herself, and realizes she is a good student who might some day get to college. More comfortable with their view of religion, she is now not alone but part of a new and accepting group. "Religion must be for trusting. And trusting, what is that for? I figured it out: It helps you go on when you can't go on."

In recent years, situations and themes in stories for older readers have been changing. With today's society more open in its discussion of the many problems of growing up, recent novels have confronted subjects that were once taboo. Although there are boy-meets-girl romances, novels now explore the growth of sexuality and its effects. Stories for older children deal with impotence, premarital sex, pregnancy, forced marriage, and abortion. What has been called the perfect-parent syndrome has been broken. Books for young people show parents as imperfect and human—unreliable, perhaps, or alcoholic, or simply shallow. Other stories deal with such problems as death, divorce, drugs, and disease. These subjects attract readers partly because of their former taboo status, but also because these matters do concern today's youth.

Often these stories seem to have been written for the vast market that the pulp magazines once appealed to; often the quality of the writing seems comparable. Sometimes the young reader is carried along by sentimentality and coincidence; writing is drab in style and shallow in characterization; themes are didactic and oversimplified. However, some writers, like those just mentioned, deal with the issues of today with sensitivity and skill, writing about the problems that confront the young in ways that create suspenseful stories and make the reader care about the protagonist's problem. Style and characterization show skill and perception, while the themes show universal truths that arise from conflicts.

Take, for example, one story about a girl with a problem, *Deenie* by Judy Blume. Deenie has scoliosis and wears a back brace. While we do feel sorry for Deenie, she is so close to being a stereotyped adolescent—interested only in boys and beauty—that we soon find her uninteresting. One theme of the book, that even girls with back braces can find friends, seems didactic and unconvincing because we have little interest in or understanding of the flat protagonist.

Although two readers may have essentially the same experience of theme, their words to state the theme may be somewhat different. Look back again at *The Watsons Go to Birmingham:* the theme might be stated as "Life can be unjustly difficult for African Americans, but personal strength can remain and grow." Walter Dean Myers's story of the integration of an orphaned White girl into an all-Black baseball team might suggest a theme for *Me, Mop, and the Moondance Kid:* "There are no easy victories, but a strong ego can mask failures." The title of *Beware of Kissing Lizard Lips* by Phyllis Shalant may suggest humor only, but there is more. Too-tall Lizard Lips hates being ignored by the boys, Zach hates being small, and Nikki's Korean immigrant English arouses jeers: "Growing up is not easy." Natalie

Babbitt's lasting favorite *Tuck Everlasting* explores the idea of living forever and concludes: "Being forever young is not totally desirable." Bruce Brooks's story *What Hearts* explores the idea of faking feelings, his own about his pushy stepfather and his mother's about her second marriage. "It's best to be honest with oneself."

In keeping with our contemporary interest in the vast varieties of human lifestyles, mores, and traditions, many recent books are broadening our understanding to encompass life in other lands. An engrossing example is *Shabanu* by Suzanne Fisher Staples, who writes of a twelve-year-old girl living a nomadic life on the desert of Cholistan, Pakistan, in a culture far different from the West's. With Shabanu we see what it is to herd camels, to survive extreme drought and deadly sandstorms, to live in a close family structure knowing that at the age of thirteen a girl leaves her home and moves to the household of her husband, there very soon to produce sons. The father of girls struggles to accumulate sufficient wealth to provide the dowry necessary for a daughter's good marriage to an adolescent boy. Carefully breeding camels for their strength and ability to dance, moving from dry water hole to small stream, avoiding marauding clans, caring for the infirm elderly, and finding an appropriate burial spot are just some of the challenges Shabanu's story reveals. We follow the growth of her pet, an orphaned camel, and note that the animal's difficulty in fitting into a new life is similar to what faces Shabanu. Although in our own society one is still a child at the age of twelve, in Shabanu's culture one must struggle at a tender age to be grown, to leave home and family for a new identity.

Today's themes often involve cross-cultural change. Gary Soto's story *The Skirt* is about a Mexican girl who, on moving to the United States, wants to retain the tradition of Mexican dances, *folklorico*, for the school recital. She is given a new and vivid skirt to replace her mother's old and now drab one, but the dance must still be traditional. "Moving to another country does not necessitate leaving all tradition behind." But when she proudly takes the skirt to school, she forgets it on the bus. Her adventures in recovering it from the bus are the story, but the theme concerns the pride one feels in one's heritage.

Current stories often deal with realistic problems. They can show us real characters; they can explore the problems of today's youth. However, what is true for other literature seems to be true here, as well: When we believe in the character, we believe in the experience, and are then prepared to accept the theme. When, however, theme seems to have been the first motive for writing—"Now I'll write a story about the evils of smoking pot"—the stories may become didactic, as does *The Grass Pipe*. If we look beneath the surface of many realistic stories for young people, we find didacticism and sentimentality. The well-written stories, however, will convince us of the truth of the theme and thus contribute to the reader's growth and discovery. Mature themes can be explored in children's literature; they contribute to understanding when they meet the requirements of excellence.

When we believe in the character, we believe in the experience and can accept the theme.

Summary

Theme, stated explicitly or implicitly, is essential to a children's story if it is to merit the name of literature. A narrative with action and people but without theme is a story without meaning that leaves the reader wondering at the close, "So what?" A piece of writing—a collection of words with plot, character, setting, style, and meaning (without preaching)—is literature for children just as it is for adults. The theme we take to become part of ourselves is the one that enlarges our understanding and the one we ourselves discover, not the one delivered didactically by the author. "Look for truth, not for reality," says playwright Brian Dykstra. "Want reality? Ride the subway."

Notes

1. Social historian Stephanie Coontz comments on such themes in *The Way We Never Were: American Families and the Nostalgia Trip* (New York: Basic Books, 1992).
2. Wayne Booth makes this comment in *The Rhetoric of Fiction* (Chicago: University of Chicago Press, 1961), p. 136.
3. Booth, *The Rhetoric of Fiction*, p. 126. The satisfaction of knowing causality in children's literature is most obviously demonstrated in cumulative tales like the humorous "Old Woman and the Pig" or the verse story "This Is the House That Jack Built."
4. Jack Zipes, in *Fairy Tales and the Art of Subversion* (London: Heineman Educational Books, 1983), discusses the tales of Grimm and Andersen. The former shows girls and women their subordinate roles; the latter, though commonly thought to show a triumph over misfortune by the poor and lowly, actually admires the hierarchy.
5. *I Want to Be a Homemaker* by Carla Greene (New York: Children's Press, 1961) is shelved in many libraries among picture books as JE or Juvenile. Commenting on the book here calls to mind the difference between real stories and instructive narrative. Others in the series of fifty-four books describe jobs; *I Want to Be a Homemaker* seems to describe a role.
6. See "The Shape of Things to Come" in James Gunn's *Alternate Worlds: The Illustrated History of Science Fiction* (Englewood Cliffs, NJ: Prentice-Hall, 1975), pp. 225–239.

Recommended Books Cited in This Chapter

ALCOTT, LOUISA MAY. *Little Women.* 1868–1869. Reprint. New York: Dutton, 1948.

ANDERSEN, HANS CHRISTIAN. "The Ugly Duckling," "The Swineherd," "The Nightingale," "The Princess and the Pea," and "The Tinderbox." In *The Twelve Dancing Princesses,* ed. Alfred David and Mary Elizabeth Meek. Bloomington: Indiana University Press, 1974.

AVI. *Crispin: The Cross of Lead.* New York: Hyperion, 2002.

BABBITT, NATALIE. *Tuck Everlasting.* New York: Farrar, Straus & Giroux, 1975.

BROOKS, BRUCE. *What Hearts.* New York: HarperCollins, 1992.

CARROLL, LEWIS. *Alice's Adventures in Wonderland.* 1865. Reprint. New York: Macmillan, 1963.

CHESTESEN, BARBARA. *The Myths of the Orient.* Shaker Heights, OH: Raintree, 1977.

COLLIER, JAMES LINCOLN, and CHRISTOPHER COLLIER. *Jump Ship to Freedom.* New York: Delacorte, 1981.

CURTIS, CHRISTOPHER. *The Watsons Go to Birmingham.* New York: Delacorte, 1963.

CUSHMAN, KAREN. *The Midwife's Apprentice.* New York: Houghton Mifflin, 1995.

HALEY, GAIL. *A Story, A Story.* New York: Atheneum, 1970.

HAMILTON, VIRGINIA. *Cousins.* New York: Putnam, 1990.

HOOKS, WILLIAM H. *Circle of Fire.* New York: Macmillan, 1982.

HURWITZ, JOHANNA. *Class President.* New York: Morrow, 1990.

JONES, JENNIFER BERRY. *Heetunka's Harvest.* Niwot, CO: Roberts Rinehart, 1994.

KIPLING, RUDYARD. *The Just So Stories.* 1902. Reprint. Garden City, NY: Doubleday, 1986.

LE GUIN, URSULA K. *A Wizard of Earthsea.* Berkeley, CA: Parnassus, 1968.

LINDGREN, ASTRID. *Pippi Longstocking.* New York: Viking, 1950.

LOTTRIDGE, CELIA BARKER. *The Name of the Tree.* New York: Macmillan, 1990.

MacLACHLAN, PATRICIA. *Journey.* New York: Doubleday, 1991.

MILNE, A. A. *Winnie-the-Pooh.* New York: Dutton, 1926.

MYERS, WALTER DEAN. *Me, Mop and the Moondance Kid.* New York: Doubleday, 1988.

NORTON, MARY. *The Borrowers.* New York: Harcourt, 1965.

PATERSON, KATHERINE. *The Smallest Cow in the World.* New York: HarperCollins, 1991.

PORTE, BARBARA ANN. *Harry's Mom.* New York: Greenwillow, 1985.

POTTER, BEATRIX. *The Tale of Peter Rabbit.* London: Warne, 1902.

RINALDI, ANN. *A Ride into Morning: The Story of Tempe Wick.* New York: Harbrace, 1991.

ROTH, SUSAN L. *Fire Came to the Earth People.* New York: St. Martin's, 1982.

SALISBURY, GRAHAM. *Lord of the Deep.* New York: Delacorte, 2001.

SHALANT, PHYLLIS. *Beware of Kissing Lizard Lips.* New York: Dutton, 1995.

SOTO, GARY. *The Skirt.* Illustrated by Eric Velasquez. New York: Delacorte, 1992.

STAPLES, SUZANNE FISHER. *Shabanu.* New York: Knopf, 1989.

TAYLOR, MILDRED. *Roll of Thunder, Hear My Cry.* New York: Dial, 1976.

THOMAS, JANE FRESH. *The Princess in the Pigpen.* Boston: Houghton Mifflin, 1989.

WHITE, E. B. *Charlotte's Web.* New York: Harper, 1952.

WHITE, RUTH. *Belle Pater's Boy.* Putney, VT: Threshold Books, 1996.

WOLFF, VIRGINIA EUWER. *True Believer.* New York: Atheneum, 2001.

WOODSON, JACQUELINE. *Miracle's Boys.* New York: Putnam, 2004.

Binya's Blue Umbrella

Ruskin Bond

Illustrated by Vera Rosenberry

Setting

Does setting have to be important?
Change the setting and see.
What happens to the story?

Both depiction of character and working out of plot and theme occur in time and place. These latter elements are called **setting.** In an adult novel, action may occur anywhere, even in the mind of the protagonist, and may need little delineation of place or time. However, the story for children usually occurs in a time and place described in some detail.

The possibilities for setting are endless. It is possible to write of a time when humans lived in caves, or of a time when they may live on Mars. As for settings in place, from cave to Mars, the spread is equally broad. When we consider all the times and places known to us, and add to them all those we are capable of imagining, there is no limit to possibilities. Sometimes the writer wishes to make setting very clear, because the story depends on understanding and envisioning the particular setting. At other times, the writer deliberately refrains from closely examining and describing setting. Making the setting a specific time and place, for example, might limit the universality of conflict, characters, or ideas the writer is exploring. It is the writer who determines the nature of the story, and thereby determines the setting.

Sometimes it is important to know the physical description of the setting, the details of what is present, how it all looks, smells, feels, and sounds. These relevant details will directly influence character, conflict, and theme. Such details at other times—kinds of sounds and smells, kinds of buildings, quality of light and climate—may create the mood of the time and place and so create the atmosphere for the characters and the conflict.

Sometimes understanding a story depends on awareness of setting.

149

In *A Corner of the Universe* by Ann M. Martin, a small town, a boarding house, and a traveling carnival and its freak show are the setting. Hattie Owen is happy just to stay at home in a familiar world interrupted only by the traveling carnival with a few actual freaks ("How else are they going to support themselves?, she asks.") and others who merely pretend to be freaks. Into this world comes an uncle, a young man, never mentioned by her parents or grandparents, who is mentally ill. Uncle Adam's behavior is unpredictable, sometimes laughable, sometimes frightening, but nonetheless happy and loving. "Adam's moods are like a deck of playing cards with someone riffling through them—dozens of cards, one after the other in a blur." The boarders, each one odd in his or her own way, comfortably accept Adam's strange behavior. "Most of the performers in the sideshow are putting on an act, the ones who have learned how to do tricks or to wear special makeup and costumes. . . . People stare at them because of the way they were born." The small town, however, has its insensitive citizens who call Uncle Adam a freak. Finally being called "a freak" is more than Adam can take. Here setting has a strong impact on a theme that suggests acceptance of everyone, each one a "corner of the universe."

Types of Settings

In any piece of literature, whether for child or adult, there are essentially two types of setting: (1) the **backdrop,** or relatively unimportant setting, and (2) the **integral,** or essential setting.

The importance of setting—whether it is integral or backdrop—depends on the writer's purpose. For example, in a story of internal conflict, the first-person narrator may tell the progress of the plot in narrative, dialogue, action, or diary form. The reader may not need to know where or when the character lives, since understanding depends on interest in character and in the character's internal conflict as the narrator reveals the inner tension. Time and place are merely a backdrop. This kind of setting contrasts sharply with the significant integral setting in a nonfiction book such as *Anne Frank: The Diary of a Young Girl.* Although this autobiographical account, too, has internal conflict, where and when the action occurs are essential information if we are to understand conflict and character. In fact, setting working on character is the essence of conflict in this book.

The writer makes the setting clear in descriptions. Each reader may have a personal catalogue of mentally pictured settings—a beach, a farm, or a cabin—but the writer does not depend on the reader's experience or recollection of settings. If the writer wants to make the setting integral to a story, the writer must describe it in concrete details, relying on sensory pictures and vivid comparisons to make the setting so clear that the reader understands how this story is closely related to this particular place.

By contrast, if the unskilled writer insists that setting is significant, and

> Setting may influence character, conflict, and theme.

yet creates a setting superficial in concept and shallow in depiction, the reader may then reject all of the story's reality, from character through action and unifying idea. A one-dimensional setting cannot be convincingly integral, and therefore little that happens seems believable.

The title *Willie Goes to the Seashore* suggests that the setting is an integral part of the action; the seashore must be so interesting that Willie will have an exciting time. The actual case is quite different. The little cottage and the sandy beach are the setting. Willie, moving in quick succession from one to another of the activities one expects at the shore, seems to move *over* the setting rather than *in* it, finding neither conflict nor involvement in any of the activities the setting suggests. Setting does not come alive to involve character in plot. So what is exciting about a seashore? Why would Willie want to live there all the time? The setting has failed as an integral part of the story, since it does not influence character, conflict, or idea.

Integral Setting

A story has an **integral setting** when action, character, or theme are influenced by the time and place, since, as writer Eudora Welty says, setting has "the most delicate control over character . . . by confining character, it defines it."[1] These characters, given these circumstances, in this time and place, behave in this way.

Chapter 1 of Patricia MacLachlan's *Sarah, Plain and Tall* immediately draws the reader into the integral setting. Caleb sits close to the fire, the dogs "beside him on the warm hearthstones"—a pioneer home, apparently. Anna looks out the window to the prairie that reaches out and touches "the places where the sky came down. Though winter was nearly over, there were patches of snow and ice everywhere." A dirt road "crawls" across the plains, and there are "fields and grass and sky and not much else." The wind seems to blow Papa into the house. When Sarah comes in answer to Papa's ad for a wife, the family is relieved to find that she enjoys farm life, even climbing up the ladder on "the mound of hay for bedding, nearly half as tall as the barn, covered with canvas to keep the rain from rotting it." Because the issue is whether Sarah, who loves the dunes and sea of Maine, can be happy as a prairie wife and mother, we must see her involved with and enjoying the prairie farm. The setting is integral.

Knowing the nature of the river in which Tony dares Joel to swim is essential to plot and theme in *On My Honor* by Marion Dane Bauer. The red-brown water is "slithering" under the bridge. Chemicals and sewage are not visible, but Joel knows they are there. Although the water flows past like "a refreshing massage," Joel doesn't want to put his face in it; "the river smelled of decaying fish," the current dividing in a sharp V at the boys' waists. Here is not only pollution but also a threat of strong current to an inexperienced swimmer like Tony.

"Setting by confining character, defines it."
Eudora Welty

Brian, the protagonist in *Hatchet* by Gary Paulsen, is the sole survivor of the crash of a single-engine plane in Alaska; his only survival tool is his hatchet. To believe in his struggle with isolation in the rugged surroundings he must make habitable, we must see the setting clearly. A stone ridge near the lake that the plane has crashed into yields a cavelike shelter:

> At one time in the far past it had been scooped by something, probably a glacier, and this scooping had left a kind of sideways bowl, back in under a ledge. It wasn't very deep, not a cave, but it was smooth and made a perfect roof and he could almost stand in under the ledge. . . . Some of the rock . . . had . . . been pulverized by the glacial action, turned into sand, and now made a small sand beach that went down to the edge of the water in front.

Here, once he can build a fire, Brian finds protection from the black flies and mosquitoes that blanket his body.

Setting is also clearly shown in Bruce Brooks's *Everywhere,* the story of a White boy who with his Black friend Dooley tries "soul switching." The narrator is afraid his grandfather is dying, but Dooley has a secret method of being sure that it doesn't happen. Find an animal that has some resemblance to grandfather and at the moment when it seems the sick man's soul is about to leave his body, substitute that of the animal—in this case a turtle. As he fearfully awaits some indication that his grandfather is dying, the narrator has a heightened awareness of everything around him. His description of each detail is significant, particularly because he regrets never having shown his grandfather this hideaway:

> I followed [Dooley] out the gate and down the alley. It was paved with crushed coke, which crunched beneath our sneakers. When we reached the edge of the field past the old dairy building, I touched him on the elbow and angled off across it. He followed. . . . Pretty soon we came to some persimmon trees, and I cut through them to the path I had made myself over the previous four or five summers, and we wound downward through denser woods that started to thicken with cedars and pines.

Backdrop Setting

Backdrop settings may also have symbolic meaning.

The term **backdrop setting** comes from the theater. For example, some of the action in scenes from Shakespeare and from many musicals takes place on the stage before a featureless curtain, or before a flat, painted scene of an unidentified street or forest. Soliloquy, dialogue, action, or character confrontation concerns us; where the characters are positioned matters, but less than seeing and hearing them, and following them in the developing conflict. Yet, while the street or forest is unidentified, it may have importance. It may have some subtle meaning that suggests the forest as a place of physical or spiritual darkness, and the busy street as a reminder of society.

A clear example of a children's story with backdrop setting is *Winnie-the-Pooh.* A. A. Milne's Christopher Robin might live anywhere at all—from

England's Land's End to Lancashire, or from the United States' Bangor to Sacramento. Action occurs on the bank of a stream, or by a big oak tree with a honeybee hive. While time and place are not specific, they may suggest something about the action or characters when Pooh, Eeyore, Rabbit, and his assorted friends-and-relations set off on an "Expotition" to the North Pole. The Forest—with a capital *F*—is of course the proper place for Pooh and Piglet to track the fearful Woozle/Wizzle, but there is minimal description of the beech tree beyond its being in the middle of the Forest. It is the tension among the characters that matters and dominates.

In *Winnie*, setting is generalized and universal; its vividness exists in our minds merely as the place where the interesting action occurs. We do not know, for example, what Rabbit's house looks like; what matters is the memorable view of Pooh's legs serving as towel racks. Although time and place have importance, they do not influence the character and plot in the same ways that an integral setting does.

In backdrop settings, time and place do not necessarily influence action or character.

Setting in *Charlotte's Web*

Our touchstone, *Charlotte's Web*,[2] is an excellent example of integral setting literally described. This story could have occurred nowhere but on a farm, in fact only on a farm that has the traditional farm animals. This is not a sprawling ranch or a grain-growing industry, because such farms have concerns other than pigs and their barnyard friends. The Arable farm is near a country road, since Fern catches the school bus at her front door. There is a brook for playing in, with wonderfully oozy, sticky mud. This farm has a dump—or how could Templeton find essential words for the web? It has meadows that show seasonal changes, maples that redden with anxiety, and a big pasture that frightens a timid piglet. This farm, with an orchard where apples fall and the gander's family feasts, is no generalized farm; there is no other farm quite like it, where fog and rain, crickets and song sparrow are all parts of the place, the setting. However, most important of all, this farm has a barn that houses a variety of animals—or how could sheep, pigs, and geese become acquainted, advising, consoling, and taunting one another? White shows the Zuckerman barn as soon as Wilbur sees it. The reader, too, knows its smells, its sights, and its warmth:

> The barn was very large. It was very old. It smelled of hay and it smelled of manure. It smelled of the perspiration of tired horses and the wonderful sweet breath of patient cows. It often had a sort of peaceful smell—as though nothing bad could happen ever again in the world. It smelled of grain and of harness dressing and of axle grease and of rubber boots and of new rope. And whenever the cat was given a fish-head to eat, the barn would smell of fish. But mostly it smelled of hay, for there was always hay in the great loft overhead. And there was always hay being pitched down to the cows and the horses and the sheep.

No one could confuse this setting with any generalized backdrop, since each item in the description shows the singularity of this setting, home of Wilbur, Charlotte, and Templeton. We know this place as well as Wilbur does, and because its description is so vivid, we are alerted to its importance in the total story. To know the exciting Fairgrounds, we must:

> . . . hear music and see the Ferris wheel turning in the sky . . . smell the dust of the race track where the sprinkling car had moistened it . . . smell hamburgers frying and see balloons aloft . . . hear sheep blatting in their pens.

At night the lighted Ferris wheel revolves in the sky, the gambling machines crackle, the merry-go-round makes music, and a voice calls numbers from the beano booth. In the morning we hear sparrows stirring, roosters crowing, cows rattling chains, and cars whispering on the roadway.

The Fair is an essential part of the story, and it is therefore necessary that the reader see, hear, smell, and even touch and taste it. Wilbur's character is fully revealed at the Fair, where, experiencing threatened failure and final success, he remains humble but radiant. Wilbur's conflict, furthermore, cannot be resolved without the Fair. Wilbur must have time to grow, and then must prove himself worthy of being saved; the fall Fair is a traditional proving time for farm animals. Charlotte's efforts to prolong Wilbur's life produce no certainty of success until the Fair—he wins the prize for attracting so many visitors.

White must also show temporal change, since character growth and conflict, as well as several of the story's thematic discoveries, depend on the passing of time. White must make us see the seasons as they exist, merge, and change. As we hear, see, and smell, we are aware of time passing, and of weather and landscape changing.

In Charlotte's Web the passing of a full year makes clear both outcome and theme.

Spring is the time for pigs to be born; rain drips from the eaves, runs crookedly through the pigweed, and gushes from the rainspouts. Summer is everyone's holiday; lilacs are blooming, bees are dropping in on the apple blossoms, and horses are pulling the noisy mower. Birds sing and nest. However, since summer cannot last forever, the crickets' song prepares us for fall and the important Fair time. Uneasy sheep break out of their pasture, and the gander's family invades the orchard. Although little of the story's action occurs in winter, even winter is not slighted. The pasture is frozen, the cows are standing in the sun beside the straw pile, the sheep are eating snow, and the geese are just hanging about. Then, to complete the year's cycle and to prove that Wilbur has survived butchering time and that Charlotte's eggs have hatched, White returns to spring and its strengthening light, new lambs, nine goose eggs, and Charlotte's old web floating away.

The time element is important here. As the year passes, Wilbur matures from panicky child to responsible adult. In the passing of a full year we know that his victory over society is complete. We have had time to see the truth of such themes as the growth of friendship and of maturity, and the inevitability and acceptance of death. The integral setting has helped to make all this clear.

Functions of Setting

Setting That Clarifies Conflict

As *Charlotte's Web* demonstrates, an integral setting plays an important part in conflict. Time setting for a story can be any time, past, present, or future. Attitudes toward African Americans that Turner finds when he moves to a small town in Maine are made clear when Gary Schmidt describes the setting of *Lizzie Bright and the Buckminster Boy*. Turner finds life in a small town quite different from that in Boston; one of those differences becomes clear in the description of setting. Lizzie, Turner's African American friend, lives on a rocky island so wild it looks uninhabitable. Self-righteous and greedy towns-people wish to destroy the community and turn the island into a money-making resort. The writer's description of the rugged island clarifies both its natural beauty and the town's wish to exclude the inhabitants from their lives.

> Turner felt as if he was on the brink of a discovery. Ahead of him, the beach was covered with stones, their hard outsides rubbed off and smoothed so that they glowed as the waves gathered them up and down. The granite ledges were streaked by a thousand shades of gray and silver, separated by slices of pink quartz that glowed like happiness. . . . The pines threw their roots around the shore's boulders, grappling with the living rocks and wrestling them into position. And out of those rocks they thrust themselves into the air as if they might scratch the blue dome of heaven.

Historical fiction has a responsibility to show how environment affects action. For example, turn to the austere Puritan New England setting of *The Witch of Blackbird Pond* into which Kit Tyler is transported from her West Indies birthplace. Author Elizabeth Speare does not rely merely on our history-book knowledge of that time and place when witchcraft was feared; she clarifies setting by her description of the austerity of life among the Puritans: the house with hand-rubbed copper, indicative of hard work; the heavy, fortresslike door; the dim little mirror; and the severe wooden bench. Speare weaves description of the house itself into a description of Kit's tasks in a typical day. Meat must be chopped, vegetables prepared, and the pewter mugs polished with fine sand and reeds. Throughout the day Kit stirs the kettle of boiling soap with a stick, the heavy stirring tiring her muscles. Even the easiest task, making corn pudding, keeps her leaning over the smoky fire that burns her watering eyes. Walking through the little town to church with Kit, we see severity in the straight, cold lines of functional buildings with punitive devices. The unpainted Meeting House, the whipping post, the pillory, and the stocks are frightening evidence that Kit is now in a rigid and

Setting in historical fiction is very important.

uncompromising environment, one for which her carefree Barbados upbringing has not prepared her.

Gary Paulsen is in top form when he writes of struggles to survive in the wilderness. His stories about Tucket take place in the West, in midcentury. *Tucket's Ride* is the story of Francis and his adopted family as they move West in search of his own family. Captured by Comancheros, outlaws who trade with the Native American Comanches, they ride without stopping to eat or sleep, ruthlessly driving horses and children. Fear that Francis and his family will be sold provides tension enough, but the desolate setting heightens their anxiety.

> All day they rode, stopping only once to loosen and retighten cinches, to take a sip of water and a bit of jerky. All day and into the night they kept riding. . . . Finally, out in the flats of the prairie, they came upon a cut, a wide canyon that didn't show until they were almost on top of it.
>   The leader led them down a winding trail wide enough for one horse along the canyon wall. Far below Francis could see a group of small shacks in a stand of cottonwoods—little more than brush huts covered with skins—and a winding stream. . . . He could make out a fairly large herd of horses. . . . Some wagons were parked near the shacks. As they dropped down the canyon wall, Francis could hear dogs barking.

Rosemary Sutcliff, writer of historical fiction, takes great care that we see the wilderness of Britain in 600 C.E., the setting for *The Shining Company*. Here is the hunt for the white hart:

> I was running, running, as it seemed, the heart out of my breast . . . branches snatching at me, roots clawing at my feet, and always ahead of me the music of the hounds. By and by the land began to lift under us, and the trees thinned and fell back, the crowding damp oaks giving place to birch as we drew up towards the open surge of the great hills, and the sky opened to us, turning wide and shining.

We see the slave/master relationship of the times in the exchange between body-servant Conn and Prosper; Conn asks if he might learn from the smithy how to forge weapons, but Prosper explains that once he learned a trade he would become free. Even such details as how the lord Gerontius shaved are helpful in assuring us that we are living vicariously in a time long ago.

> My father was sitting in the high chair with the lion feet, rubbing his chin with a lump of pumice stone. . . . My father still went clean-shaven in the Roman way, with razor and goose grease when need be, with pumice when the traders brought any.

Historical fiction can make the past come alive, make it become reality so that the reader can live vicariously in another time. One of the shames of twentieth-century U.S. history is the incarceration of Japanese Americans in camps during World War II—an event in history that, like slavery, most citizens would like to forget. Although Japanese immigrants had lived for many years in the United States, the bombing of Pearl Harbor awakened suspicions about their loyalty. *Journey to Topaz* by Hoshiko Uchida shows the educated and assimilated Sukanes, and it is shocking to read how the family of four is divided, forced to live in a horse stall for a time, then shipped off to the Topaz camp in Utah. The parents' sorrow and the children's anger are understandable. The camp is "white powdery dust, covering everyone in a smothering blanket . . . flour-dusted cookies that had escaped from a bakery":

> There wasn't a single tree or a blade of grass to break the monotony of the sun-bleached desert. It was like the carcass of a chicken stripped clean of any meat and left all dry, brittle bone. . . . They sank into [the road] with each step as though they were plowing through a snow bank.

Regional literature, too, must show how time and place affect story. Sometimes a mode of living or of making a living help clarify the story's conflict. In such a case the setting may be integral.

Time, particularly in fantasy, has a way of lengthening or shortening, depending on the make-believe world the writer creates. Time is relative: when we're entertained, time goes quickly; when we're bored, time drags endlessly. But the writer of fantasy takes other liberties with time, perhaps by making one event, or one life, last through centuries or be over in seconds.

In fantasy time may take any form.

Setting as Antagonist

Sometimes setting itself is the antagonist, as it is for Sheila Burnford's *The Incredible Journey*. An essential part of the story, the Canadian wilderness, is not only setting but antagonist. Without clear descriptions of the dense brush, forest land, and wilderness river, such a novel would have no believable conflict to hold the reader. However, on the opening page of the novel, Burnford prepares the reader for the conflict; the rugged country of northwestern Ontario is introduced, and the description continues for a page and a half:

> [A] vast area of deeply wooded wilderness—of endless chains of lonely lakes and rushing rivers. Thousands of miles of country roads, rough timberlanes, overgrown tracks leading to abandoned mines, and unmapped trails snake across its length and breadth. It is a country of far-flung, lonely farms and a few widely scattered small towns and villages, of lonely trappers' shacks and logging camps.

In *The Talking Earth*, nature is the antagonist that Jean George describes effectively, the natural setting she knows so well. Billie Wind fights fire in Lake Okeechobee, where, in the searing heat, she sees snakes and restless alligators zigzagging just below the water's surface:

> [S]he was struck by a blast of hot air, more searing than the one she had felt in the boat. It smelled of burning grass. And then she knew, she knew why the animals ran and why the island seemed to rise.

> . . . Now she could see flames through the trees. Running to the shore,
> she pushed back the limbs and looked out. Orange blazes licked the sky like
> serpents' tongues. They shot downward and devoured the grass. They spat black
> smoke as the many-tongued beast came rushing toward Billie Wind.

Were she not so schooled in the survival tactics of her Seminole heritage, Billie Wind would not survive, but even so, the setting seems heavily weighted against her.

The setting of *Tituba of Salem Village* by Ann Petry makes clear Tituba's position in her new New England home. Sold from Barbados, where life was easy and pleasant, where she could bathe each morning in the ocean, where she might see through the window the bay as an extension of the kitchen, and where breezes but no chill winds blew, Tituba meets nothing but the bitter winter and wind of New England; the bareness of trees and shrubs makes her fear they are all dead. The contrast of benign nature in the islands and the rigorous and rigidly controlled life as a slave in the austere Reverend Parris's tiny house prepares us for the conflict. The natural way of life in which Tituba had collected healing herbs for her mistress contrasts with the suspicions surrounding healing by a Black woman. As a singular woman in Puritan society, she is suspect because of her color, and suspicions increase because of her skills at spinning, weaving, and healing.

Setting That Illuminates Character

In many examples, setting influences character. Notice the effect of isolation and crowding on the protagonist's fear in that unusual autobiography *Anne Frank: The Diary of a Young Girl*. We must see the stiflingly cramped atmosphere of the Secret Annexe or we cannot experience the yearning for freedom and privacy that Anne expresses during the twenty-five months of the family's hiding from the Nazi soldiers who are rounding up Jews for imprisonment. We must see Anne's surroundings as we follow her tensions with her parents and fellow prisoners, her awakening sense of self, and her curiosity about growing up. Just two days after the family crowds into the Annexe, Anne writes as though it is an adventure:

Setting affects character.

> Our little room looked very bare at first with nothing on the walls; but thanks to
> Daddy who had brought my filmstar collection and picture postcards on before-
> hand, and with the aid of paste pot and brush, I have transformed the walls into
> one gigantic picture. This makes it look more cheerful, and, when the Van Daans
> come, we'll get some wood from the attic, and make a few little cupboards for the
> walls and other odds and ends to make it look more lively.

But thirteen months later, we have another picture, this time of the efforts necessary when bedtime approaches:

> *Nine o-clock in the evening.* The bustle of going to bed in the "Secret Annexe"
> begins. . . . Chairs are shoved about, beds are pulled down, blankets unfolded,
> nothing remains where it is during the day. I sleep on the little divan . . . chairs

have to be used to lengthen it. A quilt, sheets, pillows, blankets, are all fetched from Dussel's bed where they remain during the day . . . creaking in the next room: Margot's concertina-bed being pulled out! Again, divan, blankets, and pillows, everything is done to make the wooden slats a bit more comfortable. It sounds like thunder above, but it is only Mrs. Van Daan's bed . . . shifted to the window.

The setting becomes overwhelming in its effect on every aspect of the characters' lives. Bickering, quarrels, arguments, and rages result from the pressures of close confinement.

Confinement in one room for two years, with extremely rare opportunities to walk outside, surely has impact on a character. That is also the case in Johanna Reiss's *The Upstairs Room,* the autobiographical account of the author's life during the Holocaust. Annie at first does not understand and is resentful that she cannot go to school, to the shops, or outside to play. As her confinement continues in the home of a Dutch farm family, she grows in understanding, but at the age of eleven is still resentful. She does not realize the life-and-death danger to her host family should she and her sister Sisi be found, nor does she see why twenty-year-old Sisi has more privileges than she does. Her resentment and frustration are like those of most children and are therefore believable.

The setting for *Al Capone Does My Shirts* by Gennifer Choldenko is Alcatraz Island where Moose lives because his mother said he had to. Moose's father is working two jobs to enable sister Natalie to attend an expensive school for autistic children. Staff must live on the penal island where the notorious gangster Al Capone is imprisoned. When Moose leaves his small house for a tour, the first thing he sees is the guard tower; from there he goes to the morgue, "a little cottage." "The dock smells like sardines and it's pretty deserted unless you count the birds." The chief warden of Alcatraz, however, lives differently from other employees and certainly from the prisoners.

> Across the road from the cell house is a fancy mansion with flowerpots on the steps and curtains in the windows. . . . That's the only tip that this is Alcatraz. There's nothing but cement clear up to the door. Even so, it's strange how one side of the road is so different from the other—high society on the left, grim and grisly on the right.

The differences in the two areas serve as a figurative device, contrasting the elegant home of the warden to the ugly environment of criminals. Moose's distrust of the warden's daughter Piper from "high society" is legitimate; privileged though she is, she instigates an illegal scheme, advertising at school that the prisoners will do laundry for a fee. She collects the kids' laundry, and pockets their fees. Setting and character are closely connected.

The title alone, *Olive's Ocean,* says that setting is important to the story. In Kevin Henke's story Martha learns that Olive, who has just been killed in an accident, admired her and that like Martha she wanted to be a writer who wrote about the sea. During her dreamy summer vacation by the sea, Martha, thinking about Olive, writes of loving the sea, the sand, the waves, and the rocks. This summer's experience is also the first thrill of liking a boy. Picnics on the shore, hand-holding walks, sharing secrets and memories, building a sand castle together, seem to be the stuff from which romance is made. But when Jimmy ruthlessly wrecks the castle, that action seems metaphorically the destruction of their closeness; his kiss captured on tape is merely a response to a challenge. As Martha sits close beside Jimmy on the couch, she hears a voice. "'The world is not what you think it is,' a voice repeated. Martha guessed it was Jimmy's voice, altered somehow, making him sound mechanical, roboticized." Setting helps to reveal character.

Setting and Mood

Setting, too, can be sentimentalized.

As several of the preceding examples demonstrate, setting affects mood. Setting is sometimes sentimentalized, as it is in Frances Hodgson Burnett's *The Secret Garden:*

> On that first morning when the sky was blue again, Mary wakened very early. The sun was pouring in slanting rays through the blinds and there was something so joyous in the sight of it that.
> . . . She clasped her hands for pure joy and looked up in the sky, and it was so blue and pink and pearly and white and flooded with springtime light that she felt as if she must flute and sing aloud herself, and knew that thrushes and robins and skylarks could not possibly help it.
> . . . And the secret garden bloomed and bloomed and every morning revealed new miracles. In the robin's nest there were eggs and the robin's mate sat upon them, keeping them warm with her feathery little breast and careful wings.

In the early pages of *Shadow in Hawthorn Bay,* Janet Lunn shows the benign Scottish setting of Mary's childhood: the brilliant sky, a pasture blazing gold, small lakes ringed with new green, cows grazing on the ridges, hills rising and falling, and fields in flower. After her emigration to join her cousin, Mary's habitat changes to the wilds of Canada. "She [heard] the sounds of the woods at night as though she had just wakened from a sleep—wolves howling nearby, owls hooting, frogs croaking, other unfamiliar cries and calls, and all around her rustlings and gruntings in the underbrush." Everything is strange to Mary, the trees, the woodland streams, the land contours, the animals, even the healing plants growing in marshes rather than on the hilly slopes. To Mary their strangeness is ominous, haunting, and until she feels at home in the north woods, she feels like an unsettled stranger.

Epic style is grand, vivid, and resonant, and setting is pictured in elevated language.

Epic style is grand style, vivid and resonant; and setting—like character and action—can be pictured in elevated language. In keeping with the heroic subject, the setting of Ian Serraillier's retelling of *Beowulf the Warrior* also has solemn majesty; its description produces a mood of great dignity. Serraillier sketches the setting briefly with phrases that ring with grandeur. Book One begins with a description of the vast and splendid hall Heorot, scene of Grendel's monstrous deeds and of Beowulf's selfless struggle:

Hrothgar, King of the Danes, glorious in battle
Built him a huge hall—its gleaming roof
Towering high to heaven—strong to withstand
The buffet of war . . .
The long hall . . .
The floor paved with stone, the roof high-raftered.

As Beowulf battles with Grendel in a struggle of awesome violence, this huge hall shudders. The struggle is greater, and therefore the victory is greater, because of the mood created by the splendor of setting.

In Avi's *Shadrach's Crossing* the author maintains mystery by picturing the island's rugged wildness, its isolation and inaccessibility:

Lucker's Island . . . was only a mile and a half at its widest. . . . The middle of the island consisted of rolling, sandy dunes, with low, wind-cut scrub pine bushes and patches of coarse grass. Here and there were piles of stones, and at the southern end, stretches of pebbles. But mostly it was sand. . . . During the last hurricane . . . [h]ouses had been blown flat, as though pressed by hands.

The vacant house where Shad meets his friend Davey, a place abandoned the year before, is the most private place for conferring: "Old wallpaper curled from walls. Floorboards had begun to twist and lift. . . . The front room, as if it were the bottom of an hourglass, had started to fill with sand." To find help in catching the smugglers, Shad and his younger brother Brian try to cross the marsh to the mainland:

Very quickly, the water reached over Shad's ankles. The black bottom became so stirred up that when he looked down he couldn't see his toes. Once, twice, he suddenly sank into a hole of black ooze. But for the most part the bottom held firm. . . . The water was almost up to his waist. Underfoot, the bottom was becoming thicker, softer. . . . But there was no other way to go. No matter which way they turned, they sank into soft, sucking mud. . . . The clutching mud made each step an effort. In the time it had taken to cover ten feet before, Shad could only move three.

In some cases, there is minimal text to evoke setting, but the pictures help to make it clear. *Where the Wild Things Are* and *Peter Rabbit* are notable examples.

Setting as Symbol

Symbols may operate in setting as they may in other elements of literature. A **symbol** is a person, object, situation, or action that operates on two levels of meaning, the literal and the figurative or suggestive. Once aware of the existence of symbols, it is easy to run wild, to read into stories all sorts of fanciful overtones not legitimately supported by the story. What seems important here is that only fairly obvious symbols will be understood by most children.

In some of the simplest of symbolic settings, forest is both a literal setting and a symbol for the unknown; the garden is both a literal setting and a sym-

A symbol operates on two levels of meaning.

bol of natural but cultivated beauty; sunlight may symbolize goodness, while darkness is evil. In this way some of the settings in folktales have symbolic meanings. Hansel and Gretel, as well as Snow White, are lost in the fearful and unknown—the forest. The forest is also the domain of ogres and giants, mysteriously frightening creatures. Despite their backdrop qualities, these symbolic settings often set the mood in traditional tales.

Symbols may be combined to create **allegory,** as they are in some stories for children. According to Northrop Frye, allegory translates into images.[3] To be a true symbol, the object must be emphasized or repeated, and supported throughout the entire story; it represents something quite different from its literal meaning. But stories for children operate on a fairly literal level. Ideas of good and evil may be translated into characters, actions, or setting, which then become symbols for ideas.

In this sense the Narnia series by C. S. Lewis is allegory. However, the Narnia books are also highly successful when read on a literal level; the young reader may or may not see the ideas symbolized by characters or setting. A child may read through the series with great excitement, think a bit, then exclaim "He's talking about good and bad!" and then reread them all, this time on an allegorical or symbolic level.

In contrast, the Forest seems a natural place for Pooh and Piglet to hunt a Woozle/Wizzle; to extend the meaning of the Forest to the point of calling it a symbol for evil is pretentious and pointless. Hannah, the supposed Quaker witch in *The Witch of Blackbird Pond,* does not live in the dark forest; a kind and harmless woman, she lives in the benign and sunny meadows. Speare chooses this setting for Hannah's home to assist in creating conflict, but calling the setting symbolic seems heavy-handed.

> "A true symbol is emphasized, repeated and supported."
> *Northrup Frye*

❋ *Special Issues of Setting in Children's Literature*

We experience with our senses an important setting.

Folktale settings are often escapes to an easier life.

Like adults, children will accept as much or as little setting as the story seems to call for. Like adults, too, they expect that when a setting is important to understanding the story, they will be made to see, to hear, perhaps even to smell the setting—to sense the setting in any way relevant to the mood, conflict, and characters in the story. Younger children will be less likely to sit still for long descriptions that take them away from the conflict and characters. For them, and for many adults as well, setting interwoven with action is the most interesting and readable. Once this setting is established, any reader of any age expects the writer to be consistent. At times we all accept settings as escapes. The scene of an exotic ball or lavish banquet in a folktale undoubtedly was a satisfying escape for the poor and oppressed who heard these stories told in the past; today setting in some adventure and science-fiction stories also seems to function as escape. But once again, the principle is that the essential setting should be integrated with character and conflict, and not a mere digression. Since folk literature and fantasy are more common in literature for children than for adults, their special considerations bear closer examination.

Traditional Literature

In most folktales action and theme are the focus of interest and the setting is backdrop. The action is usually brisk and little time is spent describing time and place. The setting is a vague long-ago-and-far-away that avoids pinning down time and place. Such a setting also suggests magically one of the most pleasurable aspects of the folktale: maybe it happened here, maybe yesterday! Thus such a setting also anticipates the equally pleasurable possibility that perhaps it could happen again, perhaps here! We have noted in discussion of character that in a folktale the protagonists are so general and universal that what happens to them might happen to anyone. Similar vagueness in setting reinforces the possibility of adventures.

Folktale settings often follow the "once upon a time" formula. A random sampling of tales from Grimm—the tales best known to a majority of Western readers—reveals the following settings, or lack of them, in their opening lines; little is added within the stories:

> Once upon a time there lived an old man and his wife who for a long time . . .
> Once upon a time there was a king who had twelve daughters. . . .
> Once upon a time in deep winter, when the snowflakes were falling like feathers . . . [4]

Occasionally a simple variation occurs: "At the edge of a great forest lived a woodcutter and his wife." Folktale settings from other cultures seem to vary little from the patterns of Grimm, with little more specific definition of time and place than the Native American "My grandfather told me . . ." It is the nature of the folktale—originally told to an audience that might become restless—to plunge into conflict and action. Such generalized settings can demonstrate more clearly a universal theme: The kindness of the daughter is rewarded; she lives happily ever after in the palace of the prince.

As Laurence Yep, reteller of Chinese tales, says, "Some tales come from a common heritage; but others are specific to the region." There are particular settings in the Captain Stormalong tales of New England, and those of John Henry from the mining regions, as well as Pecos Bill from the Southwest. Just as the people enrich our society, all these stories enrich their readers.

The African tale retold by Gail E. Haley in *A Story, A Story* begins: "Once, Oh small children around my knee . . ." A Kaffir tale of South Africa, *Mufaro's Beautiful Daughters,* retold and illustrated by John Steptoe, also begins traditionally: "A long time ago, in a certain place in Africa, a small village lay across a river and half a day's journey from . . ." *The Name of the Tree*, a Bantu tale retold by Celia Barker Lottridge, begins: "Once, long ago, in the land of the short grass, there was a great hunger." Southeastern Alaska is the scene for the pourquoi tale *How Raven Brought Light to People*. It begins, "Long ago when the earth was new . . . "

The Orphan Boy, a Masai story told by Tololwa M. Mollel, however, plunges into the action: "As he had done every night of his life, the old man gazed deep into the heavens." The resulting story seems less a folktale and more an original creation of the writer.

Other folk literature seems equally vague about setting. In fact, the fable omits setting altogether, going immediately into action and its didactic point:

> A certain Wolf, being very hungry, disguised himself in a sheep's skin.
> A mischievous Shepherd's Boy used to amuse himself by calling "Wolf! Wolf!"

Many of the fables are only a few sentences long, and since they exist to point to a moral, setting is quite logically unimportant. The lesson is universal, unlimited by time or place. Myths happened "in ancient Greece," or "in the days of the giants," and designation of time and place is barely relevant. What matters is not location of specific action, but pinning down the locale to a cultural world. Here, too, simplicity in setting reinforces the universal qualities of the myths, their comments on human vanity or greed.

Legends, those unauthenticated stories handed down from tradition and regarded by the public as figuratively possible or even true, are by their definition related to historical events or people. This relationship narrows somewhat their time and place. For example, Robin Hood's adventures occur in Sherwood Forest since, according to history, that is where Robin Hood lived. Often, however, the legends refer to mystical events occurring centuries later than the lifetime of the character, and caused supposedly by the character's onetime presence. The oases of the Egyptian desert, for example, are said by legend to have sprung up wherever the fleeing Joseph, Mary, and infant Jesus stopped to rest.

Fantasy and Science Fiction

Setting in fantasy is a special consideration, since fantasy often begins in a setting of reality and moves to a fantasy realm, then back again. Such a book as *Alice in Wonderland* moves easily from the real to the fantastic by the device of a dream; Dr. Seuss's *And to Think That I Saw It on Mulberry Street* is a fantastic daydream, a parade framed by what the narrator actually saw on the way home from school. Other transitions are more complex. In Susan Cooper's *The Dark Is Rising,* the world that Will enters is filled with the mysterious and the supernatural—integral parts of the setting and essential to the story. The castle where Will meets the Old Ones, who for centuries have been battling evil, is the setting for Will's discovery that by the exercise of his willpower he can actually bring change. Reluctantly, he learns that he must accept his power in order to use it for good:

> [He looked] across the room at the light and shadow dancing side by side across
> the rich tapestries on the stone walls, and he thought hard, in furious concentra-

---

In fables, setting exists as backdrop for the stated moral.

Legends place setting in a historical time.

Setting may move between reality and fantasy.

tion, of the image of the blazing log fire in the huge fireplace behind him. He felt the warmth of it on the back of his neck, and thought of the glowing heart of the big pile of logs and the leaping yellow tongues of flame. *Go out, fire,* he said to it in his mind, feeling suddenly safe and free from the dangers of power, because of course no fire as big as that could possibly go out.

The fire goes out. Next Will sees that each of the many tapestries on the castle walls has its own frightening image, some as terrifying as "the empty-eyed grinning white skull of a horse, with a single stubby broken horn in the bony forehead and red ribbons wreathing the long jaws." Threatened by the rising of evil, the Dark, Will sees clearly his responsibility to use the special power given him.

In the fantasy *Alice's Adventures in Wonderland,* Lewis Carroll sets all logic awry, including the logic of setting. A rabbit hole extends deep into a strange, unbounded world, and time moves in all directions to create a setting essential to our experience of the story. To us as well as to Alice, time and place are illogical and confusing; they influence nonsensical behavior that defies every rule. In defiance of time and the related laws of growth, Alice grows and shrinks; the Mock Turtle's lessons lessen; the tea party murders time by going on forever; the White Rabbit tries fruitlessly to catch up with time. As for place, nothing seems to be where it is expected to be, and nothing can be counted on to be in the same place at another moment. The great hall with glass table and tiny door vanishes, and Alice finds her way into a tidy little room. Turning her back on the tea party, Alice walks through a door into a tree—only to find herself back in the long hall with the glass table and the tiny door. Finally, cause and effect—which occur in that order and are logically related to time—defy time to appear in nonsensically reversed order: sentence first, verdict later.

Summary

Setting is of two principal types. First, it may be a backdrop for the plot, like the generalized backdrop of a city, street, or forest against which we see some of the action of a play. In traditional literature, setting is usually backdrop, so generalized that it becomes universal. Or setting may be an integral part of the story, so essential to our understanding of this plot, these characters, and these themes that we must experience it with our senses. Backdrop or integral—the choice is the writer's. The integral setting may not only clarify the conflict; it may also help the reader understand character, be cast as the antagonist, influence mood, or act as symbol. Often the sense of place prepares the reader to accept the story and the writer's personal view of life and its significance.

Whether setting is integral or backdrop does not constitute a judgment about the quality of a piece of writing. What is important, however, is that understanding may develop only when we realize that this particular setting is essential to this story. And, if setting is essential to our understanding, the writer must make the reader see, hear, touch, and perhaps even smell the setting. It is as much the writer's task when writing for children as for adults to evoke setting, described either in paragraphs or in phrases woven into action, by the details of color, sound, figurative comparisons, and other stylistic means.

Notes

1. Eudora Welty, *Place in Fiction* (New York: House of Books, 1957), p. 22.
2. Writing of his stepfather, E. B. White, Roger Angell (*New Yorker*, February 14, 2005, p. 143) notes that White waited to write *Charlotte's Web* "until he had the country stuff in it down by heart. He knew how geese sounded when they were upset, and on what day in the fall the squashes and pumpkins needed to be brought in and put on the barn floor—which is to say that he'd still be himself in writing about it, and would not put in a word that might patronize his audience." Angell comments further that he probably knew that his story of seasons and farm life would be his masterpiece. "[It] would not occur to him to feel uneasy that his best book was for children."
3. Northrop Frye, "Theory of Symbol," in *Anatomy of Criticism* (Princeton, NJ: Princeton University Press, 1957), pp. 71–128.
4. Alfred David and Mary Elizabeth Meek, eds., *The Twelve Dancing Princesses* (Bloomington: Indiana University Press, 1974).

Recommended Books Cited in This Chapter

AVI. *Shadrach's Crossing.* New York: Random House, 1983.
BAUER, MARION DANE. *On My Honor.* Boston: Houghton Mifflin, 1986.
BROOKS, BRUCE. *Everywhere.* New York: Harper & Row, 1990.
BURNETT, FRANCES HODGSON. *The Secret Garden.* 1911. Reprint. New York: Viking, 1989.
BURNFORD, SHEILA. *The Incredible Journey.* Boston: Little, Brown, 1961.
CARROLL, LEWIS. *Alice's Adventures in Wonderland.* 1865. Reprint. New York: Macmillan, 1963.
CHOLDENKO, GENNIFER. *Al Capone Does My Shirts.* New York: Putnam, 2004.
COOPER, SUSAN. *The Dark Is Rising.* New York: Atheneum, 1973.
FRANK, ANNE. *Anne Frank: The Diary of a Young Girl.* Garden City, NY: Doubleday, 1967.
GEORGE, JEAN. *The Talking Earth.* New York: HarperCollins, 1993.
HALEY, GAIL. *A Story, A Story.* New York: Macmillan, 1970.
HENKES, KEVIN. *Olive's Ocean.* New York: Greenwillow, 2003.
LEWIS, C. S. *The Chronicles of Narnia.* New York: Macmillan, 1951–1956.
LOTTRIDGE, CELIA BARKER. *The Name of the Tree.* New York: Macmillan, 1989.
LUNN, JANET LOUISE. *Shadow in Hawthorn Bay.* New York: Scribner's Sons, 1986.
MACLACHLAN, PATRICIA. *Sarah, Plain and Tall.* New York: Harper & Row, 1985.
MARTIN, ANN M. *A Corner of the Universe.* New York: Scholastic, 2002.
MILNE, A. A. *Winnie-the-Pooh.* New York: Dutton, 1926.
MOLLEL, TOLOLWA M. *The Orphan Boy.* Boston: Houghton Mifflin, 1991.
PAULSEN, GARY. *Hatchet.* New York: Bradbury, 1987.

————. *Tucket's Ride*. New York: Delacorte, 1997.

PETRY, ANN. *Tituba of Salem Village*. Binghamton, NY: Vail-Ballou, 1964.

POTTER, BEATRIX. *The Tale of Peter Rabbit*. London: Warne, 1902.

REISS, JOHANNA. *The Upstairs Room*. New York: Harper & Row, 1987.

SCHMIDT, GARY D. *Lizzie Bright and the Buckminster Boy*. New York: Clarion, 2004.

SENDAK, MAURICE. *Where the Wild Things Are*. New York: Harper, 1963.

SERRAILLIER, IAN. *Beowulf the Warrior*. New York: Walck, 1961.

SEUSS, DR. *And to Think That I Saw It on Mulberry Street*. New York: Hale, 1937.

SPEARE, ELIZABETH. *The Witch of Blackbird Pond*. Boston: Houghton Mifflin, 1958.

STEPTOE, JOHN. *Mufaro's Beautiful Daughters*. New York: Lothrop Lee, 1987.

SUTCLIFF, ROSEMARY. *The Shining Company*. New York: Farrar, Straus & Giroux, 1990.

UCHIDA, HOSHIKO. *Journey to Topaz*. New York: Scribner's, 1971.

WHITE, E. B. *Charlotte's Web*. New York: Harper, 1952.

Jamie and Angus Stories

Anne Fine

Illustrated by Penny Dale

chapter 8

Point of View

Whose story is this, anyway?

Try changing the point of view in a story. What happens?

When we hear the term **point of view,** we commonly think of opinion or attitude: "From my point of view, women's rights are . . . " Sometimes we think of a personal angle or perspective: "That may be true for you, but I'm a student, and . . . " But point of view has special meaning for literature. As we read a story, we may be aware that we are seeing the events through the eyes—and mind—of one character. Or we may feel that we are objective observers watching the events unfold before our eyes. The writer wants to tell us this story. Whose view of the story the writer tells determines the point of view. Who sees the events determines how the story will develop.

It's clear that two people to whom the same incident happens simultaneously can have different versions of the event. Each responds out of past experience, the place from where she observed the incident, or from belief in right and wrong behavior, as well as from the more obvious differences in the physical and emotional effects of the incident. Each version of the facts is a personal truth.

A similar situation exists in literature. As readers we describe point of view depending on who sees and tells about the action. The same story is a different story, depending on which side of the story we see. In the case of Louise Fatio's picture book *The Happy Lion,* the story depends on which side of the cage door the zoo lion is on. The Happy Lion thinks his visitors are pleasant, civil people. They nod, bow, greet him, and feed him—when he is inside the cage. But the day the keeper forgets to close the door, the Happy

Lion walks out and meets his friends in their territory. One faints, one screams, and another throws a bag of vegetables in his face. Now the Happy Lion's friends have become puzzling strangers. Since the point of view is the Happy Lion's innocent thoughts, we are completely sympathetic to his puzzlement. When he calls the people foolish, we agree, since we know this lion is neither vicious nor predatory. He's just taking a walk. However, if we didn't know the protagonist's thoughts, we'd be as frightened as the human citizens of the lion's town. It is all a matter of point of view—whose thoughts we know, whose view of the action we follow.

Types of Point of View

Point of view is determined when the writer chooses who is to be the narrator and decides how much the narrator is to know. The first possibility a writer might consider is the **first-person point of view,** used when a story is told in first person "I." In such storytelling, the reader lives, acts, feels, and thinks the conflict as the protagonist experiences and tells it, just as Karana does in *Island of the Blue Dolphins.* Occasionally the first-person narrator is not the protagonist, but a minor character who observes the action and tells what the protagonist is doing.

Point of view determines how we see the story.

The second possibility is the **omniscient point of view.** Here the writer, telling the story in third person (using "he," "she," and "they"), is all-knowing or omniscient about any and every detail of action, thought, and feeling—conscious or unconscious—in the past, present, or future; if the writer chooses, he may recount any and all details. This omniscience is White's choice for *Charlotte's Web.*

A third possibility is the **limited omniscient point of view,** in which the writer, again telling the story in third person, concentrates on the thoughts, feelings, and significant past experiences of only the central character or protagonist, as Wilder does in her *Little House* stories. Occasionally the writer may choose to be omniscient about several—though not all—characters; this choice, too, is sometimes called limited omniscient.

The fourth possibility is the **objective (dramatic) point of view,** again using third person, as, for example, in Burnford's *The Incredible Journey.* The meaning of this term seems clear when we refer to the fictional reality of drama or motion picture. A camera seems to record—it cannot comment or interpret. There is no one there to explain to the reader what is going on or what the characters think or feel. The camera selects and we see and draw our own conclusions.

First-Person Point of View

The first-person narrator is limited; like the reader, she cannot tell what another character thinks unless told by that other character. Although the narrator sees the action of another character, the narrator, again like the reader, can speculate only about what the other is thinking. A hasty tucking in of a shirt or a nervous shaking of the head gives evidence from which the narrator may draw conclusions, just as we draw conclusions. However, unless the second character says aloud what he or she thinks, the first-person narrator, again like us, can only guess.

The first-person narrator who tells the story may be either the protagonist or a minor character observing the action. For example, Karana, the protagonist in *Island of the Blue Dolphins*, is a first-person narrator. At no time does Karana pretend to know what is in the minds of others, not her brother, the hunters, Tutok the Aleut stranger, or the animals. Tutok comes out from the brush quickly; Karana says, "She must have been waiting nearby." That possibility is all that Karana can know about Tutok's motives. Tutok hugs Karana when she receives the shell necklace. Karana says, "She was so pleased that I forgot how sore my fingers were." From a hug—action from another character—Karana concludes that Tutok is pleased. Although Karana knows her dog, Rontu, very well, she describes only his actions, never his thoughts, concluding that the dying Rontu wishes to bark only because he always had:

> [Rontu] raised his ears at the sound, and I put him down, thinking that he wished to bark at [the gulls] as he always did. He raised his head and followed them with his eyes, but did not make a sound.

Had author Scott O'Dell violated the first-person point of view by telling us Rontu's feelings, we might have turned our concentration from Karana, and the story would have been less real.

One of the strongest assets of first-person narration is its great potential for pulling the reader into what appears to be autobiographical truth. Because Karana's thoughts are credible, the reader sympathizes with her. Because what she claims to know is believably limited, she is consistent. Because solitary Karana—like solitary Robinson Crusoe—tells her own realistic story, the vicarious experience of survival is a powerful reality, convincingly immediate to the reader. If the story had been filtered through an omniscient writer, the immediacy of the experience would be less intense. The intervention of someone who wasn't there but who still knows and can tell it all would create an intervening omniscience between the solitary protagonist and the reader. The story would then be more remote, less immediate, and less intensely real.

Clearly the danger in first-person narration lies in the possibility of "I" ignoring appropriate limitations, reporting thoughts of others, and predicting, when such prediction would not naturally fall within "I's" ability to predict. Credibility is then lost.

The lives of the Blackfeet tribe of Canada in the 1800s were filled with the struggle to survive as well as great harmony with the cycles of growth and natural change. In her first-person novel *Sweetgrass*, Jan Hudson graphically shows both the struggle and the harmony. Although at the age of fifteen she is the oldest unmarried woman in her tribe, Sweetgrass cannot convince her

First-person point of view creates a sense of autobiographical truth.

father she is mature enough to be first-wife-who-sits for Eagle Sun. She must continually prove herself. As told in consistent first-person narration, Sweetgrass struggles with her anger at her father; with her wish to be with Eagle Sun; with her envy of her betrothed or married younger cousins; and finally with her desperate battle against smallpox and starvation. There seems no better way to understand the customs and mores of the Blackfeet culture and its role demands than seeing into the protagonist's mind as she wrestles with what she would like to do and what she, as a dutiful daughter and tribe member, must do.

In a time when the topic of attention deficit disorder and hyperactivity is frequently discussed, readers can get a rare glimpse of what it is like to live with it with *Joey Pigza Swallowed the Key* by Jack Gantos. In a first person account, Joey tells how it feels:

> I must have looked pretty calm on the outside, like I was really normal. . . . But inside my body I felt like a big bottle of warm Coke when you drop it in the grocery story and it begins to fizz out the top like a bomb about to blow. . . . Then I picked at my finger bandage until I had it unrolled. And then I started rocking back and forth, but the chair wouldn't rock. So I heaved myself from side to side. It still didn't move. I gripped the arms and jerked myself around and hung way out over the arms like some rodeo rider on a wild bull. But the chair didn't budge an inch. When I looked down at the legs I saw it was bolted to the floor. Bolted, as if I was some kind of a circus freak. So I rocked even harder.

Joey's narrative shows his inability to control his actions, his hurt at being seen as different. When he realizes how his behavior makes life difficult for his mother, he is sad for her, but he cannot control the highs and lows of his attention span. The doctor gives Joey a patch: "The goal is to give you a fighting chance to maintain a normal attention span."

Matters of vocabulary and word use are restrictions, as the person telling the story is limited to diction compatible with age and personality. Vicky Austin's view of events in Madeleine L'Engle's *A Ring of Endless Light* is shaped by her sixteen-year-old experiences. The story opens at the funeral of Leo's father, where Vicky comments: "I looked at Leo and his face was all splotchy as though he had cried and cried, but he hadn't cried, and he needed to." Later that day, she comments:

> I held Leo and he held me and we rocked back and forth on the old elm trunk, weeping. . . . And I discovered that there is something almost more intimate about crying that way with someone than there is about kissing, and I knew I'd never again be able to think of Leo as nothing but a slob.

And of Adam she says, "He wasn't particularly gorgeous . . . but he had a kind of light within that drew me to him like a moth to a candle." This is the diction of a sixteen-year-old speaking her feelings and thoughts, and not presuming to know what she cannot know: "I don't think Adam realized how nervous I was."

E. L. Konigsburg uses first person in her suspenseful novel *Silent to the Bone*. Bran has been traumatized and has retreated into silence, but Connor,

Diction is compatible with age and personality of the narrator.

who has found a method to help Bran out of his silence, worries about the effectiveness of his method. Days go by, and Bran remains silent. With her frequent touch of humor, Konigsburg reveals Connor's thinking about how hard it is to wait:

> Waiting takes up a lot more energy than people give it credit for. Say you are sitting in a theater, knowing there is a lot of stuff going to happen behind the curtain, but the curtain is stuck and can't go up; I give waiting for the curtain to go up a *three.* Say you are late for a soccer game, and your mother has to stop for a red light, and the line of cars in front of her is so long, she has to wait for a second green before she can go; I give waiting for the second light a *five.* Say you are in math class waiting for the teacher to hand back the results of a test you had not studied for; I give waiting for the test results a *ten.* Waiting for something to begin is harder than waiting for something to end, so I give waiting for Nikki . . . *a twelve.*

Later, Connor says that "waiting for Branwell to speak is a *twelve point five.*"

The same story can be told by different participants, each one in first-person point of view. In Sharon Creech's story *The Wanderer,* cousins Sophie and Cody tell in their journals in alternating chapters their views of a life-threatening voyage across the Atlantic to Ireland in a sailing vessel. At first each thirteen-year-old is uncertain about the other, but over the voyage, they become strong and appreciative friends. Each wonders about the other, but due to the author's careful use of point of view, neither seems to pry nor to "know" the other's thoughts.

First-person point of view is effective in *Coast to Coast.* By following Birch's thinking, Betsy Byars shows the close relationship of thirteen-year-old Birch to her grandfather. While helping to get his house ready for a yard sale before his move to California, she finds a box of her grandmother's poems, a treasure that makes her want even more to be close to her grandfather. She persuades him to do what he has long dreamed of doing: fly his Piper Cub across country to California. While on the flight, Birch wants to speak of what is on her mind; she has just found evidence she may have had a twin sister. But Pop is uncommunicative and preoccupied with the flight. As we follow Birch's thinking, she conveniently speaks it all aloud to the dog, Ace:

> It was about a baby that died, Ace, on my birthday. And all of a sudden I knew that poem meant one of two things. Either my mom's natural baby died, or lived just a little while . . . And so maybe . . . someone else in the hospital had had a baby and was going to put her up for adoption, and that was me.

In their travels across the states, Birch and her grandfather become closer.

Occasionally a writer experiments successfully with different points of view, as does Alice Childress in *A Hero Ain't Nothin' but a Sandwich.* Using first-person point of view, each of Childress's characters tells the story from her or his own perspective of events and relationships. From the total of their stories, we see events, characters, plot, and theme, as well as setting. The story, set in the inner city, concerns Benjie's experience with drugs, and to be convincing, each of the speakers must reveal self through distinctively personal diction:

> [*Benjie:*] "My block ain't no place to be a chile in peace. Somebody gonna cop your money and might knock you down cause you walking with short bread and didn't even make it worth their while to stop and frisk you over."

> [*Grandmother:*] "This house is my jail, only I pay rent. I'm afraid to go out in the street alone, day or night. Bad boys will beat [us] and take away our little money."

> [*Nigeria Greene, teacher:*] "Bernard Cohen is not to be believed. His whole mission in teaching is to convince Black kids that most whites are great except for a 'few' rotten apples in every barrel. It burns me."

> [*Benjie's mother:*] "I try to keep the neighbors out of my business because every friend has a friend, and if I can't keep a secret, how can I ask them not to tell what I told?"

In *Bronx Masquerade* Nikki Grimes uses an unusual variation on first-person point of view. The novel's structure is a series of first-person comments from a group of students, all describing in prose how they see themselves. Each prose comment is followed by a revealing poetic or rap selection about him- or herself. Mr. Ward, the teacher, holds Open Mic Fridays, when students read their personal descriptions. One dislikes her name, another her Jewish heritage in a class predominantly Black, another wishes she were darker like the others, and still another reveals a truly personal but hidden skill. Race, skill, and interest differences no longer matter. Each now sees something new in the others, a reason for lack of confidence, a self-conscious wish not to seem different, or something common to all. As one poem says, "Is your heart /like an onion, too? . . . Your turn/Peel away." "It don't matter what your skin color is, or what name you call yourself. Everybody is different inside. We're all trying to fit in. Ain't nothing new about that." As the weeks go by, the class discovers what each person is truly like; pictures of self, spoken aloud, help the class to become an accepting family.

The King of Dragons by Carol Fenner uses two first-person narrators to keep high our suspense and concern about a homeless eleven-year-old who lives in an abandoned city courthouse, a place that is secure, safe, and secret. Left alone, Ian fears that his father has been hurt, and worries that he will be discovered and relegated to the streets once again. Throughout the novel, italicized accounts of hospitalized patient number 227 appear, the nightmares of a survivor reliving the horrors of his war experience. As we follow Ian and his life in hiding, and are puzzled about who patient 227 might be, Fenner's use of two first-person narrators holds us wondering how the two may be related. When we realize that this patient is Ian's father, hope grows for their being together again.

Avi's use of first-person narrator in *Nothing But the Truth* presents an interesting situation, that of the "unreliable narrator." Although the jacket blurb suggests that the issue confronted is the importance of communication, a more important idea is that false communication can wreak havoc. Bent on squeezing from his teacher an unearned grade so he can run track, Phillip, the narrator, is totally rebellious. He blames his poor grades not on neglected homework, but on a popular teacher; to goad her, and to annoy her in class, he hums the national anthem under his breath. When she reprimands him, Phillip claims patriotic motives. Phillip's parents believe him, his story is publicized, his teacher humiliated, and his classmates angered. No one hears "nothing but the truth," and only Phillip knows what he has done—told *anything but* the truth to serve his own purposes.

Written in the "I" form of letter narration, *Letters from Rifka* by Karen Hesse is set in 1919, when Jewish Rifka is detained on Ellis Island. Writing imaginary letters to her Russian friend on the margins of a volume of Pushkin's poems, Rifka records her impressions of the United States, and of the immigration process; again, the first-person point of view creates a convincingly personal account.

Letter or diary form uses first person comfortably.

At one time it was thought that small children found stories written in first person difficult to follow, but in recent years many books written in a childhood vernacular make the voice of a young narrator far easier to recognize.

Omniscient Point of View

A distinct change from the limitations of the first-person point of view occurs when the writer chooses the freedom of the omniscient point of view. The writer in this case may recount relevant information about any and every character—their thoughts, ideas, and feelings about themselves as well as others. The writer may flash back into past experiences, feelings, and thoughts, or forward into what will happen in the future. The omniscient writer may relate anything he or she believes is relevant to the story, moving around, in, and through the characters, knowing everything, explaining motives, and giving the reader helpful information. In William Armstrong's *Sounder,* for example, how the boy feels when his father has been taken to jail becomes clear.

> The loneliness that was always in the cabin . . . was heavier than ever now. It made the boy's tongue heavy. It pressed against his eyes, and they burned. It rolled against his ears. His head seemed to be squeezed inward, and it hurt.

In adult fiction, details may be more subtly and less obviously related to the conflict and characters, but in children's stories, the writer concentrates on what is essential to the reader's understanding.

Adult fiction may have details subtly related to character and action.

White finds the omniscient point of view best for *Charlotte's Web.* The objective, third-person statement that Fern wore a very pretty dress to the Fair has little significance until the young reader has the omniscient writer's interpretation: she thought she'd see boys there. When Wilbur learns of Charlotte's bloodthirsty appetite, he thinks that although Charlotte is pretty and clever, she is everything he doesn't like—scheming and fierce. The reader is as uncertain as Wilbur until White adds that fears and doubts go with new friendships. We know why Templeton finds the dirty junkyard his favorite spot; he thinks it's a good place to hide. If we had merely heard speeches and seen actions, we might have interpreted the details quite differently. White knows and tells what is in the minds of all his characters: Fern thinks the world is blissful; Lurvy feels weak at the sight of the dew-covered words in the miraculous web; Wilbur can't bear loneliness; Templeton is miserable when his rotten egg breaks. And when Wilbur tries to spin a web, Charlotte watches him delightedly, pleased that he is no quitter. White is truly the omniscient narrator. The reader knows everything because of the point of view.

Limited Omniscient Point of View

Often a story is told from a *limited* omniscient point of view. Here the writer chooses to see action usually through the eyes of one character—occasionally several characters—and to report that character's thoughts. In children's literature, this character is usually the protagonist. The writer shows not only what the character sees and hears, but also what the character feels and believes. The writer is inside as well as alongside the character.

When Dicey of *Dicey's Song* by Cynthia Voigt is asked in her classroom if her portrait-essay of a person she knows is really her relative, Dicey stands accused of showing fiction as fact, and even of plagiarism. She lifts her chin, and deliberately concentrates on something else—the sailboat Gram has let her refinish:

> She didn't answer. There was no way anybody could make her answer. In her mind, she made a picture: the little boat, she'd have painted it white by then, or maybe yellow—it was out on the Bay beyond Gram's dock and the wind pulled at the sails. Dicey could feel the smooth tiller under her hand; she could feel the way the wooden hull flowed through the water.

This is Dicey's story, her mind and feelings.

In Wilder's *Little House in the Big Woods*, limited omniscient narration shows what pioneer life was like to a child. First, however, Wilder shows the universal child Laura. Laura had never had more fun than when she fell from a stump into the soft snow and made pictures shaped like herself. Like everything else in the Wilder series, the understanding of Santa Claus and the giving of Christmas gifts are suited to the child's view of reality. "Santa Claus did not give grown people presents, but that was not because they had not been good. . . . It was because they were grown up, and grown people must give each other presents." Through Laura's innocent point of view we get the literal interpretation of a Bible story. As Adam names the animals, Laura envies him his clothing:

> Adam sat on a rock, and all the animals and birds, big and little, were gathered around him anxiously waiting to be told what kind of animals they were. Adam looked so comfortable. He did not have to be careful to keep his clothes clean, because he . . . wore only a skin around his middle.

Because through limited omniscience Laura's simplicity and innocence are visible, we accept her account of pioneer life. In detailed description Laura tells what butchering an animal was like. As one detail follows another, from playing with the pig's bladder to roasting the pig's tail, the modern city child, who knows only that meat comes from the supermarket, is prepared to believe the truth of butchering on the frontier. By recognizing the feelings of childhood, the reader accepts the particular and specific routines and actions of Laura's life—different though they are from the reader's own. Wilder is successful in large part because she chooses Laura's point of view.

Yolanda of *Yolanda's Genius* by Carol Fenner is smart, tough, and a new arrival in Grand River; she defends and cares for her younger brother Andrew, and finally persuades the great B. B. King of Andrew's musical genius. Yolanda, whose thoughts are always on one of two things—Andrew or food—arranges for Andrew to fake being lost at Chicago's big blues concert weekend, and, when "found," to be seen onstage with celebrities. There Andrew plays his harmonica and his pipe, imitating the sounds of the city, from the wind off Lake Michigan and the shushing or roaring of the crowd, to the strength and queenliness of oversized Yolanda. Andrew's musical genius is recognized. Because the point of view is limited omniscient, we know the thoughts and feelings of both Andrew and Yolanda. Six-year-old Andrew closes his eyes through it all and finally decides to learn to read—so he can read music. For Yolanda, being both smart and independent are good, but finding a new best friend with whom to share things is wonderful.

The skillful writer recognizes and presents a child's views.

To cite another example, when Van, the boyfriend of Jamie's mother in Carolyn Conan's *What Jamie Saw*, tries to throw baby Nin against the wall. Jamie catches her, and the three of them escape to live in friend Earl's tiny trailer in the woods. Jamie's "nosey" teacher finds help for the three cold, hungry people, and slowly they begin their painful efforts for a normal life. The story is told in limited omniscient point of view: Jamie worries about Nin's safety, and while the baby sleeps in a drawer, he wonders if she'd fit if he pushed the drawer in when he was in a hurry. Perhaps he could punch holes in the drawer, as he had when he kept bugs in a jar. When Van shows up, Jamie lifts infant Nin from the drawer, then hides under the bed, crawling in first, then pulling her in after him. Characters are few in this short novel, but its effectiveness is largely due to knowing Jamie's fears as we live within his body.

Gary Paulsen, telling a story quite different from his usual action/suspense novels, writes *Sisters/Hermanas* about two girls, both fourteen years old, seeking their own ways to similar goals. Rosa from Mexico sells herself on the streets to send money home to her mother, meanwhile dreaming of wealth as a beautiful model. Traci sells her individuality to fulfill her mother's dream of financial success bought by beauty and superficiality. The two girls' paths nearly cross when Traci, shopping for the perfect outfit, finds Rosa hiding from immigration officials. Traci looks into the eyes of the young streetwalker and sees herself: she, too, has sold herself but in another way. In alternating chapters, the similarity of the two girls' motives is revealed. The novel is very short, bound as two related stories told in limited omniscient point of view, one in English and the other in Spanish.

Objective (Dramatic) Point of View

In the objective or dramatic point of view, the writer does not enter the minds of any of the characters. The action speaks for itself as it unfolds and the reader hears speeches and sees action. The term *dramatic*, of course, comes from *drama*, where characters reveal themselves by what they say, what they do, and what others say about them. Drama permits the audience to see and hear, but to draw inferences only from what it sees and hears. Inner thoughts or feelings must be revealed by visible action. In most plays there is no interpreter standing at stage left to tell the audience what thoughts run through the speakers' minds. The audience must sometimes figure out for itself the meaning of the actions and speeches, deciding from a character's voice inflections or actions what—beneath or in spite of the words—may lie in that character's mind.

The objective or nearly objective point of view in some stories makes heavier demands on the imagination and understanding of the reader. Adults guess that when a character looks at the floor, scuffs the dust with a toe, or twists a lock of hair, that person is shy or embarrassed, but the ability to interpret body language is a skill few children have. It is the writer's responsibility when using the objective or dramatic point of view to describe and report action that, since it is without interpretation, must be within the child's understanding.

The Incredible Journey is an example of the use of omniscience for the minor human characters and of relative objectivity for the major animal characters. Realistically, we can never know what, if anything, is in the minds of the three animals:

> The old dog walked gingerly into the shallow water, shivering . . . turning his head away. Once more the Labrador swam the river, climbed out . . . shook himself, and barked. There was no mistaking the command. The old dog took another reluctant step forward, whining piteously, his expressive tail tucked under. . . . Again the Labrador swam across.

Because we see the reluctant step of the old terrier, hear the piteous whine, and note the tucked-under tail, we draw conclusions about how the dog feels. Burnford does better than most writers of animal stories, but even she uses animal/human comparisons, calling the terrier a white cavalier; he is like a "shipwrecked mariner after six weeks at sea on a raft."

Allan W. Eckert, in his portrayal of the badger in *Incident at Hawk's Hill*, is perhaps more successful; his objectivity falters less frequently. Eckert mentions instinct and experience as aids to the badger as she digs a tunnel five feet into the earth to a point she chooses for a nesting chamber. He describes the digging, the earth moving and scattering, and the choosing of a spot fifty feet away to start a longer escape tunnel connecting with the chamber. An incredible engineering feat now accomplished with unerring skill, the badger wheezes with fatigue. We observe the badger's actions, but we do not know her thoughts.

Variations in Point of View

E. L. Konigsburg in *The View from Saturday* uses a combination of omniscient point of view in her story about four students. The omniscient author tells how Mrs. Olinski appointed the team representing the school in the Academic Bowl; each seemed to her to be a loner. The four students—Ethan, Nadia, Julian, and Noah—speak, each one revealing family and history as well as fears and insecurities. Nadia: "Dividing my time was part of the divorce settlement. I was to spend Thanksgiving, spring vacation, and one month over the summer with Dad." Noah is visiting his grandpa and helps with the wedding plans: "On the day of the wedding I was in great demand to take things over to the clubhouse in my wagon. The African violets alone took three trips, and the briskets took two. . . . Fact: I did a wonderful job."

Julian invites the three others for a mystery meeting that soon evolves into "The Souls," a compatible group of students who develop a kinship and who act together for the benefit of both school and teacher.

Kate DiCamillo uses authorial intervention, a variation of the omniscient point of view, in *The Tale of Despereaux,* a fantasy about a mouse and a rat. Deep in the dungeons below the castle of the king, Despereaux seeks an opportunity to be a knight in shining armor who rescues Princess Pea, while the rat Roscuro enjoys being a mean rat. Caught as a castle invader, Despereaux is destined for punishment in the dungeon—until his mother Antoinette intervenes.

> At the last moment, Antoinette came out of her faint and shouted one word to her child.
>
> That word, reader, was *adieu.*
>
> Do you know the definition of *adieu?* Don't bother with your dictionary. I will tell you.
>
> *Adieu* is the French word for farewell.
>
> "Farewell" is not the word that you would like to hear from your mother as you are being led to the dungeon by two oversize mice in black hoods.

Such comments by the authorial voice appeal to some readers, while others find them an interruption in the narrative that does little to advance conflict, create suspense, or clarify theme.

A skillful writer can make variations in point of view easily understood. *Antar and the Eagles* by William Mayne begins with Antar's point of view, limited omniscience that despite conversation with his family stays only with Antar's thinking. Without permission, Antar has climbed the ladders to the

A skillful writer may vary the point of view.

church steeple to his father. "They saw on one side the sea glittering under the sun, and on the other the distant mountains, where snow lay all summer. Below them all the town lay busy not knowing it was being watched." But this is a fantasy. Antar is snatched away by the Great Eagle to live with eagles so that he may complete the mission of retrieving from a distant star the eagle egg that will hatch to become the next Great Eagle. During Antar's stay in the nest with fledglings, he learns the language of eagles, and the point of view now includes what they think and feel as well. "They want" Antar to climb the mountains and are "extremely annoyed" when he slides and tumbles; they "insist" that he continue to climb, "but let him take the zigzag way." After a time, they are talking to Antar, who understands their language: "You must climb higher. . . . You will fly from the height and glide down to the Great Eagle's pinnacle. There is no other way for you to get there." The gradual way in which Antar and the eagles come to communicate in eagle language helps to suspend disbelief. Had Antar and the eagles understood one another immediately, credibility would have suffered.

William Mayne, in the story *Drift*, tells two versions of the same story. The first thirteen chapters are third-person limited omniscient as the White boy Rafe tells what happened when he and the Native American girl Tawena get lost in the storm while idly hunting Bear. The ice of the lake breaks, and they are unable to return to their village; Tawena "disappears," and Rafe is led home by two Native American women seeking ransom. Chapter 14 begins "Tawena's Story." Now events are shown through Tawena's mind, and we realize that she had been close behind Rafe during the long trek through the forest, under the waterfall, and in the wolf pack, helping (when she could remain hidden) and guiding (by pretending to be the voice of Bear, messenger of the god Maneto). The two stories, each with its own point of view, completely support and verify each other.

❂ *Special Issues of Point of View in Children's Literature*

Why all these words about point of view? Is it that important?

Yes, it is. Credibility of the story often depends on a successfully maintained point of view. If we didn't know what Wilbur was thinking in *Charlotte's Web*, we'd wonder why he runs madly about once he gains his freedom. Or how in the world a spider and a pig—two creatures most of us would find unappealing—could forge a friendship. And what motivates that rat, anyway? The three pets of *The Incredible Journey*, who wander across the Canadian wilderness, would be characters from fantasy if we knew what they thought. The resulting destruction of realism would mar the story. Speculate as we may about whether our own lost pets would care about returning home, this story is a reassuring confirmation of their reciprocated loyalty—it doesn't happen only in the newspapers. In the Little House series, Wilder's remarkable consistency in using the growing child Laura's view makes the frontier credible and real. "Enough of forest animals, frontier heroes and the legends; this is what it was like for a child like me."

The point of view of seventh-grader Anastasia Krupnik in Lois Lowry's books by that name (*Anastasia at This Address,* for example) is successfully maintained. She is interested in boys, and yet realizes that the boys unfortunately aren't ready for romance. Following her thinking, we see her fantasies about an older man, a "SWM" whose ad she answers, and her misgivings make sense. She finds herself in a corner. Lowry keeps the humor coming: she never condescends or laughs *at* Anastasia while she takes the youthful point of view. It's easy to see how confusing the vocabulary and actions of the adult world are to a thirteen-year-old. After all, you'd think that having one's earlobes pierced might logically be called a lobotomy.

Maturity of the Reader

It is not possible, or even relevant, to make authoritative statements about the best or most successful point of view for children's literature. A few sensible inferences, however, are possible. The first-person point of view *may* present difficulties for the smallest child. A child just learning his or her own "I" identity may have trouble identifying with the strange "I" of the story.

The older child, however, may find first-person stories exciting proof of understanding, and of the capacity to project self into another "I." First person is an increasingly popular choice in stories for children. When Twain wrote *Huckleberry Finn* in first person, he probably had adult readers in mind, but when Robert Louis Stevenson wrote *Kidnapped* and *Treasure Island,* he must have wished to involve young readers in you-are-there adventures. Since that time there are many more first-person stories for older readers; they seem to explore the growing-up tensions in a child or young adult.

As for the objective point of view, children are inexperienced in drawing conclusions from speeches and from descriptions of actions; they may find the dramatic point of view hard to understand. This necessity for objectivity, therefore, presents a particular kind of challenge to the writer whose audience is the young child. If the story relies, however, on pictures showing the characters' feelings through facial expressions—as they may in picture books—the interpretive words about emotions and thoughts are not so essential.

Animal Realism

Animal realism presents special problems in point of view. Look back at *Charlotte's Web,* a story in which the characters are animals. White's story is not a realistic story about pigs and spiders and rats that live in barns; we know that. Such a story would have to show characters living and moving like animals, making animal noises. It would have to be told from a point of view that does not imagine or report the thoughts of nonhumans acting human.

There is no "best" point of view in a story for children.

Inexperienced in drawing conclusions from action, children may find omniscience easiest.

White had no intention of being realistic; he chose to portray his animals living as animals and yet similar to people. So successful is White that we have a distinct feeling that they *are* people. In fact, since they all think and worry and love and hurt and laugh and needle one another as people do, White's animal story reveals human truths of friendship and continuity, death and maturity. His careful control of what is animal and what is human in each character, never confusing the two, is a source of his success.

The objective or dramatic point of view, however, seems to be the logical choice for a realistic animal story. *Black Beauty* by Anna Sewell presents a distinct contrast. The book may give the impression of being a realistic story because the horses lead "horse lives." *Black Beauty*'s first-person narrator, however, is a horse using human language to tell us his horse emotions and thoughts. Sewell inconsistently mixes and confuses Black Beauty's animal and human natures. The point of view destroys realism. The horse's feelings would be believable assuming that animal feelings are identical to our own. It is, furthermore, inconsistent with realism that we should know the animal's feelings by anything but observation and speculation, although perhaps accompanied by a hearty dose of our sympathy. Black Beauty, speaking in the first person "I," says, "Day by day, hole by hole, our bearing reins were shortened, and instead of looking forward with pleasure to having my harness put on . . . I began to dread it." Black Beauty decides to do his duty despite his discomfort. But worse things come; the sharp bit cuts his tongue and his jaw, and he froths at the mouth. He feels "a pressure on my windpipe, which often made my breathing very uncomfortable . . . my neck and chest were strained and painful, my mouth and tongue tender, and I felt worn and depressed." While it is perhaps true that the story makes us feel like a horse, as Frances Clarke Sayers says, the reverse is more nearly accurate; this horse feels the way we would feel if we were living in horses' bodies. In a realistic animal story, however, at least a relatively objective point of view is important, whether the story is for child or adult.

Choice of point of view, then, affects the reader's acceptance of a story. Some writers of animal stories manage to avoid the temptation of sentimentality; they seek to convey the reality of animal life by picturing the animals' natural habitat, showing the impact of predators, weather, seasons, and maturity cycles on animal lives. Such a writer is Felix Salten, author of *Bambi*. Sometimes Salten successfully evokes wonder; through the mind of Bambi the deer, the reader watches the approach of winter, feeling the cold rain and hearing the shushing of falling leaves. It pleases Bambi "to see the milk-white veils of mist steam from the meadow in the morning. . . . They vanished so beautifully in the sunshine. The hoar frost . . . with such dazzling whiteness delighted him too." Salten clearly and believably carries the suspense through a winter in which Bambi's first enemy is starvation and his second is Man. However, when Salten depicts as human Bambi's love for his doe, or his admiration for the wise owl, the other information—the accurate natural history—seems less reliable. Salten begins to falsify when he humanizes even

A realistic animal story needs an objective or dramatic point of view.

Choice of point of view affects acceptance of a story.

the leaves and is totally omniscient. By assuming unlimited knowledge, he causes us to question his otherwise accurate portrayal of nature and its forces. Such complete omniscience may be traceable to the translation, but it creates doubts about what is really true.

In Bruce Coville's compilation of horse stories and poems, called *Herds of Thunder, Manes of Gold,* the quality is consistently high. Each story maintains the point of view of the human owner or observer; each one is consistently and convincingly accurate. Coville's own retelling of "The Taming of Bucephalus," of how Alexander the Great met the horse that carried him to conquer Europe, is as convincing as any. In "White Horses," Anne Eliot Crompton tells the story from the point of view of a cave girl grown to womanhood, and in Peter Roop's "Prairie Lightning," the Native American grandfather tells his grandson of another horse of great speed. Nathaniel Hawthorne tells of the capture of the winged horse Pegasus by Bellerophon, but as is often the case when Hawthorne writes for children, his coy asides disturb the mood of the otherwise interesting tale. The overall quality of the stories, however, makes the book a pleasure for lovers of horses.

Fantasy

If fantasy is to be successful, a reader must willingly suspend disbelief. If the story's characters, conflict, and theme seem believable, it is plausible and even natural to know the thoughts and feelings of animal characters or tiny people. In fact, the story may be so good that we wish it *were* true. This persuasion that the writer wishes to bring about—persuasion that "what if" is really "it's true"—is most successful when the writer is consistent about point of view.

Point of view is an essential part of Mary Norton's *The Borrowers.* Norton's central characters are diminutive; most of the action is seen through the eyes of young Arrietty. The Clock family is only six inches tall, and everything in the story, from postage stamps to primroses, is seen in relationship to the characters' size. To believe that Arrietty is so tiny, the reader must enter the dimensions and scale of her world. Pushing through the grass, she is startled by something glittering and discovers "It was an eye. Or it looked like an eye. Clear and bright like the color of the sky. An eye like her own but enormous." While "human beans" find a walk across the carpet easy, to tiny Arrietty it is like pushing through a dense field of grain. The yard and garden are huge; here is Arrietty's glimpse:

> A greenish beetle, shining in the sunlight, came toward her across the stones. She laid her fingers lightly on its shell and it stood still . . . when she moved her hand the beetle went swiftly on. An ant came hurrying in a busy zigzag. She danced in front of it to tease it and put out her foot. . . . Cautiously she moved . . . in amongst the green blades. As she parted them gently with her bare hands, drops of water plopped on her skirt . . . pulling herself up now and again by rooty stems into this jungle of moss and wood-violet and creeping leaves of clover . . . she sat down suddenly on a gnarled leaf of primrose.

A story may be so good we wish it were true.

No wonder disbelief is suspended to convince readers that the Clock family lives. Not only do safety pins and postage stamps have a way of disappearing, but everything from furniture to flowers is from the point of view of Arrietty, who sees everything from a six-inch height. The scale is relative to a tiny borrower, and point of view is thoroughly consistent.

This same strongly established point of view and its detailed development helps to account for some of the greatest successes in children's fantasy, like, for example, Carroll's *Alice's Adventures in Wonderland* and the fantasies of Ursula Le Guin and Robin McKinley.

Stories of Various Cultures

Stories of children from other countries are a particular problem for the writer. Early in the twentieth century, a series of books was published about children of other lands—*The Eskimo Twins, The Japanese Twins,* and others. These stories stressed what seemed to be peculiarities of life in other countries. Flat and unreal children lived in exotic and uninhabitable lands. Fascinating as it was to learn about children eating whale blubber or octopus, or wearing wooden shoes or tatami sandals, the stories now seem condescending. At this point in the discussion, however, once we believe in the reality of character we believe in the vicarious experience of the character's way of life. A story about other countries can show how life is lived there without making the country and its people seem weird and wondrous, strange and unbelievable, or all alike.

Children, like adults, may first see the obvious differences in people: he has black hair and I have blond; she is tall and I am short. From these outward physical traits, our attention shifts to more subtle differences, like names, houses, pets, and games—differences expected and looked for. One effective way in which the writer can picture a different country accurately, make the story credible, and at the same time present the truth of human nature, is to make careful use of point of view. An objective point of view in a story about life in Morocco, for example, might leave a child puzzled by uninterpreted facts, but some degree of omniscience achieves several results. First of all, since thoughts can be known, the character can more easily be shown to be like us. Then, once recognized, the character is believable; the character's way of life is different but interesting, rather than strange or beneath us—a significant contribution to international understanding.

Point of view also reveals other things about people. Through Meindert DeJong's use of limited omniscient point of view in *House of Sixty Fathers,* North American readers not only discover experiences unfamiliar to themselves and to this Chinese child, but also how familiar parts of American experience must look to a child of another land. We, who automatically peel paper from chewing gum and pop the gum into our mouths to chew continuously and without purpose, find the action nothing unusual, but Tien Pao is mystified. Here he rides for the first time in a jeep, a "small, open carriage":

People can be like us although their lives are different.

Various cultures may be more easily understood through omniscience.

"The man behind the strange wheel did things with his hands and feet. The carriage suddenly roared, shot ahead. It hopped and jumped and bounced in swiftness over the little road. It went still faster." Each aggressive action Tien Pao sees is committed by impersonal war equipment, every kind act by a person Tien Pao comes to know.

An interesting corollary to consider beside *Sixty Fathers* is *Dragonwings*, Laurence Yep's story of a Chinese immigrant boy coming to California, the "Golden Mountain." As he approaches the California coast, he is disappointed; it is only "a brown smudge on the horizon," the wooden houses "like shells of wood which terrible monsters had spun about themselves." As the narrator tries to learn the new language, the "letters keep on rearranging themselves in the most confusing patterns." Because Americans can use their great powers for good or evil, the Chinese immigrants call them "demons"— demons whose calendars are not properly arranged, not based sensibly on the movements of the moon or on the ten-day week.

Aware of their feelings, we find ourselves breathlessly involved in the life of the Chinese family and fearful for its members' safety. Although their lives are different from our own, they are themselves like us. We see people, countries, cultures, and ways of life—all through the point of view and wide eyes of a child—and are persuaded that a child is a child in any culture.

Summary

Point of view, an integral part of storytelling, determines the view the reader gets of events, character motivation, suspense and climax, and theme. There are four major kinds of point of view: first person with an "I" narrator; omniscient with an all-knowing writer; limited omniscient with focus on one or a few characters; and objective or dramatic with a report only of what can be seen and heard. Each one, when suited to story and reader, accomplishes a significant task.

Since the limited experience of children makes it hard for them to draw their own inferences from objective description of action and speech, the writer often clarifies the story by use of some degree of omniscience. The pleasure of literature comes from style, character, plot—all the literary elements. In literature for children, understanding of character and the other elements is aided by a sensitive choice of point of view adapted to subject matter, type of conflict, and expected maturity level of readers.

Recommended Books Cited in This Chapter

ARMSTRONG, WILLIAM. *Sounder.* New York: Harper & Row, 1969.
AVI. *Nothing but the Truth.* New York: Orchard, 1991.
BURNFORD, SHEILA. *The Incredible Journey.* Boston: Little, Brown, 1961.
BYARS, BETSY. *Coast to Coast.* New York: Delacorte, 1992.

CHILDRESS, ALICE. *A Hero Ain't Nothin' but a Sandwich.* New York: Coward, 1973.

CONAN, CAROLYN. *What Jamie Saw.* Arden, NC: Front Street Press, 1995.

COVILLE, BRUCE, ed. *Herds of Thunder, Manes of Gold.* New York: Doubleday, 1989.

CREECH, SHARON. *The Wanderer.* New York: HarperCollins, 2000.

DEJONG, MEINDERT. *The House of Sixty Fathers.* New York: Harper, 1956.

DICAMILLO, KATE. *The Tale of Despereaux.* Illustrated by Timothy Basil Ering. Cambridge, MA: Candlewick Press, 2004.

ECKERT, ALLAN W. *Incident at Hawk's Hill.* Boston: Little, Brown, 1971.

FATIO, LOUISE. *The Happy Lion.* New York: McGraw-Hill, 1954.

FENNER, CAROL. *Yolonda's Genius.* New York: Simon & Schuster, 1995.

GANTOS, JACK. *Joey Pigza Swallowed the Key.* New York: Harper Trophy, 1998.

GRIMES, NIKKI. *Bronx Masquerade.* New York: Dial, 2002.

HESSE, KAREN. *Letters from Rifka.* New York: Henry Holt, 1992.

HUDSON, JAN. *Sweetgrass.* New York: Putnam, 1989.

KONIGSBURG, E. L. *Silent to the Bone.* New York: Atheneum, 2000.

———. *The View from Saturday.* New York: Atheneum, 1996.

L'ENGLE, MADELEINE. *A Ring of Endless Light.* New York: Farrar, Straus & Giroux, 1980.

LOWRY, LOIS. *Anastasia at This Address.* Boston: Houghton Mifflin, 1991.

MAYNE, WILLIAM. *Drift.* New York: Delacorte, 1986.

NORTON, MARY. *The Borrowers.* New York: Harcourt, 1965.

O'DELL, SCOTT. *Island of the Blue Dolphins.* Boston: Houghton Mifflin, 1960.

PAULSEN, GARY. *Sisters/Hermanas.* Translated into Spanish by Gloria de Aragon Andojar. New York: Harcourt, 1993.

SALTEN, FELIX. *Bambi.* New York: Grosset & Dunlap, 1929.

STEVENSON, ROBERT LOUIS. *Kidnapped.* 1886. Reprint. New York: Scribner's, 1913.

———. *Treasure Island.* 1883. Reprint. New York: Scribner's, 1911.

TWAIN, MARK. *Huckleberry Finn.* 1884. Reprint. New York: Dutton, 1955.

VOIGT, CYNTHIA. *Dicey's Song.* New York: Random House, 1982.

WHITE, E. B. *Charlotte's Web.* New York: Harper, 1952.

WILDER, LAURA INGALLS. *Little House in the Big Woods.* 1932. Reprint. New York: Harper, 1953.

YEP, LAURENCE. *Dragonwings.* New York: Harper & Row, 1975.

"[Man] is immortal . . . because he has a soul, a spirit capable of compassion and sacrifice and endurance. The poet's, the writer's duty is to write about these things. It is his privilege to help man endure by lifting his heart, by reminding him of the courage and honor and hope and pride and compassion and pity and sacrifice which have been the glory of his past."

—*William Faulkner, 1949*
Nobel Acceptance speech

Bandit's Moon

Sid Fleischman

Illustrated by Joseph A. Smith

Style

Is it possible to identify the sources of distinctive style?

See what happens when you eliminate imagery and figurative language.

Consider now the literary element that makes language memorable—its style. Frequently someone asks, "But does the writer know what he or she is doing with words?" Yes. The author has added, subtracted, experimented, and substituted, creating the style that best tells her story. The skilled writer chooses words that become setting, plot, character, and theme to make a piece of literature.

Style is basically words, *how* an author says something as opposed to *what* he says. From an infinite number of words available, the writer chooses and arranges words to create a particular story, the words and arrangement best for that story. For example, on the first day of school:

> [Rufus Moffat] felt a slight impulse to run home and play as he used to. Play what? . . . Mud pies? he asked himself sarcastically. Pooh! He was too old for all that business now. He was going to school. Soon he would be going home to lunch.

This is Rufus, his own style—that is, author Eleanor Estes's choice of the style suited to situation and character in *The Moffats*.

By contrast, Scott O'Dell's formal and restrained language and simple sentence structure constitute the style suited to the setting, conflict, and character in *Island of the Blue Dolphins*. The protagonist, who lives a life totally dependent on nature, says in the opening lines:

> I remember the day the Aleut ship came to our island. At first it seemed like a small shell afloat on the sea. Then it grew larger and was a gull with folded wings. At last in the rising sun it became what it really was—a red ship with two red sails.

O'Dell uses nature comparisons throughout the survival story. Ramo has eyes "half-closed like those of a lizard lying on a rock about to flick out its tongue to catch a fly." An invader's beard is combed until it "shines like a cormorant's wing." Karana says the enemy's mouth is "like the edge of a stone knife." Word pictures and comparisons describe characters, action, and setting, but in a style suited to this story of a protagonist who lives with her antagonist, nature. The styles of *The Moffats* and *Island of the Blue Dolphins* could not be interchanged. In each case the style is right for that particular story.

Similarly, the style of *The Midwife's Apprentice* is suited to the medieval setting. Karen Cushman's sentences are sometimes long and rhythmic, as though the story were being told to attentive listeners. She often lists the tasks of apprentice Alyce, and the ancient healing herbs with their curative powers. She takes and stores "in her brain and her heart what she heard the midwife say and do about babies and birthing and easing pain":

> She discovered that an eggshell full of the juice of leeks and mallows will make a labor quicker, that rubbing the mother's belly with the blood of a crane can make it easier, that birthwort roots and flowers can strengthen contractions in a reluctant mother, and that, if all else fails, the midwife can shout into the birth passage, "Infant, come forward! Christ calls you to the light!"

In fiction, style at its best increases not only our pleasure in words and sounds, but also our belief in the characters' reality. We come to know them through the words they say, through the words that describe how they look and how they act. Eager to believe in the characters' experiences, we follow the plot and visualize the action described in the chosen words. Through words, we see, hear, and even smell the setting, realizing its effect on characters and conflict. Style is the product of all the choices the writer makes.

A writer's style is a personal choice dependent on setting, plot, and characters.

These choices are, of course, an entirely personal matter, since style and writer are inextricable. Mark Twain's style is no more Ogden Nash's style than Twain is Nash. One writer deals with the nature of reality or fantasy in one way; another expresses his vision in quite another way. A writer does, of course, vary style. Since one story differs from another, styles will differ as the writer suits style to story. Notice how O'Dell's restrained and dignified style in the opening of *Island* differs from his brisk and active language in the opening of *The King's Fifth*. This is not Karana but a different character:

> It was eight bells of the morning watch, early in the month of June, that we entered the Sea of Cortés. On our port bow was the Island of California. To the east lay the coast of New Spain.
>
> I sat in my cabin setting down in ink a large island sighted at dawn, which did not show on the master chart. The day was already stifling hot, so I had left the door ajar. Suddenly the door closed.

Style is not something applied to a finished piece of writing; rather, it is the writing, conveying both the idea and the writer's view of the idea. Henry James says that each word and every punctuation mark directly contribute to meaning; the content of a story and how it is told are inseparable.[1] Tone, word choice, grammatical structure, devices of comparison, sound, and rhythm—all are style. All these elements vary with the author's purpose, as the idea, the incidents, and the characters vary. Style gives the whole work its distinction and makes the story memorable.

One of *Harry Potter*'s many charms is the originality of J. K. Rowling's style. In *Harry Potter and the Sorcerer's Stone* some people among the Muggles actually "don't approve of imagination" But in the fantasy world of Hogwarts school of magic, broomsticks have names, like the new "Nimbus Two Thousand—fastest ever," a phrase reminiscent of a magazine ad for a new model car. Sweets come in a variety of forms: Chocolate Frogs, Drooble's Best Blowing Gum, Cauldron Cakes, and Every Flavor Beans that occasionally taste like liver or tripe, spinach or sprouts. The dirty Sorting Hat, patched and frayed, twitches and opens a mouth near the brim. Rowling describes the Great Hall at Hogwarts as lit by infinite numbers of candles that seem to float in the air. Tables glitter with golden serving pieces, and the many faces of the wizardry students seem to flicker in reflected light.

Originality and style are not the same, but they are related in the sense that a writer is an original. Nor should novelty be confused with style, for novelty is sometimes mere gimmickry—as it often is in Paul Zindel's novels, for example—rather than unique and personal expression. If the writer's way of telling the story and its truth is distinctively the writer's own, then that expression has a personal mark, and the style should become the best possible one for a particular work. Reading a work aloud is a pleasurable way to discover style as senses awaken, rhythms appear, and comparisons become vivid.

> Style is not *applied* to writing. It *is* the writing.

Devices of Style

The most easily identified element of style is the writer's use of certain specific devices of language. Many stylistic devices are listed in dictionaries of literary terms; our concern here is with those most often used in children's literature.

Connotation

Connotation is the associative or emotional meaning of a word. Connotative meaning, when added to dictionary meaning, or **denotation,** adds significance and impact to a term. Charlotte, for example, is not as big as a thimble, or as small as a fingernail, or as round as a button—all denotative comparisons that might convey her proper size and shape but that have no emotional impact. Charlotte is, instead, "about the size of a gumdrop." Now there's a reassuring comparison for a bloodthirsty spider. The stomach of gluttonous

> Words often have emotional meaning.

Templeton is not bulbous, or enlarged, or even like a ball. Instead, "as big around as a jelly jar" expresses comparative size and shape, but adds pleasant connotations. No spider egg sac ever had the appeal of Charlotte's; it is neither orange nor pink but peach-colored, and looks like cotton candy. Cotton candy, jelly jar, and gumdrop are all favorites with children; each of these comparisons describes size, color, and shape, but adds pleasant and positive emotional meaning.

Imagery

By far the most frequently used device, and the most essential, is imagery. **Imagery** is the appeal to any of the senses; it helps create setting, establish a mood, or show a character. We use imagery in our everyday conversations to describe sounds, smells, and sights. We say the sky is sapphire blue, the carpet is celery green, a jacket is fire-engine red; we describe the nature of a sound as clanging, buzzing, humming, or thundering. We say that tastes are bitter, sweet, or salty, that smells are acrid or musty, and that texture is scaly or slimy.

Imagery, or appeal to the senses, is part of conversation, too.

The writer relies on imagery to give the reader impressions of what the writer wishes to depict. But verisimilitude, or description to duplicate reality, is not the writer's only goal; suggestion and release of the imagination are important. The writer, by the choice of details and of the words used to describe the details, stirs the reader's imagination; the impact may be recognition or delight.

Charlotte's Web demonstrates the use and effectiveness of imagery. In the opening pages of the third chapter, Wilbur has just come to live in the manure pile of the Zuckerman barn, and we explore the building with him. No barn was ever more real, more suggestive of security and activity. The imagery convinces us as we smell the variety of odors, feel the warmth and coolness, and see the clutter of equipment. We may not settle down snugly in the manure pile, but we are as much at home in the barn as Wilbur is.

White describes the silence of the barn, but by sound imagery of a negative kind. The quiet itself is described by White's noting the absence of the customary noises; animals are so quiet that we hear only the weather vane:

> The sheep lay motionless. Even the goose was quiet. Overhead, on the main floor, nothing stirred: the cows were resting, the horses dozed. Templeton had quit work. . . . The only sound was a slight scraping noise from the rooftop, where the weather-vane swung back and forth.

When Wilbur first arrives at the fairgrounds, that setting is created for the reader by imagery. As White lists the senses one by one, a specific image appeals to each:

> They could hear music and see the Ferris wheel turning in the sky. They could smell the dust of the race track where the sprinkling cart had moistened it; and they could smell hamburgers frying and see balloons aloft. They could hear sheep blatting in their pens. An enormous voice over the loudspeaker . . .

White relies on imagery to make the reader aware not only of setting, but also of character and action. When Wilbur gets his buttermilk bath, we see him; he stands with closed eyes, feeling the buttermilk trickling over his sides. When he greedily opens his mouth and tastes the delicious buttermilk, Wilbur's childlike character is revealed. He stands in the pig trough and drools with hunger, while White itemizes the slops, each particle a distinctly visual image with a taste of its own:

> It was a delicious meal—skim milk, wheat middlings, leftover pancakes, half a doughnut, the rind of a summer squash, two pieces of stale toast, a third of a gingersnap, a fish tail, one orange peel . . . the scum off a cup of cocoa, an ancient jelly roll, a strip of paper from the lining of the garbage pail, and a spoonful of raspberry jello.

As we visualize slops, each item has color and shape in our minds. At the same time, White appeals to taste by listing foods a child knows and likes. And finally, the variety has the distinct quality of slops, since it is punctuated by a fish tail and a bit of garbage pail liner. Imagery not only helps create setting, but pictures action and character as well.

Figurative Language

Another device of style is **figurative language.** The writer uses words in a nonliteral way, giving them meaning beyond their usual, everyday definitions and thereby adding an extra dimension to meaning. Personification, simile, and metaphor are the most common kinds of figurative language in stories for children.

Children's stories often make use of **personification,** the giving of human traits to nonhumans or inanimate objects. In *Charlotte's Web* a large cast of nonhuman characters is personified, from Wilbur to the maple trees and even crickets:

For childen, pets and toys can be personified.

> The crickets sang in the grasses. They sang the song of summer's ending. . . .
> The sheep . . . felt so uneasy they broke a hole in the pasture fence. . . . The gander discovered the hole and led his family through. . . . A little maple tree . . . heard the cricket song and turned bright red with anxiety.

We hear the crickets singing, rather than chirping. The sheep are "uneasy," the goose "family" eats apples, and nearby the "anxious" maple turns autumn colors. Human qualities are given to everything. Where Salten fails in *Bambi,* White is successful because his personification is fresh and the story is fantasy, not sentimentalized realism.

In *The Jamie and Angus Stories* for young children, Jamie loves his toy Highland bull, whose "silky coat looked smooth as bath water and white as snow." Anne Fine's style aptly shows a child's devotion to a personified toy, the many ways in which that toy is part of a child's life, and stimulates imaginative play. Firm but loving parents treat both Jamie and Angus with affection.

One of the simplest figurative devices is the **simile,** a stated comparison between unlike things, using *as, like,* or, occasionally, *than.* Straw fluttered down "like confetti" at the exciting news from the Fair loudspeaker. When Charlotte is weary, she is swollen and listless and feels "like the end of a long day." These very specific comparisons are easy to see, since they are directly stated. Their combination of imagery and comparison makes them distinctive enough to stir the reader's imagination.

Implied comparisons, such as the sapphire sky and the celery green carpet, are called **metaphors.** They are sometimes so neatly put, so recognizably clear that we scarcely notice them—like the familiar "beads" of water decorating Charlotte's web. As Charlotte catches and stings her insect fare, she metaphorically "anaesthetizes" them. Templeton hears the Fair is a figurative "paradise," where he'll find a "veritable treasure" of leftovers, enough for "a whole army of rats." Paradise is great happiness, treasure great wealth, and army a vast number; all are metaphors.

Hyperbole

We are so accustomed to exaggeration as humor that we scarcely recognize it as a figure of speech; we often stretch a comparison to create **hyperbole.** When, for example, Mrs. Zuckerman is scared to death, or Wilbur threatens to die of a broken heart, the author uses hyperbole that has become part of our daily conversation. But when Templeton, grousing that he did not come to the Fair to be a newsboy, refuses to "spend all my time chasing down to the dump after advertising material. . . . Next thing you'll want . . . is a dictionary," his grumbling and sarcasm are hyperbole. Wilbur uses self-pitying hyperbole when he says, "I'm less than two months old and I'm tired of living." But we may laugh at the words of the sheep whose hyperbole is sheer imaginative extremism. He speaks to Templeton: "If Wilbur is killed and his trough stands empty day after day, you'll grow so thin we can look right through your stomach and see objects on the other side."

Much of Robert Newton Peck's *Soup's Hoop* is sheer nonsense hyperbole. Rob and Soup's new friend Piffle Shootsensinker, a seven-foot native of Pretzelstein, is unable to play basketball without the music of his native spitzentootle. So that Piffle can help Learning School win the basketball game, the two boys create a spitzentootle from this and that. Throughout the story, Rob speaks in hyperbole. Janice is the school scourge who, when she knocks out a fellow student's tooth, would take it home, "stuff it full of sugar, and watch it ache." When she lassos the boys, she finds a bug "not quite the size of a Shetland pony," and thinks it might fancy "a nasal excursion." The cereal the boys eat is called Soppies, because when touched by milk it is fit "only to be eaten by . . . starving maggots." In the earth-floored cellar, the boys see a rat, big "as a golden retriever. A kid could have throwed a saddle on that rat and rode it to school." In each case, the image such exaggeration creates in our minds is visually vivid.

Godless is written by Pete Hautman in the hyperbole of adolescence. For

Exaggeration or hyperbole often adds humor.

example, Jason, who has climbed inside the town water tower, wonders "what it would sound like to crank up some Metallica or Eminem inside that enormous metal cavern. If you got it loud enough, maybe people would hear it coming out their faucets." Arrested, he spends the night in jail: "I'm hungry and scared and I'm gagging at the reek of my neighbor's winey vomit. I lay wide-eyed on the narrow cot, staring at some pink chunky glop stuck to the ceiling. What is it? How did it get up there? My stomach churns."

Note the combination of similes and metaphors, personification, hyperbole, and imagery or appeals to the senses in a short paragraph from Gary Schmidt's *Lizzie Bright and the Buckminster Boy*. Turner has just heard that a developer wants to destroy the island homes in the African American settlement and to build a resort on the island.

> The afternoon had become as hot as meanness, and since the shirt he was wearing had enough starch in it to mummify two, maybe three, pharaohs, he began to feel he could hardly breathe. The only thing that saved him from absolute suffocation was the sea breeze somersaulting and fooling, first ahead, then behind, running and panting like a dog ready to play. And he followed it, pulling at his collar, trying not to wish what a minister's son should not wish.

Hyperbole adds interest to the regional way of speaking captured by Richard Peck, author of many books for children. In *A Year Down Yonder*, Mary Alice, sent to live in rural Illinois with Grandma Dowdel, finds her taciturn and fearless, managing to maintain dignity and humor while the Great Depression overwhelms the country. When Mary is nauseated, Grandma Dowdel says she "fights with her supper." She speaks of trick-or-treat as "vittles or vengeance."

Understatement

The reverse of exaggeration is **understatement,** or playing down. Like hyperbole, it may be used for comic effect. When Fern bites into a raspberry with a concealed "bad-tasting bug" and gets "discouraged," discouragement seems minimal. When Avery removes from his pocket the frog that has traveled back and forth on the barn swing all morning, scrunched and dried in a tight pants pocket, we read that the frog seems tired from a morning of swinging. Merely tired?

Like Karana in *Island of the Blue Dolphins,* the protagonist of Jan Hudson's *Sweetgrass* does not mention her sorrow but describes factually— and with restraint—the tragedy of her baby sister's death:

> Her tiny tummy was swollen already, puffed out like that of a corpse of many days. . . . Soon her shape would not be human at all.
> I knew what had come amongst us, then. Only one sickness killed so fast and turned its victims to foul black dung. Smallpox. The white man's smallpox had stolen into our camp and was now bent . . . over our little baby.
> I stumbled out and vomited into the snow.

Sometimes understatement can be more effective than hyperbole.

Sweetgrass searches for a blanket to wrap around the decaying corpse, as she considers ways in which to satisfy burial customs and yet make it possible for her to stay and nurse Almost-Mother and her two brothers. Finally, knowing she cannot properly satisfy custom, she makes her compromises. Restraint marks the descriptions, restraint that avoids sentimentality and yet convinces us that Sweetgrass grieves for her baby sister while she struggles.

While style in *The Jamie and Angus Stories* cannot be called understatement, notice how Anne Fine adapts style to the age of her audience of younger children, using simple and childlike sentence structure.

> Jamie folded up his clothes and found his pajamas, and climbed over Uncle Edward and Angus to get out onto the landing to put his socks and pants in the laundry basket. Then he climbed back over them both to draw his curtains and put on his reading lamp and turn his clock to face the exact right way.

Kira-Kira by Cynthia Kadohata is also told in the style of a young child. As Katie tells of caring for little Sam, of her parents' exhaustion, and of sadness as the family watches Lynn's death approach, she writes in the simple sentences of childhood.

> I cried and cried. For a while as I cried I hated my parents, as if it were their fault that Lynn was sick. Then I cried because I loved my parents so much.
>
> Then I didn't feel like crying anymore. I just felt barren, my eyes felt dry. The sky was still gray. Everything was gray, the sky and the store and even my hand when I held it in front of myself.
>
> And yet I knew Lynn was dead. I could feel the place inside me where she had [lived]. This place was empty.

Katie describes with simple vividness the love sweet Auntie and volatile Uncle Katsuhisa share.

> Uncle's face got wistful as he stared into the sky. Auntie kissed his face. He put his arm around her, and they leaned against each other.

Allusion

One figure of speech, **allusion**, probably has meaning only to the mature reader, since it relies on recognition of a reference to something in our common understanding, our past, or our literature. Few adults will miss an allusion—for example, to a disastrous experience, an exam perhaps—when it is called "my Waterloo." White adds an opportunity for pleasure for the adult reader when he alludes to the call of the white-throated sparrow that must have come all the way from Boston: "Oh, Peabody, Peabody, Peabody!" Some adults may recognize reference to the Peabody sisters of Salem, but if not, no meaning is lost; it remains a New Englander's description of the bird song, as well as a standard description of the birdcall. Again, one of the delights of

Alice in Wonderland for Victorian readers was the wealth of allusions they could recognize, although contemporary readers, young and old, may miss them. Allusion is difficult for children to catch, since it relies on a background they lack.

Symbol

A **symbol** is a person, object, situation, or action that operates on two levels of meaning: the literal and the figurative or suggestive. Certain symbols are universal: the dove is the symbol for peace, a flag symbolizes a certain country. Other symbols are particular to a story. Clearly, the necklace of shells Karana gives to Tutok in *Island of the Blue Dolphins* is a symbol of friendship. Less obvious is the Borrowers' emerald watch among all the unneeded and unmissed items borrowed from Aunt Sophie's household. It might be called a symbol for the latent materialism in Pod, and particularly in Homily.

> To be a symbol, a term needs meaning beyond its literal meaning.

In a picture book, too, symbol can help us understand a thematic point. *Fly Away Home* by Eve Bunting tells of a homeless father and his small son who live at the airport, moving constantly so as not to call attention to themselves. When a bird flies in, the boy watches it dash itself repeatedly against windows, trying to be free. Wounded, then rested, it finally manages to "fly away home," symbolic of the boy's hopes that he and his father will be able to fly away to a home.

A symbol, then, has significance beyond its literal self. At times we may think that a repeated sight or object is a symbol, but because the writer does not connect it with an idea, a mood, or some other meaning, it fails as a symbol. Clay in Paula Fox's *Monkey Island* uses a red crayon to add his own graffiti to others' on the walls of the elevator of the welfare hotel. Seeing a tiny "Stop" crayoned here and there, its red color standing out from the other scrawls, a reader may think it is a symbol for something. Vaguely, it connects with the problems in Clay's life as a homeless and abandoned child, but unfortunately its significance is never made clear.

Puns and Wordplay

An imaginative writer who enjoys the pleasure of words is tempted to echo words of other literary works. When White says that Templeton has no "milk of rodent kindness," we may recognize an echo from *Macbeth*. Wilbur is lured back to his pen by the promise of slops and the goose warns, "It's the old pail trick, Wilbur. Don't fall for it!" Here are echoes of "the old shell game." A sly grammatical error slides in, one that parents frequently correct in their children: "He also has a smudge on one side where he lays in the manure." And instead of correcting the grammar—*lies* for *lays*—Zuckerman corrects the facts: "He lays in clean straw." Then White adds a bad **pun** using another word: "untenantable" is implied.

"If that ancient egg ever breaks, this barn will be untenable."
"What's that mean?" asked Wilbur.
"It means nobody will be able to live here on account of the smell."

Finally, White plays with words in still other ways. Naive Wilbur uses faultless logic when he argues with the lamb that he is not less than nothing:

"I don't think there is any such thing as less than nothing. Nothing is absolutely the limit of nothingness. It's the lowest you can go.... If there were something that was less than nothing, then nothing would not be nothing."

Devices of Sound

Onomatopoeia

One sound device called **onomatopoeia,** or words that sound like their meanings, dominates an occasional paragraph of *Charlotte's Web*. For example, as White describes Wilbur eating his slops, he uses the onomatopoeic words "swishing and swooshing," which suggest Wilbur's happy gluttony. While these slushy sounds suggest one kind of eating, the explosive sounds of "gulping and sucking" describe another.

Alliteration

Another easily recognized sound device is **alliteration,** repetition of initial consonants, as in, "They *s*ang the *s*ong of *s*ummer's ending." The effect of the sentence is musical, but its movement is slow and the music sad and final. By contrast, the Zuckerman dump becomes exciting as visual imagery rhythmically piles up interesting debris, layer upon layer. Alliteration then adds to the pleasure of the passage: "*b*roken *b*ottles ... *d*iscarded *d*ish*m*ops ... last *m*onth's *m*agazines."

Assonance

A device that enhances meaning by the repetition of similar vowel sounds within a phrase is called **assonance.** When we hear the crickets' song, "*a* sad, m*o*n*o*t*o*nous s*o*ng," the neutral *a* and the similarly sounded *o*'s suggest the feeling of sorrow and sameness. Reading the passage aloud shows how sadness and monotony are here extended by assonance.

Consonance

The close repetition of consonant sounds is called **consonance.** In the phrase "emp*t*y *t*in cans and dir*t*y rags and bi*t*s of me*t*al and broken bo*tt*les," repetition of the abrupt *t*'s in varying positions in the words emphasizes the idea of ragged remains of unrelated items—junk. Again, reading the sentence aloud is the best test for sound devices, since sound rather than spelling shows how meaning is affected.

Rhythm

So closely is **rhythm**—from the Greek word rhythmos, meaning flow— associated with poetry and verse that we often forget that it is also part of prose. Stories that are read aloud to children can make particularly effective use of rhythm, which in prose is sometimes called **cadence.** White uses the word *and* to create rhythm as he shows the Zuckerman dump, an accumulation of one item after another, each joined to the others by *and.* Reading aloud is the test for rhythm as it is for other sound devices. Here is:

> . . . an astonishing pile of old bottles and empty tin cans and dirty rags and bits of metal and broken bottles and broken hinges and broken springs and dead batteries and last month's magazines and old discarded dishmops and tattered overalls . . . and useless junk of all kinds, including a wrong-size crank for a broken ice-cream freezer.

The rhythmic list slows to a halt with the last comma, followed by the final, jerking phrase filled with abrupt and explosive consonants: "a w*r*ong size cran*k* for a *bro*k*en* ice-cream *f*reezer." The changed rhythm brings the astonishing pile to an end.

Rhythm or cadence suits meaning.

An unusually effective example of cadence occurs in White's description of the rope swing as it flies back and forth. The first phrases of the passage anticipate "and jumped," and then the swinging begins. Again, by reading aloud, we hear each of the phrases shorten as the arc of the swing shortens. Abruptly the words bring the swing to a halt, and the swinger jumps to the ground:

> Then you got up all your nerve, took a deep breath, and jumped. . . . The rope would twist and you would twist and turn with the rope. Then you would drop down, down, down out of the sky and come sailing back into the barn almost into the hayloft, then sail out again (not quite so far this time), then in again (not quite so high), then out again, then in again, then out, then in; and then you'd jump off and fall down and let somebody else try it.

Rhythm ceases completely with the series of short, explosive words and phrases at the end of the paragraph. As the successive phrases shorten, there is pleasure in the description of action as well as in the understanding of the experience. Rhythm is the key.

❂ *Special Issues of Style in Children's Literature*

Trite Versus Fresh Style

A story written in clichés is dull, just as a person who thinks and speaks in clichés is dull. Some of the drabbest stories for children are often those that tie into children's television shows, like *The Muppets* or *Sesame Street.* Other popular fiction for children may rely exclusively for interest on subject matter focused on early adolescence. Many of Judy Blume's books are written in trite language. Here there are no surprises. For lack of figurative or connotative language or appeals to the senses through imagery, nothing is vivid. In *Then Again, Maybe I Won't,* the first-person narrator has just found that his friend is shoplifting:

> The salesman told me the mitt I liked was $37.50. I thought that was a lot of money. . . . I'd have to think about it. . . . I walked back to the cash register where Joel was waiting. I wanted to know if he thought $37.50 was too much for a mitt. But I never asked him because he was smiling his crooked smile and humming some tune.
>
> I thought, oh no! Please, Joel. I don't want to be sick again. I don't want to go back to the hospital. I know what you've done. I can tell by just looking at you. What'd you take this time, Joel?

We've heard this before. Or even worse—we feel we must have, even if we know we haven't. Nothing is distinctive here. The first-person narrator gives no sense of the personality of the speaker because the words spoken in vernacular lack individuality and freshness. Similarly, the style of writing in *Keep the Lights Burning, Abbie* is monotonous, although the subject—Abbie Burgess, the girl who, left alone in 1856, kept Maine lighthouse lamps burning—is potentially interesting. Simple sentences repeat words and information unnecessarily, and the reader grows impatient waiting to get on with the story.

Story and style work together for a coherent whole, but occasionally we encounter a combination that seems an uncomfortable mix. Such is the case with Walter Wangerin, Jr.'s *Elizabeth and the Water-Troll.* The story begins with a long and rhythmic line that promises a folktale, but in folktales we know who is good and who is not. Here we are confused by the ugly Troll who lives in the Well of Despair and resembles a conventionally drawn devil who "grins" and "creeps"; his teeth "flash" as he "speaks through his fangs," and his "claws [come] toward her face" as he "snarls." This Troll, we are to believe, loves Elizabeth, and yet the terms describing him portray a fearful monster. These are terms quite unlike those describing Beauty's sad and lonely but kind and thoughtful Beast in that folktale. Held to the Troll's breast, Elizabeth "feels his hurt as though it were her own," "a suffering," "a pain" we know nothing of, unrevealed to us now or later; he is "an injured creature whom she loves." Is his ugliness or his loneliness the source of his sadness? What causes her to love him? Further stylistic dissonance occurs when "He is frowning on account of a difficult thought," and in such double-negative phrases as "No, I won't trust nobody, nobody, since everybody lies." Elizabeth's father rushes "out of doors. 'Happy day! I know where Elizabeth's at!'" Abrupt shifts in what at times is folktale style, then ungrammatical colloquialism, prevent our feeling compassion for the Water-Troll or believing in Elizabeth's love for him.

In contrast, vernacular language may be clear and descriptive, like that of Jerome Foxworthy in Bruce Brooks's *The Moves Make the Man*. Jerome, a basketball player, strings his words together without breaks or pause; we feel and hear and see the shot, a pleasure in many sensory ways:

> [C]radling the ball and at the last minute pulling my left hand away like Oscar Robertson and snapping that lubricated right wrist and knowing, feeling it right straight through from the tips of the fingers that had let fly the ball and touched it all the way to the last, straight down the front edge of my toes just before they hit the ground again, that the shot was true, feeling the swish and tickle of the net cords rushing quick down my nerves, and landing square and jaunty in time to watch, along with everybody else, as the ball popped through the net without a single bit of deceit, so clean it kicked the bottom of the cords back up and looped them over the rim, which is called a bottoms up and means you shot perfect and some people even count them three points in street games.

Although Jerome does not slip fully into the vernacular, he manages to sound like a credible boy.

The use of the word "rap" in the title *The Mouse Rap* by Walter Dean Myers makes style immediately significant. Each chapter begins with a piece of rap as with, for example, the lines that open Chapter 2:

> *Phoomp! Phoomp! . . . Phoomp! Phoomp!*
> *Phoomp Phoomp Phoomp! Phoomp! Phoomp! Phoomp!*
> High waters run fast, still waters run deep
> 'Cause a man look old don't mean he asleep
> Those old-time dudes were big and bold
> And I'm glad I heard their stories told
> They were sometimes right, and sometimes wrong
> Their days were short but their stash was long
> A million bucks will blow your mind
> But your hand can't spend what your eyes can't find
> *Phoomp! Phoomp!. . .*

Rap style may convince some readers that there is something interesting in this story. Mouse, the first-person narrator, continues in the rhythm of African American idioms, and a reader follows the suspenseful story to find the money hidden by a gang years ago.

The style of Gary Paulsen's *The Winter Room* is unlike that in his adventure stories, but perfectly suited to the storytelling skills of Eldon, an eleven-year-old living on a farm in northern Minnesota. Many of his questions gain from his father and Uncle David only puzzling answers, "with words around the edges." "And sometimes Uncle David is never wrong so that might be the way of it." Time to thrash is Father's favorite time "if there's been good rain and the oats and wheat are good, and his sad time if it's been dry and the oats and wheat didn't make right." Fall is the time when "all the grain is up and the barn is full of hay and the fields are tucked in with haystacks waiting to be used and everything is done." Eldon describes arguing with his brother:

> Wayne says there aren't any divisions in things. We had a big fight one time over whether or not there was a place between days when it wasn't the day before and it wasn't tomorrow yet. I said there were places, divisions in things so you could tell one from the next but he said no there wasn't and we set to it. By the time we were done I had a bloody nose.

In his survival story *Hatchet,* Paulsen's style is very different. Brian finds seventeen leathery turtle eggs and knows that to survive he must eat them raw. He sharpens a stick to poke a hole in the shell, widens it with a finger and looks inside to see a yolk of dark yellow. We watch him as he brings the egg to his lips, closes his eyes, squeezes the flexible shell, and swallows as fast as possible. Despite its oily taste, it was an egg. "His throat tried to throw it back up, his whole body seemed to convulse with it, but his stomach took it, held it, and demanded more." The vivid sensory images show Brian's struggle to do what he must to survive.

Retellings and Translations

When a story is no longer protected by copyright laws, publishers may ask other writers to retell the story in "simple" language. *Peter Rabbit,* for example, has been retold countless times, sometimes with didactic messages for children or with new and trite illustrations. Hans Christian Andersen's "The Ugly Duckling" is another such example. For instance, a major children's author, a Newbery Medal winner, retells the classic Andersen story in such choppy sentences and drab phrases that it loses all its artistry; sensory appeals vanish with the vanished setting, and characters change to become dull and uninteresting. It is then a plot summary, not the story. As the mother duck sits on the eggs, she speaks in the most ordinary language, occasionally punctuated by "quacks" and self-congratulatory remarks. She is impatient with the last egg, slower to hatch than the others, then shocked that the last one is not as pretty as the others, but instead is a fat, ugly duckling. Meanwhile, the other ducklings add their "peep-peep"s to the dull story.

Now look at what Andersen actually wrote, as translated by R. P. Keigwin.[2]

> Summertime! How lovely it was out in the country, with the wheat standing yellow, the oats green, and the hay all stacked down in the grassy meadows! And there went the stork on his long red legs, chattering away in Egyptian, for he had learnt that language from his mother. The fields and meadows had large woods all around, and in the middle of the woods there were deep lakes.

Yes, it certainly was lovely out in the country. Bathed in sunshine stood an old manor house with a deep moat round it, and growing out of the wall down by the water were huge dock-leaves; the highest of them were so tall that little children could stand upright underneath. The place was as tangled and twisty as the densest forest, and here it was that a duck was sitting on her nest. It was time for her to hatch out her little ducklings, but it was such a long job that she was beginning to lose patience. She hardly ever had a visitor; the other ducks thought more of swimming about in the moat than of coming and sitting under a dock-leaf for the sake of a quack with her.

At last the eggs cracked open one after the other—"peep! peep!"—and all the yolks had come to life and were sticking out their heads.

"Quack, quack!" said the mother duck, and then the little ones scuttled out as quickly as they could, prying all round under the green leaves; and she let them do this as much as they liked, because green is so good for the eyes.

"O, how big the world is!" said the ducklings. And they certainly had much more room now than when they were lying in the egg.

"Do you suppose this is the whole world?" said their mother. "Why, it goes a long way past the other side of the garden, right into the parson's field; but I've never been as far as that. Well, you're all out now, I hope"—and she got up from her nest—"no, not all; the largest egg is still here. How ever long will it be? I can't bother about it much more." And she went on sitting again.

Here are a manor house, a deep moat, enormous dock-leaves so huge children can stand beneath them, a dense, figurative forest all tangled and twisted, an onomatopoeic "scuttling," the nonsensical granting of permission to the ducklings to look all around because green is so good for the eyes, the understatement about the size of the world—right into the parson's fields. The stork speaks Egyptian, and a patient mother continues her lonely vigil waiting for her last egg to hatch.

Our memories of *Tom Sawyer* include adventures and characters recalling Tom's runaway trip to the pirate island, his surreptitious night visit to Aunt Polly, and Tom, Huck, and Joe as they attend their own funeral. We remember hunting treasure by moonlight and getting lost in the cave, but we may not be aware that these memories are so vivid because of Twain's style: his use of the right word in the right place.

Twain meticulously describes Tom's and Becky's wandering farther and farther away from the cave mouth, intrigued by the possibility of exciting discovery. Notice the imagery and the figurative devices in Twain's description:

> Presently they came to a place where a little stream of water, trickling over a ledge and carrying a limestone sediment with it, had, in the slow-dragging ages, formed a lace and ruffled Niagara in gleaming and imperishable stone. Tom squeezed his small body behind it in order to illuminate it for Becky's gratification.

A reteller of *Tom Sawyer,* author Albert O. Berglund, matter-of-factly substitutes monosyllables and clichés and eliminates the allusion to Niagara

Retelling does not always improve a story, but may instead make the story drab.

Falls.[3] While Twain's Tom *squeezes* behind the ruffled Niagara, the reteller's Tom *steps* behind the falls:

> Soon they came to a place where a little stream, carrying limestone matter with it, had formed a falls of beautiful stone. Since Tom was small, he stepped behind the falls with his candle so that Becky might see the lacy stone lighted in all its glory.

Twain's description is filled with imagery; he uses details to describe the cave:

> In one place they found a spacious cavern from whose ceiling depended a multitude of shining stalactites of the length and circumference of a man's leg. They . . . presently left it by one of the numerous passages.

The reteller eliminates the long words; he substitutes for stalactites a trite comparison to ice that fails to create a picture, and he turns the children's awed exploration into a pleasant walk through a hallway:

> In one place they found a cave from whose top hung something that looked like ice. Parts of this were nearly the size of a man's leg, and when Tom held his candle up toward them, they shown in the light. The children walked all about this cave, wondering and admiring, and finally left by one of the halls.

Twain shows the children wondering, admiring, marveling, and being bewitched by turns. He creates mounting suspense, his imagery showing the enormous, endless caverns and corridors of the cave. His verbs change from those of appreciative awe to verbs of vigorous action that show Tom's fear and arouse fear in the reader: seizing, hurrying, darting, striking, chasing, plunging. However, when Berglund substitutes more ordinary verbs—saw, flew, put out, hurried—the action loses its suspense. As for the cave, Twain's is a labyrinth of endless passageways and a limitless lake; we fear Tom and Becky will never find their way out. In the reteller's version of the story, two children merely come to a small hall.

We might point out many more contrasts in the two versions of *Tom Sawyer*, each one showing how the loss of freshness in style results in the loss of suspense in the action, depth in characterization, and vividness in setting. The two stories are vastly different, even though the same events are reported in the retelling. The reason for the difference is not what happens, but how the writer selects and uses words to show what happens. This is style.

Translations may present other problems. In an otherwise beautifully translated story, *The Island on Bird Street* by Israeli author Uri Orlev, translator Hillel Halkin occasionally lapses from informal language into American slang. Polish Alex, the first-person narrator who is hiding in the ruins of the Warsaw ghetto of Holocaust days, is "bushed" (exhausted); feels "like a dope"; and is told to "shut up." Although these lapses seem trivial, in an otherwise seamless narrative that is totally convincing—rooted as it clearly is in the reality of Orlev's experience—they call attention to the story as a translation from another language in a way that *Island of the Blue Dolphins* does not.

A slang term may be so out of place that it disrupts credibility.

Lest these brief comments detract too much from an excellent and engrossing narrative, notice the convincing language describing Alex's scavenging efforts:

> I decided to make just one bundle of clothes. Into it went a few things that fit me, the suits for father, the coat, and some towels and sheets. I found a beat-up Polish army hat, the kind tough Polish kids like to wear, and stuck it happily on my head. Then I filled a second blanket with books and dragged the two bundles to the entrance to the cellar, where I took them apart and carried in a few things at a time. Before it got dark I went back again and took a mattress. I picked a nice soft one. And then I made one last trip for a folding chair that I managed to fit through the opening too.

Stories of Other Periods and Places

Word choice, or **diction,** should give the reader the flavor of the time, the place, and the events; this the writer does by use of language that seems native to the period and locality of the story.

Fantasy is maintained in *The Moorchild* by Eloise McGraw not only by using folktale elements like the changeling traded for a human being, but also by the rich cadences and unusual figurative language.

> Eavesdropping on the activities of the "Folk": . . . they boasted of their pranks around the cookfires; one had stripped a farmer's honeycombs, another emptied a fisherman's basket as fast as he filled it. . . . [Life] as it was meant to be . . . went on, seamlessly, until she and the other younglings had finished their night-time learning and began to go abroad by day—to find out about dogs and iron and crosses, and humans who were not safely asleep but awake and wary.

Here fantasy creates another world or society that uses its own vocabulary. An argument becomes an argle-bargle, a trundle bed a truckle bed, a fool a lack-brain, disciplinary detention a tether, and to hurry is to skimble-skamble. When the moorchild is angry, she "vents her baffled spleen," and when meaning is clear, it is "clear as a shout." Flavor and color are appropriate in *The Moorchild;* they apply to time, place, characters, and genre.

Another example, *Anpao: An American Indian Odyssey* by Native American author Jamake Highwater, is written in the style and form of the oral tale. The holy man Wasicong tells the story of Anpao's lengthy and dangerous quest, a task set for him by the beautiful Ko-ko-mik-e-is, whom he wants to marry. With his contrary twin Oapna, he must travel to the Sun and get his permission for the marriage. As we follow Anpao, the storyteller maintains a serious, mystical tone achieved by the evocation of the natural world, the formality of the language, and the long cadences of oral telling:

> Once again the sacred pipe was lighted and, under the new stars and among all the people of the land, it was passed around the great circle where the twins sat with the old swan-woman. The campfire rose into delicately twisting flames and the drums sang. . . .

Language can give "flavor" to an account.

Style is also compatible with setting.

Oapna had fallen asleep while the old woman told her story, and he lay wrapped in a blanket of swan feathers. But even in his sleep he seemed to ebb and drift in the new light of the Sun.

Laurence Yep's novel *The Star Fisher* tells of a fifteen-year-old Chinese American girl who has moved from the big city of Toledo to a small town in West Virginia, there to face the bigotry of an insular society that has never met anyone of Chinese heritage. Yep's story chronicles a variety of discriminatory experiences met by the children in school and in the town, a situation comparable to that in the old Chinese tale for which the book is named. It tells of star fisher birds, mystical creatures or changelings who are not at home on earth as people but nevertheless must stay. The necessity for each of us to understand groups in a multicultural society is well served by the realistic story. It is interesting, however, to note the difference in style between the narrator Joan's language as she tells the Chinese folktale to her little sister, and her speaking style for the rest of the story:

> "[The three women] were dressed in silken gowns—though the farmer could not decide what color they were because they seemed to change every moment. Around the women's shoulders were cloaks of golden feathers that rippled with a soft light of their own like the sunlight on the surface of a pond."

Style varies with genres.

The melodious language of the folktale evokes images of beauty through such terms as "silken gowns," "cloaks of golden feathers," "rippled," "sunlight on the surface"; the remaining narrative is the crisper speech of a schoolgirl:

> I snatched up Bobby's [lunch bag] just before the wind sent it swirling away. And as I sat folding up old paper bags, I could hear the laughter and happy shouts all around me; and I felt as I were trapped inside some glass cage—cut off from the laughter and happy voices that surrounded me.

Grab Hands and Run by Frances Temple is the story of escape to the North made by fugitive slaves. Not only is it a pleasure to be caught up in the excitement of a successful escape, but the account is made stylistically interesting by its vivid imagery and figurative language. Fear grips the small family, "making a hole in my brain," thinks Felipe. "Mama is like a balloon about to burst, a volcano ready to explode." Later:

> [A voice] comes from the shadow of a boathouse at the end of the dock. A man steps out suddenly, silently. He has on a leather hat and a gray serape. He smells of fish and sour tequila, and his eyes in the lantern light are red and vivid. . . . The man's voice comes out in short growls.

Style increases suspense as the reader wonders if the newcomer is friend or foe.

Stories of other cultures and times make special demands on the writer. Before we can accept them as believable, we must first believe that the characters are human like ourselves. To understand the new culture, we must see the particular differences between our own lives and those of other people. Style makes the difference.

High Fantasy

Since the most significant struggle in all human experience is that between the forces of good and evil, it seems appropriate that the language of high fantasy should have dignity. Spicing her serious tone and elevated diction with occasional humor—in descriptions of her pets, the foltstza and the yerig, for example—Robin McKinley uses long, complex sentences and slow cadences in *The Hero and the Crown*. Here elevated language appears in the final lines of the novel as we read of the years following Aerin's defeat of the dragon Mauer and the ascent of Tor and Aerin to the throne:

> Perhaps the memory of the reek of Mauer's despair made her a little forgetful too, for she began to think of the wide silver lake as a place she had visited only in dreams; for the not quite mortal part of her did sleep, that she might love her country and her husband.

Summary

Few of us are content with plot summary as a substitute for the story itself. What happened to the Ugly Duckling was not merely plot, since action alone does not make absorbing hours of reading. Helpful as Charles and Mary Lamb are in *Tales from Shakespeare,* the book is no substitute for Shakespeare, and a quick look at a book of plot summaries reminds us that *Tom Sawyer* and *Little Women* were never like this. Any good story is words, many words, selected and arranged in a manner that best creates character, draws setting, recounts conflict, builds suspense to a climax, and ties it all together with some significance.

Style involves the use of comparisons or figurative language appropriate to the story; imagery that describes for the senses what is happening or how things look; exaggeration or understatement to entertain or to heighten feelings; allusions to people or events already known; wordplay with puns or echoes; and sound devices to give pleasure and to heighten meaning. Appropriateness and freshness—the sense that these words are the best possible words for this particular story—are not only the style of the story; they *are* the story.

Notes

1. Henry James, *The Art of Fiction and Other Essays* (New York: Oxford University Press, 1948).
2. Hans Christian Andersen, *The Ugly Duckling,* translated by R. P. Keigwin, illustrated by Adrienne Adams (New York: Scribner's, 1965).
3. *Tom Sawyer,* adapted by Albert O. Berglund (Glenview, IL: Scott, Foresman, 1949).

Recommended Books Cited in This Chapter

ANDERSEN, HANS CHRISTIAN. *The Ugly Duckling.* Translated by R. P. Keigwin. New York: Scribner's, 1965.

BROOKS, BRUCE. *The Moves Make the Man.* New York: Harper & Row, 1984.

CARROLL, LEWIS. *Alice's Adventures in Wonderland.* 1865. Reprint. New York: Macmillan, 1963.

CUSHMAN, KAREN. *The Midwife's Apprentice.* New York: Houghton Mifflin, 1995.

ESTES, ELEANOR. *The Moffats.* New York: Harcourt, 1941.

FINE, ANNE. *The Jamie and Angus Stories.* Illustrated by Penny Dale. Cambridge, MA: Candlewick Press, 2003.

FOX, PAULA. *Monkey Island.* New York: Orchard, 1991.

HAUTMAN, PETE. *Godless.* New York: Simon & Schuster, 2004.

HIGHWATER, JAMAKE. *Anpao: An American Indian Odyssey.* Philadelphia: Lippincott, 1977.

HUDSON, JAN. *Sweetgrass.* New York: Philomel, 1989.

KADOHATA, CYNTHIA. *Kira-Kira.* New York: Atheneum, 2004.

McGRAW, ELOISE. *The Moorchild.* New York: Simon & Schuster, 1996.

McKINLEY, ROBIN. *The Hero and the Crown.* New York: Greenwillow, 1985.

MYERS, WALTER DEAN. *The Mouse Rap.* New York: Harper & Row, 1990.

O'DELL, SCOTT. *Island of the Blue Dolphins.* Boston: Houghton Mifflin, 1960.

———. *The King's Fifth.* Boston: Houghton Mifflin, 1966.

ORLEV, URI. *The Island on Bird Street.* Translated by Hillel Halkin. Boston: Houghton Mifflin, 1984.

PAULSEN, GARY. *Hatchet.* New York: Bradbury, 1987.

———. *The Winter Room.* New York: Orchard Press, 1989.

PECK, RICHARD. *A Year Down Yonder.* New York: Dial, 2000.

PECK, ROBERT NEWTON. *Soup's Hoop.* New York: Dell, 1992.

ROWLING, J. K. *Harry Potter and the Sorcerer's Stone.* New York: Arthur A. Levine Books, 1997.

SCHMIDT, GARY D. *Lizzie Bright and the Buckminster Boy.* New York: Clarion Books, 2004.

TEMPLE, FRANCES. *Grab Hands and Run.* New York: Orchard Press, 1993.

TWAIN, MARK. *The Adventures of Tom Sawyer.* 1876. Reprint. New York: Macmillan, 1966.

WHITE, E. B. *Charlotte's Web.* New York: Harper, 1952.

YEP, LAURENCE. *The Star Fisher.* New York: Morrow, 1991.

"Authors must write with the conviction that what they are writing can help others become more free, more sensitive, more clear-sighted; yet without righteousness."

—*Mario Vargas Llosa*

Toad Triumphant

William Horwood

Illustrated by Patrick Benson

Tone

Can you identify tone in a children's novel?

Why does it matter?

Try changing the story's tone and see what happens.

We hear the command from old cowboy movies—"Smile when you say that!"—and we know what the speaker means: "If you call me your friend, a smile will say you mean it, a frown will mean the opposite." Although identical words are used, friend or enemy can change meaning by adding a smile. The same words spoken by a teacher to a child acquire a different tone for different situations by the change in voice inflection. Pulling a rebellious child into the classroom, a teacher says, "Come on!" Encouraging a child to try the new word puzzle, the teacher says, "Come on!" Rejecting a long-winded excuse from the child who must clear the worktable, the teacher says, "Come on!" Each time, the words have a different meaning because inflection, or vocal tone, changes meaning.

Just as tone of voice reveals how a speaker feels about her subject, **tone** in literature tells us how the author feels about her subject. In literature, however, readers cannot rely on inflection in a writer's voice, but rely entirely on words. Words express the writer's attitude toward his work, subject, and readers. Without vocal inflection to help convey tone, the writer must choose words with great care.

The author's **style** conveys the tone in literature. Sentence structure, word choice, patterns, and arrangements—all influence style. Figures of speech are chosen for their sounds as well as for their meaning. All these choices create the style and determine the tone of the writing, revealing the attitude of the writer toward both the subject and the reader.

You may feel that tone is too subtle a literary element to be found in children's literature. But this is not so. For example, most readers would agree that Rudyard Kipling's tone in *Just So Stories* is humorous. Kipling's way of saying "This is the way it all happened—just so" is his own unique combination of matter-of-fact and humor:

> So the Elephant's Child went home across Africa frisking and whisking his [new] trunk. . . . When he wanted grass he plucked grass up from the ground, instead of going on his knees as he used to do. When the flies bit him he broke off the branch of a tree and used it as a fly-whisk: and he made himself a new, cool, slushy-squshy mud-cap whenever the sun was hot.

We suspend our disbelief and say wouldn't-it-be-fun-if, toying with the idea that it might really have happened this way. Fondness for the pompous Bi-Coloured-Python-Rock-Snake, and the Crocodile with his "musky tusky mouth" who stretches the "mere smear nose" into a handy trunk, makes a reader play along with Kipling's "facts" about how the elephant got his trunk. The tone here is the feeling resulting from all the elements working together—the mock-serious situation Kipling is reporting, the tongue-in-cheek characterization, the playful language, the deliberately overplayed, pretentious style. The humorous tone results from all of these.[1]

Tone in the *Just So Stories*, like tone in any writing, cannot be isolated from the words of the story. More specifically, words of all kinds, as well as the sounds of these words, show tone, and tone influences meaning. "Frisking," "whisking," and "plucking" are playful and lighthearted kinds of action expressed in short vowels and quick consonants. Their kinds of action are quite different from the action suggested by, for example, "slamming, banging, and breaking." If the light, rapid sounds of "fly whisk" became "fly-swatter," tone would become more serious; if the Elephant Child's "schloopy-sloshy mud-cap all trickly behind the ears" became instead an objectively described "cold, messy, runny mudpie dripping behind the ears," the harsher consonants and the longer vowels would influence and change the tone. Kipling's choice of playful words and quickly moving cadences makes his pretense of factual reporting into humorous spoof.

The literary meaning of point of view is the mind or minds through which we see the story—the voice telling the story, whether a character or an omniscient author. Tone is different. It is the author's *attitude* toward story and readers. By the writer's choice of materials, the writer almost inevitably reveals something about his or her own personality. If the author told the story orally, voice tone would reveal attitude and self; since the author is telling the story in print, the choices of words must be the means of showing attitude.

Tone cannot be isolated from the words of a story.

Tone in *Charlotte's Web*

How do we discover tone? Sometimes it's easier to describe a writer's tone than it is to be aware of how it is discovered. Tone seems to creep into our consciousness without our awareness. But tone, like the showing of action, depiction of character, and description of setting, is created by the writer's choice of words. If we look carefully at a few passages from *Charlotte's Web*, we may see how White's tone is revealed.

The first pages of the book are filled with kindness and affection: Mr. Arable looks at Fern "with love," and speaks to her "gently." Fern kisses her father and mother, pleased that the runt pig is safe. White describes the setting and the characters in the same kinds of affectionate terms. The action—Wilbur spinning a web, for example, or fainting at his honors—is humorous and yet affectionate.

The chapter "Summer Days" begins with a description of setting:

> The early summer days on a farm are the happiest and fairest days of the year. Lilacs bloom and make the air sweet, and then fade. Apple blossoms come with the lilacs, and the bees visit around among the apple trees. The days grow warm and soft. School ends, and children have time to play and to fish for trouts in the brook. . . .
>
> All morning you could hear the rattle of the machine as it went round and round, while the tall grass fell down behind the cutter bar in long green swathes. Next day . . . the hay would be hauled to the barn in the high hay wagon, with Fern and Avery riding at the top of the load. Then the hay would be hoisted, sweet and warm, into the big loft, until the whole barn seemed like a wonderful bed of timothy and clover. It was fine to jump in, and perfect to hide in.

In this selection, there are none but pleasant sensory images—fragrant lilacs, apple blossoms visited by friendly bees, children fishing for trout. Summer work goes on, but the sights and sounds are pleasant; work is another kind of sensory pleasure—rhythmic "round and round," colorful "long green swathes," sweet-smelling clover, a soft timothy bed for playing in. The abstract terms "happiest," "fairest," "warm," and "soft" describe the days, while "wonderful," "fine," and "perfect" describe the fun the days bring. Both the abstract words and the vivid appeals to the five senses have pleasant connotations. Summertime is not marred by a single unpleasant image or connotation. Summer fun is also humorous; Avery carries in his pocket a stiff, warm trout to be fried for dinner, or finds a slender grass snake and pockets it. Like the rest of the story, this chapter is filled with descriptions of a serene and pleasant world. White loves the summertime, the farm, the children, and the animals. Although White later builds suspense to a strong climax, his affectionate descriptions of all that summer brings have assured us that he will not permit disaster to come. While his emphasis on the cycle of seasons prepares for change, he never suggests in his choice of words that the change will bring tragedy or despair. Summing up White's attitude toward his story, we can best

Both sensory and abstract terms may have connotations.

characterize it as humorous affection. As White goes on to compare a gray spider to a gumdrop, the contours of a gluttonous rat to a jelly jar, and to describe a pig as terrific, radiant, and humble, affection and humor are apparent in all that happens in the story. White's word choices—style—have determined tone.

Humor

Humor has long been an important tone in children's literature. Much of the humor comes from situation, that is, incongruous happenings that make children laugh. The cow jumping over the moon, the barber shaving a pig—these situations are funny to a small child. Situation or action is also the source of humor in Astrid Lindgren's *Pippi Longstocking* and Robert McCloskey's *Homer Price.* But these stories are more than pie-throwing cartoons; they have invention and absurdity expressed in straightforward language.

Other stories depend for their humor on style or unexpected phrasing as well as on situation. Ludwig Bemelmans's *Madeline,* for example, in which the diction is precise and brief, not only shows a humorous situation, but also describes the situation in fresh and unexpected wording, rhythm, and rhyme. The crack upon the ceiling whose habit it is to look like a rabbit is situation nonsense; it is also humorous absurdity because of the unexpected internal rhyme and the personification that accompanies cracks having habits. The source of humor in *Winnie-the-Pooh* does not lie in the situation alone—sailing off on an overturned umbrella or disguising oneself as a black cloud. The humor rises as much from the quiet, almost solemn wording of conversations and descriptions surrounding the absurdities.

Few writers use humor as skillfully and pervasively as does Betsy Byars. Open any of her stories to any page, and you are likely to find reason to chuckle. In *The Burning Questions of Bingo Brown,* for example, the class bully moves into the house next door to Bingo, a bully so objectionable that he insults everyone:

> Mamie Lou's insult was, "Mamie Lou, you are a perfect 10. Your face is a two, your body is a two, your legs are a two. . . . "
> Tom Knott's was, "Tom, your nose is so big it has its own zip code."
> Melissa's was, "Melissa, you have the face of a saint—a Saint Bernard."
> "Harriet, you may not have invented ugliness, but you sure are the local distributor."

In *Bingo Brown, Gypsy Lover,* Bingo pedals to the post office to mail his Christmas gift earrings to Melissa:

> Bingo stepped up and took the post office pen. He had always wanted a reason to use this pen.
> On the inside of the card he wrote, "Well, here they are, Melissa. I hope you like them. I wish I could see your ears with them in them."

He regretted that "them in them." It wasn't topnotch writing. But the post office pen didn't erase.

He added:

"Merry Christmas forever."

A humorous tone carries Phyllis Shalant's *Beware of Kissing Lizard Lips* as each of the agonies of early adolescence comes along, from "muscles like pimples" to first boy-girl parties and unexpected hormone rages. Zach spends every spare minute trying to grow in both height and strength, and will try anything. After he connects with Nikki, who can teach him tae kwon do, he joins her at the ice rink despite his wobbly ankles.

A humorous situation described in serious terms is funny, too.

> Zach took a deep breath and pushed off with his right leg. But the ground refused to stay still. He brought his left foot down too quickly, snagging the ice so that he almost tripped. To catch himself, he threw his body backward, except then his right skate began sliding out from under him. To regain his balance, he waved his arms.
>
> "Quack! Quack!" someone called.

Laughter is a contagious kind of pleasure, and tone is often the source of it. Situation humor fills the pages of *The Canning Season* by Polly Horvath, but additional pleasure bubbles up from the verbal nonsense. While her mother and father tried to agree on a name for their baby, they noticed a tool left on the windowsill of the hospital room. Father called it a lug wrench, and Mother a ratchet. Mother won, and hence, the baby's name: Ratchet. The table cloth at Aunt Tilly's and Penpen's is a deep maroon, especially ordered to catch the "drippings" when their mother "offed herself" by "cutting her head off." She'd not been prepared for her head to "bounce." While this tone may be too slapstick for some children, others may enjoy it thoroughly.

In writing *Ali Baba Bernstein*, Johanna Hurwitz shows clearly how well she knows eight-year-olds. Each chapter begins with a different, exact recitation of David's age: eight years, four months, and sixteen days. Tired of being one of many Davids, he has changed his name to Ali Baba, another gambit common to eight- and nine-year-olds. Ali Baba, who fancies himself a detective, follows every false clue to its humorous conclusion. Finally, he invites all the David Bernsteins in the phone book to his birthday party. The tone is sustained throughout, and there is laughter on every page.

Humor is much evident in *Owen Foote, Soccer Star* by Stephanie Greene. Owen loves soccer and persuades his best but klutzy friend Joseph to play on the town team, but Joseph is worried:

> [Owen] didn't have to see Joseph's face to know what it looked like. Joseph could look worried better than anyone Owen knew. His eyebrows rose up in the middle. Like a mountain. . . . Even his eyeballs looked worried.

The cover announces tone in *Surviving the Applewhites*, by Stephanie Tolan. Despite its serious theme, it's a funny book all the way. The Applewhites run a special school—the Creative Academy. A family home school, it also takes in students expelled from other places. Jake, the new arrival, is dressed all in black and "scowling his most ferocious scowl ... his silver-spiked leather collar and his Vampire Zombies from the Beyond T-shirt with the skull and fangs that dripped bright red blood." Jake is accused of burning down a school, and looks tough enough to do it. In short order, the reader meets the Applewhite clan, including Winston the bassett hound, "his stubby front paws on each side of the cereal bowl, lapping up milk and leaking foamy saliva." Brother Hal is a reclusive artist, sister Cordelia a choreographer in black leotard appearing as she wrestles a recalcitrant goat to his pen. At first glimpse four-year-old Destiny, mouth agape, is shouting his version of the "itsy bitsy spider," but in a moment is endlessly interrogating Jake. Lucille, the "burbling" schoolmistress, appears in "capri pants and a billowy blue-and-green flowered shirt, her hair clamped on top of her head and spilling curls in every direction." Paulie the parrot has an extensive vocabulary of forbidden words. One after the other, the Applewhites are introduced, each showing evidence of a chaotic household. Not only people but also plot happenings are wild and strange and funny. The motley assortment of characters is humorous, and many situations as well.

Humor is not the predominant tone of many stories, but it often increases a story's pleasure. *Bud, Not Buddy,* Christopher Paul Curtis's story about a boy's search for his father, is far from somber, but Bud's hardships seem less threatening when relieved by humor. Bud lives by a series of survival rules, "Bud Caldwell's Rules and Things for Having a Funner Life and Making a Better Liar Out of Yourself." He is understandably cynical about his life being better if he's in a foster home; his experiences don't support that idea. From his mother Bud has posters showing an African American jazz band led by a bass player called Calloway, a name rather like his own. During the Great Depression, when jobs are tight, African Americans may have even less, but Bud finds they give help along the way to a hiking child who fights fear, vampires, and hunger. The topic he thinks about, losing that first tooth at six, is humorously recounted:

> At first you think it's kind of funny, but the tooth keeps getting looser and looser and one day, in the middle of pushing the tooth back and forth and squinching your eyes shut, you pull it clean out ... you lose control of your tongue at the same time and no matter how hard you try to stop it, it won't leave the new hole in your mouth alone, it keeps digging around in the spot where that tooth used to be.
>
> Unless you're as stupid as a lamppost you've got to wonder what's coming off next, your arm? Your leg? Your neck?

Bud's friend Bugs tells about how it feels to have a roach crawl into your ear and be removed by tweezers:

> "Well, bugs ain't so different from us as you'd think, soon as he saw those tweezers coming at him he was pretty terrified and commenced to screaming, screaming in English too, not some bug language like you'd expect from a roach."

Even during Bud's stealthy and frightening trek from Flint to Grand Rapids, Michigan, in the dark, Curtis interjects humor, describing how Bud hears bugs and toady-frogs and mice and rats playing tag. "Instead of being tagged and called 'it' like the way human beans play the game, out here the ones that got got, got ate up."

As for tone, Cynthia Voigt in *Bad Girls* makes us laugh. Two fifth-grade girls, both new to the school, find their initials, ME, are the same and from an assortment of similarities decide they are friends. Michelle (or Mikey) is a scrappy girl who challenges the boys at games, and fights with her fists at any provocation. Margalo, however, is shy and retiring, wishing to be more like Michelle. The "witch" teacher announces pet day just two weeks into the semester, and the two talk about their plans. Margalo will bring either her brother's gerbil or six kittens, and Mikey says it's irresponsible not to have the mother cat spayed.

> "That's not necessarily true."
> "It's irresponsible not to have her spayed."
> Margalo stared at Mikey and didn't say anything.
> Mikey thought maybe Margalo wanted to talk about something else. "So what's this gerbil's name you're bringing?" She hoped it was a friendly smile she was putting on her face. She couldn't be sure; she didn't have much practice with friendly smiles.
> Then she had an idea. "Maybe," she said, before Margalo could even start to answer the question, "I could bring in a roadkill. You know? In a shoe box, and I could make holes in the side of the box, with a pencil or the points of scissors."
> "That's really barfmaking," Margalo said and her face lit up. "They'd scream their heads off. I bet, don't you think? I mean, they'd really scream, all the girls, especially the Gap girls, I bet."
> "You wouldn't," Mikey said. She was glad to say something that would make Margalo feel good. She guessed maybe she wouldn't mind if Margalo did want to be friends.
> "No. But I'd already know it's already dead. When something's already dead, the horrible part is all over with."
> Mikey was relieved to hear that. She wondered if Margalo had seen a dead person.
> "You can't hurt a dead body," Margalo said. "It's true," she said.

Bring-a-pet day is chaotic, with an escaped rat and threats of a snake and a Rottweiler.

Many stories might not be called humorous in tone, and yet have moments of humor. E. L. Konigsburg uses humor throughout her stories. In *The View from Saturday,* each of the loners, the four members of The Souls, tells a personal story, some with more humor than others. For example, as Nadia expresses her curiosity about Nathan, grandson of her new grand-mother, she says this:

Serious stories often have moments of humor.

> Why had Margaret said nothing about his coming when we had seen each other at Sunday's brunch? Most grandmothers of her species carry a coffee-table-sized photo album in their tote-bag-sized pocketbooks. Either Margaret was a strange subspecies of grandmother or her grandson Ethan had done something strange to his hair. When grandmothers disapprove of grandsons, it is usually their hair.

Their hair or their music. Or both. She must have known about his visit for at least two weeks because everybody I know has to buy airline tickets that far in advance to get the discount.

Commenting on her grandpa's affection for his new bride, she says:

He seems to find it difficult to keep himself from pinching her or pinching himself for having had the good fortune to find and marry her. Such public displays of affection can be embarrassing to a prepubescent girl like me who is not accustomed to being in the company of two married people who like each other.

The Lemony Snicket series relies for most of its interest on suspenseful threats and possibilities, and is humorous as well. For example, in *The Ersatz Elevator*, Snicket turns common phrases around to contradict meaning: "It's all uphill from here," gives the reader pause: It "merely means that things will get better in the future." The names of the threatening forces are ominous: Dark Avenue, the Squalors who are the new caretakers, the Quagmires, Mr. Poe whose name suggests Edgar Allan Poe's spooky stories, and his business, Mulctuary Money Management. In elaborately formal language, the reader must dread the Beaudelaire's climbing the stairs in darkness, stairs to the Squalor's penthouse. Each step is lit only by a candle, and there are "forty-eight, but might be eighty-four" floors. Violet and Klaus are accompanied by little Sunny who speaks only nonsense, wordlike sounds that the author interprets. Sunny says, "Onesew," which means "Yes, ma'am," or "Lakry" "which meant something like 'There are no ropes.'" "It was darker than a pitch-black panther covered in tar eating black licorice at the very bottom of the deepest part of the Black Sea."

Stories for very young readers need not be written in drab prose, but may be as lively and entertaining as those for older readers. Patricia Reilly Giff, who writes for children in the primary grades, successfully holds attention with humor and real understanding of the concerns of that age group. In *Matthew Jackson Meets the Wall*, for instance, the worries about moving to a new town, a new home, a new school, and new friends are central. Matthew has much to hide or hide from: his poor reading and spelling skills, the new house that looks haunted, his cat Barney's disappearance, and The Wall, the boy next door who, he's been told, is fierce. Vivid prose shows Matthew practicing karate stance and shadowboxing to prove to himself that he's tough, but then finds there is nothing to worry about.

Children are expected to laugh at situation humor, since it is easy to see. But children are underestimated if it's assumed that is all they can find humorous. Children's discovery is limited by their exposure to the simplest and most obvious. A double row of beds and a double file of children is the situation humor of *Madeline*. However, "lived twelve little girls in two straight lines" is the sophisticated humor of style. Children deserve this source of humor, too.

Small children can appreciate verbal as well as situation humor.

Parody

Parody is usually a device for older readers, since it relies on the reader's memory of a known piece of writing or of a way of talking. It retains the form of the original but changes the words and the tone for humorous effect. "An hour of freedom is worth a barrel of slops" is a simple parody of an old saying—"An ounce of prevention is worth a pound of cure." A parody reminds of something known, then gives fresh pleasure by duplicating form that contrasts to new and humorous meaning. A clear parody for children is the bedtime story that Charlotte tells Wilbur. It has the traditional beginning, as well as the fluid phrasing, of folk- or fairy tale. Within the folktale parody is a description of the struggling fish trapped in the spider web. Read the paragraph aloud and notice its similarity to a prizefight account:

> "There was my cousin, slipping in, dodging out . . . dancing in, dancing out, throwing her threads and fighting hard. First she threw a left around the tail. The fish lashed back. Then a left to the tail and a right to . . . "

And again, try square dancing while Charlotte spins her web:

> "Now for the R! Up we go! Attach! Descend! Pay out line! . . . Whoa, girl! Steady now! . . . Now right and down and swing that loop and around and around! O.K.! Easy, keep those lines together! . . . "

The child catches some of the pleasures of White's parody and wordplay, but the adult catches many more; the result is pleasure for everyone. Lewis Carroll's literary parodies are extremely witty—Robert Southey's "The Old Man's Comforts" becomes "You Are Old, Father William," for example. But with the exception perhaps of "Twinkle, twinkle, little bat," White's parodies are unrecognized by the child—or by most of today's adults, for that matter. White, however, parodies word patterns from three familiar situations—folktale, prizefight, and square dance. Wit explained loses its wittiness, and these need no explanations.

A rare triumph in parody for small children occurs in *Santa Cows,* a picture book by Cooper Edens illustrated by Daniel Lane; success results from children's familiarity with "The Night Before Christmas." Using the exact rhythms and general outline of the original, the story tells of cows floating down through the chimney, singing carols with the family, giving game-play gifts, and stopping to play baseball in the snow of Christmas Eve.

Differing Tastes in Tone

We all bring to a story our own backgrounds and experiences, and the story has a personal meaning for us because we respond out of our own emotional history and present feelings. Readers, however, can take from a story only something already put into the story by the writer; tone is the effect of the

Response to literature is a transaction between reader and writer.

writer's words. If two readers describe tone differently, it is often the result of personal definitions of their descriptive terms, or the result of differing personal taste and experience.

Frances Hodgson Burnett's *The Secret Garden* is a story about an unloved young girl sent to live with a grieving uncle, who pays little or no attention to her. Mary's loneliness sends her out into the unkempt but once luxurious garden, where she finds a secret door to a secret garden that she tends lovingly. Finding in the huge mansion an equally isolated and unloved boy named Colin, she joins him, and together they restore the garden and themselves to health. To some readers Burnett's tone may seem cute, coy, or sentimental as her use of the omniscient point of view takes us into the minds of birds and flowers:

> The bulbs in the secret garden must have been much astonished. Such nice clear spaces were made round them that they had all the breathing space they wanted, and . . . they began to cheer up under the dark earth and work tremendously. The sun could get at them and warm them, and when the rain came down it could reach them at once, so they began to feel very much alive. . . .
>
> The first moment [the robin] set his dew-bright black eye on Dickon he was not a stranger, but a sort of robin without beak or feathers. He could speak robin (which is quite a distinct language not to be mistaken for any other). To speak robin to a robin is like speaking French to a Frenchman. . . . The robin thought he spoke this gibberish to them because they were not intelligent enough to understand feathered speech.

Recently *The Secret Garden* has once again become loved by many children. The many beautiful colored and black-and-white illustrations by Shirley Hughes placed throughout the story in a recent edition no doubt play a part, as does a reawakened interest in fantasy, to say nothing of the successful musical of recent years.[2] But perhaps after a lengthy run of severely despairing books, violent films, and news stories about the horrors of reality, *The Secret Garden* returns readers to a peaceful and hopeful world where children enjoy innocent play and awaken love in an idealized world.

The tone of *Winnie-the-Pooh* may seem to some readers whimsically affectionate. Pooh and Piglet do not converse in fragments the way we do, but in long, complex sentences filled with "that" clauses. And all the time, what they discuss so gravely is near nonsense:

> "I think that I have just remembered something. I have just remembered something that I forgot to do yesterday and shan't be able to do tomorrow. So I suppose I really ought to go back and do it now."
>
> "It isn't the sort of thing you can do in the afternoon," said Piglet quickly. "It's a very particular morning thing, that has to be done in the morning, and, if possible, between the hours of—What would you say the time was?"

One reader calls the tone whimsical and playful. Another reader, thinking the playfulness and sentiment excessive, reads Christopher Robin's words, "Oh, Bear . . . how I do love you!" and says this is not a lightly affectionate tone, but sentimentality—an adult talking the way children never talk. The same words

Appreciation of tone may change with generations.

Tone may be described by different people in different ways.

Tone may attract some readers and annoy others.

are used by the writer; two different readers receive them. The differing opinions might be called a matter of taste. Children, like adults, have their personal preferences. They may not define their reactions in terms of tone, but they may think the Pooh stories are "funny," or "silly," or "boring." On questioning them, we may find that these children are responding to Milne's attitude toward his material and his readers—in other words, tone.

Tone Related to the Author's Choice of Materials

Any kind of tone can be found in any kind of genre of children's literature. A fantasy, for example, may be serious in tone to fit its serious themes, as is Jacqueline Woodson's *Miracle's Boys.* Or the tone may be lighthearted, as it is in *The Wind in the Willows,* which—with its little universe of peace, its pictures of natural beauty, and its variety of friendly and harmless animal characters in a quiet country setting—shows in its tone Kenneth Grahame's attitude toward his characters and his story. In gentle and kindly acceptance, Grahame not only observes but also enjoys the differences among the characters, their styles of living, their preferences, and their habits. Bountiful leisure, filled with lunches, snacks, picnics, and breakfast extending into lunchtime, and all surrounded by profound good will, occupies a benevolent world.

First, notice how the setting reflects Grahame's tone. Rat loves his river. When the brown flood water "all drops away and shows patches of mud that smells like plum-cake," Rat "can potter about dry-shod over most of the bed of it and find fresh food to eat." "Plum-cake" and "potter about" are connotative of comfort and happiness. The river is Rat's world and its banks are covered with his friends. Mole learns to love it, too, to enter "into the joy of running water."

Badger is the perfect host in his house "behind comfortable-looking doors," a cozy home with "wide hearth," chairs grouped "sociably," "spotless plates" winking from the shelves, and rafters hung with stored harvest; "The ruddy brick floor smiled . . . the oaken settles, shiny with long wear, exchanged cheerful glances with each other; plates on the dresser grinned at pots on the shelf, and the merry firelight flickered and played over everything without distinction." Everything in Badger's house is friendly; each item is personified and made to smile, to glance cheerfully, to grin, to play and be merry.

Mole's underground home also has a welcoming front yard that shows love of home and a hospitable welcome: "A garden-seat stood on one side of the door . . . On the walls hung wire baskets with ferns in them . . . a skittle alley, with benches along it and little wooden tables marked with rings that hinted at beer-mugs." Here, also, the setting shows tone: the pleasant game court, lined with spectator benches and tables, shows a generous host who serves his friends refreshments in leisurely comfort.

This same kindness and acceptance appear in the characters' attitudes toward one another. Impetuous braggart Toad is "the best of animals. . . . So simple, so good-natured, and so affectionate . . . Perhaps he's not very clever—we can't all be geniuses; and it may be that he is both boastful and conceited. But he has got some great qualities, has Toady." Such terms as "accepting," "kindly," "friendly," or "genial" might describe tone, but all spring from the close relationship between the idyllic country setting and the gentle, accepting characters.

In her several books about Lynn, Mouse, and Mrs. Toggle the witch, Phyllis Naylor tells a spooky story, successfully awakening the reader's fear. Seeing their behavior in a totally realistic story of two girls in school, at home, on their bikes, in the cemetery where they talk staring up at the clouds, convinces readers that these are normal girls and everyday occurrences and behaviors. But in *The Witch's Eye,* whenever the glass eye—all that remained when Mrs. Toggle was killed in her burning house—is present, the tone becomes mysterious. The eye causes Lynn and her younger brother, Stevie, to be drawn to the river, to behave cruelly to family and friends, to sing the frightening song that croons, "Hear the shadows whisper back." They even seem to age and become the evil Mrs. Toggle. The eye winks; it sings a spooky song, and seems to bring a flock of crows that circle Lynn's house. Naylor successfully balances the realistic and the fantastic by adhering to suitable tone in each instance.

A humorous tone dominates the first part of *The Watsons Go to Birmingham* by Christopher Paul Curtis. Ten-year-old Kenny is taunted by his teasing older brother, King Cool Byron, who continually works at being a bad boy. When Kenny and his sister Joetta complain about wearing piles of warm clothes that their Southern mother insists on, lest they "freeze solid," Byron claims it's true. Furthermore, they mustn't ever look inside the garbage trucks with the huge mouths because early each morning the workers pick up all the bodies so frozen they "won't bend in the middle" and dispose of them. The tone becomes serious, however, once the family reaches Birmingham, where the Watsons experience racism. Now By is strong and tender, comforting the panicked family when the Sunday School where Joetta is thought to be is bombed. Tone changes as the situation changes.

> As a story's tension rises, tone may change.

Tone is hopeful in Lois Lowry's fantasy *The Giver.* A new society is examined, and its shortcomings suggest its end. In the impersonal but efficient society, people are in artificially constructed groups of spouses and "new-children" known by their functions assigned by the governing council. As the Receiver of history and memories, Jonas, the narrator, receives all past memories from the elderly Giver. As he learns bit by bit about something called "family"—that something called "love" connected people with one another, that old people were not "released" but kept in the family as beloved grandparents—Jonas becomes uneasy. When he learns that being "released to Elsewhere" is really being killed, he can no longer stay in his honored role as Receiver; with baby Gabriel, whose development is ominously slow, he takes off on his bicycle for an old-fashioned community where love and family live. Optimism wins as he looks ahead.

Literature for children usually touches on their particular concerns in today's world; one of these is the single parent. Ivy Ruckman in *Who Invited the Undertaker?* focuses on Dale's worry about the depression of his mother, Cathy, following her husband's death, and about the family's financial struggle. As children often do, Dale seeks a partner for his mother. Although his letter to the personal ads describing her interests draws women callers because he alludes to her only as "C," Dale does manage to set up a meeting with John that seems promising. The title of the story relates to the young undertaker-in-training who is attracted to his mother and may be fun, but is also struggling financially. John has the advantage. Cathy becomes a fighter for all single parents when she insists that father-son and mother-daughter programs are discriminatory. Although these are serious issues, Ruckman maintains a humorous tone in dialogue and in sustaining Dale's point of view.

Such a mixture is also apparent in Phyllis Naylor's *Reluctantly Alice,* a story filled with Alice's concern for her father's happiness, but also with humor and the usual traumas of a seventh-grade girl who wants everyone to like her. Elizabeth and Pamela talk about seeing boys naked. They have made a pact to tell each other everything, even embarrassing things, and not to laugh:

> "Well . . ." Elizabeth raised her shoulders and took a deep breath, then stared down at her feet. "I'm twelve years old, I'm in junior high, but I've—I've never seen a boy naked."
>
> I was waiting for her to get to the point, then realized that *was* the point.
>
> "So?" I said. "Elizabeth, you can still graduate."

Science fiction and high fantasy need carefully controlled tone to persuade us to suspend disbelief willingly. Throughout the high fantasy, *A Wizard of Earthsea* by Ursula Le Guin, the elevated language, often with long and sonorous line, emphasizes the seriousness of the struggle between good and evil in the soul of Ged. Le Guin preserves such departure from ordinary language when she describes the otak, a small animal Ged carries with him on his travels. Using inverted word order, she sets the otak apart from earthly animals. "They are small and sleek, with . . . fur dark brown or brindle. . . . Their teeth are cruel and their temper fierce, so they are not made pets of. They have no call or cry or any voice." Although not all high fantasy is written in so formal a tone, such word choice seems highly appropriate.

Ian Serraillier in his retelling *Beowulf the Warrior* uses the language of today and yet retains the tone and qualities of the folk epic as it was first recorded a thousand years ago. The intent of the folk epic is serious, since the long narrative centers on a national hero and makes clear the values of a people. Serraillier has respected this intent by maintaining a consistently dignified tone. He keeps the elevated language, the compound synonyms or kennings, the imagery, the alliteration, and the extended metaphors. In the passage below, Beowulf and his band set sail:

> They ran up the white sail. And the wind caught her,
> The biting wind whipped her over the waves.
> Like a strong bird the swan-boat winged her way
> Over the grey Baltic, the wintry whale-road.

At times a sympathetic tone may cause us to accept the unacceptable.

Heroes and their deeds deserve a tone of awe and respect.

The voyage across the sea is no happy, lighthearted sail across the bay; Beowulf and his valiant warriors face a sea worthy of their courage. Hand-to-hand combat with a monster has a dignity heightened by long, rhythmic lines, richly connotative terms, and alliterative descriptions with long vowels and hard consonants:

> Spilling the benches,
> They tugged and heaved, from wall to wall they hurtled.
> And the roof rang to their shouting, the huge hall
> Rocked, the strong foundations groaned and trembled.

The long sounds (extended *a*'s and *oo* sounds, slowly moving consonants—*l*'s, *g*'s, and *r*'s, for example) make the poetic lines move slowly to create a sense of dignity that accompanies the awesome struggle. After Beowulf defeats Grendel, Hrothgar praises Beowulf, and thereby shows his own generous and humble nature. But here shorter vowel and consonant sounds quicken the pace and so lighten the tone:

> . . . the grateful King,
> All glooming gone, his countenance clear and cloudless
> As the sky in open radiance of the climbing sun,
> Gave thanks to God for deliverance. "Beowulf," he said,
> "Bravest of men, I shall love you now as my son.
> All I have is yours for the asking."

Rosemary Sutcliff has retold the hero tales of Anglo-Saxon Beowulf and of Finn MacCool and Cuchulain of Ireland, Wales, and Scotland. Sutcliff, too, retains the elevated style of the epic, even while she describes characters that to us seem horribly bloodthirsty. These were days of fierce combat and intense loyalty to king and country. Cuchulain's story, *The Hound of Ulster,* is filled with such wars.

> For a long time after the fight at the ford and the death of Ferdia, for a long while after the wounds of his body were healed, it was as though Cuchulain were wounded in his mind; he had no joy left to him even in hunting, no joy in harp song, nor in the touch of [his wife] Emer's hands. But little by little, as the months passed into years, that wound also healed, though maybe the scar of it never ceased its aching. . . . The fire of life burned high in him again, and he answered as of old to the call of any adventure that came his way.

In the retelling of the epic about Finn MacCool, the supernatural element common to epics often intervenes, particularly as related to war. Here is a gentler passage about Finn's marriage to Saba, one of the Fairy Kind, but the language is nonetheless serious and dignified rather than sentimental:

> So she became Finn's wife, and their happiness was like the happiness of the immortals in the Land of Youth where spring never turns to winter, and magic birds sing always in the branches of the white apple trees whose blossom never falls, even when the apples sweeten and turn gold.

✪ *Special Issues of Tone in Children's Literature*

Condescension

Looking down on people, treating them as unintelligent or immature, is called condescension. In the original writings of the Greeks, Homer, Hesiod, and Pindar, the myths conveyed religious truth; they expressed the depth and seriousness of ancient faith. As Edith Hamilton says, we know Greek mythology best through the Greek writers who believed in what they wrote. One of Hamilton's examples is the story of Perseus and the Gorgon's head, a story that moves us, its brief descriptive phrases giving horror and urgency to the tale:

> And they are three, the Gorgons, each with wings
> And snaky hair, most horrible to mortals.
> Whom no man shall behold and draw again
> The breath of life.

By contrast, in Nathaniel Hawthorne's retelling in *A Wonder Book,* the Gorgons become snake-fairy-butterfly concoctions:

> Why, instead of locks of hair, if you can believe me, they had each of them a hundred enormous snakes growing on their heads, alive, twisting, wriggling, curling, and thrusting out their venomous tongues, with forked strings at the end! . . . and they looked very dazzling, no doubt, flying about in the sunshine.

By making the Gorgons into cartoonlike characters, Hawthorne has turned the tone of the story into ridicule; in descriptions of the hero himself—Perseus who slew the Gorgon Medusa—there is none of the expected dignity. Instead, in casual, quick-paced language, Hawthorne describes Perseus as pathetically vulnerable. His turning to stone would be a "very sad thing to befall a young man." Perseus's motives seem selfish and glory-seeking, as he "wanted to perform a great many brave deeds, and to enjoy a great deal of happiness in this bright and beautiful world." Perseus could hardly keep from crying. He felt "greatly ashamed . . . like a timid little schoolboy." "What would my dear mother do, if her beloved son were turned into stone?" "Dear me . . . I shall be afraid to say a syllable." All grandeur is lost in Hawthorne's version.

The tone in Hawthorne's retelling of the myth is condescending. He seems to be saying to the reader, "Now, children, isn't this a silly little story about foolish people?" There is no awe at the size of Perseus' task, no admiration for the courageous and liberating act. The myths of ancient people, myths that have come to us from those who believed in them, were filled with reverence and mystery, since by myth humans attempted to explain the wonders of humans and of nature. Hawthorne, although he may have followed the traditional details, has changed the myth completely by his condescending tone.

A modern example of condescension is Walt Disney's *Wonderful World of Knowledge,* volume 10, which does include the traditional details of the myths.

Myths should be told without condescension.

Although the diction is condescending, it is not as offensive as the illustrations: Pluto is Icarus and King Arthur; Mickey Mouse is Jason, Roland, Sigurd, and Galahad; Tinker Bell is one of the ondines, or water sprites, from the Norse Eddas. Despite color reproductions of classical artworks showing myths, the total effect is destroyed by the cartooned heroes.

Does this condescending tone matter? When a retelling so completely violates the original tone or the spirit in which it was told, the story is changed beyond recognition; a child meeting such condescension may be turned off by tone that talks down, and may never be encouraged or interested enough to find a better version of the myth. In original fiction, too, literature that talks to children as "dear little readers" demeans them; they may even be insulted. No one likes condescension, and the child who meets it may reject the pleasures and discoveries of literature.

Sentimentality

"Cute" stories are often condescending.

Sentimentality, or the overuse of sentiment, is a kind of condescension. Thornton W. Burgess, still in print and on some library shelves after many years, in telling his story *Mother West Wind's Animal Friends* is not only trite in language but also sentimental in tone. Burgess creates talking animals that have few traits to convince us either of their likeness to people or of their animal natures—except that those with wings fly, and those without, walk. Open a Burgess story and find this:

> Then old Mr. Toad picked up his cane and started down the Crooked Little Path to the Green Meadows. There he found the Merry Little Breezes stealing kisses from the bashful little wind flowers. Old Mr. Toad puffed out his throat and pretended that he disapproved, disapproved very much indeed, but at the same time he rolled one eye up at jolly, round, red Mr. Sun and winked.
> "Haven't you anything better to do than make bashful little flowers hang their heads?" asked old Mr. Toad gruffly.

The many capitalized nouns and adjectives, the personification of breezes, flowers, and sun, the repetition of words and phrases ("disapproved, disapproved very much indeed") and the clichés ("anything better to do") do little to convey conflict or to make the story move. Peter Rabbit (a nod to Beatrix Potter) and the "little meadow people and forest folk" are organizing an Easter Egg Rolling for everyone in the Green Meadows, the Purple Hills, and the Green Forest. The long-winded combination of sentimentality and the omniscient point of view create a coy tone and fail to reveal character or to describe actions. Burgess lacks respect for his readers as well as his characters; his condescension makes a shallow story.

By contrast, Scott O'Dell in *Island of the Blue Dolphins* never condescends, never demeans Karana's life by sentimentality. Her people have always lived on the windswept island, dependent on themselves and their own capacities to use what is provided by nature and to avoid death at nature's impersonal hands.

A product of this culture, living close to the elements, Karana quietly accepts what faces her. Life is sometimes cruel; humans survive by self-control. Ramo's being killed by wild dogs does not make Karana wild in her grief; we sense instead her feeling of inevitability and of necessity for restraint:

> All night I sat there with the body of my brother and did not sleep. I vowed that someday I would go back and kill the wild dogs in the cave. I would kill all of them. I thought of how I would do it, but mostly I thought of Ramo, my brother.

O'Dell's restraint makes us feel sympathy for and understanding of Karana in her isolation and loneliness; there is no sentimentality here.

The story of Paul Edward, who is of mixed race and suffers discrimination from both Whites and African Americans, might easily become sentimental. But Mildred Taylor in *The Land* successfully promotes understanding by a sympathetic rather than sentimental tone. A prequel to *Roll of Thunder, Hear My Cry*, this is Paul Edward's story; he is the son of a Southern farmer and his African American slave. Just after the Civil War, Paul Edward grows up in a close family of five children: Cassie, his true sister, and three older half-brothers born to the White farmer and his White wife. With his fair skin and hair, Paul is ostracized by both the White people who regard him as Black, and the African Americans who distrust him as part of the White world. In his struggle to be himself and be in control of his life, Paul encounters prejudice on every side. An argument with his close White brother Robert opens for him a realization that follows him through adulthood.

> I thought on my brother Robert. "If you're colored, that white man's going to always think of you with your color in mind, and I don't care how close you think you are, if that white man figures it's in his interest to turn his back on you, that's just what he's going to do."

Paul Edward's valuable palomino, won in fair competition, is killed by a White man, and although his friend does not understand, Paul does.

> Digger was a little man who had nothing. Out of his own meanness he had killed that magnificent animal because he had belonged to me, a man of color. He had killed my horse and he had killed my friend.

In his effort to save enough money for the land he loves, Paul says, "I worked with fever and I worked with pain. . . . I pushed myself until I could push no further." But White landowners do not believe he has the money, and bankers cannot believe he will repay a loan.

Nor is there sentimentality in Katherine Paterson's portrayal of Jess's grief at the death of his friend in the flood waters. In *Bridge to Terabithia* Jess's stomach "felt so odd." And yet, the morning after the news, pancakes doused in syrup taste "marvelous." Jess's sister accuses him of not caring, and he is puzzled: "The coldness curled up inside of him and flopped over." As Jess's mother and sister talk, he "could hear them talking and they were

Even the death of a loved one can be described without sentimentality.

farther away than the memory of a dream." He cannot leave the table, but he doesn't know what to do. Then, his mind a blank, he mumbles, "What little girl?" Paterson's depiction is not sentimental, filled with sighs and tears and sobs; we nonetheless see that Jess is shocked and grief-stricken.

The Winter Room is dedicated to the author's father. Gary Paulsen might easily have let his story of boyhood in northern Minnesota fall into the trap of sentimentality, but he doesn't. In the second chapter, "Spring," he describes his family, including his parents, his brother, Wayne, and his elderly Uncle David. Spring on a northern farm, the rooms and furnishings in the house, the farm buildings, the weaning of the calves, playing cowboys with his brother, and Wayne's jump from the hay mow to the old horse's back are the events of the chapter. In later ones, the first-person narrator tells the stories Uncle David told in the Winter Room (the parlor used only in winter), and concludes with a moving tale about a "strong young man" who could split a log from the ends by swinging two axes, one axe in each hand to meet perfectly in the center. To the narrator's horror, Wayne calls Uncle David a liar, and then, hiding in the loft, the boys see old Uncle David enter the barn and quietly, with great strain, manage the old trick. The story's poignancy comes from Paulsen's underplaying the incident while we see how the old man yearns for his youth and strength—and tries one more time to prove his strength to himself.

Missing May by Cynthia Rylant is a tale of love. Summer misses May, the most loving human anyone can imagine; in the little trailer, May was the source of all good for her husband, Ob, as well. Since May's death, life is empty. Ob is about to give in to grief, but Summer tries to keep him involved, to find new purpose for his life. A new focus for Ob is Cletus, an odd but beloved boy. It seems that love does not die but can keep adding new love objects. Without sentimentality, tone supports theme.

Nory Ryan's Song by Patricia Reilly Giff is about an Irish family, staving off starvation during the potato famine; it could easily lapse into sentimentality, but never does. Mother died in childbirth, Da has gone to sea, and the family awaits his return with fish and the rent money. Nory's older sister, Maggie, has married and gone off with her husband to live in the States, and Celia in desperation begins a walk to Belfast to find employment. Nory is left to care for three-year-old Patcheen, but there is no food. Desperate, she tucks her brother into a cleft in the rock and, with Sean holding the rope, climbs down the cliff to steal birds' eggs. She must not worry about his safety, but must attend to finding food:

> I'd think of the eggs round and warm in my hands. I'd think of opening them, one for me and one for Patch. Thinking of spooning a warm egg soup [into the mouths of Anna the starving healer, and her little brother]. . . .
>
> I touched [Sean's] hand, made the sign of the cross over myself . . .
> And took a step.
> And another.

Appreciation and respect avoid senti-mentality.

And turned my back away from the sea.

And lowered myself down, one rock at a time, feeling with my toes, testing each rock as Sean had said, to make sure it would hold me. And rested, catching my breath, leaning my head against a slab of rock, my feet on a wide flag.

Sentimentality is avoided; at no point in the story does a miracle happen. Facing reality and cruelty, Nory's struggle is clear and unabating.

Sun & Spoon by Kevin Henkes is quietly reassuring in tone. Spoon's Gram has recently died, and Spoon fears he will forget his wonderful grandmother unless he has something tangible to remember her by. Her solitaire cards seem appropriate until Spoon realizes that Pa treasures them, too. Then he remembers what Gram said about her name, "There's always an *M* in Martha," and discovers that the lines in his hand—and those of his parents—all carry an *M* for Martha. Gram will not be forgotten, because there will always by an *M*.

Janet Taylor Lisle also avoids sentimentality in *Afternoon of the Elves,* the story of friendship between Hillary and Sara-Kate, her impoverished neighbor. Sara-Kate's village of tiny elf houses made from twigs is the focus for their play—empty houses and invisible elves. Little by little, Hillary recognizes them to be the empty house Sara-Kate lives in with her sick mother—unfurnished, cold, and without electricity or telephone. Sara-Kate must resort to theft and hiding so that she and her mother can eat and survive. We suspect some of these conditions, but follow Hillary's gradual discoveries as appreciation grows for Sara-Kate's pride and her insistence on privacy.

The dedication in Bruce Brooks's *Everywhere* reads, "For my dad, and his," a dedication that could signal a story's lapse into sentimentality. In this case, the slim book tells of the ten-year-old narrator's experience of his grandfather's heart attack, and the remarkable "soul switch" his African American friend Dooley manages with the help of a box turtle, some nail polish, and a frozen chicken neck. Dooley, nephew of Lucy the nurse, knows some Native American lore that will get the soul of the turtle to switch with that of the dying man, so that the boy's grandfather will not die. The boy remembers making things with his grandfather, regrets that he has never shown him his secret place by the stream, and is fearful as he climbs to the bedroom window and sees the old man's body jerking in what may be death throes. Then he calms as he makes eye contact with the old man. The story is filled with the love of boy and grandfather, but despite the brush with death it never becomes maudlin or tearful.

Sensationalism

Sensationalism, as noted in the discussion of plot, is another kind of tone. Paula Fox's *The Slave Dancer* and the Colliers' *My Brother Sam Is Dead,* for example, might have been sensational in many places. The writers, however, have carefully chosen words that convey meaning and control tone but avoid sensationalism.

A sensational tone occurs in many books published for children. Pop stars are often accused of sensationalism in their concert appearances and song lyrics, resorting to highly flamboyant behavior to pull in the crowds. In fiction, sensationalism may often appear as the gratuitous and unwarranted inclusion of violence, or perhaps explicit sexuality, for the sake of selling books. Writers and publishers are not above such unnecessary and excessive sensationalism, and at times this tone takes over. Like overused sentimentality, sensationalism may dull the reader's reaction to emotional pain or physical discomfort in real life.

When Robert Cormier's *The Chocolate War* was first published in 1974, some criticism was leveled at what at first glance seemed sensational violence in the final boxing match that punished Jerry Renault for his refusal to join in the Vigils' behavior. That section of the novel, however, is an integral part of the whole and not added for sensational reasons; we know that unfortunately such behavior is not uncommon among the young. Cormier, who wrote *The Chocolate War* for his adult audience, was persuaded to make some changes for a younger audience. He is a fine writer whose work reflects the concerns and lives of young adults, while offering well-developed characters and strong themes.

Other stories with sensational segments are out there now. When first published, Judy Blume's *Forever* was much castigated for what by today's standards seems tame sexual allusion. A quick glance at books for young adults shows that Blume's book has been overtaken by those that include everything from four-letter words to a sixteen-year-old as mistress to a man of forty, a book in which the writing is not sensational, although some may consider the topic so.[3]

One kind of tone misunderstood by those who castigate folktales or nursery rhymes for their violence is **distanced tone,** a dispassionate view of the people, places, and events in a literary work. *Aesthetic distance* objectifies an emotion or experience. It depends on the reader's ability to recognize the separateness of art and reality. Form, as noted earlier, is strong in folktales, in their plotting as well as their characters, and because they are unlike anything known to them, readers do not identify with the characters or situation. Aesthetic distance results.

Didacticism

Didacticism, or preaching, is expected of sermons that point to moral lessons, and teaching from textbooks that spread before us the truths of concept or fact.[4] In folk literature, the fable exists only to make visible or tangible a moral lesson. In fact, that may be one of the pleasures of the fable: Once heard, a reader can say, "I know what that story means." Fable form requires didacticism, but in other imaginative literature it is a negative quality.

Literature for young adults often resorts to sensationalism.

Fables are meant to make clear a lesson or concept.

Perhaps one reader sees an obvious theme that appears didactic, while another reader will not find the story to be teaching or preaching, but merely to be developing a second theme.

By giving the protagonist a few personal traits and setting him or her into a narrative, the writer may seem to have created a story. (Remember the earlier discussion of *Willie Goes to the Seashore.*) But pleasure comes from a good story told well and understanding grows from a discovery about human nature; stories lacking these qualities often fail as literature.

Look, for example, at the picture book *I Want to Be a Homemaker.* Jane's mother gives her advice about her doll children. She says that they need good food—milk, eggs, vegetables, meat, and so forth—so they will grow. As Jane pours tea into her doll teacups, her mother adds that some foods will build bones and others muscles. Others give "pep" for running, jumping, and playing. "You see, Jane, we need many kinds of food." Moments later Jane tells a visitor about her doll children, who sometimes won't behave, won't brush their teeth, often get their feet wet, and even run into the street. Mother replies that a good homemaker is a teacher all day long.

Like the results of adding a statement to *The Tale of Peter Rabbit,* "Good bunnies always obey," a didactic story seems to have been conceived only in order to teach. Characters are undeveloped, conflict is nonexistent, and style is dull. All that survives is a didactic message: homemakers (that is, women) must know about child care. While *Homemaker* is an unfortunate example of sexist stereotyping, many "stories" seem to have as their purpose the underlining of a moral or the teaching of a lesson. Pleasure and understanding are lost.

Didacticism will always be with us. The degree of acceptance varies with the reader, but the pleasure is diminished for many when the moral seems more important than the characters and their significant experiences.

Changing Values

Styles in writing change—for children as they do for adults. Sometimes tone forces the retirement of a onetime classic. Such, it seems, may be the case in E. Nesbit's *Five Children and It,* a book that continues to appear on lists of classics but is no longer read by many children. While an occasional child today may still respond to the playful fantasy of *Five Children,* it is perhaps the sentimental and condescending tone that has retired it from the active shelf. Lamb, who is too old to be called a baby today, kisses the Gypsy woman, "a very nice kiss, as all his kisses are, and not a wet one like some babies give." Robert asks Lamb to "come and have a yidey on Yobby's back." Sentimental and stereotyped characterization combines with condescension toward Gypsies, "Eyetalians," and "Red Indians." Condescension and whimsy also contrast artificially the views of children and adults on what is real and true:

> Grown-up people find it very difficult to believe really wonderful things, unless they have . . . proof. But children will believe almost anything, and grown-ups know this . . . they tell you that the earth is round like an orange, when you can

Tone in a classic of the past may retire it from today's list.

see perfectly well that it is flat and lumpy; and why they say that the earth goes round the sun, when you can see for yourself any day that the sun gets up in the morning and goes to bed at night like a good sun as it is, and the earth knows its place, and lies as still as a mouse.

For contrast, look at Eleanor Estes's *The Moffats,* or Beverly Cleary's *Ramona and Her Father,* two other family stories. We might call the tone of such stories "wonder"—a kind of wonder that says "Aren't everyday, ordinary things remarkable?" Ramona, who has made herself a crown of burs and now must have her hair cut off in order to remove them, begs Daddy not to cut any more than he has to. "Does it look awful?" she asks. And her father replies with humor, "It will never be noticed from a trotting horse." Ramona lets out a "long, shuddery sigh, the closest thing to crying without really crying." When Ramona, whose father has lost his job, wishes she might earn a million dollars like the boy on the hamburger commercials, her father replies:

> "I'll bet that boy's father wishes he had a little girl who fingerpainted and wiped her hands on the cat when she was little and who once cut her own hair so she would be bald like her uncle and who then grew up to be seven years old and crowned herself with burs. Not every father is lucky enough to have a daughter like that."

Although the events of *Five Children* are fantastic and those of *Ramona* are humorously everyday, *Ramona* is far more successful in its creation of a sense of surprise. True, the children of *Five Children* live in an era more remote and foreign, but time distance is not the issue, since to a child time is not measured by decades. Possibly, what makes one story old-fashioned and relegates it to book lists and what keeps the other alive and read may be to a great extent tone, or how the author feels about the story's subject and readers. Our tastes in tone change. Baby talk was more acceptable in Victorian fiction than it is today.

Surprises often hold a reader's interest.

Variety of Tone

Some writers vary tone as the situation in the story changes; they use various tones to comment on people as individuals and as social groups. While such a story can often be read as a fast-paced, character-conflict-theme story, the perceptive reader who catches the shifts and shading of tone may find added pleasure in the story. As the readers recognize human manners and behavior, they also discover the author's attitude, and a whole new level of pleasure can be uncovered.

Note the various tone shifts in Andersen's "The Ugly Duckling." Andersen is sometimes humorous, sometimes tender, often critical, and even, sometimes, almost cynical. The child may read "The Ugly Duckling" often during the early years; because of the range of tone, at each reading the child discovers a new tone and added meaning.

Alice Childress, as she changes point of view with each chapter in *A Hero Ain't Nothin' but a Sandwich,* shows each of the speakers with a different tone. The principal's tone is resigned: "No matter what I do or don't do there are drug addicts." Benjie is naive when he says of his addiction, "I kicked once and I can kick any time I wanta." Walter the pusher, angry and protesting that anyone who sells anything is a pusher, says he is "pushin' for cops, when you get right down to it. You heard me! When I pay off, what the hell you think I'm payin' with? . . . I gotta hustle ten bags before I can pay the fuzz five singles, dig?"

Jean Fritz, too, varies tone. In the foreword to *Homesick: My Own Story,* she calls the book "my story, told as truly as I can tell it."[5] In an accepting and reminiscent tone touched with occasional gentle humor, Fritz observes people and events through the eyes of a child. When Jean's mother takes over her education, she insists on arithmetic, for example, figuring how long a train takes between Hankow and Peking at x miles an hour, stopping y times on the way. Jean, who hates arithmetic, protests the unnecessary study: "I knew that grown-ups never figured out such problems; they just looked at timetables." When Jean meets American girls and is asked to speak some Chinese, she obliges with Chinese insults, then refuses to translate: They are "worthless daughters of baboons," with big turtles for mothers. But Fritz is often serious. When her nurse Lin Nai-Nai returns from her home in besieged Wuchan, Jean finds her swaying in her chair, trouser legs rolled, foot bindings gone, "her stumps of feet, hard little hooves with toes bent under," painful from running "like a stumbling duck."

Few stories have greater variety and complexity in tone than *The Adventures of Tom Sawyer,* a story that offers great excitement on the level of character and plot alone. Mark Twain ranges over human attitudes from tenderness to sarcasm, from delight to cynicism. In his depiction of boyhood and adolescence, Twain admits that life is varied and contradictory; he uses tone to show its complexity and perversity. In reading the following passages from the novel, notice Twain's distance from, and yet smiling acceptance of, the self-deception and self-absorption of the young:

> [*On crushes:*] He had been months winning [Amy]; she had confessed hardly a week ago; he had been the happiest and the proudest boy in the world only seven short days, and here in one instant of time she had gone out of his heart like a casual stranger whose visit is done.

> [*On ceremony:*] The oath was complete. They buried the shingle close to the wall with some dismal ceremonies and incantations, and the fetters that bound their tongues were considered to be locked and the key thrown away.

Twain, in commenting on human behavior, is sly and faintly satirical:

> [*On theft:*] There was no getting around the stubborn fact that taking sweetmeats was only "hooking," while taking bacon and hams and such valuables was plain simple stealing—

> [*On the forbidden:*] Huckleberry was cordially hated and dreaded by all the mothers of the town, because he was idle and lawless and vulgar and bad—and because all their children admired him so, and delighted in his forbidden society, and wished they dared to be like him.

Complexity in tone contributes to complexity of understanding.

Although *Tom Sawyer* may be remembered as enjoyable, Twain is ironic, sarcastic, even cynical at times:

> [*On showing off:*] [The Sunday school superintendent] by bustlings and activities. [The librarian] by making a deal of the splutter and fuss that insect authority delights in. [The teachers] by bending sweetly over pupils that were lately being boxed.
>
> [*On accusation:*] The public are not slow in the matter of sifting evidence and arriving at a verdict.

And finally, on public sentimentality he becomes almost sardonic:

> This funeral stopped the further growth of one thing—the petition to the governor for Injun Joe's pardon . . . a committee of sappy women . . . in deep mourning . . . wail around the governor, and implore him to be a merciful ass and trample his duty underfoot . . . scribble their names to a pardon petition, and drip a tear on it from their permanently impaired and leaky waterworks.

By giving his novel a great variety of tones, Twain has increased the scope and significance of his story. He has shown what pleasure can come from observing all of life and from taking a stand on any and every aspect of it. By varying tone yet maintaining an overall attitude of humor and enjoyment of each experience, he has managed to create not only a novel of suspense and excitement, but also one that continues to amaze and delight, no matter what the age of the reader or the number of rereadings.

There are kinds of tone that seem unsuited to children's stories. Satire with its intent to reform is often too intellectual an exercise. It demands breadth of experience and ability to see and interpret exaggeration and understatement. Some stories are so strong that they carry the child's interest and the satire may be missed completely without loss to the reader—the *Alice* books, for example. As overall tone, sarcasm with its intent to wound is also too complex and thus questionable for children. To children, all experience is a subject for wonder. Condemnation, as well as fear and pessimism, seem to have little place in their literature; without experience to place these negative tones in perspective, they may be overwhelmed and moved to despair.

For a time, children's literature took increasingly honest looks at all areas of life, adding suffering, pain, and futility to stories for young readers. As long as these negative attitudes are not unrelieved, they have their place. However, children are less able than adults to defend themselves against despair, and so find the pessimistic messages more meaningful if they are presented within a story in which the tone is basically hopeful.

In addition to the opportunity to live with Laura and her frontier life, the tone of Laura Ingalls Wilder's Little House books may be a significant reason for their popularity. In each of the nine successive volumes, Laura is older and the reader follows with interest as she grows and matures. But an additional appeal is the consistent tone of quiet security, wild animals, hard work and deprivation, many moves and new houses, long and bitter winters, the long wait for Pa's return, and Mary's blindness. These surely hold us, but

Stories of other times and places let the reader live vicariously.

despite these and other inevitable uncertainties, they are never sensational-ized. In fact, some might say the stories are sentimental because hardships are minimized—or even forgotten—when we once again glimpse the firelit room, and hear Pa's fiddle and the click of Ma's knitting needles. Laura's content-ment with her life holds us as it concludes each volume.

What matters is that tone for children's literature be, if not optimistic, at least positive, or perhaps objective. For children, all the world is opening up; there is much to be appreciated and marveled at—and improved upon. If lim-iting tone to optimism and affirmation narrows it too much, consider only condescension and unrelieved sensationalism or despair as unsuitable. But in defending these kinds of tone, we remind ourselves of the functions of litera-ture. Futility and despair do not give pleasure or necessarily increase under-standing; there are dozens of other possible attitudes that may do this for young readers.

Summary

Tone, the author's attitude toward subject and readers, is an integral part of a story, since it is created by the writer's choice of words. It is not created by any single, obvious decision of the author; instead it is the result of all the choices made in telling the story. Tone can make the same story—one of heroes and valiant deeds, for example—either a series of trivial anecdotes or a monument to human valor. Tone can fill us with affection and acceptance, or rouse us to examine ourselves and even to laugh with delight at the frail-ties we find.

Notes

1. For further discussion of style and its relationship to humor in Kipling's *Just So Stories*, see Lukens, "Kipling's Humor in All Its Promiscuous Parts," in *Studies in American Humor*, Winter, 1986–1987, pp. 255–266.
2. See "To the Instructor" for comments about changes made in onetime classics (including *The Secret Garden*), changes necessary to appeal to today's children. Peter Hunt in *Children's Literature Quarterly*, Winter, 1996–1997.
3. Today's crop of novels for young adults, some fine and some disappointing, underlines the injustice of the continuous ban on that insightful novel *The Catcher in the Rye*, the story of Holden Caulfield's yearning for an ideal world.
4. Joanna Gillespie, in her article "Schooling through Fiction" (*Children's Literature*, New Haven, CT: Yale University Press, 1986), quotes from early litera-ture for children, part of the Sunday School movement: "It has been my design . . . to direct the minds of children to subjects of higher importance than those which generally occupy the pages of books put into their hands. . . . The silly stories which their fathers read in their childhood will soon be, perhaps in a double sense, 'tales of other times!' " (quote from writer William M'Gavin, 1849).

5. Jean Fritz has reconstructed her China childhood with true incidents but feels that the possibility of inaccuracy in chronology necessitates calling *Homesick: My Own Story* fiction.

Recommended Books Cited in This Chapter

BEMELMANS, LUDWIG. *Madeline.* New York: Viking, 1939.

BROOKS, BRUCE. *Everywhere.* New York: Harper & Row, 1990.

BURNETT, FRANCES HODGSON. *The Secret Garden.* 1911. Reprint. New York: Viking, 1988.

BYARS, BETSY. *Bingo Brown, Gypsy Lover.* New York: Viking, 1990.

———. *The Burning Questions of Bingo Brown.* New York: Viking, 1988.

CHILDRESS, ALICE. *A Hero Ain't Nothing but a Sandwich.* New York: Coward McCann, 1973.

CLEARY, BEVERLY. *Ramona and Her Father.* New York: Morrow, 1977.

COLLIER, JAMES LINCOLN, AND CHRISTOPHER COLLIER. *My Brother Sam Is Dead.* New York: Four Winds, 1974.

CORMIER, ROBERT. *The Chocolate War.* New York: Pantheon, 1974.

CURTIS, CHRISTOPHER. *Bud, Not Buddy.* New York: Delacorte Press, 1999.

———. *The Watsons Go to Birmingham.* New York: Delacorte, 1995.

EDENS, COOPER. *Santa Cows.* Illustrated by Daniel Lane. New York: Greenwillow, 1991.

ESTES, ELEANOR. *The Moffats.* New York: Harcourt, 1941.

FRITZ, JEAN. *Homesick: My Own Story.* New York: Putnam, 1982.

GIFF, PATRICIA REILLY. *Matthew Jackson Meets the Wall.* New York: Doubleday, 1990.

———. *Nory Ryan's Song.* New York: Delacorte Press, 2000.

GRAHAME, KENNETH. *The Wind in the Willows.* 1908. Reprint. New York: Scribners, 1953.

GREENE, STEPHANIE. *Owen Foote, Soccer Star.* New York: Clarion Books, 1998.

HENKES, KEVIN. *Sun & Spoon.* New York: Greenwillow, 1997.

HORVATH, POLLY. *The Canning Season.* New York: Farrar, Straus & Giroux, 2003.

KIPLING, RUDYARD. *Just So Stories.* 1902. Reprint. New York: Doubleday, 1946.

KONIGSBURG, E. L. *The View from Saturday.* New York: Atheneum, 1996

LE GUIN, URSULA K. *A Wizard of Earthsea.* Berkeley, CA: Parnassus, 1968.

LINDGREN, ASTRID. *Pippi Longstocking.* New York: Viking, 1950.

LISLE, JANET TAYLOR. *Afternoon of the Elves.* New York: Orchard, 1989.

LOWRY, LOIS. *The Giver.* New York: Doubleday, 1993.

MCCLOSKEY, ROBERT. *Homer Price.* New York: Viking, 1943.

MILNE, A. A. *Winnie-the-Pooh.* New York: Dutton, 1926.

NAYLOR, PHYLLIS. *Reluctantly Alice.* New York: Atheneum, 1991.

———. *The Witch's Eye.* New York: Delacorte, 1990.

O'DELL, SCOTT. *Island of the Blue Dolphins.* Boston: Houghton Mifflin, 1960.

PATERSON, KATHERINE. *Bridge to Terabithia.* New York: Crowell, 1978.

PAULSEN, GARY. *The Winter Room.* New York: Orchard, 1989.

RUCKMAN, IVY. *Who Invited the Undertaker?* New York: Harper, 1991.

RYLANT, CYNTHIA. *Missing May.* New York: Orchard, 1992.

SERRAILLIER, IAN. *Beowulf the Warrior.* New York: Walck, 1961.

SHALANT, PHYLLIS. *Beware of Kissing Lizard Lips.* New York: Dutton, 1995.

SUTCLIFF, ROSEMARY. *The Hound of Ulster.* New York: Dutton, 1963.

TAYLOR, MILDRED. *The Land.* New York: Putnam, 2001.

TOLAN, STEPHANIE. *Surviving the Applewhites.* New York: HarperCollins, 2002.

TWAIN, MARK. *The Adventures of Tom Sawyer.* 1876. Reprint. New York: Macmillan, 1966.

VOIGT, CYNTHIA. *Bad Girls.* New York: Scholastic Press, 2000.

WHITE, E. B. *Charlotte's Web.* New York: Harper, 1952.

WILDER, LAURA INGALLS. *The Little House* books. 1932–1943. Reprint. New York: Harper, 1953.

WOODSON, JACQUELINE. *Miracle's Boys.* New York: Putnam, 2000.

Hippopotamustn't and Other Animal Stories

J. Patrick Lewis

Illustrated by Victoria Chess

From Rhyme to Poetry

Children naturally respond to the rhythms and rhymes of verse, but some never move on to poetry.

Are these children missing anything you can describe?

When do children first meet literature? If they are lucky, they meet it in infancy, as early as the time they are making valiant efforts to "pat-a-cake, pat-a-cake, baker's man." Because nursery or Mother Goose rhymes use the elements of literature and the devices of style, and because the rhymes are sources of pleasure—sheer delight in sounds and stories shared by child and adult—they can legitimately be called the earliest literature for the youngest child. These **rhymes** are brief stories that have been passed orally from generation to generation, and are the beginning of poetry for children.

Nursery Rhymes

Few narratives in literature for child or adult are told with the joyful economy of the nursery rhyme. Many of them, like "Pussy cat, pussy cat, where have you been?" are the most tightly constructed stories. "Sing a song of sixpence, a pocketful of rye" tells a complete tale in three short verses. "Three wise men of Gotham" could hardly be more condensed:

Three wise men of Gotham
Went to sea in a bowl.
If the bowl had been stronger,
My story had been longer.

Small children—whose attention spans are limited—are introduced to brief fictional tales in rollicking rhythms and rhyming forms. While the rhymes are not poetry, they are the most natural introduction to poetry.

Literary Elements

The pleasure of stories begins with Mother Goose or nursery rhymes.

Many of the Mother Goose or nursery rhymes are the simplest and briefest of stories. The **characters** are the Queen of Hearts who made some tarts, the old woman tossed up in a basket, and Old Mother Hubbard whose cupboard is bare. **Setting,** too, is quickly sketched in some rhymes. Amazingly, the Old Woman lives in a shoe, and Peter Pumpkin Eater's wife lives in a pumpkin shell. The brief narratives have simple **plots.** The crooked man uses his crooked sixpence to buy a crooked cat that "caught a crooked mouse/And they all lived together in a little crooked house" for a happy closed ending. Action in these stories varies from the simplest of tumbles taken by Humpty Dumpty to the more complex involvements of "The House That Jack Built" and "Who Killed Cock Robin?"

Ideas also occur in Mother Goose rhymes, ideas a small child can grasp. Some of the simple rhymes are surprisingly clear in their insights, and oftentimes the short verse-stories have slight **themes.** Life is a fleeting thing, we discover from "Solomon Grundy":

Solomon Grundy
Born on Monday,
Christened on Tuesday,
Married on Wednesday,
Took ill on Thursday,
Worse on Friday,
Died on Saturday,
Buried on Sunday,
That's the end
Of Solomon Grundy.

Because of Dapple Gray, we know that "a pet is worth more than money":

I had a little pony; his name was Dapple Gray.
I lent him to a lady to ride a mile away.
She whipped him, she slashed him,
She rode him through the mire—
I would not lend my pony now
For all that lady's hire.

A child's understanding is increased in other ways.[1] Curiosity about the environment is roused when the commonplace is made exciting. The trip to the grocery store is no longer ordinary: "To market, to market, to buy a fat pig." And a walk beside the flower beds is time for "Mistress Mary's garden" with "silver bells and cockle shells and pretty maids all in a row."

Style

In a pleasant, regular beat of rhymes there is **rhythm** that may correspond to walking, breathing, and the heartbeat within us; rhythm is a way into poetry:

> Hickory, dickory, dock.
> The mouse ran up the clock.
> The clock struck one,
> And down he run,
> Hickory, dickory, dock.

The quick rhythmic movement makes a child jump to a beat:

> Jack be nimble, Jack be quick.
> Jack jump over the candlestick!

Children clap hands to "The Farmer in the Dell," and swing their arms to "London Bridge." Rhythm, which is determined by patterns of accented and unaccented syllables and by long or short vowels, moves the lines quickly and happily.

The variety of **sound effects** in nursery rhymes, although simple, acquaints children with poetic devices and gives pleasure. "A tisket, a tasket," "Hey, diddle, diddle," "Hickety, pickety," or "Rub-a-dub-dub" use **internal rhymes, assonance,** and **consonance. Alliteration** occurs in "Daffy-down-dilly," or "Peter Piper picked a peck of pickled peppers"; consonant and vowel repetitions exist in "Tommy Snooks and Bessie Brooks went walking out one morning." There is **onomatopoeia** in "Hark, hark, the dogs do bark!" and "Bow-wow-wow, whose dog art thou?" The enjoyable sounds of tongue-twisters are endless challenges. And of course the usual **end rhyme** is pleasing:

> Little Boy Blue, come blow your horn!
> The sheep's in the meadow, the cow's in the corn.
> Where's the boy who looks after the sheep?
> Under the haystack fast asleep!

Figurative language is another stylistic trait of Mother Goose rhymes. Dishes and spoons, ravens and daffodils, cats and mice, and ladybugs are excitingly **personified.** "Frogs and snails and puppy dogs' tails" contrast to "sugar and spice and everything nice," **metaphors** for "bad" and "good" qualities in little boys and girls. Jack Sprat and his wife figuratively—or literally if we prefer—"lick the platter clean"; in **simile** form, a snail is "like a little Kyloe cow."

As for **tone,** humor with delight is more prevalent than any other. There is laughter in:

> Barber, barber, shave a pig.
> How many hairs will make a wig?
> Four and twenty, that's enough.
> Give the barber a pinch of snuff.

Delight in sounds begins with nursery rhymes.

Humor, wonder, and play are parts of the earliest rhymes.

And there is seriousness in:

> Ding Dong Dell, Pussy's in the well!
> Who put her in? Little Johnny Green.
> Who pulled her out? Little Johnny Stout.
> What a naughty boy was that
> To try to drown poor pussy cat
> Who never did him any harm
> But killed the mice in his father's barn.

Verbal **irony** is found in:

> A diller, a dollar,
> A ten o'clock scholar,
> What makes you come so soon?
> You used to come at ten o'clock,
> And now you come at noon.

Wonder at romance and possible adventure is awakened in the melodious "Bobby Shafto's gone to sea," or in "I saw a ship a-sailing."

Emotional intensity may be more commonly thought of as a quality of fine lyric poetry, but there is also intensity and excitement in children's play and the rhymes that accompany this play. Children chant a teasing rhyme, "Tattle-tale, tattle-tale, hanging on a dog's tail!" Carried along by rhythms and sounds, children sing out variations on names:

> Sally-bum-balley, tee-alley-go-falley,
> Tee-legged, tie-legged, toe-legged Sally.

Or in the universal taunts of childhood, children adapt verses to their playmates' names:

> Janie's mad and I'm glad,
> And I know how to please her.
> A bottle of wine to make her shine,
> A bottle of ink to make her stink
> And all the boys to tease her.

Caught up in what Robert Frost calls the catchiness of rhythm and rhyme, children recite and improvise.

In the nursery or folk rhymes, children also find the intrigue of riddles. They ask each other rhythmic or rhyming questions:

> What can go up the chimney down,
> But can't go down the chimney up?

They are surprised that "umbrella" is the answer. And children don't forget this involved question:

> As I was going to St. Ives,
> I met a man with seven wives.
> Each wife had seven sacks;

In each sack were seven cats;
Each cat had seven kits.
Kits, cats, sacks, wives,
How many were going to St. Ives?

In addition to the rhymes we commonly call Mother Goose, children are made ready for poetry by many other folk rhymes that may have general similarities and local geographical variations. Children from many parts of the country know the ball-bouncing rhyme "When Buster Brown was one/He learned to suck his thumb." Some children, perhaps from a particular section of a particular state, seem to share common variations of similar rhymes, like the jump-rope verses with the refrain:

Folk rhymes vary from region to region.

Here comes the doctor,
    Here comes the nurse,
Here comes the lady
    With the alligator purse.

Other rhymes seem to appear by some magic, known at first only to an inside group on a particular playground. If the rhymes are catchy enough, they are soon carried across the country by a child who moves away, or by a visitor who returns to a hometown. It seems unlikely that those who have jumped rope to this rhyme will forget it:

When children memorize their own choices, appreciation of poetry thrives.

Fudge, fudge,
Call the judge.
Mama's got a baby.
Ain't no girl,
Ain't no boy,
Just a plain old baby.
Wrap it up in tissue paper.
Put it on the elevator.
First floor, miss!
Second floor, miss!
Third floor, miss!
Fourth floor—
Kick it out the door.[2]

Nonsense

Nursery rhymes and sidewalk jingles merge with nonsense; there is no line of demarcation. While each is joyful in itself, both prepare the child for poetry. When the cow jumps over the moon, that's nonsense. Of all the animals that Adam named, the least likely moon-jumper is the stodgy cow. Nonsense plays on our delight in the illogical and the incongruous, on our pleasure in words cleverly used or misused, on some secret yearning to see the immutable laws overturned. The best nonsense can do all these things. Edward Strachey wrote in 1894 in his introduction to Edward Lear's *Nonsense Omnibus* that nonsense is not "a mere putting forward of incongruities and absurdities, but the bringing out of a new and deeper harmony of life in and through its contradictions." Strachey called nonsense the "true work of the imagination, a child of genius, and its writing one of the Fine Arts."

Commonly used phrases can be confusing to a small child, and Jack Prelutsky capitalizes on that confusion in his nonsense verse, "I Wave Good-bye When Butter Flies":

> I wave good-bye when butter flies,
> and cheer a boxing match.
> I've often watched my pillow fight,
> I've sewn a cabbage patch,
> I like to dance at basket balls,
> or lead a rubber band.
> I've marveled at a spelling bee,
> I've helped a peanut stand.

Children thrive on nonsense. They make up and invert words or make illogical comparisons; one child tells another "It's cold as a bumblebee out!" and both children roll on the floor in glee. They repeat nonsense words in series, just for the pleasure of tasting and hearing their sounds: "Eenie-beenie-pepsi-deenie"; "Hogan-Bogan-Mogan was her name." Nonsense relies on rhythm, sound patterns, figurativeness, compactness, and emotional intensity—the intensity of laughter that may be repeated, stored in the memory, then shared again and again.

Rhythm and Sound

The **limerick** form, first popularized by Edward Lear in the nineteenth century, is the most traditionally structured nonsense verse. It clearly shows how important to nonsense are rhythm and sound:

> There was an old lady named Crockett
> Who put a new plug in a socket
>   But her hands were so wet
>   She flew up like a jet
> And came roaring back down like a rocket.

Suitable to the tone—lighthearted laughter—the rhythm is quick, with the syllables more frequently unaccented than accented. The sounds are short, with happy rather than serious overtones.[3]

Compactness and Surprise

Much of the humor in nonsense verse comes from the surprise of names, events, or words. Look, for example, at Harry Behn's "Circles," which surprises us by the consistency of its plural word endings, all distorted to rhyme with "compasses":

The things to draw with compasses
Are suns and moons and circleses
And rows of humptydumpasses
Or anything in circuses
Like hippopotamusseses
And hoops and camels' humpasses
And wheels on clownses busseses
And fat old elephumpasses.

Laura E. Richards's "The Owl and the Eel and the Warming Pan" is made up of perfectly assorted incongruities, since more unlikely characters and events would be hard to assemble:

The owl and the eel and the warming-pan,
They went to call on the soap-fat man.
The soap-fat man he was not within;
He'd gone for a ride on his rolling-pin.
So they all came back by the way of the town
And turned the meeting-house upside down.

The lighthearted treatment of disaster or the slightly macabre are often subjects for nonsense; nonsense verses often comment on current fads as well, as does X. J. Kennedy in "A Choosy Wolf":

"Why don't you eat me, wolf?" I asked.

"It wouldn't be much fun to.
Besides, I'm into natural foods
That nothing has been done to."

In the rhythm and rhyme of nonsense, ordinary creatures become extraordinary, as this anonymous verse notes:

What a wonderful bird the frog are—
When he stand he sit almost;
When he hop, he fly almost.
He ain't got no sense hardly;
He ain't got no tail hardly either.
When he sit, he sit on what he ain't got almost.

Lewis Carroll wrote some of the most compact and intense nonsense, so witty that not a word is wasted, not a sound is out of place. "The White Rabbit's Verses" from *Alice in Wonderland,* for example, uses more than forty pronouns, and yet has only five nouns to which the multitude of pronouns might refer. The twenty-four lines are written in such logical word order—subject, verb, complement—that they thoroughly convince us of their truth. And yet, when we finish the six verses, we have no idea what we are now convinced of.

Carroll's most admired nonsense is "Jabberwocky," a mystifying tale of valor:

> 'Twas brillig, and the slithy toves
>   Did gyre and gimble in the wabe;
> All mimsy were the borogoves,
>   And the mome raths outgrabe.
>
> "Beware the Jabberwock, my son!
>   The jaws that bite, the claws that catch!
> Beware the Jubjub bird, and shun
>   The frumious Bandersnatch!"
>
> He took his vorpal sword in hand:
>   Long time the manxome foe he sought—
> So rested he by the Tumtum tree,
>   And stood awhile in thought.
>
> And as in uffish thought he stood,
>   The Jabberwock, with eyes of flame,
> Came whiffling through the tulgey wood;
>   And burbled as it came!
>
> One, two! One, two! And through and through
>   The vorpal blade went snicker-snack!
> He left it dead, and with its head
>   He went galumphing back.
>
> "And hast thou slain the Jabberwock?
>   Come to my arms, my beamish boy!
> O frabjous day! Callooh! Callay!"
>   He chortled in his joy.
>
> 'Twas brillig, and the slithy toves
>   Did gyre and gimble in the wabe;
> All mimsy were the borogoves,
>   And the mome raths outgrabe.

Perhaps the best-known popularizer of nonsense verse for several decades was Ogden Nash, many of whose verses are known by adult and child alike. Nash's nonsense employs rhythm and made-up words. For compactness, one could not improve on:

> Dentists' anterooms
> Give me tanterooms.

Poetry

We move from nursery rhymes and nonsense to poetry with a feeling, perhaps, that now the discussion will become somber and difficult to follow. Not so. Something about the idea of getting meaning beyond amusement from brief groups of words in short lines, each line or phrase usually beginning at the left margin, seems to frighten many readers. Strange to say, readers read along easily in paragraphed pages, but if the same words are placed in stanza form, the meaning seems less quickly apparent, and readers may feel lost.

Prose and Poetry

The difference between poetry and prose is not as great as it may seem. Much of what we encounter in poetry we have already met in rhymes or in prose. Flow or cadence in prose may become more regular in poetry and be called rhythm, or meter. Sound patterns in prose, like alliteration and onomatopoeia, exist in poetry to an even greater degree. Connotative meaning in prose acquires heightened significance in poetry. Figurative language that compares unlike things exists in prose, but occurs more frequently in poetry. What seems to take us by surprise and to make us feel that the two forms are totally different lies elsewhere. When poet Octavio Paz, a Nobel prize winner, was asked about writing poetry, he replied, "You compose it, and some way, well, silent but aloud. You are hearing with the mind, the sounds."

The principal difference between prose and poetry is *compactness.* A single word in poetry says far more than a single word in prose; the connotations and images hint at, imply, and suggest other meanings. In a sense, the poet distills meaning in brief and vivid phrases. Economy and suggestion evoke our response.

The characteristics of poetry that set it apart from prose are essentially *rhythm, sound patterns, figurativeness, compactness,* and *emotional intensity.* The last two qualities are to a large extent the results of effective use of rhythm, sound patterns, and figurative language to produce compressed expression in words. This compactness in turn results in emotional intensity, a particular quality of poetry.

Analysis of rhythm in such metrical patterns as anapestic or iambic, or of such line patterns as dimeter or tetrameter, seems irrelevant to our discussion of rhythm in poetry for children. We focus here not on naming the forms of meter, but on the *use* of rhythm.

One question seems in order. What is the difference between poetry for adults and poetry for children? Once again, the difference is not in kind, but in degree. We may arbitrarily divide poetry for adults by theme and subject—love or nature lyrics, death or war lyrics, for example. Adults are also concerned about the passage of time, the inevitability of death, and the changing of relationships. Just as the interests of adults are the subjects of their poetry, the concerns of childhood are the subjects of children's poetry. Since much of childhood is spent in play, or in wonder at what is common and yet not commonplace, what surrounds children in their constantly unfolding world are the subjects of children's poetry.

Some poetry appeals to both children and adults, and it seems impossible

Compactness presents a challenge, not a mystery.

"There are no good poems ... suitable only for children."
W.H. Auden

and unnecessary to designate it as poetry for either group. However, in discussing rhyme and poetry for children, we *can* be somewhat more concise, although no less arbitrary. Nursery or Mother Goose rhymes are the happy rhythmic verses of early childhood; they can also be said to include riddles, chants, and tongue twisters. As the inventive rhymes focus more on the incongruous and the surprising or unexpected, they become more nonsensical, and we tend to call them nonsense rather than nursery rhymes. Where the division comes, anyone and no one can say. When nonsense seems masterfully created, we may find ourselves calling it poetry, and yet where poetry and nonsense begin and end—again, anyone and no one can say. What does seem important is that we appreciate the particular qualities of language form that are distinctively poetic. In our discussion of the arbitrary categories—nursery rhymes, nonsense, and poetry—the focus is on these qualities. The essential point remains that poetry is poetry, and that poetry for children differs from poetry for adults in degree, but not in kind. Subject matter may differ, but standards remain the same.

Many have tried to define poetry, and most have found such definitions difficult. A. E. Housman sardonically calls poetry a secretion, "whether a natural secretion, like turpentine in the fir, or a morbid secretion like the pearl in the oyster." Robert Frost calls it simply "a performance of words." Most definitions of poetry, however, return to at least one central idea derived from the Greek origin of the word. A poet is a *maker*, and poetry is *made;* every word counts.

Unlike the word "created," which implies inspiration and mystery, the term "made" suggests materials and effort. If poetry is made, it does not emerge perfect from the writer's pen. Like anything that is made, poetry follows a pattern of development: conception, effort, technical discipline, and refining and polishing before the maker is pleased with the thing made. Most likely the poem is written and rewritten; words are crossed out; substituted for, perhaps replaced with earlier words; rewritten, crossed out, substituted for again—until the maker-poet feels the poem is finally right. Of course, effort alone does not make a poem, any more than it makes good fiction. Skill, patience, and the critical judgment of the disciplined mind are a more likely combination.

> "Being inspired" is passive. "Making" a poem takes energy and effort.

Verse and Poetry

First, let us say that **verse** differs from poetry. Merriam Webster defines verse as "metrical writing distinguished from poetry especially by its lower level of intensity." *American Heritage* goes further to say that verse is metrical writing "that lacks depth or artistic merit." What matters is not that we distinguish between them, congratulating the poet for poetry and denigrating the versifier for verse. That is not the issue. Once again, we are aware of a continuum; at one end is trite doggerel and at the other the finest of lyrics. Such distinction may suggest that verse is of a lower order than poetry, which is, by one definition, the most imaginative and intense perceptions humans can express concerning themselves, others, and their relationships to the world outside themselves. Another definition—noble emotions, noble thoughts, expressed by noble minds—seems a forbidding description. Far more inviting is Shelley's statement. "Poetry is the record of the best and happiest moments of the best and happiest minds." Such a definition includes an extensive part of the continuum.

The content of poetry is emotion; its contribution to humans is significance. Perhaps one person will insist that beauty—and beauty is a matter of preference—must illuminate a familiar object with newness and sensitivity; as Coleridge says, poetry's immediate object "is the communication of pleasure," again an end achieved through a wide spectrum of sources. Or, as Wordsworth says, it is "the spontaneous overflow of powerful feelings recollected in tranquility." Note that these statements suggest both joyful intensity and serene happiness, but not all poetry is tranquil or serene. Some is somber, even upsetting. Such feelings may come to us from what one critic might call verse and another poetry, but the possibility of such emotions arising from the experience of doggerel seems highly unlikely. Emily Dickinson had criteria for poetry that few poets can achieve; her statement surely sets poetry apart. "If I read a book and it makes my whole body so cold no fire can ever warm me, I know that it is poetry. If I feel physically as if the top of my head were taken off, I know that it is poetry."

> Not all poetry is joyful, beautiful, or serene. Other feelings are also appropriate.

Given the inevitability of difference of opinion, and perhaps even the irrelevance of making a distinction, it might still be worthwhile to look at how some critics have defined verse. They maintain that while poetry is an end in itself, verse has a specific purpose. Poet-critic T. S. Eliot, for example, who seems almost to dismiss verse as "a superior amusement," describes poetry by contrasting it to verse. He says that while feeling and imaginative power are found in real poetry, verse is merely a matter of structure, formal metrical order, and rhyme pattern. Its structure, furthermore, may seem more important than its meaning. Proverbial wisdom occurs in verses as simple as "A stitch in time/Saves nine." The purpose of other verses is to sell diet drinks and chewing gum; still others convey traditional sentiments. We know what greeting card verse is, and, perhaps without knowing why, have a feeling that it is not poetry. Some of such verse is humorous, some sentimental, and some so incongruous that it may provoke a condescending smile: "To love a father is no fad/When he's a father like my dad."

> According to T. S. Eliot, the structure of verse often seems more important than its meaning.

Verses can be pleasant and entertaining; they can remind us of sentiments and ideas with which we agree, but often their expression is trite and awkward, with rigid metrical structure, ordinary images, obvious rhymes, or phrases twisted to produce rhyme. They are not poetry as T. S. Eliot has described it— the distilled and imaginative expression of feeling. Annette Wynne's "I Keep Three Wishes Ready" is a pointless verse with an incongruous, marching rhythm that takes over the meaning; the speaker expects to meet a fairy and has three wishes ready. But fairies float, they flit, they drift—never march.

Prose would say more clearly and with greater brevity the idea expressed in sixteen lines filled with empty, throwaway words.

We have a tendency to see the name of a poet, like Robert Frost or John Ciardi, and assume that everything that person writes is fine poetry. That is not the case. Both Frost and Ciardi, as well as many, many other poets, have written verse that is clever and some that is pedestrian. We assume, too, that Robert Louis Stevenson's *A Child's Garden of Verses* has been around so long, it is all poetry. Or that A. A. Milne, who delights us with his Winnie-the-Pooh tales, is writing poetry in *When We Were Very Young*. The division may sometimes be difficult to distinguish, but the difference between verse and poetry lies in intensification of feeling and in distillation of language, not in regular end rhymes and predictable figures of speech.

Large quantities of both verse and poetry are available to children. With exposure, children grow in awareness of the pleasure that artful poetry can bring. Greater experience with imaginative poetry can lead children to an awareness and appreciation of Walter de la Mare's "rarest of the best." But children enjoy verse as well; each has its place.

The difference lies in the distillation and feeling of language.

Kinds of Poetry

We sometimes simplify the classification of poetry and say there are two kinds of poems: **narrative,** situational or story poetry; and **lyric,** or song poetry. Two familiar examples of narrative poems are Alfred Noyes's "The Highwayman" and Robert Browning's "The Pied Piper of Hamelin," found in many anthologies.

Poems may use a narrative form as well as convey emotion. Kaye Starbird often mingles slight narrative with personal poetry rich in imagery and figurative language, as she does in "That Morning in June":

That morning in June when I wakened
   at sunrise
And walked alone,
I followed a path through the country,
   half-hidden
And overgrown,
Where everything, everywhere glittered
   and sparkled.
Everything shone.

Along with the shimmering grass near
   the dewy
Path that I took,
The tipped-over bowl of the sky had
   a gleaming
And polished look,
And so did the glimmering fishes
   that circled
The see-through brook.

It seemed as if Someone important
   had ordered
The world to shine.
And suddenly everything listened
   and glistened,
Each leaf, each vine
And even the numberless needles
   on every
Steeple-topped pine.

In case (when I'm older) I find I'm forgetful
Of things I've known.
I hope I'll remember forever that morning
I walked alone,
That morning when everything,
   everywhere sparkled.
Everything shone.

Narrative poems for children may be of any length, of course; surprisingly, even in eight short lines, a story comes alive. Kristine O'Connell George in "New Friends Talking" captures the experience of finding a new friend.

Talking all the way, we're suddenly at my house.
We're not done, so much more to talk about,
so we turn around, keep on walking and talking
all the way back to Kori's house, but we're *still* not
finished, so we walk around the park (twice), then we
keep walking and talking halfway back to my house.
Then

                  We run straight home
                  To phone.

One type of narrative, the **ballad,** comes to us from traditional or folk literature. Other ballads are of known authorship; both may show supernatural intervention, themes of physical courage and love, and incidents common to ordinary people. Developing the story through dialogue and using little characterization or description, ballads traditionally have abrupt transitions, are frequently incremental in structure, and rely on refrains. "John Henry," like other folk ballads originally sung, flows with songlike cadence, and exemplifies many ballad qualities.

Other poems are **lyrics,** or songlike poems that use sounds, rhythms, and figurative devices to express emotional response to some brief moment of experience. Some adult poems are a pleasure to both children and adults, and most children's poems can be enjoyed by adults. The intense experience of lyric poetry, however, is often given to children in some kind of situation or story form.

Rhythm

In the best poems, rhythm does not distract, but reinforces meaning.

Look now at the characteristics of poetry, several of which are known to children through rhymes and nonsense. The recurrence of stress is called **rhythm.** In our discussion of rhythm in prose, we mention cadence or flow, but when rhythm is set into a more regular pattern as it often is in verse or poetry, we speak of **meter.** The poet uses rhythm to enhance the feeling that the poet's words express. In choosing the rhythm for a poem, whether it be unvarying metrical form or more freely flowing lines, the poet makes several commonsense choices. When we are happy, we speak quickly; when we are sad, or serious, or matter-of-fact, our words come more slowly. In the same way, the poet uses a quickly moving line with many unaccented syllables and short vowels to express lightheartedness in lines that may move as quickly as those of the limerick. When the poet is expressing serious thoughts, the rhythm moves more slowly, with longer vowels and a higher proportion of accented syllables. Within the line, rhythm may also vary as the poet wishes to stress an idea or a single word. And within the poem, the rhythm slows or quickens to vary the mood or shift the tone.

The best poetry uses rhythm to add meaning to words, as does Robert Francis's "The Base Stealer." The sense of the baseball player poised on base, almost on, back again, teasing with sideways shuffles and teetering motions, is clearly shown by the irregular rhythm and the increasingly quick vowels:

> Poised between going on and back, pulled
> Both ways taut like a tightrope-walker,
> Fingertips pointing the opposites,
> Now bouncing tiptoe like a dropped ball
> Or a kid skipping rope, come on, come on,
> Running a scattering of steps sidewise,
> How he teeters, skitters, tingles, teases,
> Taunts them, hovers like an ecstatic bird,
> He's only flirting, crowd him, crowd him,
> Delicate, delicate, delicate, delicate—now!

As we note the variation in phrase length, the surprise of the longer phrasing of "come on, come on," then the short vowels, the plosive *t*'s and *c*'s, the sibilant *s*'s, we recognize how the quickening rhythm leads up to an admonitory "Delicate, delicate, delicate, delicate," and the final emphatic "now!" sending him off to steal the base, perhaps to score!

In a few tight lines, Arnold Adoff uses rhythm in "Let the Biter Beware" to produce sharp images of what dangers lie ahead for the candy-lover. Irregular beats and line length reproduce the jerky chewing, as caramel and nuts lurk, ready to glue or shock:

In the center of each

                pale
                milk
c h o c o l a t e   l u m p
there is a hard nut
waiting to bump your
front tooth into the
d e n t i s t ' s   c h a i r

In the center of each

                dark
                deep
c h o c o l a t e   h u n k
there is a car a mel
chunk just waiting to
                glue
your teeth to geth er
           for ev er.
T a k e
c a r e .

Abrupt and halting rhythm and frequent accented syllables in Myra Cohn Livingston's "74th Street" create the sense of a beginner on roller skates, struggling to get and maintain balance, then to take another jerky stroke:

Hey, this little kid gets roller skates.
She puts them on.
She stands up and almost
flops over backwards.
She sticks out a foot like
she's going somewhere and
falls down and
smacks her hand. She
grabs hold of a step to get up and
sticks out the other foot and
slides about six inches and
falls and
skins her knee.

And then, you know what?

She brushes off the dirt and the
blood and puts some
spit on it and then
sticks out the other foot

again.

The astonishing news that a single stroke, shown almost entirely in words of one syllable that create a jerky rhythm, has resulted from all this activity is the delight of the poem.

One caution: When we read prose, we pause at punctuation marks, but the poet also starts and stops lines in units of meaning; this requires that at the end of the line we make a stop, minute though it may be. Here ending lines with conjunction or adverb, like "and" and "almost," forces the rhythm into even more abrupt pauses, just like the jerkiness of the skater's strenuous efforts and continuous failures.[4]

Robert Louis Stevenson creates the movement of the swing arc by his use of regular and lilting rhythm in "The Swing":

> How do you like to go up in the swing,
>   Up in the air so blue.
> Oh, I do think it the pleasantest thing
>   Ever a child can do!
> Up in the air and over the wall,
>   Till I can see so wide,
> Rivers and trees and cattle and all
>   Over the countryside—
> Till I look down on the garden green,
>   Down on the roof so brown—
> Up in the air I go flying again,
>   Up in the air and down!

But notice, by contrast, the rhythm of "Falling Snow." The words fall into a regular, thumping pattern of beats, a strong accent on alternating syllables, and a far cry from the gentle and noiseless falling of actual drifting flakes that accumulate so slowly. The hard, rhythmic beat denies the meaning rather than enhances it:

> See the pretty snowflakes /ˑ/ˑ/ˑ
>   Falling from the sky; /ˑ/ˑ
> On the walk and housetop /ˑ/ˑ/ˑ
>   Soft and thick they lie. /ˑ/ˑ/

Here regular meter seems more important to the writer than the experience of snow; rhythm in this verse seems to exist for itself, because a marching rhythm cannot describe falling snow.

As Eve Merriam says in "Inside a Poem," rhythm is important:

> It doesn't always have to rhyme, ˑ/ˑ/ˑ/ˑ/
> but there's the repeat of a beat, somewhere ˑ/ˑˑ/ˑˑ/ˑ/
> an inner chime that makes you want to ˑ/ˑ/ˑ/ˑ/
> tap your feet or swerve in a curve; /ˑ/ˑ/ˑˑ/
> a lilt, a leap, a lightning split:— ˑ/ˑ/ˑ/ˑ/

The quick, changeable beat contributes to meaning, saying that poetry is joyful discovery of meaning, assisted by rhythm. Here the first line is a serious

As rhythm starts and stops, it enhances meaning.

Reading poetry aloud is different from reading prose aloud.

statement about rhyme, and Merriam's rhythm enforces the factual meaning of the line by regularity and uniformity. The first line has four accented syllables, as do all the others. The second line has the same number of accented syllables, but the line's rhythm picks up speed with the use of two additional unaccented syllables, a ratio of six light to four heavier syllables. The more unaccented syllables, the more quickly the line runs, and the more lightness the meaning acquires. Line 3 also has four accented syllables, but it includes five unaccented ones; in line 4 the final anapestic foot ◡◡/ also adds to the lightness and the unexpected quality of the rhythm. Again in line 5, there are four accented syllables, but this time the internal punctuation interrupts the rhythm. The scansion looks the same as that of the first line. ◡/◡/◡/◡/, but the commas cause us to stop and start, stop and start. The surprise we feel as we pause for the final *t*'s of "lilt" and "split" and the final *p* of "leap," when added to the short vowels and the plosive consonants, is all part of what Merriam is saying about rhythm: rhythm need not be absolutely regular, but it should suit meaning. The idea of "Inside a Poem"—while a poem need not rhyme, its rhythm exists to clarify meaning—is clear. Note, too, that while Merriam says a poem need not rhyme, she uses rhyme, but in unexpected places. The sound of "rhyme" reappears in "chime" a bit later; "repeat of a beat" and "swerve in a curve" are not the regular and predictable rhymes occurring in end positions, but are rhymes nonetheless. Merriam uses rhyme as she uses rhythm— not as an end in itself as the versifier does, but as a way to enforce meaning.

Poor choice of rhythm may negate or cancel meaning.

Sound Patterns

In "Lost," Carl Sandburg uses musical devices and sound patterns that are exceptionally helpful as they add to meaning. The poet personifies the fogbound boat as a lost child, and the harbor as a mother:

> Desolate and lone
> All night on the lake
> Where fog trails and mist creeps,
> The whistle of a boat
> Calls and cries unendingly,
> Like some lost child
> In tears and trouble
> Hunting the harbor's breast
> And the harbor's eyes.

The long sounds of the words "calls and cries" are not the only lonely ones, since every line echoes the feeling of desolation. The long vowels in "lone," "all," "long," "fog," "trails," and "creeps" give added duration to the words. Sandburg calls the vessel a "boat," its long *o* adding to the loneliness far more than would the word "ship" with its short *i* sound. Consonants are largely liquid *l*'s and *r*'s or nasal *m*'s, *n*'s, and *ng*'s held together with sibilant *s*'s. The long vowel duration and the consonants that further pull and stretch the words, called **phonetic intensives,** create the slow groping of the fogbound boat.

Patterns of vowels and consonants also influence meaning.

The sounds of the two lines dealing with the "mother," the protective harbor, are quite different. Because vowels are short and decisive, and the words are spoken more swiftly, the effect of the lines is reassuring.

As for rhythm, stressed syllables in "Lost" are far more frequent than unstressed syllables, and the effect is a slowly moving poem—movement like a fogbound boat. Sound devices combined with imagery and figurativeness have created a visible and audible scene. The short poem has given us a fresh picture, and its sound has strengthened both the meaning and the impact.

Figurativeness

Comparisons "say
twice as much in half
the time."
Christopher Fry

As noted in the earlier discussion of style, figurative language is a means by which a writer says one thing in terms of another, and by which the writer makes comparisons. It is this quality of which Christopher Fry speaks when he says that poetry "has the virtue of being able to say twice as much as prose in half the time, and the drawback, if you do not . . . give it your full attention, of seeming to say half as much in twice the time." Emily Dickinson said of her writing, "When I tell the truth, I tell it slant." In other words, not straight-out obvious.

When a poem makes either implied or explicit comparisons, the images called up may acquire connotative meaning, or may be seen in a fresh way. For example, Dorothy Aldis in "On a Snowy Day" describes a fence post topped by the little white cylinder of snow; the personified posts wear metaphorical marshmallow hats. The shapes are aptly compared and the metaphor and image are not only vivid, but also connotatively pleasant.

In "Mama Is a Sunrise," Evelyn Tooley Hunt uses figurative language effectively, comparing Mama by implication to the quiet warmth and light of sunrise:

> When she comes slip-footing through the door,
>   she kindles us
>   like lump coal lighted,
>   and we wake up glowing.
> She puts a spark even in Papa's eyes
> and turns out all our darkness.
>
> When she comes sweet-talking in the room,
>   she warms us
>   like grits and gravy,
>   and we rise up shining.
> Even at night-time Mama is a sunrise
> that promises tomorrow and tomorrow.

"Slip-footing" is Mama's quiet step as she sets her children glowing, kindling them just as she kindles the spark in Papa's eyes. We say that we "turn on the light," but the poet says Mama "turns out the darkness." Her sweet talk warms the family to make them rise shining. Using tactile and taste imagery, the simile of warming "like grits and gravy" provides pleasant connotations. The final lines state clearly that at night, too, Mama is just as reassuring that all will be well "tomorrow and tomorrow," when another pleasant sunrise is in store. This is not a mother who flips the window shade to a loud snap and cries out "Rise and shine!" These children are eased serenely into day.

The moon is intriguing to us all, a favorite object for poets' contemplation; its changes are mysterious, particularly to the child. Emily Dickinson's poem noting the moon's changes begins with a figurative picture of the crescent moon:

The moon was but a chin of gold
    A night or two ago—
And now she turns her perfect face
    Upon the world below—
Her forehead is of amplest blond;
    Her cheeks like beryl hewn—
Her eye unto the summer dew
    The likest I have known.

If the crescent moon is "but a chin of gold," then the full moon must be a "perfect face," with forehead, cheeks, and eyes. The metaphor is perfectly suited to the changing shape of the moon.

Like the jigsaw puzzle already put together, the poem with obvious figurative comparisons—the moon is a golden ball—denies the reader the excitement of a personal search and discovery. When the figurative comparisons are ineptly chosen, they confuse meaning rather than reveal it.

Obvious comparisons awaken no discovery.

Because of figurative language, Nikki Giovanni's brief poem "the drum" can say a great deal in just five lines. The impenetrable drum, sealed and resonant, is impossible to invade, says daddy. But the speaker doesn't care. This child will make his own life as he pleases, pounding, sounding, and succeeding:

daddy says the world is
a drum tight and hard
and i told him
i'm gonna beat
out my own rhythm

The poet's use of metaphors may delay our discovery of meaning. However, at the same time, these comparisons make the puzzle more intriguing and the discovery more exciting. Look, for example, at the completely compatible figurative devices that John Updike uses in his poem "October," each one a reference either to autumn weather or to Halloween:

The month is amber,
    Gold, and brown.
Blue ghosts of smoke
    Float through the town.

Great V's of geese
    Honk overhead,
And maples turn
    A fiery red.

Frost bites the lawn.
    The stars are slits
In a black cat's eye
    Before she spits.

At last, small witches,
    Goblins, hags,
And pirates armed
    With paper bags,

Their costumes hinged
    On safety pins,
Go haunt a night
    Of pumpkin grins.

Sometimes we may be puzzled by the figurative language in a poem; the more complex the poem, the more subtle the metaphors may be. The simplest way to check the meaning and suitability of comparisons is by means of simple "this=that" equations. The similes and metaphors in Lilian Moore's "Bike Ride" form a series of figurative comparisons:

Look at us!

We ride a
road
the sun has paved with   sun = paving machines
shadows.   shadows = pavement

We glide
on leaf lace   leaf lace = shadow pattern
across tree spires   spires = steeplelike shadows of tree tops
over
shadow ropes   ropes = telephone wire shadows
of droopy wires.

We roll
through a shade tunnel   tunnel = overhanging branches
into light.

Look!
Our bikes
spin
black-and-white
shadow
pinwheels.   pinwheels = shadows of whirling
                                                       bicycle wheels

"We ride through the shadows on the road" is a summary statement of the lines, but surely the experience of these words is not the same as the poem. The rightness of Moore's figurative comparisons has made a fresh experience from what might have been an ordinary one.

Imagery, the appeal to our senses, makes additionally vivid the figurative comparisons, as we clearly see in Dorothy Aldis's "Fourth of July Night":

Pinwheels whirling round
Spit sparks upon the ground,
And rockets shoot up high
And blossom in the sky—
Blue and yellow, green and red
Flowers falling on my head . . .

Blossoming flowers and pinwheels spitting sparks make the bright display a picture in our minds. In her collection of poems called *Hailstones and Halibut Bones,* Mary O'Neill uses another figurative device called **synesthesia,** in which stimulation of one sense (colors, sight) results in our seeing concrete images of smells and sounds as well.

Imagery further stretches our perceptions; we see details and figurative comparisons we might otherwise only vaguely note. Aileen Fisher personifies the cat, giving a clear visual metaphor in her poem "At Night":

When night is dark
my cat is wise
to light the lanterns
in his eyes.

The sight of a backpack dumped on the floor is vividly described by reference to shapes and colors, to show a credible jumble of typical possessions in "Passing Notes:"

I dump my backpack
my notes flutter out
Hearts, squares, some folded
smaller than my fingertip.
Some arrived
hidden inside markers
or pinned to pink erasers.
Veterans of covert operations
during language arts,

Top Secret conversations
    scatter silently across the floor.

Poet Kristine O'Connell George neatly uses unexpected metaphors of combat: "veterans," "covert operations," not "martial" but "language arts," and finally "Top Secret."

The value of such images is clear when we contrast these poems to verse that minimizes sensory appeal. As Herbert Read says, "Poetry is not made up of words like pride and pity, or love and beauty. . . . The poet distrusts such words and always tries to use words that have a suggestion of outline and shape, and represent things seen as clear and precise as crystal."[5] For example, although Stevenson, in his poem "The Swing," successfully duplicates the rhythm of the swing, his terms are not sensory. "Rivers," "trees," "cattle," "countryside," and "pleasantest thing" make little appeal to our senses. Although the roof is brown, we do not see truly vivid sights. We do not smell,

Abstract terms do not appeal to our senses. Concrete ones do.

hear, taste, or touch them, and both reader and poem are the poorer for lack of sensory appeal.

Whispers, however, are a very common part of life, and might be vaguely described. But whispers are titillating, bringing secrets for cherishing, then for sharing, and perhaps for embellishing. Once whispers were merely audible, but never again, because "Whispers" by Myra Cohn Livingston captures other sensory qualities. Notice, too, the pleasant connotations of the many sensory appeals:

> Whispers
> tickle through your ear
> telling things you like to hear.
>
> Whispers
> are as soft as skin
> letting little words curl in.
>
> Whispers
> come so they can blow
> secrets others never know.

Whispers will never be the same, because not only do we hear them, but we also feel whispers when they "tickle," "blow," and are "soft as skin"; we see them as the "words curl in." Because of the connotative meanings of the words, we delight in whispers, feeling their tender softness and seeing their spiral curl headed for listening ears.

In a series of combination words made up of a noun and a verb form, Douglas Florian creates vivid descriptions of action caused by "The Wind:"

> Blow-drier
> Kite-flier
> Leaf-dancer
> Seed-prancer
> Hat-tosser
> Earth-crosser.

Connotative words may either add or detract.

The best chosen words for a poem add by **connotations** new dimensions of meaning to words we have always known. However, sometimes the connotations of words are distracting rather than helpful in uncovering the meaning of the poem. This is the case in "Feeding the Fairies," where fairies are compared to hens and roosters:

> Fairies, fairies, come and be fed,
> Come and be fed like hens and cocks;
> Hither and thither with delicate tread,
> Flutter around me in fairy flocks.

First, the title deceives us. Instead of finding ourselves in a quiet grove or a magic circle where we might hope and expect to find fairies, we are taken to the barnyard where clucking, pecking chickens live their unmagical lives. Next the chickens' "flutter" and "delicate tread" (an incongruous phrase because *delicate* connotes the opposite of *tread*) have connotations incompatible with the fragile appearance and delicate movement of fairies. The connotations are wrong for this comparison.

Compactness

Poetry exists as an end in itself. It has no mission or message beyond discovery, beyond the emotion and thought of the reader as he explores the lines. A poem is best said in few and artfully chosen words; it follows that if we change a word, we change the poem. As Charlotte Zolotow says so succinctly, "Some people touch your hand/and music fills the sky." Nothing can be altered in Langston Hughes's simple yet eloquent lament for a lost friend:

> I loved my friend.
> He went away from me.
> There's nothing more to say.
> The poem ends,
> Soft as it began—
> I loved my friend.

Hughes's purpose is not to instruct or to inform us, but through his words to make us experience profound loss. Change a single word and we change the experience. "I miss my friend" is no substitute for these six lines; the poem says far more than that. Even the repeated last line does not repeat the first idea, but adds to it. So compact is the poem that it can bear no paraphrase; it says twice as much in half the time.

On a similar subject, Nikki Grimes has written a book of poems called *What Is Goodbye?* Each is spoken by a family member or friend about the loss of a boy named Jaron. The early poems are filled with shock; shock turns to sadness, and in Jesse's poem, "His Name—Jesse," to questions or memories:

> Mommy won't say Jaron's name
> so I write it everywhere,
> on the walls, my book, his chair,
> If I'm punished, I don't care.
> Let her take away my pens.
> I'll write it on the air!

Another of Grimes's books in picture-book style, *Come Summer,* is arranged around a single theme.

Poems are brief and condensed. The poet must make the best possible use of each word, often choosing one term to convey many meanings, or relying on connotation to extend our awareness of the experience.

Emily Dickinson compresses the experience of reading a book into a poem of eight lines. To make her poem compact she relies on three figurative comparisons, each one expanded in meaning by its richness in connotations:

> There is no frigate like a book
>   To take us lands away,
> Nor any courser like a page
>   Of prancing poetry—
> This traverse may the poorest take
>   Without oppress of toll—
> How frugal is the chariot
>   That bears the human soul!

Dickinson does not say that a book is like a mere boat, or even a sailboat; she calls up romance by using the term "frigate." Frigates are sailing vessels used by explorers seeking new lands, by pirates pursuing treasure and adventure, by merchants carrying silks and spices from Asia to far-flung shores. A book is like a "courser," not a mere horse. "Courser" connotes knights charging off on missions fraught with danger and the promise of rescue. No car or wagon could have the mystery of a "chariot," a fragile royal cart flying along behind the hoofs of a thoroughbred. Other words as well, like "prancing," "frugal," and "toll," are rich in connotative meaning. Specific terms with rich meanings expand the ideas in the compact comparisons. By means of these connotations, the total experience of a book becomes adventure, wealth, discovery, suspense, intrigue, danger, romance, and a multitude of other possibilities. This poem, like the one Eve Merriam describes in "How to Eat a Poem," has nothing unnecessary, nothing to throw away—not a seed or a pit, a stem or a core or a rind.

Intensity often derives from compactness, and brevity exists in Jim Hall's "White Trash," a title with double ironic meaning. The many images and figurative comparisons are accurate, and more effective in poetry than prose:

> Now it's Styrofoam pellets
> that blow across the yard.
> They settle in the new grass
> like the eggs of Japanese toys.
> It's a kind of modern snowing.
>
> The boy next door opened a box,
> and took out the precious present
> and shook these white spun plastic
> droplets into the wind.
> It's how his family thinks.
>
> Hundreds of them. Shaped like
> unlucky fetuses or the brains
> of TV stars.
>
> Now they burrow in the lawn,
> defy the rake, wriggle like the toes
> of the shallow buried.
>
> They'll be there when we're gone.
> Bright tumors, rooted in the dark.
> Crowding the dirt. Nothing makes them
> grow. But nothing kills them either.

Specific terms are preferable to general ones.

Emotional Intensity

Like fiction at its best, poetry at its best lets us enjoy an old experience with new insight or understand one that we have never met. However, unlike the writer of fiction, the poet condenses the experience. Poetry attempts to capture the reader where she is, and to involve the reader briefly but intensely.

The successful poem is an intense emotional experience. "There Is No Frigate" is an experience of a book. It is not a description of a book, or of the feelings a child might have while reading a book. By its richly connotative words and its varied sensory images, the poem becomes an intense emotional experience.

We have noted the verse of Robert Louis Stevenson as he describes the swing. A similar verse of his describes the wind. But William Carlos Williams, in "The Winds," shows how its effects can figuratively change everything, from parts of the physical world to the minds and hearts of humans:

> flowing edge to edge
> their clear edges meeting—
> the winds of this northern March—
> blow the bark from the trees
> the soil from the field
> the hair from the heads of
> girls, the shirts from the backs
> of men, roofs from the
> houses, the cross from the
> church, clouds from the sky
> the fur from the faces of
> wild animals, crusts
> from scabby eyes, scales from
> the mind and husbands from wives.

We have noted how rhythm, sound, and figurative language contribute to compactness, and compactness to emotional intensity. Langston Hughes writes out of the Black experience but gives nonetheless a universal reaction to waiting for a dream to come true. "Dream Deferred" has emotional intensity, intensity created particularly by his skillful use of unusual figurative comparisons and sensory appeals:

> What happens to a dream deferred?
>
> Does it dry up
> like a raisin in the sun?
> Or fester like a sore—
> And then run?
> Does it stink like rotten meat?
> Or crust and sugar over—
> like a syrupy sweet?
> Maybe it just sags
> like a heavy load.
>
> *Or does it explode?*

A poem is not a description, but an experience in itself.

From the poem we have an intense emotional experience of frustration. A festering sore, stinking meat—these are ugly images causing us to experience the emotions that accompany frustration. The images connote neglect, usefulness turned to decay. What was a simple sore is now painfully infected; what was edible meat is now stinking uselessness.

Countee Cullen's speaker in "Incident" evokes both our sympathy for the Black child and shame about the White racist, all in a few brief lines of the following poem:

> Once riding in old Baltimore,
>   Heart-filled, head-filled with glee,
> I saw a Baltimorean
>   Keep looking straight at me.
>
> Now I was eight and very small,
>   And he was no whit bigger,
> And so I smiled, and he poked out
>   His tongue, and called me, "Nigger."
>
> I saw the whole of Baltimore
>   From May until December;
> Of all the things that happened there
>   That's all that I remember.

Poetry can point out stereotypes as well. In four short lines, Janet Wong reminds readers of their prejudices:

> "Asians are supposed to be good at math."
> Mr. Chao can't figure me out.
> "Asians are quiet. Asians like numbers."
> Me, I like to shout.

Negative Qualities in Poetry

The negatives of literature—**didacticism, sentimentality,** and **condescension**—make their appearances in poetry, too, but only in poor poetry. These qualities are often expressed in words with distracting connotations, in trite comparisons, commonplace imagery, repetitive and unvaried beat, or in sound unsuited to meaning and tone. Kipling's didactic verse "If" is representative of the preaching verse adults often hear in the so-called inspirational speech. But children are even more often subjected to verses with preaching purpose, and Abbie Farwell Brown's "A Music Box" is one. The first stanza sets up a metaphor; the two that follow preach a sermon:

Preachy verses have little appeal to children.

> I am a little Music Box
>   Wound up and made to go,
> And play my little living-tune
>   The best way that I know.

If I am naughty, cross, or rude
   The music will go wrong,
My little works be tangled up,
   And spoil the pretty song.

I must be very sweet and good
   And happy all the day,
And then the little Music Box
   In tune will always play.

Intrigued with the metaphor, we are fooled into thinking that "A Music Box" will be a pleasurable experience; then we learn that our sins spoil the song. By the final stanza—"I must be very sweet and good"—we are thoroughly disenchanted, disappointed that what began by intriguing us ends by instructing us to be happy models of perfection.

As for sentimentality and condescension, a poem that speaks to a worm about pain, assuming its pain to be comparable to the pain a person might feel if jumped on by a giant—that poem surely condescends to readers as it tries to rouse our emotions beyond justification:

No, little worm, you need not slip
Into your hole, with such a skip;
Drawing the gravel as you glide
On to your smooth and slimy side.
For my part, I could never bear
Your tender flesh to hack and tear,
Forgetting that poor worms endure
As much as I should, to be sure,
If any giant would come and jump
On to my back, and kill me plump,
Or run my heart through with a scythe,
And think it fun to see me writhe![6]

It is not the subject of the poem that is inappropriate for poetry; it is the sentimental tone. In contrast, note the quality of wonder in Elizabeth Madox Roberts's poem "The Worm." The poet duplicates a childhood experience, relying almost exclusively on imagery to draw us into experiencing the children's intent wonder. As the children dig with broken shell, tin, and spade, they find a small clod with a worm inside. They marvel at the sheen of the wet skin of the worm, and forget to dig their wells. Like children everywhere, they wonder if the worm knows it is a worm.

Digging up a worm and looking at it intently can be an experience of poetry, an experience so compact that even adults become children once again during their involvement in twenty-four lines. In Roberts's poem there is neither sentimentality nor condescension.

The best poetry is made with care and artistry. Sometimes, in fact, poetry is found in paragraph form; the writer has chosen each word for its imagery and

Poetry may look like prose on the page, and prose like poetry.

connotative power, asking of the reader concentration and imagination to discover meaning. And sometimes prose and prosaic writing are put into the form usually reserved for poetry—irregular lines and stanza arrangement. But by failing to use words rich in connotative meaning, by failing to make figurative comparisons or to use rhythm to enhance meaning, the writer has written prose. Line or stanza arrangement has not made poetry out of prose.

The best prose and the best poetry are written with care and skill. The difference between them lies primarily in the compactness and the intensity of the expression. Figurative devices, rhythmic flow, and sound patterns occur in prose. There is then no line to be drawn between prose and poetry; the difference is simply in degree. As rhythm becomes more significant, imagery more vivid, and statements more compact, emotions become more intense. The reader feels the increased intensity and becomes aware of the expression as poetry.

Summary

Nursery rhymes and sidewalk jingles are many children's first experience with literature, and surely their first introduction to verse and poetry. The rhymes may not only provide an easy and loving bridge between the parents' childhoods and the new generation, but also their simple stylistic devices of rhythm, sound, and comparison, their colorful characters involved in elementary tensions, and their occasional themes about the lives of humans are sufficient reasons for including them as literature for the youngest child. They may or may not influence children's understanding, but the joy they give is undeniable.

The nursery and nonsense rhymes of childhood contain on different levels many of the elements of literature—of poetry and its style. Rhymes give pleasure through story and sounds. Nonsense delights us by its inventiveness, its unexpected turns and surprises. With its rapid rhythms and unexpected rhymes, and its topsy-turvy, no-sense way of looking at the logic of life, nonsense provides children with a great deal of pleasure—whether the joy is awakened by a patterned limerick, a gem of concentrated wit, or by children's own creations. Nonsense, too, is a way into poetry.

Poetry stands as an aesthetic experience in itself. Rhythm, sound, and connotation expand meaning; imagery heightens our sensory awareness; and apt figurative comparisons tempt our imaginations. A distilled representation of an experience, poetry at its best permits the reader to participate, but without the burden of didacticism or sentimentality.

Since the whole range from rhyme to nonsense to imaginative poetry is available to children, it seems only fair to introduce them to it all. Led easily from simple rhymes and nonsense to poetry, children, as Herbert Read says, deserve to be enticed and invited, wheedled and persuaded by poetic art. The experience of the best efforts of skillful poets is enlarging; it gives pleasure and promotes understanding. To keep that pleasure forever, children should be allowed to memorize what *they* choose—because we are all different.

Notes

1. Poet Myra Cohn Livingston, in "Don't Cook Mother Goose" (*New York Times Book Review*, July 26, 1988), calls attention to occasional new versions of Mother Goose that refuse "to free fancy," but interpolate "didacticism, moralism, and parochialism"; "they destroy the charm to tongue and ear and blind the child's inner eye."

2. Francelia Butler, in her study of jump-rope rhymes around the world, discovered more brutality and violence in rhymes from the United States than in those from other countries. Violence, however, is not peculiar to children's rhymes. Consider the controversy about song lyrics for young adults.

3. Morris Bishop, writing in *Smithsonian* (September 2002) makes an intriguing comment in limerick form:

   The limerick is furtive and mean,
   You must keep her in close quarantine,
      Or she sneaks to the slums
      And promptly becomes,
   Disorderly, drunk and obscene.

4. Listen to a recording of a poet reading his or her own poetry. Line breaks are recognized by the poet.

5. Herbert Read, "What Is Poetry? An Afterthought," in *This Way, Delight* (New York: Pantheon, 1956), p. 140.

6. Ann Taylor (1782–1866) published verses during a period when instruction was the only excuse for poetry to be published for children. *Original Poems for Infant Minds*, written by Ann, Jane, and their brother Isaac, was published in 1804.

Books Containing Poems Cited in This Chapter*

ADOFF, ARNOLD, ed. *Chocolate Dreams*. New York: William Morrow, 1989.

ALDIS, DOROTHY. *Hop, Skip and Jump*. New York: Putnam, 1934.

BEHN, HARRY. *The Little Hill*. New York: Harcourt Brace, 1949.

BROWN, ABBIE FARWELL. *Pinafore Palace*. Edited by Kate Douglas Wiggin and Nora Archibald Smith. New York: Doubleday, 1907.

CARROLL, LEWIS. *Alice's Adventures in Wonderland*. 1865. Reprint. New York: Macmillan, 1963.

CULLEN, COUNTEE. *On These I Stand*. New York: Harper & Row, 1927.

DICKINSON, EMILY. *The Complete Poems of Emily Dickinson*. Boston: Little, Brown, 1960.

FISHER, AILEEN. *Out in the Dark and Daylight*. New York: Harper & Row, 1980.

FLORIAN, DOUGLAS. *Autumblings: Poems and Paintings*. New York: Greenwillow, 2003.

FRANCIS, ROBERT. *The Orb Weaver*. Middletown, CT: Wesleyan University Press, 1948.

GEORGE, KRISTINE O'CONNELL. *Swimming Upstream: Middle School Poems*. New York: Clarion, 2002.

GIOVANNI, NIKKI. *Spin a Soft Black Song*. Toronto: Collins Publishers, 1985.

GRIMES, NIKKI. *What Is Goodbye?* New York: Hyperion, 2004.

———. *Come Summer.* Grand Rapids, MI: Erdman's, 1996.

HUGHES, LANGSTON. *Selected Poems of Langston Hughes.* New York: Knopf, 1926.

JANECZKO, PAUL, ed. *Looking for Your Name.* New York: Orchard Books, 1993.

KENNEDY, CHARLES W., ed. *Anthology of Old English Poetry.* London: Oxford University Press, 1960.

KENNEDY, X. J. *The Phantom Ice Cream Man: More Nonsense Verse.* New York: Atheneum, 1979.

LEAR, EDWARD. *Nonsense Omnibus.* New York: Frederick Warne, 1943.

LIVINGSTON, MYRA COHN, ed. *What a Wonderful Bird the Frog Are.* New York: Harcourt Brace Jovanovich, 1973.

———. *Whispers and Other Poems.* New York: Harcourt Brace Jovanovich, 1958.

MERRIAM, EVE. *Inside a Poem.* New York: Atheneum, 1962.

MOORE, LILIAN. *Think of Shadows.* New York: Atheneum, 1980.

NASH, OGDEN. *The Face Is Familiar.* Garden City, NY: Garden City Publishers, 1941.

O'NEILL, MARY. *Hailstones and Halibut Bones.* New York: Doubleday, 1989.

PRELUTSKY, JACK. *Something Big Has Been Here.* New York: Wm. Morrow, 1990.

ROBERTS, ELIZABETH MADOX. *Under the Tree.* New York: Viking, 1930.

SANDBURG, CARL. *Chicago Poems.* New York: Harcourt Brace Jovanovich, 1944.

STARBIRD, KAYE. *The Covered Bridge House.* New York: Four Winds, 1979.

STEVENSON, ROBERT LOUIS. *A Child's Garden of Verses.* 1885. Reprint. New York: Watts, 1966.

UPDIKE, JOHN. *A Child's Calendar.* New York: Knopf, 1965.

WONG, JANET S. *Good Luck Gold and Other Poems.* New York: Macmillan, 1994.

WYNNE, ANNETTE. *More Silver Pennies.* New York: Macmillan, 1938.

ZOLOTOW, CHARLOTTE. *Everything Glistens and Everything Sings.* New York: Crowell, 1987.

* Because of their very nature, anthologies and collections of poetry are not always consistent in their quality. Therefore, this list is only of books containing poems cited in this chapter.

"How can we live an exemplary existence. . . .
How can we, in our often naturally dormant
lives, be inspired to action, sometimes even at
the sacrifice of our own immediate well-being?
We derive those inspirations from heroes."
—*President Jimmy Carter*

So You Want to Be President?

Judith St. George

Illustrated by David Small

Biography

Some children get "hooked" on biography, and others may never discover it.

What reasons are there for leading children to biography?

Sometimes curiosity leads children to wonder about people. How did this writer start writing? Who proved the world is round? Who wondered about the stars? Who led millions of people to understand racism? What made so many women become nurses?

Biography Defined

Facts, concept, and attitude are essential to biography.

Biography is the history of the life of an individual. It includes three essentials: facts, a concept that the facts relate to, and an attitude toward the subject and the reader. First of all, the facts are expected to be accurate, up-to-date, and authentic as they depict the subject and the period in which the subject lived. The objective biographer must include or omit events and details as they suit the interests and age level of the readers for whom the biography is intended. As for concept, we assume that the subject of the biography is worth reading about, just as it is worth the writer's time in research and writing. A subject for biography has done something or been something, discovered or demonstrated something that makes her or his life significant—more significant, say, than your life or your sister's or brother's. The attitude of the writer reflects interest and enthusiasm, even delight in the person. If the writer finds the subject worth writing about, she finds the subject

271

worth writing about with the skill we call style. The skillful biographer uses words imaginatively, even in the simplest biographies for younger readers.

Autobiography, written by its subject, cannot be totally objective because the narrated events are filtered through the writer's own consciousness. A particularly moving series of personal accounts can be found in Julius Lester's collected slave narratives, *To Be a Slave.* No mere researcher, or even observer, could have written with such insight.

Biography often gives a picture quite different from traditional stereotypes. The cruel emperor and successful conqueror Genghis Khan might seem a strange figure for a biography for the picture-book crowd, but writer-illustrator Demi seems to have been tempted by the story's colorful and unusual opportunities for illustration. Each page of the brief text is accompanied by an elaborately detailed picture of the action. The account does not glorify cruelty, but instead rewards loyalty and military skill.

We often turn to the lives of significant people because we wish to discover more about what it was like to be alive and aware in a period of history we have just discovered. Or we may become curious about the "what if" of being a frontier hero—"What if I had been one?"—or a winning athlete, or a worker in the slums. We may be wondering how people become writers or architects. Or we may have discovered that once people didn't know about bacteria, and we wish to know about that discovery and its relationship to disease. Curiosity, wonder, the possibility of discovery, or increased appreciation—a number of related motives may lead us to read about the lives of individuals.

Curiosity may lead the reader into a subject and beyond it.

The Writer's Obligations

Within the definition of biography—biography is the history of the life of an individual—are two terms, *history* and *individual,* and each presents a separate obligation for the writer. The first term, *history,* implies facts, and biography, like all nonfiction, should be factually accurate. Information about the life of the subject comes from such sources as letters, journals, diaries, court records, interviews, newspaper accounts, recorded conversations, and interviews, wherever feasible. Although not all biographies for children include a bibliography, it is a useful addition. A quick glance at the foreword or acknowledgments tells something about the writer's research, and perhaps suggests other readings to the curious child. A closer look at the text itself will reveal dates, quotations, places, and names as they fit into the narrative. Often the last pages of a biography list in detail the sources the biographer examined. The reader is thus convinced of authenticity. But again, the numbers of such details depend on the age of the intended readers. Such data make the book seem factually authentic.

Bibliographies and other sources certify authenticity.

The term *history* implies another obligation on the part of the writer: History, when properly written, is reported objectively. The respected historian neither shows personal bias nor assumes omniscience about thoughts and feelings of historical figures. The conscientious biographer, despite interest in the subject, is bound by similar limitations; he does not presume to know the mind of the subject, but limits the information to verifiable matters and to emotions, fantasies, or thoughts the subject has spoken of or recorded. For example, in *The Double Life of Pocahontas,* Jean Fritz is faithful in her documentation; notes and bibliography are complete enough for the child reader. As extensive as her research seems to have been, Fritz could not know what Pocahontas thought as she was being "civilized" by the British at Rock Hall. "Perhaps she thought [she would] become one of them. . . . In her long skirts she may already have felt less like an Indian." John Rolfe and Pocahontas "probably first met at church. . . . Perhaps he was falling in love." All Fritz can do is speculate.

In the recent flood of interest in the discoveries of explorers Lewis and Clark, biographers have unearthed masses of information, thanks in part to journals written by the twenty-nine adventurers. In writing her biography of York, the one African American who was part of the journey, Rhoda Blumberg had to imagine, or to suppose certain actions on his part as she wrote *York's Adventures with Lewis and Clark: An African-American's Part in the Great Expedition.* Knowing that York had grown up with William Clark as his personal "body servant," and that the two had played together as boys Blumberg assumes, with Clark's own written comments as support, this loyal involvement continued throughout the journey. Although York, a big muscular man, was uneducated, he was the personification of strength and loyalty, his skills as carpenter, swimmer, hunter, butcher, and hiker invaluable. "Greatly agitated for our wellfar [welfare]," York was "invaluable." He could clamber up steep slopes in the "awesome" mountains. Because York was Black and the Indians had never seen a Black man, he was an entertaining curiosity whose color could not be washed off. Unlike the Indian warriors who had to paint their faces black, York was thought to be "a powerful warrior," "big medicine" to the Shoshoni. Even the warlike Nez Perce's were awed by his presence. At journey's end, the explorers were given at least 320 acres of land, but since York was a slave, he received no pay for his rigorous work.

Letters, journals, newspapers, concert reviews, books, and music manuscripts in libraries and universities, were available sources for Susanna Reich as she worked on the biography *Clara Schumann: Piano Virtuoso.* Clara, daughter of a demanding piano teacher who even brutalized her brothers when they performed poorly, was identified early as a musical genius. Reich speculates that perhaps the chaotic fury in her home led her to express herself only through music, which kept her content and happy by the hour as she lost herself in beautiful sound. She was a virtuoso at nine who played a heavy schedule of concerts; as a young woman she was forbidden to see fellow musician Robert Schumann, whom she loved. Only by an act of rebellion did she manage her own career, taking her father to court over her rightful earnings. Clara's musician husband, less in demand than his wife, died young; in order to support their eight children Clara carried a heavy concert schedule, traveling and performing even during pregnancies. One of the elements that make this life of an artist an interesting, even fascinating story is the evidence of conflict, the struggles of a vibrant woman for whom "art is life."

By definition, a biography is about an *individual,* and here lies a second responsibility. Children who become interested in the lives of presidents, for example, often have difficulty sorting out the life of one president from the life of another, because aside from living in different historical periods, presidents in children's biographies unfortunately may become stereotypes of all that is good. Their differences are slight: Washington is honest, Lincoln compassionate, Woodrow Wilson scholarly, Theodore Roosevelt nonconforming but commanding. Servants to society like Jane Addams, Clara Barton, and Florence Nightingale are unselfishly devoted to helping others; freed slaves like Amos Fortune may be cardboard figures of self-denial.

Incomplete biographies omit socially disapproved behavior.

The process of writing biography, like that of writing informational books, is a process of constant decision making: what to select and what to omit. The biographer wishes to show the individual as a believable human, complete with such flaws as occasional self-interest, irritability, or faulty judgment. Although there is a trend toward showing the less admirable traits in the character of the subject, writers usually ignore socially disapproved behavior. Poor biographies, however, often ignore completely any negative qualities and present only the good. The result is sometimes a book colored by an approving tone that may be disproportionate to the subject's achievements or character, and in any case is unrealistic.

While he narrates the story of her remarkable life in *Martha Graham: A Dancer's Life,* Russell Freedman does not hesitate to tell of Martha Graham's weaknesses: her furious temper and her exploitation of the competitiveness in her dance troupe in order to heighten tension for a spirited performance. As she aged, she worked through her arthritis, choreographing as well as performing, but with far fewer accolades. Nor does Freedman neglect the fact that Graham frequently reeked of alcohol when she appeared in public. This detail, however, does not negate the dancer's great artistry.

In *Christopher Columbus,* Susan Heimann gives her subject credit for his achievements; nonetheless, she does show him as a believable person. Columbus, in writing about the Native Americans in the newly discovered land, says of them: "They ought to be good servants and of good skill . . . they would easily be made Christians, because it seems that they belonged to no religion." Heimann goes on to say that Columbus has revealed in these words that while the one public motive for the voyage—bringing religion to the natives—is still important, it now seems to come second to "using" these people as skillful servants. Since children often read biography because of curiosity about a hero to emulate, it seems important that the subject of the biography not be so unreal, or so saintly, that the reader feels emulation is impossible. When honestly described, the subject is real enough to encourage the reader to similar efforts and achievements.

Biography and Fiction

We see the terms *biographical fiction* and *fictional biography* and wonder what they mean. Both admit that the writer has dramatized or invented parts that perhaps cannot be verified, or that the writer wishes to make facts into a story to show how the subject *might* have behaved, given her character. The problem for the writer of biography for children lies to a great extent in the answers to two basic questions: How much fact shall I include? How much narrative may I invent?

F. N. Monjo, for example, used some of the facts of Lincoln's life along with a fictional storytelling device: Lincoln's son Tad is the first-person narrator of *Me and Willie and Pa.* Tad tells, among other things, of crawling into Pa's bed when he was lonely after the death of Willie, his brother. The book uses historical facts, but the child's interest is held by the imagined narrative. A biography as brief as a picture book can also be effective nonfiction, telling only the most significant events. *The Glorious Flight* by Alice and Martin Provensen tells of Louis Blériot, his five children, and the family's fascination with the clacking flying machine overhead. Blériot's keen interest turns to obsession, and he builds one machine after another, until in 1909 the Blériot XI flies the twenty miles across the English Channel. The text does not try to describe differences in the eleven models, but the book pictures their differences one by one.

Biography for the older child might fall closer to the factual end of the spectrum; the older child can absorb more facts and may require less story. Too much factual detail, however, makes the page dense with dates, events, and the capital letters of names and places; the appearance is that of an encyclopedia. The response to such a biography may be, "This is more than I really want to know." And yet, too much dramatization or inclusion of probable dialogue prompts the response, "What can I really believe?" Carl Sandburg, in writing about his biography of Lincoln, stated that he did not invent dialogue or incident to prove a point; he adhered to fact. And yet Sandburg's longer biography, from which he developed *Abe Lincoln Grows Up* remains unsurpassed as a definitive biography of young Lincoln, both for accuracy and interest. It is possible to stick to the facts and to write an interesting book. But if the writer does dramatize, these inventions should be historically true to the times and not merely possible, but probable. Such dramatization often occurs when the subject of the biography is long dead and has left few written records.

The carefully researched *Lincoln: A Photobiography* by Russell Freedman is very convincing, largely because Freedman quotes from Lincoln's handwritten notes and occasional journals. He catches the tone of Lincoln's writing, interpreting what happens in light of the insights gained from personal glimpses. Lincoln's last day, for example, rings true to what we know of his compassion. After lunch he "revoked the death sentence of a Confederate spy." And he pardoned a deserter, signing his name with the comment, "Well, I think this boy can do us more good above ground than under ground!"

For younger children some invented narrative seems acceptable.

Members at the last Cabinet meeting heard his wish that no retaliatory "bloody work" be done, adding that blood enough had been lost.[1]

People who live active lives are naturally and easily made interesting for children; when adventure is part of the subject's life, the narrative pulls the reader along. Few people have led more active lives than the female athlete Babe Didrikson Zaharias, for six years named by the Associated Press as the Woman Athlete of the Year, and this at a time when "nice girls" just didn't do aggressive athletic things. Freedman's biography is highly entertaining, in large part because Babe herself was entertainment. Starting in high school as a basketball player, she became an American Athletic Union All American, went on to track and field wins in javelin throw, baseball throw, shot put, high jump, and broad (or long) jump. "And then she began to train." She made a bracelet of her first ten golf medals. When Babe began playing golf, she entered a world dominated by socially elite women; she was called by reporters "Muscle Moll," subjected to insulting comment, but played to the crowd successfully. When she flubbed a shot, she grinned, and said, "All that work and a dead baby!"—hardly a comment likely to be made by her sophisticated competitors.

Biographies of philosophers, poets, artists or musicians who lived quietly with little drama or action in their lives are more difficult to make interesting, especially for younger readers. The obligation remains, however, for the biographer to focus on the nature of the person as well as on the exciting events of his life. Where the subject's achievement is less filled with action or adventure, the writer faces the necessity of holding interest in the subject and yet keeping invented action to a minimum. This dual responsibility is not easy to fulfill, particularly when the subject has left few recorded statements. Invention is sometimes the biographer's compromise, but should be acknowledged.

Lives of the Artists: Masterpieces, Messes (and What the Neighbors Thought) is a complex title for any book. But Kathleen Krull's collection of brief biographies of nineteen artists does what her title implies. The life and work of each artist is described, but each has a wondrous quirk that holds interest. Chagall threw paintings out the window; van Gogh was run out of town by his neighbors; Michelangelo rarely bathed and so rarely took off his dogskin boots; Anguissola was so old that she had to get a document saying she was alive; Rembrandt painted a family who owned no monkey but whose picture included one, so the family refused to pay; Hokusai drew pictures on a grain of rice; Andy Warhol had 175 cooky jars; Kathe Kollwitz's empathic art was so disliked by the Nazis that she carried a vial of poison—so she could kill herself rather than be taken alive. Each short account is not merely odd information about an artist, but is complete with descriptions of an artist's life and work.

Tone and Style

The reader of biography ought to expect suitable tone and appropriate style. In five different accounts of Columbus's landing in what he thought to be the Indies, the biographers refer to the "Indians" and explorers in different ways.

> Invention, a biographer's compromise, should be acknowledged.

One account calls undue attention to the Native Americans' nakedness, and by using quiet verbs and exotic descriptions condescends with a romantic, fairy tale tone. Consider the effect of "scarlet" instead of red, for example:

> Columbus and his men saw a new beautiful world.
>
> Here were brown men with no clothes at all. Their bodies were painted red and other bright colors. . . . They were pleased to take gifts of bells and beads and scarlet caps. They were a gentle and friendly people.

A second account by its tone of wonder makes Native Americans seem to be children and the explorers seem to be gods.

> [All Columbus saw] were naked, red-skinned savages. They threw themselves to the ground and worshiped Columbus and his bearded men. . . . They thought that gods had descended from the heavens on white-winged birds. They led the white gods to their homes.

And a third writer, Susan Heimann, wins our belief by narrating facts in a convincingly objective tone:

> Curiosity quickly overcame fear on the part of the people of the island, and soon they came out to meet these strange men from another world. These "very handsome people" were Tainos. . . . Columbus called them Indians. He described them as gentle and helpful in every way. They wore no clothes, and many of the men painted their bodies.

Jean Fritz, in *Where Do You Think You're Going, Christopher Columbus?*, shows Columbus as a very ordinary man who miscalculated the distance to the Indies as well as what the "Indians" would look like; his impressions had been gained from inaccurate descriptions by Marco Polo and Sir John Mandeville.

> The only sign of gold was the gold rings that the natives wore in their noses. Indeed, that was all they wore. The people were as naked, Columbus said, "as their mothers bore them," which of course, was pretty naked. Otherwise, they were normal looking. They didn't have umbrella feet or eyes on their shoulders.

Fritz's description of Native Americans retains the light, humorous tone of the whole book, and therefore it does not condescend to them any more than to the explorers. The biography seems essentially accurate, and is a thoroughly enjoyable "story" complete with endnotes.

The number and variety of books about Columbus published for the five-hundredth anniversary of the "discovery" of America seems infinite. One of the most controversial is *Encounter*, Jane Yolen's imaginative and sympathetic picture book narrated in first person by a Native American boy who distrusted the explorers from the start and whose distrust proved to be justified when he was taken captive. The worst elements of the explorers' behavior become very real when we see their effect on a young boy.

The oversized history book by Richard Humble called *The Voyages of Christopher Columbus,* in the Exploration Through the Ages series, is beauti-

Anniversaries tend to bring a flood of relevant biographies.

fully illustrated with pictures of Native Americans, small maps, large action pictures aboard sailing ships, and glimpses of the explorers' clothing and of Columbus on his death bed. Dates make the account authoritative, and rarely noted facts are interesting additions. For example, it was not Columbus but later Spanish arrivals who made slaves of the Native Americans. The admiring tone of this account, however, covers up the explorer's character flaws.

In *Christopher Columbus,* part of the Junior World Biographies, Norman L. Macht begins his Columbus story with the influential effect of the writings of Marco Polo as he described the exotic wealth of the Grand Khan of China. In the sixteenth century, people feared that at the equator the sea was boiling hot, ships would burn up, and monsters would eat the sailing crews. They also feared that if the earth were truly round it would be impossible to turn around and sail upward toward home. The text, using a more critical tone, reveals Columbus's weakness as governor of Hispaniola, his harsh treatment of rebels, and his irritation as he saw others who had sailed with him going out later to achieve a new glory while he stayed behind in Spain to plead endlessly with the monarchs for new ships and sailors.

> The same individual may be quite different in different books.

Many other Columbus books are longer and more detailed. Nancy Smiler Levinson, in her author's note to *Christopher Columbus: Voyager to the Unknown,* has the objectivity of the historian as she tells of the difficulties of researching events five hundred years old, the early translations that seem to contradict one another, and the controversy regarding which island was Columbus's first landfall.

Look next at a group of biographies of Martin Luther King. The first, *Martin Luther King, Jr.: A Man Who Changed Things,* is part of a series called "Rookie Biography." The book bores the reader immediately by its simple sentences in repetitive form:

> Next Martin studied in Boston.
> There he met a girl.
> Her name was Coretta Scott.
> She was pretty and smart.
> On their first date, Martin asked her to marry him.

Happy Birthday, Martin Luther King is a bare-bones account of his life. Racist society is briefly described in a few sentences about drinking fountains, restaurants, and segregated schools, while King's philosophy of nonviolent protest is oversimplified into "Love one another in peace."

Martin Luther King, Jr., and the March toward Freedom, however, plunges immediately into showing reasons for readers to know about King. "Movements are born when many people share a belief that things must change. But every great movement needs a leader. Often it takes a single person to shape a clear vision of how the world can be." Although her purpose is laudatory, not all of Rita Hakim's writing is interesting; she, too, falls at times into simple, repetitive sentences. In chapters with titles like "The Minister and the Boycott," "The Movement," and "The March on Washington," the narrative follows the principal events in King's life. His "I Have a Dream" speech is partly quoted, and Mahatma Gandhi's method of nonviolent protest explained. The book ends with a useful list of suggestions for books, movies, and places to look for further information.

A number of picture books also tell King's story. Faith Ringgold's *My Dream of Martin Luther King* is unlike others. In the narrator's dream, great crowds of people of all creeds and colors are gathered, each with a bag containing ignorance, fear, and hatred. The essential facts of King's life and times—his family, the country's racism, nonviolent protest, Rosa Parks—all are there in the narrator's illustrated dream, but the crack of an assassin's gun ends King's life. When the dream crowd gathers to mourn his death, they empty their bags of hatred and racism, which go up in a burst of flame as "emblazoned across the sky," words are seen by the crowd: "Every good thing starts with a dream." The biography is effective, a personal and artistic reaction to King's life and work.

Some biographies may be highly personal.

Martin Luther King by Rosemary L. Bray, paintings by Malcah Zeldis, has an unusual combination of dense and lengthy text on a full 10-by-12-inch page across from a full-size illustration. It tells of the bus strike initiated by Rosa Parks, encouraged by the NAACP, and organized by King. With text that is not oversimplified, but well written and surprisingly complete, the book shows King as what he was: a martyr to civil rights. The book is intended for a picture-book audience, however, and deserves a more appropriate format.

Writers of biography may use all of the devices of style. In *Stonewall,* stylist Jean Fritz describes Stonewall Jackson as experiencing painfully hard years between the deaths of his father and his mother. She calls this time a figurative "hard knot at the very root of his character." Using imagery and onomatopoeic language, she tells us that he lived with his mother's relatives for a time, where the "rumble of wagon wheels, the slip-slopping of water, the buzzing of machinery formed a background music for all the farm work." Life on his uncle's farm was rough; men "from all over the country came and . . . bet and drank and smoked and swore and spit and carried on." Using five sentences of repeated subject-verb order, Fritz's style emphasizes Jackson's determination: "He decided . . . he had to find rules for his life and then follow them strictly. He wasn't going to let life just happen to him. He wasn't going to be like his father and slip carelessly into errors and from errors to ruin. He was going to be in charge."

In his collection of critical essays about children's literature, *Should We Burn Babar?*[2] Herbert Kohl examines textbooks that mention Rosa Parks and the 1955 Montgomery boycott. He concludes that some versions lack proper comment on the reasons for the African American seamstress refusing to move to the back of the bus, suggesting that Rosa's fatigue kept her from moving. "Rosa was tired" then gives the false impression that her arrest brought on a spontaneous boycott and from then on everyone rode together in happy integration. Kohl charges that such a statement misrepresents the carefully planned movement for social change, as well as ignoring her long service to the cause and her willingness to submit to arrest

The biographer, facing the need to arouse and hold the reader's interest,

Arousing and holding
a reader's interest
may tempt a writer to
use inappropriate
tone.

may be tempted to create sympathy for the subject and to make a tearjerker out of early trials. One biographer of the composer Beethoven as a young man has made from very brief factual information a sentimental story of Beethoven's being victimized by a tyrannical teacher. He says, "Poor Ludwig!" and describes his day as long, hard, and wearying. Ludwig stumbles off to bed, but is shaken awake in the middle of the night and called a lazy rascal. Then he is made to stay awake and write music. His unreasonable teacher stands over him, thunders at his drowsiness, forces the exhausted boy back to work, then goes to bed, leaving the weary boy struggling with fatigue as he finishes the writing. Here again, it is not the facts we question so much as the tone.

Paderewski the pianist might have been treated with equal sentimentality as he goes off to the Warsaw Conservatory. However, in *Paderewski*, Charlotte Kellogg is unsentimental: "More than discouraging was his first experience in a piano class. 'Not hands for playing,' the teacher declared. 'That thumb, that third finger, too short.' He gave Ignace a trial, then told him to leave, to take up some other instrument."

Concepts and Didacticism

Concept is needed in biography as it is in other literature; preoccupation with fact must not blind us to idea.

Biography needs not
only facts, but also a
reason for the choice
of subject.

Buddhism is one of the world's major religions, and Susan Roth in *Buddha* introduces her subject by recounting Buddha's mother's dream of his princeliness before his birth. Buddha's childhood in a totally protected environment, where he was pampered in every conceivable way, left him ignorant of aging, pain, illness, and poverty, but following his marriage he moved outside the palace and saw the real world. He then devoted himself to simplicity and prayer for the unfortunate. Buddhists are increasing in numbers in North America, and Roth's lyrical text and vivid collages introduce Buddha to young children.

The title *Invincible Louisa* suggests a concept behind the biography; the same can be said for *Carry On, Mr. Bowditch*, or *Up from Slavery*. Other biographies, while they may not indicate the unifying idea in their titles, do have a concept that is implicit within them, perhaps the reasons for writers choosing these people as subjects. This leader unified his or her country; this scientist persisted until research bore fruit; this athlete overcame difficulties; this composer was an innovator. Any of these reasons for writing the biography can unify the account to make it a coherent whole.

Concept unifies Fritz's biography *Stonewall*, a nickname that characterized Jackson's determination in everything, from his health to his battle plans. "I'm going to make a man of myself if I live. What I will do, I can do." Learning of his self-control, which dictated posture, prayers, and health maintenance, helps the reader picture Stonewall standing erect to keep his alimentary canal straight:

Reason for choice of
subject does not
make preaching
acceptable.

> [He put] himself on a diet of stale unbuttered bread and lean meat. No tea, coffee, or stimulants of any kind. And he exercised. Fast walks accompanied by leaps

and arm-whirlings. . . . One arm, he decided, was heavier than the other so he developed the habit of thrusting the heavy one up in the air at regular intervals. This way the blood would run back into the body . . . and lighten the arm.

However, having a reason to choose a subject for biography does not give the writer license to preach. Intent on making a point about the worthiness of the subject, the writer may lapse into didacticism. Writing of Louisa May Alcott's early life, Cornelia Meigs insists that we recognize the idealism behind the efforts of her father, Bronson Alcott, to form the perfect social community. Such insistence intervenes between the readers and Louisa, the real subject; it shakes a finger at the readers to make them accept Meigs's views. In *Invincible Louisa,* she writes:

> We must remember, however, that Bronson and his friends, wise in some ways, mistaken in others, had the courage to find out, by the only possible means, where they were right and where they were wrong. There is only one method of testing a system of living; that is by living it.

Louisa saw Concord soldiers march away to the Civil War, and such a picture is relevant to the biography. But here, too, Meigs intervenes:

> There is no experience in the world that can ever match that of seeing soldiers go away, of seeing the gaiety and the excitement and of knowing the black and hopeless tragedy which is behind it all. There is little that is so terrible as seeing strong, wholesome young men, every one of them beautiful in the flush of their high patriotism, as watching them go and knowing that they are surely to die.

Some biographies have strong themes, as does *Be the Best You Can Be* by Kirby Pucket with Greg Brown. Because the book is autobiographical and is for the picture-book set, the theme as expressed in the title seems didactic. There is further didacticism on the last page, under the heading "Kirby's Extra Innings," where quotations from athlete Pucket tell children to "Say Nope to Dope," "Get an Education," and "Treat People Right." In a sense, it is healthy for young readers to discover that some athletes strive for more than merely the high salary and have some principled views on life. Pardoning the didacticism is left to the reader.

There is information coupled with vitality in *Carry On, Mr. Bowditch.* Jean Lee Latham tells of Nathaniel Bowditch's discovery of a new and simpler way to make lunar calculations at sea. Without preaching, she simultaneously explains the process, records the action, and reproduces the excitement of discovery:

> Tonight ought to be a good one for a lunar. The moon was due to pass over a star that was bright enough to see in spite of its nearness to the moon. . . . Just when the moon neared the bright star, a cloud got in the way. Nat shrugged and sighed. There ought to be a better way to work a lunar! He studied the glittering heavens. Was there another star bright enough tonight—that the moon would pass over? Of course not. He knew that. That one . . . the moon would pass below it . . . that one . . . the moon would pass above it . . . that one . . .

The idea hit Nat so suddenly that he gasped. He raced below and for the second time that night crashed into Prince's cabin without knocking.

The straightforward, factual tone of Russell Freedman's *The Wright Brothers* carries conviction. Letters add personal touches of feeling, both optimism and disappointment, and photographs illustrate the efforts of the bachelor brothers as they confront flight problems of lift, propulsion, and control. Bishop Wright's two sons Orville and Wilbur worked to improve machines by Lilienthal, Langley, and Chanute. Their favorite niece wrote of the two brothers' early helicopter as particularly fascinating: it was made of cork and cloth, harbinger of their intense interest in flight. Newspaper accounts tell of the curious crowds that gathered at Kitty Hawk as they tried one variation after another in search of perfect solutions. The brothers first camped on the Outer Banks of North Carolina, played their harmonica and mandolin—and thought. They thought alike, rising each morning filled with enthusiasm and new ideas to try out. The effect of the biography is that these were real men with enormous curiosity and imagination, who without years of schooling were persistent in their project, loving it not for imagined financial rewards but for the joy of invention.

Many of the facts in *Eleanor Roosevelt: A Life of Discovery*, also by Freedman, are taken from Eleanor Roosevelt's own writings—her letters, newspaper columns, and autobiography—along with transcriptions of interviews and conversations with those she knew, as well as from a variety of other carefully researched sources. The unifying concept comes from one of her own statements, used as an epigraph: "You gain strength, courage and confidence by every experience in which you really stop to look fear in the face. . . . You must do the thing you think you cannot do." Roosevelt's early years and the first years of her marriage to Franklin were filled with experiences for which she looked fear in the face, doing what she felt she could not do—but did. In 1946, the plain and awkward child once demeaned by her beautiful mother was a grown woman given a standing ovation in the United Nations. Freedman's biography concludes convincingly with a return to the concept expressed in the words of the epigraph: "And having learned to stare down fear, I long ago reached the point where there is no living person whom I fear, and few challenges I am not willing to face."

It was Eleanor Roosevelt whose strong commitment to civil rights shamed the Daughters of the Revolution for refusing to host Marian Anderson's concert in Constitution Hall. Russell Freedman in *The Voice That Challenged a Nation: Marian Anderson and the Struggle for Human Rights* opens the biography with an exciting glimpse of 75,000 people waiting on the Washington, D.C., Mall to hear "one of the great voices of the time." The president's wife had arranged for Anderson to give a free concert before the Lincoln Memorial, where the audience was much larger. Because Freedman often quotes from Anderson's autobiography, the great singer becomes a real person.

"There were times when we heard our relatives and friends talking. . . . and we knew we might come in contact with [racial discrimination]. In some stores we

Quotations from the subject may provide the unifying concept.

might have to stand around longer than other people before we were waited on. There were times when we stood on a street corner, waiting for a trolley car, and the motorman would pass us by."

At first Marian was given one or two dollars for her singing, but she nonetheless shared it with her sisters, or with her mother who was taking in laundry and scrubbing floors. On some Sundays, the pastor took up a collection to buy Marian a dress to perform in. When she applied for admission to a music school, she was ignored until all applicants were heard, then she was asked, ""What do you want?" Anderson was a striking performer in a society that regarded African Americans as comic dolts, illiterate and lazy.

The concept underlying Ruby Bridge's autobiography *Through My Eyes* might be stated in this way: "Being the first African American child to integrate New Orleans schools had its effect upon me as well as upon the nation." In a profusely illustrated book, Ruby remembers her preschool years working at home in the garden and kitchen, then being escorted to school by federal marshals as she walked through the crowds of racist cries and threats. Now a mature adult, she recounts the legal and judicial issues, remembers the loneliness of being the only child in her classroom, the surprise that a few White children were coming to her school but she remained the only child in the room. Her close relationship with her teacher influenced her to unwittingly adopt Boston speech. Throughout the book, a running comment at the bottom of pages quotes the reaction of the *New York Times*, the description of angry taunts from racist neighbors in the school yard made by writer John Steinbeck, as well as comments from sympathetic people like Eleanor Roosevelt, and the loving teacher Lucille Bridges. Add to them the words of the man who fired Ruby's father: "I wouldn't have a nigger working for me with a child in a white school. Would you?" A new friend says, "I can't play with you. . . . My mama said not to because you're a nigger." Final comment is a quotation from Martin Luther King Jr. that a nation can be improved only by both "Negroes and white people of good will."

Biography of a historical figure can bring to life a whole historical period, as does *Joan of Arc* by Diane Stanley, the story of a young woman who felt she was chosen by God to restore the prince to the throne. The large volume with a rather complete text has words on the left page, accompanied by a picture on the right that resembles an illustrated manuscript. "Joan gave Charles a sign to prove she came from God. No one really knows what the sign was, but witnesses said that as she spoke, her face grew radiant and he was much changed." The effect is that history's events are colored by a spiritually motivated young woman in a religious society.

The man who in 1853 opened Japan to world trade was Commodore Perry, and the opening paragraphs of *Commodore Perry in the Land of the Shogun* by Rhoda Blumberg show the people's panic at the arrival of his mysterious ship. It is filled with "aliens," monsters the Japanese fear, and arrives with the threat of horrors including "Great giants puffing smoke." "Alien ships of fire" might invade to kill, kidnap, or destroy all of Japan, Land of the Rising Sun. Over a period of weeks spent anchored in the harbor, the curious

Americans come to respect the courteous and inquisitive Japanese, and an amicable diplomatic relationship develops. This well-researched book, whose footnotes defend its accuracy, is illustrated with numerous drawings and a few black-and-white photos.

Finally, an illustrated collection of brief biographies of six Native American chiefs, Freedman's *Indian Chiefs,* describes the life histories of men who were chiefs because they were advocates of either peace or war. Within tribes there were often leaders who advocated compromising with the White traders and settlers, and others who wished to drive them all back to the territories where, in their treaties, they had promised to stay. Hence, there were chiefs of war and chiefs of peace. Freedman discusses Red Cloud of the Oglala Sioux; Santana of the Kiowa; Quanah Parker of the Comanche; Washake of the Shoshone; Joseph of the Nez Percé; and Sitting Bull of the Hunkpapa Sioux.

Summary

Biography is the history of the life of an individual. The word *history* implies fact, and the term *individual* requires that the portrayal avoid stereotyping and show the subject as unique. Readers choose biography out of curiosity about a person, curiosity aroused perhaps by having read a reference to that person, or by a reference to a discovery or a period in time. A well-written biography helps the reader toward knowledge—knowledge as contrasted to mere information or fact. Naturally, techniques of writing and illustration should be subordinated to this end. Within each biography, the reader seeks facts, concepts, and the writer's attitude toward the subject. Curiosity or wonder, one motivation for children, is stimulated by the quality of what they read, tempting them to discover more about people and their relationships to far-off times, scientific concepts, or ways of solving society's problems.

Since the order in which facts and concepts are presented influences how well readers understand, a chronological narrative is usually best for younger children. Tone influences biography, just as it does imaginative literature. Condescension looks down on the subject, sentimentality distorts it, and propaganda invalidates it. Style, although it must be clear and factual, need not be banal or trite; imagery, figurative language, and varied sentence structure stimulate a reader's response: I want to know more.

Notes

1. See "Abe, Honestly and Otherwise," by Henry Mayer (*New York Times Book Review,* February 12, 1989, p. 24), for a comparison of Lincoln biographies for children.
2. Herbert Kohl, *Shall We Burn Babar?* New York: The New Press, 2005.

Recommended Books Cited in This Chapter

BLUMBERG, RHODA. *Commodore Perry in the Land of the Shogun.* New York: Morrow, 1985.

————. *York's Adventures with Lewis and Clark: An African-American's Part in the Great Expedition.* New York: HarperCollins, 2004.

BRAY, ROSEMARY L. *Martin Luther King.* Illustrated by Malcah Zeldis. New York: Greenwillow, 1995.

DEMI. *Chingis Khan.* New York: Henry Holt, 1991.

FREEDMAN, RUSSELL. *Babe Didrikson Zaharias: The Making of a Champion.* Boston: Houghton Mifflin, 1999.

————. *Eleanor Roosevelt: A Life of Discovery.* Boston: Houghton Mifflin, 1993.

————. *Indian Chiefs.* New York: Holiday House, 1987.

————. *Lincoln: A Photobiography.* New York: Tichnor & Fields, 1987.

————. *Martha Graham: A Dancer's Life.* New York: Houghton Mifflin, 1998.

————. *The Voice That Challenged the Nation: Marian Anderson and the Struggle for Equal Rights.* New York: Clarion, 2004.

————. *The Wright Brothers.* New York: Holiday House, 1991.

FRITZ, JEAN. *The Double Life of Pocahontas.* New York: Putnam, 1983.

————. *Stonewall.* New York: Putnam, 1979.

————. *Where Do You Think You're Going, Christopher Columbus?* New York: Putnam, 1980.

HAKIM, RITA. *Martin Luther King, Jr. and the March toward Freedom.* Brookfield, CT: Millbrook Press, 1991.

HEIMANN, SUSAN. *Christopher Columbus.* New York: Watts, 1973.

HUMBLE, RICHARD. *The Voyages of Christopher Columbus.* Illustrated by Richard Hooks. New York: Watts, 1991.

KELLOGG, CHARLOTTE. *Paderewski.* New York: Viking, 1956.

KRULL, KATHLEEN. *Lives of the Artist: Masterpieces, Messes (and What the Neighbors Thought).* New York: Harcourt Brace, 1995.

LATHAM, JEAN LEE. *Carry On, Mr. Bowditch.* Boston: Houghton Mifflin, 1955.

LEVINSON, NANCY SMILER. *Christopher Columbus: Voyager to the Unknown.* New York: Lodestar, 1990.

MACHT, NORMAN L. *Christopher Columbus.* New York: Chelsea House, 1992.

MONJO, F. N. *Me and Willie and Pa.* New York: Simon & Schuster, 1973.

PROVENSEN, ALICE, AND MARTIN PROVENSEN. *The Glorious Flight.* New York: Viking, 1983.

REICH, SUSANNA. *Clara Schumann: Piano Virtuoso.* New York: Houghton Mifflin, 1999.

RINGGOLD, FAITH. *My Dream of Martin Luther King.* New York: Crown, 1991.

ROTH, SUSAN. *Buddha.* New York: Doubleday, 1994.

SANDBURG, CARL. *Abe Lincoln Grows Up.* New York: Harcourt Brace, 1931.

STANLEY, DIANE. *Joan of Arc.* New York: Morrow Junior Books, 1998.

YOLEN, JANE. *Encounter.* New York: Harcourt Brace, 1992.

Black Potatoes: The Story of the Great Irish Famine

Susan Campbell Bartoletti

Informational Books

How does nonfiction become propaganda? Is propaganda ever justified?

Check for bias when generalizations seem unsupported by information.

Adults range widely in their reading interests, from the financial page of the daily newspaper to a favorite comic strip, and on to particular curiosities, whether they be genealogy or strip-mining. In between, they experience floods of enthusiasm for "everything *that* writer ever wrote" to "everything I see about earth warming." And yet we are continually surprised at the diversity in children's taste or at their sudden enthusiasm for rocks, space, or baseball players. People are alike, and often we find that the interesting adult with a multitude of curiosities is the grown child whose reading may have begun with an omnivorous—and simultaneous—devouring of animal fantasy and atomic fission.

What does interest a child in nonfiction? Of course, older children may go in search of information, but young children frequently find fiction and nonfiction shelved in the same section of their libraries. In search of another good book "like the one last week about the ducklings in the park," they encounter another good book—but this time it is about the color wheel and how one color merges with another to form tones and shades and tints and other colors. Both books may be equally fascinating. At other times, children who have moved away from the picture book section may happen upon a shelf where there are cataloging numbers on the spines of the books, instead of just the initial *E* or *J*. And there, wonder of wonders, are all kinds of books about how animals really live, and eat, and raise their babies, and fight to survive. From this discovery, children may take off on a nonfiction binge. In all of this meandering there seems to be a thread that holds one book or group of books to another—curiosity.

The line between fiction and nonfiction is a fine one in books for children. In a great many storybooks, there is much information about the world: animals, people, history, nature. After all, we learn about spinnerets and the parts of the spider's legs in *Charlotte's Web*. But when we discuss nonfiction, we are really less interested in how suspense is built and more interested in how facts are presented; we are less interested in character and more in discovery of the relationship and application of concepts to society or the natural world. Sometimes the writer uses a chronological arrangement of some kind, a narrative, that makes the nonfiction resemble fiction. Sometimes the writer speaks of "you" and "we" to make the explanation personal or like a story. However, the fact remains that the functions of fiction and poetry are pleasure and understanding, while the purpose of nonfiction is the discovery of factual or conceptual information. Although we look at the two somewhat differently, pleasure derives from both.

The function of informational books is discovery of facts and concepts.

The pages that follow will make clear that the informational writer is concerned with *facts* first of all. But in addition to presenting facts, the writer tries to show the reader that these facts add up to or lead into a *concept,* just as the facts about chemical composition inside the egg lead us to the concept of how it becomes an embryo and then a chick. Affecting our acceptance of fact and concept is *tone,* the writer's attitude toward the subject and the readers. We shall be concerned with all three.

Nonfiction Defined

Anyone who has spent time with a child knows that children have enormous curiosity and delight in satisfying that curiosity. They are filled with questions that lead to more questions that, when answered, lead to still other questions. Many of these questions can be answered by the right informational book, whether it is a book about a single topic like trees, an explanation of a concept like energy, or a book that awakens awareness to an issue like overpopulation. As Margery Fisher says in *Matters of Fact,*[1] an information book evokes many responses:

Order is extremely significant.

> A child uses information books to assemble what he knows, what he feels, what he sees, as well as to collect new facts. His reaction to something as ordinary as a loaf [of bread] may be, at one time or another, one of wonder, excitement, interest, aesthetic pleasure, physical satisfaction, curiosity.

When adults seek answers, they may turn to encyclopedias; a solid page of factual information does not frighten or confuse them. Their experience helps them sift out the specific items they need from the mass of information; they can extract the essential from the nonessential, the clear from the too complex. The child, to whom the world is new and perhaps confusing, may also, with the help of a book, recognize order in what she already sees or knows. This recognition of order and this assembling and sorting help to organize and stabilize the multitude of surrounding facts. The curious child moves from order to comparison, and on to new understanding of concept. To make these transitions, the child must have books that combine individuality with clarity in a combination of words that give significance to the subject and make it clear.

Wonder as Motivation

The limited experience of the child poses specific problems for the nonfiction writer. First, the writer must satisfy curiosity without squelching a sense of wonder, yet the writer must avoid suggesting miracles. "Wonder" connotes curiosity and interest, while "miracle" connotes mystery and the unknowable. The successful writer of nonfiction opens a door to discovery but does not suggest that the facts are miraculous or beyond ultimate comprehension. There are facts as yet unknown and principles as yet undiscovered, it is true, but if the child is to be led to discovery, the child must feel that the search will be rewarding and will not merely dead-end at unknowable mystery.

Adults usually choose their nonfiction for utilitarian purposes; they need to know. However, to a child, for whom everything in the world is astonishing, wonder is more often the motivation. Curiosity is the force that leads to discovery of all kinds. It led, for example, to the discovery of electricity; the unexplained needed explanation.

Curiosity and wonder open the door to discovery.

In *How Did We Find Out About Electricity?* Isaac Asimov begins his explanation with a narrative situation very similar to the reader's search for answers. Something piques a boy's curiosity, as it does the reader's. Asimov takes us back 2,500 years, to the village of Magnesia on the coast of Turkey, where a shepherd boy uses an iron-tipped stick to help him climb. As the iron sticks to a stone, the boy is mystified, but he can find nothing sticky on either surface. The odd rock comes to the attention of a wise man named Thales. Thales experiments with the stone and discovers that it attracts only iron. Asimov's account follows a pattern very similar to that which our curiosity follows as it is provoked by the unusual; we notice, we experiment, we seek to discover what we can, and when we need help we go to an authority.

While Asimov stimulates wonder in one way, Jean George in her Thirteen Moons series relies on facts both surprising and truthful. Simple, clear language that avoids ordinary terms sets the stage for *The Moon of the Salamanders:* "In the third moon of the year the first thaw came. Warm winds blew for days and nights. Lakes of ice turned to water. The snow slipped away. The frost let go of the soil." Notice how ice "turns to water" rather than melts; snow does slip away because the change in form seems almost invisible, and the hard grip of frost does "let go." George is not timid about mature language, but tells of "ephemeral ponds" that are "sequestered" among trees; words that follow make meaning clear. Cold ponds are "filled to their brims," and a "dark stage" is set for the "ancient ritual" of the salamanders. The language, as quiet as the woods itself, evokes wonder, as the salamanders "act out a strange and ancient drama just as they did 330 million years ago." Other fascinations may lie ahead in *The Moon of the Salamanders*.

In the opening paragraphs of *The Sea Around Us*—which almost single-handedly initiated the environmental movement—Rachel Carson, writing for more mature readers, rouses wonder by means of surprise. First Carson reminds us that we cannot really know how the oceans were formed, since there were no people there to see and to report:

> Beginnings are apt to be shadowy, and so it is with the beginnings of that great mother of life, the sea. Many people have debated how and when the earth got its ocean, and it is not surprising that their explanations do not always agree. For the plain and inescapable truth is that . . . in the absence of eyewitness accounts, there is bound to be a certain disagreement.

The skillful writer provokes the child to seek more information.

Carson goes on to suggest the range of estimated age for rocks found on the earth—2.3 billion to 2.5 billion years, an astonishing figure for us who find a month or a year a long time. As we follow Carson's speculations about the earth changing from a ball of whirling gases to a molten mass, and then to patterns of layered materials, wonder leads into Carson's hypothesis about the origins of the oceans.

The function of the nonfiction book for children, as for adults, is to give this desired information. If the book is to stimulate the reader to reach for more, it must be written with strict attention not only to factual accuracy, but also to tone and style that attract and lead to discovery.[2] The successful nonfiction book manages to supply information and yet makes the reader sense that discovery is open-ended. There is more to be known, and finding out is exciting. Because the attitude of wonder is stimulated, we assimilate the facts and come to understand a concept.

Informational Books

Organization and Scope

Common sense says that facts cannot be dumped on a reader all at one time, or we would have to make order out of masses of information, a task for an authority, not an inquirer. The writer of nonfiction must select the key ideas, put them in simple forms, relate them to facts already known or to concepts already understood, and from this point begin to clarify. Breaking down the ideas into component parts that can be easily understood, the writer arranges

Order must be logical.

them in coherent sequence from *simplest* to *most complex*, from *familiar* to *unfamiliar*, or from *early development* to *later development*.

Since this task is not as easy as it sounds, not all writers are successful in finding the natural order. Some writers—like some teachers we may know— have a difficult time communicating concepts to those without backgrounds comparable to their own. These writers may have the understanding, but they lack the capacity to recall what it was like when they were uninformed and needed elementary and orderly explanations.

An Indian Winter is skillfully written by Russell Freedman. The historical facts of Prince Maximilian's trip up the Missouri River to learn about the Mandan Indians of North Dakota are set out in a carefully researched book. Verifying his story are the journals of Maximilian and the many paintings of his companion, the artist Karl Bodmer. During a severe winter, Bodmer illustrates family and tribal customs as well as paints portraits and landscapes. Authenticity in the narrative account is further strengthened by Bodmer's illustrations, painted at the time of the difficult trip, creating a convincing picture of the Mandans and their neighbors.

By contrast, as occasionally happens in picture books, pictures sometimes seem to have been conceived before text; that is the case in *The Stream*, a book that was probably intended to show how water gets to a stream. It begins with clouds, moves to underground water, then to snow melting into a stream. Next come waterfalls, rivers, lakes, reservoirs for cities; then the focus shifts to the ocean and back to the dry mountains where heavy rainfall evaporates into the clouds. Although at first glance the circle seems complete because it begins and ends with clouds, the movement itself is not coherent. Another book, *Follow the Water from Brook to Ocean* begins with the sound of rainfall and water dripping from eaves into gutters, then moves to the brook beside the house, to a stream, a big river, and then to puddles. Rain and snow go through the ground to a brook where algae, frogs, salamanders, and trout live; no acknowledgment is made that algae live in stagnant water and trout in quickly moving streams. Next we move from brook and stream to underground rock and a spring, and on to how moving water carves the land and otters live there. The Grand Canyon exemplifies how water carves rock, but we move immediately to the flatlands and a meandering stream, to dams, electricity, garbage, and on to the mouth of a river, where the word "delta" goes unexplained. Too much is covered; the process backtracks, and all is disjointed.

The writer of *Rivers and Lakes* does not know how much to focus on or where to quit, and also has problems of logical order. The table of contents begins with looking at rivers and lakes, showing how rivers begin in runoff from the mountains, meander through slightly sloping lands in the middle, and at the end move through flatlands to the ocean, order that seems logical. Then the text moves to how water shapes the land, shapes civilization, forms lakes, then is controlled; how water is used at work and at play, how people live beside rivers and lakes; and concludes with "The Story of Rivers and Lakes," a return to the earlier order once anticipated. All this is followed by facts and figures. The reader follows the water's movement to the ocean, then must return to the riverbanks to see its effects. A more logical order would show the shaping of land, civilization, and lakes *as* the water moves.

True, water is a complex topic, its uses many, its forms varied, but by limiting the text to a clear explanation of a simpler issue in *The River*, David Bellamy is successful. The text begins with clear water, goes on to how clean water becomes polluted and then restored so that pike, gulls and frogs can

Text should not seem a mere excuse for pictures.

live in and beside it once again. Wendell Tanghorn in *Glacier* uses a logical order and sticks to his more limited subject of how glaciers are formed and how they melt and move a distance that varies from ten feet to a few inches in long or brief time periods, showing how ice cracks off and moves, taking with it huge boulders and dropping them off along the way. An excellent and beautifully illustrated book, *Oceans* by Seymour Simon, begins with the startling news that seventy percent of the Earth's surface is water, then writes of ocean depths and water quantities, how water moves up and down on the surface and below it. It then explains horizontal movement like currents, tides, tidal waves, crests and troughs, storm-driven waves, and surf and its effect on flat beaches. Simon concludes that using the ocean as a wastebasket prevents the ocean from renewing itself. The organization is logical and easy to follow.

Organizing text from early to later developments is clearly shown in David Macaulay's *Cathedral.* Beginning with the gratitude of some thirteenth-century French villagers for peace, health, and plenty, we learn how a medieval architect is hired to design a cathedral to the glory of God, hire the master craftsmen who own shops staffed with apprentices learning trades, and add laborers, many just returning from the Crusades. Cutting the timber, quarrying the stone, clearing the site, building workshops and forges, digging the foundation proceeds to walls, piers, buttresses, temporary wooden frames, and then arches, and up, up to beams, vaulted ceilings, and towers, and finally to sculpture placed in niches. Process, from beginning to end, is a logical plan for organization.

Macaulay has written and illustrated another remarkable book called *The Way Things Work.* In large, clear drawings with a limited color palette, he shows how everything works, from nail clippers to nuclear power plants, from axles to holograms. The book defies description. Macaulay's illustrations and his text are amazingly clear. Lest we feel overloaded with information, a fanciful text about the woolly mammoth provides a thread of regular humorous breaks to show how difficult a process is, even for a mammoth, without the simple and ever more complex machines of human invention.

Although in *The Wright Brothers: How They Invented the Airplane* Russell Freedman is telling the history of the airplane, he leaps ahead in Chapter 1 with an account of the first dramatic flight, lasting one minute and thirty-six seconds. Then he returns to the chronology of experimentation that led to that exciting minute. Notice the opening sentences in the first five chapters, each one an attention-grabber:

> No one had ever seen what Amos Root saw on that September afternoon in 1904.

> "From time to time we were [like] little children," Wilbur Wright once said, "my brother Orville and myself lived together, played together, and, in fact, thought together."

> While the Wright brothers were building bicycles in Dayton, an engineer named Otto Lilienthal was conducting gliding experiments from the top of a small hill in Germany.

Organization may proceed from early development on, or from start to finish.

Otto Lilienthal's gliding experiments in Germany, and his dramatic death in 1896, had aroused the Wright brothers' curiosity.

The experiments that Wilbur and Orville had carried out with their latest glider in 1901 were far from encouraging.

With a very different subject, the history and culture of a society, *People of the Breaking Day* uses chronology to describe the family relationships and responsibilities, lifestyles, trading, and sports of the Wampanoags, who lived in southeastern Massachusetts. The final and fitting topic that Marcia Sewell treats is burial customs and procedures.

History or events long past can still grab attention.

Narrative Form

In nonfiction for the younger child, the writer may weave information into a narrative. Robert McCloskey in his picture book *Time of Wonder* demonstrates that a slight unifying narrative can convey information about the New England shore. The island has a very old rock at the point, a rock that was hot as fire when it was new to a new world, and as cold as ice when the weight of the glacier ground into it. The seal sniffs, while the fish hawks and eider ducks listen and watch. The colors of the fern change from green to yellow and brown. The robins have flown, and the swallows have left their boathouse nest, but their places are taken by birds that rest in migration as they fly south. Gulls and crows fuss and feud, and hummingbirds find the late petunias. Trees that have fallen during the storm leave jagged holes where their roots have been, showing the wind's power. A snow-white heap of shells left long ago by Native Americans crumbles at a touch; other people once lived where we are standing, before the White people came. We have moved down the beach, discovered a bit about geology, seen the effect of the storm on the trees, and then sensed the aging agelessness of the Maine seacoast. These facts are tied together by the slight narrative.

Narrative may provide sequence in books for children.

To cite another example from picture books, *Sugaring Time* by Kathryn Lasky moves chronologically from trail-breaking through the snow to the sugar maples, cutting runner marks on the trail, tapping trees with drill and bit, then collecting into a gathering tank the maple sap that runs like a river, and finally boiling the sap, with the accompanying tasks of skimming, temperature testing, and fire stoking.

Although Jeanne Bendick does not use a continuous narrative to hold together her book *Why Can't I?* she does use the device of children wondering about the things they see. A series of comparisons shows why we can't breathe under water like a fish or walk on the ceiling like a fly. On the bottom of each of the fly's six feet is a pad of stiff and sticky hairs. As the fly walks on a smooth surface, these pads flatten and make the fly stick. Able to hold more than just the fly's weight, they keep him on the ceiling. "The bottoms of *your* feet are smooth and slippery," she points out. "You can make them a *little* sticky by wearing sneakers. But you're still too heavy to walk up a wall or

Wonder pulls the reader to follow time, change, and difference.

across the ceiling." The relating of the facts to the reader, the "I" of the title and the "you" of the text, makes these facts personal, interesting, and remarkable. Comparisons are understandable and have some narrative quality. The young reader is involved in this explanatory situation by the simplest of narrative elements.

The Great Fire by Jim Murphy is a remarkable effort to show the devastation of the Great Fire of Chicago in 1871. The many illustrations and news stories taken from periodicals of the day, the quoted personal recollections of fire survivors, the carefully researched facts about a Chicago made almost entirely of wood before and after the fire—all add up to a disaster of highly personal proportions. *The Great Fire* owes much of its success to Murphy's use of concrete and specific language to make the fire credible. The awesome destruction of four square miles of the booming wooden city becomes real through newspaper accounts and survivor narratives. Careful research details the effect of sweeping winds of tempest strength, alight with coals and embers that land on rooftops, church steeples, and protective blankets, then cross the river to ignite another area. Human errors in judgment are often caused by spreading panic, and sobbing parents fruitlessly seek their children, many of them among the dead. More than 100,000 are left homeless. Updrafts catch strange items like a burning shirt and send them aloft among the flying embers. A leather cap misshapen from the heat, a burst fire hose, a dribble of water from another, a stalled fire engine awakened by a hammer tap, and an undertaker's coffins carried upright out of the fire by young boys, as well as 50,000 tents pitched by General Sheridan's troops—all detail the devastation.

What history portrays as a city's disaster becomes a disaster for individuals who lose lives, homes, livestock, and businesses. For example, the first call of "Fire!" is made by Daniel "Peg Leg" Sullivan, whose wooden leg gets caught in the uneven floor of the O'Leary barn; hopping on his other leg, he is hit by a calf racing for the door, hangs on to it, and is saved. As these personal accounts show, this fire as personal disaster is increasingly real. Account after account of efforts to save the sick or infirm, the animals, homes, and businesses, is interesting in itself; the wealth of individual stories means far more than numbers of victims. For example, William Lee, checking on his crying seventeen-month-old child, looks out the window and sees the sky lit by flames that generated flying embers:

> Lee hesitated a moment, shouting to his wife to take care of the baby and rushed out of the house. He ran the three blocks to Bruno Goll's drugstore, determined to do what no one else in the neighborhood had thought about doing: turn in a fire alarm. At this point, the fire was barely fifteen minutes old. What followed was a series of fatal errors that set the fire free and doomed the city to a fiery death.

Too much emphasis on narrative may cloud facts.

Occasionally, however, the writer, intent on narrative suspense, may not make the facts clear. In *How People Live in the Big City*, for example, we wander through the city learning that some people live in very tall buildings with walls of glass. Such buildings sometimes are called glass houses, but there is no mention that they are far more often called apartment houses. Riding on the stairs that move is like "floating up, up, up," but no mention is made that these stairs are called an "escalator." Some writers seem to fear that words of more than two syllables will not be understood by children, but children's vocabularies are filled with big words; after all, *hamburger* has three syllables, and *refrigerator* five.

Sometimes, for the sake of the narrative, information is completely lost or so distorted that it is untrue. *When the Root Children Wake Up*, for example, is a misleading fairy tale explaining the coming of spring:

> Wide awake at last, in their root house, the root children work busily on their new Spring dresses. Each chooses the color she loves best—violet, yellow, blue, white, orange, or red—and with needle, thread and thimble, sews happily till her work is done.

Personification is not the only cause for distortion here; the writer, eager to interest the reader in the changes brought by spring, has replaced facts with additional fantasy.

In writing of the pecking order among hyenas, Alice L. Hopf in *Hyena* is accurate without personifying animals.

> Hyenas have order and rank in their packs. Because females are larger than males, they stand at the top. Or two females are the leaders in each pack, with others ranged below. . . . [T]he female . . . leads the pack on the hunt . . . decides where and when to go. She takes her packmates on a boundary-marking expedition or rushes ahead into battle with the neighboring packs of hyenas.

Citing the work of several naturalists, Hopf describes the ways of animals that seem a hybrid of dogs and cats, adding in a humorous touch that Sir Walter Raleigh did not believe Noah would have saved hyenas in the Ark because he would not have saved hybrids.

Robert McClung is highly successful at weaving facts of nature into narrative form. In a factually accurate narrative called *Possum*, McClung faces the reality of the possum's life. Following a family of nine babies we discover that they are easy prey; one is caught by a fox, another by a great horned owl, a third by a rattlesnake, another by a giant snapping turtle, and a fifth is run over as it crosses the road. These are the facts of life in the possums' world: nine babies, four survivors. Within the narrative form, *Possum* remains factually accurate. A more ambitious purpose unifies McClung's *Samson, Last of the California Grizzlies*. In this vivid narrative, Samson, to satisfy the frontiersmen's craving for excitement, is pitted against Diablo the bull:

> The crowd roared as the two great beasts tangled again. Samson crouched low, trying to seize the bull's head in his huge paws, while Diablo thrust his horns downward in a deadly twisting sweep. As Samson rolled sideways to parry the blow, the tip of one of the bull's horns caught in a link of the chain that held the bear. There was a sudden loud snap as the chain broke, and Samson rolled free.

Concrete, specific terms clarify.

In a verifiable narrative of action on the frontier, there is sympathy for the two struggling animals forced to fight till death, but there is no sentimental distortion.

Style

Style cannot be sepa-
rated from meaning.

How the writer uses language is style. In nonfiction, as in fiction or poetry, style is an integral part of meaning, and not merely decoration or embellishment added to explanations and descriptions. Style is part of all written matter. Some writers of nonfiction ignore artistry in language as a means of making their subjects interesting. Others are keenly aware of their responsibility to use language effectively.

As noted in the work of Jean George, simplicity need not be either trite or banal. Comparisons are one way to make concepts clear to the reader, and some writers use comparisons simply and effectively. Irving Adler in *The Story of Light* uses a reference to the familiar Aladdin story: Aladdin rubbed a lamp to summon the Jinni. We flick a switch to summon light. Adler reminds us of how difficult it is to get rid of light; it streams in through windows and drapes, or through keyholes. Light cannot be held by force; although we try to grab it, it slides through our fingers. But if we learn about its tricks, we can put the energy of light to work. Referring next to the common experience of bumping into things in the dark, Adler then compares light to a messenger that guides people around obstacles.

Comparisons of
known and unknown
are useful.

In *Volcano: The Eruption and Healing of Mount St. Helens*, Patricia Lauber is also successful in her use of comparisons. Explaining how a blast of steam tore the mountain open, she says that the water was heated by the magma rising inside. Then, by means of a comparison, she goes on to tell how this could happen:

> Normally water cannot be heated beyond its boiling point, which is 212 degrees Fahrenheit at sea level. At boiling point, water turns to gas, which we call steam. But if water is kept under pressure, it can be heated far beyond its boiling point and still stay liquid. . . . If the pressure is removed, this superheated water suddenly turns, or flashes, to steam. As steam it takes up much more room—it expands. The sudden change to steam can cause an explosion.

Frequent comparisons are particularly helpful in the explanations of complex ideas or startling facts. In one picture book, for example, we read the factual statement that the temperature on the sun's surface is close to 10,000 degrees Fahrenheit, and that the temperature at the sun's center may be close to 32,000 degrees. But the book doesn't offer a frame of reference for these facts. Referring to familiar temperatures like our body heat of about 98 degrees, or water that boils and steam that scalds at 212 degrees would make such high temperatures with so many zeroes even more startling and somewhat more comprehensible.

Some writers strive to simplify their texts by relying on the simplest sentence structure—subject, verb, complement. Such writers risk losing the interest of children who may weary of the monotonous rhythm created by repeating word patterns. In *What's Hatching Out of That Egg?* Patricia Lauber, describing the many animals that hatch from eggs, is factually accurate, and the picture-book format is inviting. The style, however, is jerky and halting. Describing the hatching of a monarch butterfly, she uses short simple sentences: "The young animal will spend its days flying about and feeding. But it will no longer eat leaves." Children, after all, do talk in compound and complex sentences; they are more able to read complex sentence forms than some writers assume. *The First Book of New Zealand* is filled with generalizations that suggest that all New Zealanders are alike—an unjust and inaccurate statement. The style of the book is often monotonous and repetitious as well. We are lulled into boredom and disbelief by its declarative sentences, the drumbeat of omniscient authority:

> The New Zealanders of today are law-abiding, practical, and conscientious people. They dislike extremes of any kind. They usually own their own homes. The houses are surrounded by flower gardens, for New Zealanders like to plant and grow things. . . .
>   Maori women practice as doctors and dental assistants; they teach school where both the Maoris and *pakehas* are students. They also work as news commentators on the radio. Maori girls are extremely clever.

Take a Trip to Argentina is filled with informative detail, but its brief sentences make it read haltingly. Its failure to relate or compare details about Argentina to what readers know about the United States diminishes the impact of the information. We find ourselves asking questions:

> The picture shows Cordoba, Argentina's second largest city. It was founded in 1573. [When was Boston founded?] . . . Argentina declared itself independent on July 9, 1816. [How many years after the United States declared its independence?] . . . It consists of a 254-member House of Deputies [like our House of Representatives?] and a 46-member Senate [like ours?]. Argentina is a republic and an elected President is Head of State. [We elect our President. Are we a Republic?]

Under the illusion that they are making their meaning more accessible, other writers simplify their language by breaking up compound sentences into halting and choppy fragments:

> How did the glacier do it?
>   A glacier works just like a plow. But instead of one blade, it has a thousand. For every rock frozen into its bottom acts like a plowshare.

By contrast, notice the clear and vivid description in *Gorilla Gorilla* by Carol Fenner. This book has facts, facts given in sentences of varying length, with words and phrases in varying orders:

> The hoots grew louder and faster, faster and faster still. Suddenly the huge leader thrust himself to his short legs. He tore up great clumps of bush and vine, tossed them with a furious heave high into the air, and began to thump his massive

Repetitious sentence structure puts the reader to sleep.

chest like a frenzied drummer. The drumming boomed and leapt into the leafy jungle, across the high meadows and jutting cliffs of the rain forest—an increasing chorus of beats. The hoots melted into a blurred growl.

Variety in sentence length and construction gives interest to this passage. Fenner creates further interest by the use of imagery. We hear the drumming and thumping of the huge gorilla, and we see his actions. As the leader is compared in a simile to a "frenzied drummer," the drumming booms and leaps. We see the "leafy jungle" and the "jutting cliffs," and we hear the "blurred growl," words chosen to convey precise meaning by creating sight and sound images. Because of Fenner's style we learn the facts of the gorilla's hooting, and of his feats of strength. Seeing and hearing him in his natural habitat shows something about the concept explored in the book: Captivity influences gorilla behavior.

Any impression that all dress in early America was extremely simple, sensible, and drab is contradicted in *Colonial Living* by Edwin Tunis's word pictures of Dutch apparel. Relying on imagery for clarity, Tunis vividly describes the New Netherlanders' dress:

> In an age of ballooning britches, a Dutchman's outswelled all others. His hat was a big plumed hat, not too well suited to his stocky build. Shoe buckles seem to have been popular. . . . The prosperous among the Dutch clung to the starched ruff. . . .
>
> Ruffs were a great nuisance and a great expense. They had to be laundered by experts. . . . The starched flutes . . . were arranged on "setting sticks" and fixed into shape with hot metal "poking sticks." Even then it was necessary to wear a wire "under-propper" to hold a ruff up.

Detailed imagery may also serve to make action clear. In vigorous language, Robert Leckie in *The World Turned Upside Down* shows and explains the process of loading Revolutionary War guns. Notice Leckie's use of action verbs in differing forms:

> [The British soldier] bit the cartridge open . . . [and] sprinkled a little powder on the pan of his piece. Then, placing the musket butt-downward, he poured the rest of the powder down the barrel. Next, he pushed in the ball. Crumpling the paper into a wad, he crammed that in afterward. Finally, seizing his rifle rod, he rammed all—powder, ball, and paper—down tight inside the barrel.
>
> To fire the musket, he placed the butt against his shoulder and pulled the trigger. This released a cock which struck its flint against a piece of steel to send a shower of sparks into the pan. When the powder here ignited, it flashed through a touch-hole into the bottom of the barrel and exploded the charge, which propelled the bullet down the barrel.

A child reading such a description sees that readying the Brown Bess for action was a slow and complicated process, and may understand that wars of missiles, bombers and fighter pilots differ from the battles of the American Revolution.

Images and figurative comparisons not only contribute to an interesting style, but also clarify meaning. To create visual pictures filled with comparisons, Jean George uses color imagery and figurative language. In *The Moon of the Monarch Butterfly,* she expresses wonder at the beauty of the monarch by comparing its wings to stained-glass windows and its antennae to knotted wands:

> Before sundown she came to rest on a wisteria vine that entwined the porch of a small white house in the country. Clinging to a purple flower, she closed her wings above her back, as butterflies do. Her wing tops were burnt orange, their undersides yellow. Black veins spread through them like lead in a stained-glass window and their edges seemed as if the night and day had been knitted together into sparkles of white and black. Her antennas were like wands, slender, with knots on the ends for sensing the flowers, the winds, and other monarch butterflies.

Scientific details and various kinds of eating equipment are made surprisingly clear and easy to understand when Millicent Selsam makes vivid figurative comparisons. In *How the Animals Eat,* the chapter on dinner in the water has several subheadings and captions, each an image suggesting a comparison. Sea Soup, or plankton, is a mixture of tiny animals that drift together with tiny plants. In some animals, Sea Strainers, or gill rakers, work as built-in strainers holding the Sea Soup back for the fish to swallow as water passes out through mouth and gills. A Sea Sword is the upper jaw of the fish grown out into a bony, sharp point; it stabs a hole in a big fish and kills it. A Flexible Snout is a trunklike tube that can poke around among the stones in the mud on the bottom of the sea, picking up little sea animals the same way the hose of a vacuum cleaner sucks up dirt. Each of the metaphors compares in words the unfamiliar manner of eating to something already known to the child. Each verbal comparison becomes vivid and clear. Style, in such cases, can serve as the agent for stimulating wonder and for starting the child's exploration of a subject.

Figurative language also clarifies.

Illustration

The writer of nonfiction relies on illustration differently from the writer of fiction. There is no need for characterization, for example, and only occasionally does text evoke mood. In nonfiction, illustration helps to clarify. Sometimes a nonfiction book makes use of photographs, but sometimes photographs can be less valuable than drawings or diagrams, since photos sometimes oversimplify, catching only the external appearances of objects and concepts. Although illustrations are necessary to nonfiction, the writer who cannot achieve corresponding effects of clarity with words deprives the child of a discovery that words can explain just as pictures can.[3]

A highly useful graphic device is a cross-section or three-dimensional section shown in a line drawing, a representation far more difficult to make clear in a photograph. Growth and change in a bud or flower, for example, are clearer in a drawing, where the changes and stages can be shown by captions designating time lapse. Views of the object are visible from all angles and positions. In Patricia Lauber's *Volcano*, which is filled with beautiful full-color photographs, the artist uses five colored drawings as verification of text: an air view of the area around Mount St. Helens, affected in differing ways by the eruption; the globe as viewed from Antarctica, showing the Ring of Fire of active volcanoes surrounding the Pacific; two cross-sections showing the earth's plates and what happens when they move; and how a small plate colliding with the larger one built the Cascade mountain range. The illustrative combination is most effective.

✪ *Special Issues in Nonfiction for Children*

Tone

Tone or attitude is important in informational books.

Tone is important to nonfiction, just as it is to fiction. Some children involve themselves more easily in nonfiction if they feel that a real person seems to convey the facts to them. Writers may become persons in their own accounts by using the pronouns "we" and "you." To satisfy further this need for person in the communication, the writer may adopt a particular attitude toward the facts and the readers.

Sometimes the writer of books about nature, science, processes, or other facts names the book *The Wonderful World of . . .* and the reader is startled to discover that our city sewer system is wonderful. Although the word *wonder* is overworked, there are a great many subjects about which it is perfectly reasonable to wonder. But when the writer uses the title *The Mystery of Chlorophyll,* he or she adopts a tone of surprise and intrigue. Science and the natural world are not miraculous, because as we discover more about them, their opening mysteries continue to provoke wonder—but become less mysterious. If books of fact are to stimulate the minds of children to further exploration, the writer's tone or attitude might better say, "Remarkable as all this is, we can know it. If we investigate it, we are amazed and enlightened."

Writers of nonfiction, like those of fiction, sometimes fall into a tone of *condescension,* oversimplifying, thinking of the readers as dear little things, or guarding their ears from the whole truth. In one book about elephants, for example, it is mystifying to read that usually peaceful males, which do not charge unless threatened, get angry and excitable once a year for a few weeks or months. This is a period known as *musth;* apparently we must be protected from awareness of the mating season. Although this condescension may occur in a purely factual account, it seems to appear more frequently in facts tied together with a slight narrative.

Tone in Jerry Stanley's *Children of the Dust Bowl: The True Story of the School at Weedpatch Camp* is appreciative throughout the account of the efforts of helpful citizens, and optimistic about good outcomes. Stanley tells of compassionate organizers, teachers and volunteers who gave meaning to the lives of impoverished Oklahoma Okies during the Dust Bowl period in U.S. history. Stanley first describes, for example, blowing dust so deep that farm animals had to be dug out, the nostrils of cows cleaned several times a day by children. Next he introduces the reader to John Steinbeck's *The Grapes of Wrath*, a compassionate fictional account of families in Dust Bowl days. Then, using authoritative accounts and a vast number of personal memories, he demonstrates how hard work, dedication, and the growth of hope and competence established a comprehensive school for deprived children. Handsomely illustrated with many pictures, the book is filled with the spirit of a dedicated educator who saw the peculiar needs of despised migrant children living in poverty. The sense of individual successes is proof that desperate lives can be changed. Tone is the reason.

History, and particularly remote history, is sometimes narrated in a pattern of condescension—which may join with questionable humor. *The Land and People of Iceland* describes the Vikings, using the accounts in the sagas, recorded about 1000 C.E. Erick Berry makes these warriors' lives ridiculous: in violent and purposeless battle, they cut off each other's heads. At nightfall their heads "were miraculously restored, so that they might all sit down together and feast and drink all night. To resume fighting again next morning. Presumably their morning-after headaches also disappeared by magic." The writer, however, does go on to explain the Vikings early governmental bodies, whose purpose was to settle disputes; "man-made words sought to wipe man-made violence from the land." The clumsy effort at humor seems out of place in a chapter that seriously traces Icelandic history from piracy to democracy.

A capable reader curious about the World War II years would find *I Am an American: A True Story of Japanese Internment* by historian Jerry Stanley a very personal account of the effect of U.S. policy after Pearl Harbor, when anyone of Japanese descent was placed in a camp. Such policy was based on assumptions and little evidence that Americans with Japanese ancestry would side with the enemy rather than with their new homeland. The book, relying on the experiences of specific internees, is readable, a look at the other side of that assumption. The final page quotes Shi Nomura, who generously says that "one of the greatest things about America is that it admits its mistakes. . . . It's easy to think that this is just a part of Japanese history. But it's really part of American history because this is what America is all about: tolerating different cultures, accepting people who look different."

Personal accounts of experience can prove a point.

Consider the realistic tone of *An American Plague: The True and Terrifying Story of the Yellow Fever Epidemic of 1793* by Jim Murphy, an attractive book about a most unpleasant subject. Illustrations are prolific, showing everything from the front pages of newspapers to plague victims themselves, portraits of researchers, and government proclamations. Chapters, which begin with the day's date and show how rapidly the disease traveled, have as titles quotations from observers: "This Unmerciful Enemy," "A Modern Day

Time Bomb." Other chapter titles are clearly informational: "Improvements and the Public Gratitude." Murphy describes the disease: "The sickness began with chills, headache, and a painful aching in the back, arms, and legs. A high fever developed accompanied by constipation." A doctor describes his illness: "These sweats were so offensive . . . as to cause me to draw the bed-clothes close to my neck, to defend myself from their smell." Origin of the plague was a mystery, so people blamed almost anything—immigrants or tobacco, bad smells or humid air—and tried almost anything to dispel it, including fires in the streets, and gunshots into the air. One newspaper contributor calling himself A.B. did suggest that a gill (about four ounces) of oil poured on rain barrels might kill mosquitoes, a possible disease origin. People scoffed. The city of Philadelphia emptied of citizens, while a few physicians struggled on.

When Edwin Tunis writes of Native Americans in *Indians,* he manages to treat objectively a subject that is often the victim of intellectual snobbery—superstition. Because of the matter-of-fact tone of the account, we accept the Native Americans' fears:

> There was no Indian who was even reasonably free from superstition: it covered
> everything in the world. When every animal and every tree, and every stream
> and every natural phenomenon was possessed of a spirit, probably malevolent, it
> took a lot of finger-crossing and wood-knocking to ward off evil. The Indian was
> afraid of everything . . . of killing snakes and wolves . . . of witchcraft and of the
> owls he associated with it . . . superstition . . . pervaded all Indian living.

Tone also convinces readers of surprising statements. For example, it may be unsettling to learn on the first page of Milton Meltzer's *All Times, All Peoples: A World History of Slavery* that "white, black, brown, yellow, red—no matter what [your] color, it's likely that someone in [your] family way back, was once a slave." The factual tone convinces us: "It was hard for [the earliest peoples] to feed themselves. . . . That is why, when they raided other people, they killed them instead of taking them prisoner. If the winners had spared the lives of the losers, they would have been unable to feed them." But as farming and food production grew and it was possible for conquerors to feed prisoners, they kept them as slaves. The book's powerful illustrations in black and white further reinforce the credibility of Meltzer's factual tone.

In books about animals, condescension often takes the form of **anthropomorphism,** an attitude that suggests a lack of interesting qualities in the animals themselves and a need to jazz up their lives by making them more nearly human. It's no surprise when pets are given human qualities, but it seems unacceptable and highly unscientific to attribute human qualities to prehistoric beasts. In one book about dinosaurs, a brontosaurus is called "terribly dumb"; the tylosaurus, described as clever, fierce, and cruel, seems vicious rather than, more accurately, carnivorous. In *Here Come the Wild Dogs,* about the life of a fox family, the father fox thinks to himself:

Anthropomorphism may be condescending.

What a fine morning for racing with the dogs!
Excitement!
Adventure!
And yes, even danger!

Following the race in which the fox outwits the dogs, we hear the victorious fox say, "What fun!" While these may be reasonable emotions for people, the child is misled about reality, even led to believe that foxes relish the danger and adventure of being hunted. Animal stories are great favorites with children; it is important that when the child expects a factual report, a factual report is given. Any narrative should be kept within the realm of real possibility. Wild animals' lives are filled with serious battles with hunters, blizzards, mountain lions, wolves, and starvation. Books should show more convincingly how an animal responds physically to its natural enemies.

The writer of *Ookie, the Walrus Who Likes People* goes a step further than the writer of the fox book; he regards the walrus as almost totally human.[4] She wasn't much interested in the penguin pool—didn't think they'd be the sort of creatures that would be fun to play with. The huge yet sleekly graceful walrus becomes cute and coy, like a cartoon character.

While accounts of the animal world are particularly subject to the condescension of anthropomorphism, some writers, Jean George for one, show great respect for their animal subjects. The reader, while absorbing detailed information about the gray wolves, acquires at the same time an admiration for their grace and intelligence. In *The Moon of the Gray Wolves*, the wolf watches the caribou herd and looks for prey:

> The black wolf waited until the main herd passed around the bend of the Toklat. Then, studying the forest and tundra for laggers, he tightened his muscles and sprang into a trot. His narrowly spaced wolf-shoulders gave him the stride of a horse rather than that of a dog, and in the manner of all wolves he glided along the ridge like a thoroughbred.

The wolf, an essential predator, "harvests" the weak and the old, keeping the caribou herd healthy, and their numbers balanced with the available food supply. George's tone is objective and respectful, suitable for her description.

Phyllis and Raimondo Borea are even more factual in tone in their account of *Seymour, a Gibbon*. In order to make the descriptions clear, the Boreas often compare the monkeys' actions to those of people, but carefully avoid lapsing into personification:

> Gibbons . . . live in family groups—father, mother, one or two youngsters, and sometimes a very old gibbon, perhaps a grandfather or mother . . . only gibbons enjoy this close way of living rather like our own. The family wakes at dawn after a night together in their sleeping tree, because, also like us, the higher primates sleep at night and are up and about during the day.

Animals can be compared to people without personifying them.

Although the Boreas compare gibbon families to human families, the two are said to be "perhaps" similar, but never the same. Because the authors cannot know the reasons for the gibbons' morning cries, they only speculate:

> For an hour or more after waking, they greet the dawn and their neighbors with cries that have been called songs and set down on paper like music. . . . Their morning songs may be a way of letting other gibbon families know these particular trees are lived in. The songs may also be just for the fun of it.

Herbert S. Zim is another writer intent on giving the reader the facts and the facts alone. He makes few human comparisons, and gives only verifiable information. In *Monkeys,* Zim's tone is completely objective and matter-of-fact.

> Records kept at zoos show that monkeys have a fairly long life span compared to other mammals. A mandrill has been known to live 27 years, a macaque up to 29, and a baboon to 45. But these may be special cases, and wild monkeys, on an average, may not live much over 10 or 12 years.

Didacticism and Propaganda

When a writer chooses a controversial topic such as drugs as a subject for a children's book, he or she is probably impelled by a desire to persuade the readers, or to influence their thinking, about the dangers of narcotics or of smoking. The writer, however, has an obligation to make generalizations supported by factual information. Experiments, statistics, descriptions of studies, and references to authorities should be the meat of the book. Carefully arranged, the evidence gathers and builds to prove the point. Preachment is unnecessary.

If, however, the book lacks sufficient evidence and relies on generalizations that the writer has not bothered to support with evidence for the reader's examination, the book then raises questions. How do we know? Who says so? When did that happen? Left unanswered by the data, the reader says, "That's just opinion; it's never been proved." The effect on the reader's mind is a quick write-off: "Propaganda. Pure propaganda." Doubt and distrust result.

Some concepts have been well researched and a variety of experiments has led to the same conclusions—smoking endangers the health of smokers and nonsmokers. Scientists conduct experiments, note results, and draw hypotheses; they then test these hypotheses in an effort to reach a conclusion. But many of these series of experiments are still in hypothetical stages, insufficiently proved. It is often these hypotheses that turn into propaganda for unproved theories.

The writer of nonfiction has a responsibility to use and to foster the scientific attitude. When dealing with theory not fully proven, the writer is obliged to make us aware that there are theories and countertheories on the subject. Perhaps—if society is lucky—the child-readers will be so intrigued by the puzzlement of scientists that they will wish to find the solution some day. *Black Potatoes: The Story of the Great Irish Famine, 1845-1850* suggests

Proof needs facts, not generalizations.

from its title a focus only on the famine; the book, however, goes further and establishes the famine as a source of the Ireland–England battles of succeeding generations. The first words of the introduction are taken from the traditional Irish folktale: "In Ireland long ago, there were good times, not your time nor my time but somebody's time. . . . " Using a variety of black-and-white illustrations, including historical documents, Susan Campbell Bartoletti writes of the starving Irish who died for lack of their dietary mainstay destroyed by rot. Landlords destroyed the huts of the starving because without a crop owners could not pay their taxes. Families ate only what they could dig up elsewhere; children went to school outdoors in "hedge schools" or at "soupers," where they might get meager food if they renounced their Catholic faith. Succeeding pages show the starving people living in caves or "scalps" dug into the sides of a ditch, and the coffins with false floors so that once a body drops into the grave the coffin can be used again and again. Some people blamed the fairies, the fogs, or themselves, but others blamed the starving for being lazy or having large families. Bartoletti continues, telling of mass migration, of a generation with poor health and little if any education.

Adults often seek nonfiction books because they wish to know a particular expert's opinion or attitude toward a subject. The child, however, not knowing that the facts can be interpreted through individual perspectives, approaches a book expecting to find facts and objectivity. The child will then be less likely to detect bias. It seems reasonable to say that children's books that inform should not be propaganda. If a writer has a bias, we should expect it to be stated openly. Freedom to draw our own conclusions from the facts is a precious right.

Confusing theory with truth concerns the scientist with integrity. In *The Seeds of Tomorrow,* Ben Bova cites the published projections of eminent scientists from the Massachusetts Institute of Technology regarding the disastrous effects of overpopulation. Listing the kinds of information fed to the computer, he mentions pollution, farm production, famished continents, infant mortality and increased longevity, and depletion of natural resources, then contrasts them with expected birth rates. Science and technology, while they have produced many of these "problems," are essential parts of a better future; "they offer a chance to avert the total world collapse that awaits us." Describing the evolution of Homo sapiens, he credits the curiosity of humans with solving problem after immediate problem, and points to the use of "second generation technology [that] would feed, cure, and protect us without long-term damage to the environment."

In *Hunger on Planet Earth,* Jules Archer focuses primarily on overpopulation as the source of hunger. Noting that wars are often started over too many people with too little space, he says that wealthy nations have helped very little because food aid only results in higher birth rates. Using a particularly vivid illustration, he says that "each time your heart beats, three more new hearts start to beat elsewhere on earth and three more mouths must be fed." He then cites the hard-nosed views of some scientists: "If people breed like rabbits they must be allowed to die like rabbits." Next, the moral argument is cited, followed by mention of countless efforts to solve overpopulation problems at world conferences, acknowledging at the same time the varied objections to family planning. Titles of his final chapters indicate Archer's emphasis on population control: "New Ideas for Feeding Planet Earth" addresses food production, pest control, plant genetics, irrigation, energy innovation, altered diets, sea harvesting, and a variety of other issues. "Controlling World Population," however, is the topic of one whole chapter. Clearly he sees it as paramount.

Books about endangered species use varying kinds of emphasis. The Wildlife Youth Service produces a series of slender books called *Animals in Danger*, opening each volume with a serious appeal using white letters on a black page to state that animals must stay in their natural environments; people have made life difficult for animals. Tone is deliberately didactic, but when faced with facts, the conclusions seem clear.

And Then There Was One by Margery Facklam devotes a chapter to each of several ways in which animals become extinct, some natural and others the intervention of people. The Galápagos tortoise was undisturbed until pirates and sailors in search of food on long voyages caught them, stacked them up in the ship's hold, and ate one four-hundred-pound tortoise after another. Meanwhile, settlers arrived on islands and with them came domestic animals who eat tortoise eggs and young. Constant changes in land and climate necessitate animal adaptation. Animals that adapt survive; others do not. Changes in land conformation made migration possible for dinosaurs; as they moved, they may have encountered bacteria or new predators. True, hunters have destroyed whole species, like the passenger pigeon and the mammoth, but people also insist on manipulating natural populations. Immigrants, missing familiar animals or birds, imported them, only to find they became pests necessitating the import of other species to control new populations. For example, rats deserting ships became a nuisance in Jamaica, yet the imported mongoose did not control them but ate other species instead. And finally, human intervention like the disaster of the Exxon Valdez oil spill in Alaska resulted in "no place to live" for some species. A final chapter summarizes the "good news" of human efforts to counteract extinction, including education, zoo breeding and repopulation, animal refuges, and protective laws, but admits that some degree of extinction is inevitable because we cannot change the way nature makes land and climate changes. The point of view is objective, the examples extensive, and the effect is not didactic but informative.

Publishing Trends

Interest in publishing informational books for children has grown rapidly. Many of the books focus on the natural world, fueled perhaps by the many nature programs on television. Others touch on a host of issues.

Two creative and meticulously careful minds have put together a beautifully written and lavishly illustrated book about the evolution of the earth and of humans: *The Story of Life on Earth* by Margaret Munro and Karen Reczuch. Using the most current scientific research, they trace growth and constant change over a period of five billion years, including ice ages and periods of volcanic activity. They slight no period.

Another example, *Air* by Ken Crosswell, deals with all aspects of air with minimal text and fine illustrations of convection, moisture, hurricanes and tornadoes, oxidation, odors, birds, seed dispersion, windmills, sailboats, parachutes, pollution, and breath. On a subject that requires complete and logical explanation, Robbins illuminates both the ordinary and visible, and the less easily imagined, such as convection and oxidation.

What must it be like to be victims of flooding? In *River Friendly, River Wild*, Jane Kurtz uses free verse evocative of a childhood on the Red River of the North. She moves on in similar form to the family's anxious watch of the rising waters, sandbagging, packing to leave, being concerned for a pet, restoring the flood-damaged home, and expressing gratitude for support from the neighbors, all of whom experience terrible upheaval in their own lives. The reader sees people facing loss of many kinds. Illustrations in oil glaze are beautifully effective.

Perhaps the arrival of the millennium inspired Janet Wilson's idea in *Imagine That!*: what has happened in the past one hundred years, as seen through the memories of Aunt Violet who has lived through most of the period. Wilson divides the century into decades, then cites events and changes in history, society, fashion, the arts, inventions, toys, and entertainment, and illustrates each spread with a colorful collage clarified by color-keyed records at page margins. The whole is an illustrated history of the century, trivial and big events, made personal by the presence of Aunt Violet and her listening niece.

Summary

Informational books inform by attention to facts, capitalizing on children's wonder at all that is available, all the topics out there. Fueled, too, by computer search engines, curiosity is thankfully endless. When nonfiction is most effective, it suggests a wealth of information, stimulating in the young reader a wish to know more. Without the natural organization of narrative in fiction, informational books may need other kinds of planning: Major methods include moving from the simplest to most complex, from familiar to unfamiliar, or from early to later development. Style, which cannot be separated from meaning, is as important to nonfiction as it is to fiction. As the writer avoids repetitive sentence structures, variety results. Illustration of the text may in some cases be central, and text merely clarification of what the reader sees. Or, depending on the subject or the level of intended audience, text may be illustrated by graphics. A tone of didacticism or preachiness, of "Now you know it all!" is less effective than one more objective, but in either case, without supporting evidence the writer may be writing propaganda.

Notes

1. I am grateful to Margery Fisher for many of my ideas throughout this chapter. Her book *Matters of Fact* (London: Brockhampton Press, 1997, 1973) is an excellent discussion of what should be expected of nonfiction books for children.
2. Fisher contrasts two terms: A starter makes the child "want to pursue it further. A stopper can be quickly skimmed and will be as quickly forgotten because it gives the deadly impression of being self-contained and yet incomplete" (*Matters*, p. 23).
3. Discovery through words gives the child an opportunity for greater growth. Continual reliance on illustration for clarity does not expose children to new words or develop in them the habit of using words to express themselves.
4. William Bridges's book is classified as nonfiction.

Recommended Books Cited in This Chapter

ADLER, IRVING. *The Story of Light.* Irvington-on-Hudson, NY: Harvey House, 1971.

ARCHER, JULES. *Hunger on Planet Earth.* New York: Crowell, 1977.

ASIMOV, ISAAC. *How Did We Find Out about Electricity?* New York: Walker, 1973.

BARTOLETTI, SUSAN. *Black Potatoes: The Story of the Great Irish Famine, 1845–1860.* Boston: Houghton Mifflin, 2001.

BELLAMY, DAVID. *The River.* New York: Potter, 1988.

BENDICK, JEANNE. *Why Can't I?* New York: McGraw-Hill, 1969.

BOREA, PHYLLIS, AND RAIMONDO BOREA. *Seymour, a Gibbon.* New York: Atheneum, 1973.

BOVA, BEN. *The Seeds of Tomorrow.* New York: David McKay, 1977.

CARSON, RACHEL. *The Sea Around Us.* New York: Oxford University Press, 1961.

CROSSWELL, KEN. *Air.* New York: Boyd Mills Press, 2000.

FACKLAM, MARGERY. *And Then There Was One.* Illustrated by Pamela Johnson. Boston: Little, Brown, 1990.

FENNER, CAROL. *Gorilla Gorilla.* New York: Random House, 1973.

FREEDMAN, RUSSELL. *An Indian Winter.* Illustrated by Karl Bodmer. New York: Holiday House, 1992.

GEORGE, JEAN. *The Moon of the Gray Wolves.* New York: Crowell, 1969.

———. *The Moon of the Monarch Butterfly.* New York: Crowell, 1968.

———. *The Moon of the Salamanders.* New York: HarperCollins, 1992.

HOPF, ALICE L. *Hyena.* New York: Dodd Mead, 1983.

KURTZ, JANE. *River Friendly, River Wild.* Illustrated by Neil Brennan. New York: Simon & Schuster, 2000.

LASKY, KATHRYN. *Sugaring Time.* New York: Macmillan, 1983.

LAUBER, PATRICIA. *Volcano: The Eruption and Healing of Mount St. Helens.* New York: Bradbury, 1986.

LECKIE, ROBERT. *The World Turned Upside Down.* New York: Putnam, 1973.

MACAULAY, DAVID. *Cathedral.* Boston: Houghton Mifflin, 1973.

———. *The Way Things Work.* Boston: Houghton Mifflin, 1988.

McCloskey, Robert. *Time of Wonder.* New York: Viking, 1957.

McClung, Robert. *Samson, Last of the California Grizzlies.* New York: Morrow, 1973.

Meltzer, Milton. *All Times, All Peoples: A World History of Slavery.* New York: Harper & Row, 1980.

Munro, Margaret, and Karen Reczuch. *The Story of Life on Earth.* Toronto: Douglas and McIntyre, 2000.

Murphy, Jim. *An American Plague: The True and Terrifying Story of the Yellow Fever Epidemic of 1793.* New York: Houghton Mifflin, 2003.

———. *The Great Fire.* New York: Scholastic, 1995.

Selsam, Millicent. *How the Animals Eat.* Eau Claire, WI: E. N. Hale, n.d.

Sewell, Marcia. *People of the Breaking Day.* New York: Macmillan, 1990.

Simon, Seymour. *Oceans.* New York: Morrow, 1990.

Stanley, Jerry. *Children of the Dust Bowl: The True Story of the School at Weedpatch Camp.* New York: Crown Publishing, 1992.

———. *I Am an American: A True Story of Japanese Internment.* New York: Crown Publishers, 1994.

Tanghorn, Wendell. *Glacier.* Illustrated by Marc Simont. New York: Crowell, 1988.

Tunis, Edwin. *Colonial Living.* New York: World, 1957.

———. *Indians.* New York: World, 1959.

Wilson, Janet. *Imagine That!* Toronto: Stoddard, 2000.

Wildlife Youth Service. Animals in Danger series. Windermere, FL: Rourke Corp., n.d.

Zim, Herbert S. *Monkeys.* New York: Morrow, 1955.

Children's Book Awards

Children's book awards are listed on the Internet. See the Children's Literature Web Guide, Internet Resources Related to Books for Children and Young Adults (Children's Literature Awards page, copyright © 1997 David K. Brown). Listed below in alphabetical order is a representative group.

Australian Children's Books of the Year Awards

Australia gives an award for Older Readers (1946), Younger Readers (1982), Picture Books (1956), and Information Books (1993). Listed here are the winners for all categories.

1946	*Karrawingi, the Emu* by Leslie Rees
1948	*Shackleton's Argonauts* by Frank Hurley
1950	*Whalers of the Midnight Sun* by Alan Villiers
1951	*Verity of Sydney Town* by Ruth Williams
1952	*The Australia Book* by Eve Pownall
1953	*Aircraft of Today and Tomorrow* by J. H. and W. D. Martin
	Good Luck to the Rider by Joan Phipson
1954	*Australian Legendary Tales* by K. L. Parker
1955	*The First Walkabout* by H. A. Lindsay and N. B. Tindale
1956	*The Crooked Snake* by Patricia Wrightson; Picture Book: *Wish and the Magic Nut* by Sheila Hawkins, text by Peggy Barnard
1957	*The Boomerang Book of Legendary Tales* by Enid Moodie-Heddle
1958	*Tiger in the Bush* by Nan Chauncy; Picture Book: *Pickaninny Walkabout* by Axel Poignant
1959	*Devil's Hill* by Nan Chauncy; *Sea Menace* by John Gunn
1960	*All the Proud Tribesmen* by Kylie Tennant
1961	*Tangara* by Nan Chauncy
1962	*The Racketty Street Gang* by H. L. Evers
	Rafferty Rides a Winner by Joan Woodbery
1963	*The Family Conspiracy* by Joan Phipson
1964	*The Green Laurel* by Eleanor Spence

1965   *Pastures of the Blue Crane* by Hesba F. Brinsmead; Picture Book: *Hugo's Zoo* by Elisabeth MacIntyre

1966   *Ash Road* by Ivan Southall

1967   *The Min Min* by Mavis Thorpe Clark

1968   *To the Wild Sky* by Ivan Southall

1969   *When Jays Fly to Barbmo* by Margaret Balderson; Picture Book: *Sly Old Wardrobe* by Ted Greenwood, text by Ivan Southall

1970   *Uhu* by Annette Macarther-Onslow

1971   *Bread and Honey* by Ivan Southall; Picture Book: *Waltzing Matilda* illustrated by Desmond Digby, text by A. B. Paterson

1972   *Longtime Passing* by Hesba F. Brinsmead

1973   *Family at the Lookout* by Noreen Shelly

1974   *The Nargun and the Stars* by Patricia Wrightson; Picture Book: *The Bunyip of Berkeley's Creek*, text by Jenny Wagner

1975   Picture Book: *The Man from Iron Bark*, illustrated by Quentin Hole, text by A. B. Paterson

1976   *Fly West* by Ivan Southall; Picture Book: *The Rainbow Serpent* by Dick Roughsey

1977   *The October Child* by Eleanor Spence

1978   *The Ice Is Coming* by Patricia Wrightson; Picture Book: *John Brown, Rose and the Midnight Cat* illustrated by Ron Brooks, text by Jenny Wagner

1979   *The Plum-Rain Scroll* by Ruth Manley; Picture Book: *The Quinkins* illustrated by Percy Trezie and Dick Roughsey

1980   *Displaced Person* by Lee Harding; Picture Book: *One Dragon's Dream* by Peter Pavey

1981   *Playing Beatie Bow* by Ruth Park

1982   *The Valley Between* by Colin Thiele; *Rummage* by Christobel Mattingley; Picture Book: *Sunshine*, illustrated by Jan Ormerud

1983   *Thing* by Robin Klein; *Master of the Grove* by Victor Kelleher; Picture Book: *Who Sank the Boat?* illustrated by Pamela Allen

1984   *A Little Fear* by Patricia Wrightson; *Bernice Knows Best* by Max Dann; Picture Book: *Bertie and the Bear* by Pamela Allen

1985   *The True Story of Lilli Stubeck* by James Aldridge; *Something Special* by Emily Rodda

1986   *The Green Wind* by Thurley Fowler; *Arkwright* by Mary Steele; Picture Book: *Felix and Alexander*, illustrated by Terry Denton

1987   *All We Know* by Simon French; *Pigs Might Fly* by Emily Rodda, illustrated by Noela Young; Picture Book: *Kojuro and the Bears*, illustrated by Junko Morimoto, adapted by Helen Smith

1988   *So Much to Tell You* by John Marsden; *My Place* by Nadia Wheatley; Picture Book: *Crusher Is Coming* by Bob Graham

1989   *Best-Kept Secret* by Emily Rodda; *Beyond the Labyrinth* by Gillian Rubinstein; Picture Book: *Drac and the Gremlin*, illustrated by Jane Tanner, text by Allan Baillie

1990   *Come Back to Show You I Could Fly* by Robin Klein; *Pigs and Honey* by Jeanne Baker, illustrated by Jeanne Adams; Picture Book: *The Very Best of Friends*, illustrated by Julie Vivas, text by Margaret Wild

1991   *Finders Keepers* by Emily Rodda; *Strange Objects* by Gary Crew; Picture Book: *Greetings from Sandy Beach*, illustrated by Bob Graham

1992   *The House Guest* by Eleanor Nilsson; *Magnificent Nose and Other Marvels*
        by Anna Fienberg, illustrated by Kim Gamble; Picture Book: *Window* by
        Jeannie Baker

1993   *Looking for Alibrandi* by Melina Marchetta; *The Bamboo Flute* by
        Gary Fisher; Picture Book: *Rose Meets Mr. Wintergarden* by
        Bob Graham

1994   *The Gathering* by Isobelle Carmody; *Angel's Gate* by Gary Crew; *Rowan
        of Ring* by Emily Rodda; Picture Book: *First Light* by Gary Crew

1995   *Foxspell* by Gillian Rubenstein; *Ark in the Park* by Wendy Orr;
        Picture Book: *The Watertower*, illustrated by Steven Woolman, text by
        Gary Crew

1996   *Pagan's Vows* by Catherine Jinks; *Swashbuckler* by James Maloney;
        Picture Book: *The Hunt* by Norelle Oliver

1997   *A Bridge to Wiseman's Cove* by James Moloney; *Hannah Plus One* by
        Libby Gleeson, illustrated by Ann James; *Not a Nibble!* by Elizabeth
        Honey; *Killer Plants and How to Grow Them* by Gordon Cheers and Julie
        Silk, illustrated by Marjorie Crosby-Fairall

1998   *Eye to Eye* by Catherine Jinks; *Someone Like Me* by Elaine Forrestal;
        The Two Bullies by Junko Morimoto, translated by Isao Morimoto;
        A Home among the Gum Trees: The Story of Australian Houses by
        John Nicholson

1999   *Deadly, Unna?* by Phillip Gwynne; *My Girragundji* by Meme McDonald
        and Boori Pryor, photos by Meme McDonald; *The Rabbits* by Tan Shaun,
        text by John Marsden; *Going for Kalta: Hunting for Sleepy Lizards at
        Yalata* by Yvonne Edwards and Brenda Day

2000   *48 Shades of Brown* by Nick Earls; *Hitler's Daughter* by Jackie French;
        Jenny Angel by Anne Spudvilas, text by Margaret Wild; *Fishing for
        Islands: Traditional Boats and Seafarers of the Pacific* by John Nicholson

2001   *Wolf on the Fold* by Judith Clarke; *Two Hands Together* by Diana Kidd;
        You'll Wake the Baby! By Catherine Jinks, illustrated by Andrew McLean;
        Fox by Ron Brooks, text by Margaret Wilder; *Olympia: Warrior Athletes of
        Ancient Greece* by David Kennett, text by Dyan Blacklock

2002   *Forest* by Sonya Hartnett; *My Dog* by John Heffernan, illustrated by
        Andrew McLean; *"Let's Get a Pup!"* by Bob Graham; *An Ordinary Day* by
        Armin Greder, text by Libby Gleeson; *Papunya School Book of Country
        and History* by Papunya School Publishing Committee

2003   *The Messenger* by Markus Zusak; *Rain May and Captain Daniel* by
        Catherine Bateson; *A Year on Our Farm* by Penny Matthews, illustrated
        by Andrew McLean; *In Flanders Fields* by Brian Harrison-Lever, text by
        Norman Jorgensen; *Iron in the Blood: Convicts and Commandants in
        Colonial Australia* by Alan Tucker

2004   *Saving Francesca* by Melina Marchetta; *Dragonkeeper* by Carole
        Wilkinson; *Grandpa and Thomas* by Pamela Allen; *Cat and Fish* by
        Neil Curtis, text by Joan Grant; *Animal Architects* by John Nicholson

2005   *The Running Man* by Michael Gerard Bauer; *The Silver Donkey* by Sonya
        Hartnett; *Where Is the Green Sheep?* by Mem Fox, illustrated by Judy
        Horacek; *Are We There Yet? A Journey around Australia* by Alison Lester;
        *To the Moon and Back: The Amazing Australians at the Forefront of Space
        Travel Plus Fantastic Moon Facts*

Boston Globe–Horn Book Awards

These awards have been given annually in the fall ever since 1967 by the *Boston Globe* and *The Horn Book Magazine*. Through 1975, two awards were given—one for outstanding text and the other for outstanding illustration. In 1976 the award categories were changed to Outstanding Fiction or Poetry, Outstanding Nonfiction, and Outstanding Illustration. Books published in the United States but written by non-Americans are also eligible.

1967   Text: *The Little Fishes* by Erik Christian Haugaard
        Illustration: *London Bridge Is Falling Down* by Peter Spier

1968   Text: *The Spring Rider* by John Lawson
        Illustration: *Tikki Tikki Tembo* by Arlene Mosel, illustrated by Blair Lent

1969   Text: *A Wizard of Earthsea* by Ursula K. Le Guin
        Illustration: *The Adventures of Paddy Pork* by John S. Goodall

1970   Text: *The Intruder* by John Rowe Townsend
        Illustration: *Hi, Cat!* by Ezra Jack Keats

1971   Text: *A Room Made of Windows* by Eleanor Cameron
        Illustration: *If I Built a Village* by Kazue Mizumura

1972   Text: *Tristan and Iseult* by Rosemary Sutcliff
        Illustration: *Mr. Gumpy's Outing* by John Burningham

1973   Text: *The Dark Is Rising* by Susan Cooper
        Illustration: *King Stork* by Trina Schart Hyman

1974   Text: *M. C. Higgins, The Great* by Virginia Hamilton
        Illustration: *Jambo Means Hello* by Muriel Feelings, illustrated by Tom Feelings

1975   Text: *Transport 7-41-R* by T. Degens
        Illustration: *Anno's Alphabet* by Mitsumasa Anno

1976   Fiction: *Unleaving* by Jill Paton Walsh
        Nonfiction: *Voyaging to Cathay: Americans in the China Trade* by Alfred Tamarin and Shirley Glubok
        Illustration: *Thirteen* by Remy Charlip and Jerry Joyner

1977   Fiction: *Child of the Owl* by Laurence Yep
        Nonfiction: *Chance Luck and Destiny* by Peter Dickinson
        Illustration: *Ganfa' Grig Had a Pig and Other Rhymes* by Wallace Tripp

1978   Fiction: *The Westing Game* by Ellen Raskin
        Nonfiction: *Mischling, Second Degree: My Childhood in Nazi Germany* by Ilse Koehn
        Illustration: *Anno's Journey* by Mitsumasa Anno

1979   Fiction: *Humbug Mountain* by Sid Fleischman
        Nonfiction: *The Road from Home: The Story of an Armenian Girl* by David Kherdian
        Illustration: *The Snowman* by Raymond Briggs

1980   Fiction: *Conrad's War* by Andrew Davies
        Nonfiction: *Building: The Fight Against Gravity* by Mario Salvadori
        Illustration: *The Garden of Abdul Gasazi* by Chris Van Allsburg

1981   Fiction: *The Leaving* by Lynn Hall
        Nonfiction: *The Weaver's Gift* by Kathryn Lasky
        Illustration: *Outside Over There* by Maurice Sendak

1982   Fiction: *Playing Beatie Bow* by Ruth Park
Nonfiction: *Upon the Head of the Goat: A Childhood in Hungary, 1939–1944* by Aranka Siegal
Illustration: *A Visit to William Blake's Inn: Poems for Innocent and Experienced Travelers* by Nancy Willard, illustrated by Alice and Martin Provensen

1983   Fiction: *Sweet Whispers, Brother Rush* by Virginia Hamilton
Nonfiction: *Behind Barbed Wire: The Imprisonment of Japanese Americans During World War II* by Daniel S. Davis
Illustration: *A Chair for My Mother* by Vera B. Williams

1984   Fiction: *A Little Fear* by Patricia Wrightson
Nonfiction: *The Double Life of Pocahontas* by Jean Fritz
Illustration: *Jonah and the Great Fish*, retold and illustrated by Warwick Hutton

1985   Fiction: *The Moves Make the Man* by Bruce Brooks
Nonfiction: *Commodore Perry in the Land of the Shogun* by Rhoda Blumberg
Illustration: *Mama Don't Allow* by Thatcher Hurd

1986   Fiction: *In Summer Light* by Zibby Oneal
Illustration: *The Paper Crane* by Molly Bang
Nonfiction: *Auks, Rocks and the Odd Dinosaur* by Peggy Thomson

1987   Fiction: *Rabble Starkey* by Lois Lowru
Illustration: *Mufaro's Beautiful Daughters* by John Steptoe
Nonfiction: *Pilgrims of Plimouth* by Marcia Sewall

1988   Fiction: *The Friendship* by Mildred Taylor
Illustration: *The Boy of the Three-Year Nap* by Diane Snyder
Nonfiction: *Anthony Burns: The Defeat and Triumph of a Fugitive Slave* by Virginia Hamilton

1989   Fiction: *Village by the Sea* by Paula Fox
Illustration: *Shy Charles* by Rosemary Wells
Nonfiction: *The Way Things Work* by David Macaulay, illustrated by David Macaulay

1990   Fiction: *Maniac Magee* by Jerry Spinelli
Illustration: *Lon Po Po: A Red Riding Hood Story from China* by Ed Young
Nonfiction: *Great Little Madison* by Jean Fritz

1991   Fiction: *True Confessions of Charlotte Doyle* by Avi, illustrated by Ruth E. Murray
Illustration: *Tale of the Mandarin Ducks* by Katherine Paterson, illustrated by Leo Dillon and Diane Dillon
Nonfiction: *Appalachia: The Voices of Sleeping Birds* by Cynthia Rylant, illustrated by Barry Moser

1992   Fiction/Poetry: *Missing May* by Cynthia Rylant
Illustration: *Seven Blind Mice* by Ed Young, illustrated by Ed Young

1993   Fiction: *Ajeemah and His Son* by James Barry
Nonfiction: *Sojourner Truth: Ain't I a Woman?* by Patricia C. and Frederick McKissack
Picture Book: *The Fortune Tellers*, by Lloyd Alexander, illustrated by Trina Schart Hyman

1994   Fiction: *Scooter* by Vera B. Williams
Nonfiction: *Eleanor Roosevelt: A Life of Discovery* by Russell Freedman
Picture Book: *Grandfather's Journey* by Allen Say

1995   Fiction: *Some of the Kinder Planets* by Tim Wynne-Jones
Nonfiction: *Abigail Adams: Witness to a Revolution* by Natalie S. Bober
Picture Book: *John Henry*, retold by Julius Lester, illustrated by
Jerry Pinkney

1996   Fiction: *Poppy* by Avi
Nonfiction: *Orphan Train Rider: One Boy's True Story* by Andrea Warren
Picture Book: *In the Rain with Baby Duck* by Amy Hest, illustrated by
Jill Barton

1997   Nonfiction: *Lou Gehrig: The Luckiest Man* by David A. Adler, illustrated
by Terry Widener; *Leonardo da Vinci*, written and illustrated by
Diane Stanley
Picture Book: *The Adventures of Sparrowboy*, written and illustrated by
Brian Pinkney
Fiction and Poetry: *The Friends* by Kazumi Yomoto

1998   Fiction and Poetry: *The Circuit Stories from the Life of a Migrant Child*,
by Francisco Jime'nez
Nonfiction: *Leon's Story* by Leon Walter Tillage
Picture Book: *And If the Moon Could Talk*, illustrated by Georg
Hallensleben, text by Kate Banks

1999   Fiction: *Holes* by Louis Sachar
Nonfiction: *The Top of the World: Climbing Mount Everest*, written and
illustrated by Steve Jenkins
Picture Book: *Red-Eyed Tree Frog* by Joy Cowley, photographs by
Nic Bishop

2000   Fiction: *The Folk Keeper* by Franny Billingsley
Nonfiction: *Sir Walter Raleigh and the Quest for El Dorado* by
Marc Aronson
Picture Book: *Henry Hikes to Fitchburg*, written and illustrated by
D. B. Johnson

2001   Fiction and Poetry: *Carver: A Life in Poems* by Marilyn Nelson
Nonfiction: *The Longitude Prize* by Joan Dash, illustrated by
Dusan Petricic
Picture Book: *Cold Feet* by Cynthia DeFelice, illustrated by Robert
Andrew Parke

2002   Fiction and Poetry: *Lord of the Deep* by Graham Salisbury
Nonfiction: *This Land Was Made for You and Me: The Life and Songs of
Woody Guthrie* by Elizabeth Partridge
Picture Book: *"Let's Get a Pup!"* by Bob Graham

2003   Fiction and Poetry: *The Jamie and Angus Stories* by Anne Fine, illustrated
by Penny Dale
Nonfiction: *Fireboat: The Heroic Adventures of the John J. Harvey* by
Maria Kalman
Picture Book: *Big Momma Makes the World* by Phyllis Root, illustrated by
Helen Oxenbury

2004   Fiction and Poetry: *The Fire-Eaters* by David Almond
Nonfiction: *An American Plague: The True and Terrifying Story of the
Yellow Fever Epidemic of 1793* by Jim Murphy

Picture Book: *The Man Who Walked Between the Towers* by Mordecai
Gerstein
2005   Fiction and Poetry: *The Schwa Was Here* by Neal Shusterman
Nonfiction: *The Race to Save the Lord God Bird* by Phillip Hoose
Picture Book: *Traction Man Is Here!* by Mini Grey

The Caldecott Medal

Since 1938, the Association of Library Service to Children of the American Library
Association has annually awarded the Caldecott Medal to the illustrator of the
most distinguished picture book published in the United States in the preceding
year. The recipient must be a citizen or resident of the United States. The medal
is named in tribute to the well-loved English illustrator Randolph Caldecott
(1846–1886).

1938   *Animals of the Bible* by Helen Dean Fish, illustrated by Dorothy P.
Lathrop, Lippincott
Honor Books: *Seven Simeons*, written and illustrated by Boris
Artzybasheff, Viking; *Four and Twenty Blackbirds* by Helen Dean Fish,
illustrated by Robert Lawson, Stokes
1939   *Mei Li*, written and illustrated by Thomas Handforth, Doubleday
Honor Books: *The Forest Pool*, written and illustrated by Laura Adams
Armer, Longmans; *Wee Gillis* by Munro Leaf, illustrated by Robert
Lawson, Viking; *Snow White and the Seven Dwarfs*, written and illus-
trated by Wanda Gág, Coward; *Barkis*, written and illustrated by Clare
Newberry, Harper; *Andy and the Lion*, written and illustrated by James
Daugherty, Viking
1940   *Abraham Lincoln*, written and illustrated by Ingri and Edgar Parin
d'Aulaire, Doubleday
Honor Books: *Cock-A-Doodle Doo* . . . written and illustrated by Berta
and Elmer Hader, Macmillan; *Madeline*, written and illustrated by
Ludwig Bemelmans, Viking; *The Ageless Story*, illustrated by Lauen
Ford, Dodd
1941   *They Were Strong and Good*, written and illustrated by Robert Lawson,
Viking
Honor Book: *April's Kittens*, written and illustrated by Clare Newberry,
Harper
1942   *Make Way for Ducklings*, written and illustrated by Robert McCloskey,
Viking
Honor Books: *An American ABC*, written and illustrated by Maud and
Miska Petersham, Macmillan: *In My Mother's House* by Ann Nolan Clark,
illustrated by Velino Herrera, Viking; *Paddle-to-the-Sea*, written and illus-
trated by Holling C. Holling, Houghton; *Nothing at All*, written and illus-
trated by Wanda Gág, Coward
1943   *The Little House*, written and illustrated by Virginia Lee Burton,
Houghton
Honor Books: *Dash and Dort*, written and illustrated by Mary and Conrad
Buff, Viking; *Marshmallow*, written and illustrated by Clare Newberry,
Harper

1944   *Many Moons* by James Thurber, illustrated by Louis Slobodkin, Harcourt
        Honor Books; *Small Rain: Verses from the Bible,* selected by Jessie Orton
        Jones, illustrated by Elizabeth Orton Jones, Viking; *Pierre Pigeon* by Lee
        Kingman, illustrated by Arnold E. Bare, Houghton; *The Mighty Hunter,*
        written and illustrated by Berta and Elmer Hader, Macmillan; *A Child's
        Good Night Book* by Margaret Wise Brown, illustrated by Jean Charlot,
        W. R. Scott; *Good Luck Horse* by Chih-Yi Chan, illustrated by Plao Chan,
        Whittlesey

1945   *Prayer for a Child* by Rachel Field, illustrated by Elizabeth Orton Jones,
        Macmillan
        Honor Books: *Mother Goose,* illustrated by Tasha Tudor, Walck; *In the
        Forest,* written and illustrated by Marie Hall Ets, Viking; *Yonie Wonder-nose,*
        written and illustrated by Marguerite de Angeli, Doubleday; *The Christmas
        Anna Angel* by Ruth Sawyer, illustrated by Kate Seredy, Viking

1946   *The Rooster Crows* . . . (traditional Mother Goose), illustrated by Maud
        and Miska Petersham, Macmillan
        Honor Books: *Little Lost Lamb* by Golden MacDonald, illustrated by
        Leonard Weisgard, Doubleday; *Sing Mother Goose* by Opal Wheeler,
        illustrated by Marjorie Torrey, Dutton; *My Mother Is the Most Beautiful
        Woman in the World* by Becky Reyher, illustrated by Ruth Gannett, Lothrop;
        You Can Write Chinese, written and illustrated by Kurt Wiese, Viking

1947   *The Little Island* by Golden MacDonald, illustrated by Leonard Weisgard,
        Doubleday
        Honor Books: *Rain Drop Splash* by Alvin Tresselt, illustrated by Leonard
        Weisgard, Lothrop; *Boats on the River* by Marjorie Flack, illustrated by
        Jay Hyde Barnum, Viking; *Timothy Turtle* by Al Graham, illustrated by
        Tony Palazzo, Viking; *Pedro, the Angel of Olvera Street,* written and illus-
        trated by Leo Politi, Scribner's; *Sing in Praise: A Collection of the Best
        Loved Hymns* by Opal Wheeler, illustrated by Marjorie Torrey, Dutton

1948   *White Snow, Bright Snow* by Alvin Tresselt, illustrated by Roger Duvoisin,
        Lothrop
        Honor Books: *Stone Soup,* written and illustrated by Marcia Brown,
        Scribner's; *McElligot's Pool,* written and illustrated by Dr. Seuss,
        Random; *Bambino the Clown,* written and illustrated by George
        Schreiber, Viking; *Roger and the Fox* by Lavinia Davis, illustrated by
        Hildegard Woodward, Doubleday; *Song of Robin Hood,* edited by Anne
        Malcolmson, illustrated by Virginia Lee Burton, Houghton

1949   *The Big Snow,* written and illustrated by Berta and Elmer Hader, Macmillan
        Honor Books: *Blueberries for Sal,* written and illustrated by Robert
        McCloskey, Viking; *All Around the Town* by Phyllis McGinley, illustrated
        by Helen Stone, Lippincott; *Juanita,* written and illustrated by Leo Politi,
        Scribner's; *Fish in the Air,* written and illustrated by Kurt Wiese, Viking

1950   *Song of the Swallows,* written and illustrated by Leo Politi, Scribner's
        Honor Books: *America's Ethan Allen* by Stewart Holbrook, illustrated
        by Lynd Ward, Houghton; *The Wild Birthday Cake* by Lavinia Davis,
        illustrated by Hildgard Woodward, Doubleday; *The Happy Day* by
        Ruth Krauss, illustrated by Marc Simont, Harper; *Bartholomew and the
        Oobleck,* written and illustrated by Dr. Seuss, Random; *Henry Fisherman,*
        written and illustrated by Marcia Brown, Scribner's

1951   *The Egg Tree*, written and illustrated by Katherine Milhous, Scribner's
        Honor Books: *Dick Whittington and His Cat*, written and illustrated by
        Marcia Brown, Scribner's; *The Two Reds* by Will, illustrated by Nicolas,
        Harcourt; *If I Ran the Zoo*, written and illustrated by Dr. Seuss, Random;
        The Most Wonderful Doll in the World by Phyllis McGinley, illustrated by
        Helen Stone, Lippincott; *T-Bone, the Baby Sitter*, written and illustrated
        by Clare Newberry, Harper

1952   *Finders Keepers* by Will, illustrated by Nicolas, Harcourt
        Honor Books: *Mr. T. W. Anthony Woo*, written and illustrated by Marie
        Hall Ets, Viking; *Skipper John's Cook*, written and illustrated by Marcia
        Brown, Scribner's; *All Falling Down* by Gene Zion, illustrated by
        Margaret Bloy Graham, Harper; *Bear Party*, written and illustrated by
        Willian Pène du Bois, Viking; *Feather Mountain*, written and illustrated
        by Elizabeth Olds, Houghton

1953   *The Biggest Bear*, written and illustrated by Lynd Ward, Houghton
        Honor Books: *Puss in Boots* by Charles Perrault, illustrated and
        translated by Marcia Brown, Scribner's; *One Morning in Maine*, written
        and illustrated by Robert McCloskey, Viking; *Ape in a Cape*, written and
        illustrated by Fritz Eichenberg, Harcourt; *The Storm Book* by Charlotte
        Zolotow, illustrated by Margaret Bloy Graham, Harper; *Five Little
        Monkeys*, written and illustrated by Juliet Kepes, Houghton

1954   *Madeline's Rescue*, written and illustrated by Ludwig Bemelmans, Viking
        Honor Books: *Journey Cake, Ho!* by Ruth Sawyer, illustrated by Robert
        McCloskey, Viking; *When Will the World Be Mine?* by Miriam Schlein,
        illustrated by Jean Charlot, W. R. Scott; *The Steadfast Tin Soldier* by Hans
        Christian Andersen, illustrated by Marcia Brown, Scribner's; *A Very
        Special House* by Ruth Krauss, illustrated by Maurice Sendak, Harper;
        Green Eyes, written and illustrated by A. Birnbaum, Capitol

1955   *Cinderella, or the Little Glass Slipper* by Charles Perrault, translated and
        illustrated by Marcia Brown, Scribner's
        Honor Books: *Book of Nursery and Mother Goose Rhymes*, illustrated by
        Marguerite de Angeli, Doubleday; *Wheel on the Chimney* by Margaret
        Wise Brown, illustrated by Tibor Gergely, Lippincott; *The Thanksgiving
        Story* by Alice Dalgliesh, illustrated by Helen Sewell, Scribner's

1956   *Frog Went A-Courtin'*, edited by John Langstaff, illustrated by Feodor
        Rojankovsky, Harcourt
        Honor Books: *Play with Me*, written and illustrated by Marie Hall Ets,
        Viking; *Crow Boy*, written and illustrated by Taro Yashima, Viking

1957   *A Tree Is Nice* by Janice May Udry, illustrated by Marc Simont, Harper
        Honor Books: *Mr. Penny's Race Horse*, written and illustrated by
        Marie Hall Ets, Viking; *1 Is One*, written and illustrated by Tasha Tudor,
        Walck; *Anatole* by Eve Titus, illustrated by Paul Galdone, McGraw;
        Gillespie and the Guards by Benjamin Elkin, illustrated by James
        Daugherty, Viking; *Lion*, written and illustrated by William Pène du Bois,
        Viking

1958   *Time of Wonder*, written and illustrated by Robert McCloskey, Viking
        Honor Books: *Fly High, Fly Low*, written and illustrated by Don Freeman,
        Viking; *Anatole and the Cat* by Eve Titus, illustrated by Paul Galdone,
        McGraw

1959   *Chanticleer and the Fox*, adapted from Chaucer and illustrated by
Barbara Cooney, Crowell
Honor Books: *The House That Jack Built*, written and illustrated by
Antonio Frasceni, Harcourt; *What Do You Say, Dear?* by Sesyle Joslin,
illustrated by Maurice Sendak, W. R. Scott; *Umbrella*, written and
illustrated by Taro Yashima, Viking

1960   *Nine Days to Christmas* by Marie Hall Ets and Aurora Labastida,
illustrated by Marie Hall Ets, Viking
Honor Books: *Houses from the Sea* by Alice E. Goudey, illustrated by
Adrienne Adams, Scribner's; *The Moon Jumpers* by Janice May Udry,
illustrated by Maurice Sendak, Harper

1961   *Baboushka and the Three Kings* by Ruth Robbins, illustrated by Nicolas
Sidjakov, Parnassus
Honor Book: *Inch by Inch*, written and illustrated by Leo Lionni,
Obolensky

1962   *Once a Mouse . . .*, written and illustrated by Marcia Brown, Scribner's
Honor Books: *The Fox Went Out on a Chilly Night*, written and illustrated
by Peter Spier, Doubleday; *Little Bear's Visit* by Else Holmelund Minarik,
illustrated by Maurice Sendak, Harper; *The Day We Saw the Sun Come
Up* by Alice E. Goudey, illustrated by Adrienne Adams, Scribner's

1963   *The Snowy Day*, written and illustrated by Ezra Jack Keats, Viking
Honor Books: *The Sun Is a Golden Earring* by Natalie M. Belting,
illustrated by Bernarda Bryson, Holt; *Mr. Rabbit and the Lovely Present*
by Charlotte Zolotow, illustrated by Maurice Sendak, Harper

1964   *Where the Wild Things Are*, written and illustrated by Maurice Sendak,
Harper
Honor Books: *Swimmy*, written and illustrated by Leo Lionni, Pantheon;
All in the Morning Early by Sorche Nic Leodhas, illustrated by Evaline
Ness, Holt; *Mother Goose and Nursery Rhymes*, illustrated by Philip Reed,
Atheneum

1965   *May I Bring a Friend?* by Beatrice Schenk de Regniers, illustrated by Beni
Montresor, Atheneum
Honor Books: *Rain Makes Applesauce* by Julian Scheer, illustrated by
Marvin Bileck, Holiday; *The Wave* by Margaret Hodges, illustrated
by Blair Lent, Houghton; *A Pocketful of Cricket* by Rebecca Caudill,
illustrated by Evaline Ness, Holt

1966   *Always Room for One More* by Sorche Nic Leodhas, illustrated by Nonny
Hogrogian, Holt
Honor Books: *Hide and Seek Fog* by Alvin Tresselt, illustrated by Roger
Duvoisin, Lothrop; *Just Me*, written and illustrated by Marie Hall Ets,
Viking; *Tom Tit Tot*, written and illustrated by Evaline Ness, Scribner's

1967   *Sam, Bangs and Moonshine*, written and illustrated by Evaline Ness, Holt
Honor Book: *One Wide River to Cross* by Barbara Emberley, illustrated by
Ed Emberley, Prentice

1968   *Drummer Hoff* by Barbara Emberley, illustrated by Ed Emberley,
Prentice
Honor Books: *Frederick*, written and illustrated by Leo Lionni, Pantheon;
Seashore Story, written and illustrated by Taro Yashima, Viking; *The
Emperor and the Kite* by Jane Yolen, illustrated by Ed Young, World

1969   *The Fool of the World and the Flying Ship* by Arthur Ransome, illustrated by Uri Shulevitz, Farrar
Honor Book: *Why the Sun and the Moon Live in the Sky* by Elphinstone Dayrell, illustrated by Blair Lent, Houghton

1970   *Sylvester and the Magic Pebble*, written and illustrated by William Steig, Windmill
Honor Books: *Goggles!* written and illustrated by Ezra Jack Keats, Macmillan; *Alexander and the Wind-Up Mouse*, written and illustrated by Leo Lionni, Pantheon; *Pop Corn and Ma Goodness* by Edna Mitchell Preston, illustrated by Robert Andrew Parker, Viking; *Thy Friend, Obadiah*, written and illustrated by Brinton Turkle, Viking; *The Judge* by Harve Zemach, illustrated by Margot Zemach, Farrar

1971   *A Story, A Story*, written and illustrated by Gail E. Haley, Atheneum
Honor Books: *The Angry Moon* by William Sleator, illustrated by Blair Lent, Atlantic/Little, Brown; *Frog and Toad Are Friends*, written and illustrated by Arnold Lobel, Harper; *In the Night Kitchen*, written and illustrated by Maurice Sendak, Harper

1972   *One Fine Day*, written and illustrated by Nonny Hogrogian, Macmillan
Honor Books: *If All the Seas Were One Sea*, written and illustrated by Janina Domanska, Macmillan; *Moja Means One: Swahili Counting Book* by Muriel Feelings, illustrated by Tom Feelings, Dial; *Hildilid's Night* by Cheli Duran Ryan, illustrated by Arnold Lobel, Macmillan

1973   *The Funny Little Woman*, retold by Arlene Mosel, illustrated by Blair Lent, Dutton
Honor Books: *Anansi the Spider*, adapted and illustrated by Gerald McDermott, Holt; *Hosie's Alphabet* by Hosea, Tobias, and Lisa Baskin, illustrated by Leonard Baskin, Viking; *Snow-White and the Seven Dwarfs*, translated by Randall Jarrell, illustrated by Nancy Ekholm Burkert, Farrar; *When Clay Sings* by Byrd Baylor, illustrated by Tom Bahti, Scribner's

1974   *Duffy and the Devil* by Harve Zemach, illustrated by Margot Zemach, Farrar
Honor Books: *Three Jovial Huntsmen*, written and illustrated by Susan Jeffers, Bradbury; *Cathedral: The Story of Its Construction*, written and illustrated by David Macaulay, Houghton

1975   *Arrow to the Sun*, adapted and illustrated by Gerald McDermott, Viking
Honor Book: *Jambo Means Hello* by Muriel Feelings, illustrated by Tom Feelings, Dial

1976   *Why Mosquitoes Buzz in People's Ears*, retold by Verna Aardema, illustrated by Leo Dillon and Diane Dillon, Dial
Honor Books: *The Desert Is Theirs* by Byrd Baylor, illustrated by Peter Parnall, Scribner's; *Strega Nona*, retold and illustrated by Tomie dePaola, Prentice

1977   *Ashanti to Zulu: African Traditions* by Margaret Musgrove, illustrated by Leo Dillon and Diane Dillon, Dial
Honor Books: *The Amazing Bone*, written and illustrated by William Steig, Farrar; *The Contest*, retold and illustrated by Nonny Hogrogian, Greenwillow; *Fish for Supper*, written and illustrated by M. B. Goffstein, Dial; *The Golem*, written and illustrated by Beverly Brodsky McDermott,

Lippincott; *Hawk, I'm Your Brother* by Byrd Baylor, illustrated by Peter Parnall, Scribner's

1978   *Noah's Ark*, illustrated by Peter Spier, Doubleday
Honor Books: *Castle*, written and illustrated by David Macaulay, Houghton; *It Could Always Be Worse*, retold and illustrated by Margot Zemach, Farrar

1979   *The Girl Who Loved Wild Horses*, written and illustrated by Paul Goble, Bradbury
Honor Books: *Freight Train*, written and illustrated by Donald Crews, Greenwillow; *The Way to Start a Day* by Byrd Baylor, illustrated by Peter Parnall, Scribner's

1980   *Ox-Cart Man* by Donald Hall, illustrated by Barbara Cooney, Viking
Honor Books: *Ben's Trumpet*, written and illustrated by Rachel Isadora, Greenwillow; *The Garden of Abdul Gasazi*, written and illustrated by Chris Van Allsburg, Houghton

1981   *Fables*, written and illustrated by Arnold Lobel, Harper
Honor Books: *The Grey Lady and the Strawberry Snatcher*, illustrated by Molly Bang, Four Winds; *Truck*, illustrated by Donald Crews, Greenwillow; *Mice Twice*, written and illustrated by Joseph Low, Atheneum; *The Bremen-Town Musicians*, illustrated by Ilse Plume, Doubleday

1982   *Jumanji*, written and illustrated by Chris Van Allsburg, Houghton
Honor Books: *Where the Buffaloes Begin* by Olaf Baker, illustrated by Stephen Gammell, Warne; *On Market Street* by Arnold Lobel, illustrated by Anita Lobel, Greenwillow; *Outside Over There*, written and illustrated by Maurice Sendak, Harper; *A Visit to William Blake's Inn* by Nancy Willard, illustrated by Alice and Martin Provensen, Harcourt

1983   *Shadow* by Blaise Cendrars, translated and illustrated by Marcia Brown, Scribner's
Honor Books: *When I Was Young in the Mountains* by Cynthia Rylant, illustrated by Diane Goode, Dutton; *A Chair for My Mother*, written and illustrated by Vera B. Williams, Greenwillow

1984   *The Glorious Flight: Across the Channel with Louis Blériot*, written and illustrated by Alice Provensen and Martin Provensen, Viking
Honor Books: *Ten, Nine, Eight* by Molly Bang, Greenwillow; *Little Red Riding Hood*, retold and illustrated by Trina Schart Hyman, Holiday House

1985   *St. George and the Dragon*, retold by Margaret Hodges, illustrated by Trina Schart Hyman, Little, Brown
Honor Books: *Hansel and Gretel*, retold by Rika Lesser, illustrated by Paul O. Zelinsky, Dodd; *Have You Seen My Duckling?* by Nancy Tafuri, Greenwillow; *The Story of Jumping Mouse* by John Steptoe, Lothrop

1986   *The Polar Express*, written and illustrated by Chris Van Allsburg, Houghton Mifflin
Honor Books: *The Relatives Came* by Cynthia Rylant, illustrated by Stephen Gammell, Bradbury; *King Bidgood's in the Bathtub* by Audrey Wood, illustrated by Don Wood, Harcourt

1987   *Hey, Al!* by Arthur Yorinks, illustrated by Richard Egielski, Farrar
Honor Books: *The Village of Round and Square Houses*, written and illustrated by Ann Grifalconi, Little, Brown; *Alphabetics*, written and illustrated by Suse MacDonald, Bradbury; *Rumpelstiltskin*, retold and illustrated by Paul O. Zelinsky, Dutton

1988   *Owl Moon* by Jane Yolen, illustrated by John Schoenherr, Philomel
        Honor Book: *Mufaro's Beautiful Daughters,* written and illustrated
        by John Steptoe, Lothrop

1989   *Song and Dance Man* by Karen Ackerman, illustrated by Stephen
        Gammell, Knopf
        Honor Books: *Free Fall,* written and illustrated by David Wiesner,
        Lothrop; *Goldilocks and the Three Bears,* retold and illustrated by
        James Marshall, Dial; *Mirandy and Brother Wind* by Patricia McKissack,
        illustrated by Jerry Pinkney, Knopf; *The Boy of the Three-Year Nap* by
        Diane Snyder, illustrated by Allen Say, Houghton

1990   *Lom Po Po: A Red Riding-Hood Story,* translated and illustrated by
        Ed Young, Philomel
        Honor Books: *Bill Peet: An Autobiography* by Bill Peet; *Color Zoo* by
        Lois Ehlert; *Talking Eggs: A Folktale from the American South,* illustrated
        by Jerry Pinkney, text by Robert D. San Souci; *Hershel and the Hanukkah
        Goblins,* illustrated by Trina Schart Hyman, text by Eric Kimmel

1991   *Black and White* by David Macaulay, Houghton
        Honor Books: *Puss in Boots,* illustrated by Fred Marcellino, text by
        Charles Perrault, translated by Malcolm Arthur; *"More More More"
        Said the Baby: Three Love Stories* by Vera B. Williams

1992   *Tuesday,* written and illustrated by David Wiesner, Clarion
        Honor Book: *Tar Beach* by Faith Ringgold, Clarion

1993   *Mirette on the High Wire,* written and illustrated by Emily Arnold
        McCully, Putnam
        Honor Books: *The Stinky Cheese Man and Other Fairly Stupid Tales,*
        illustrated by Lane Smith, text by Jon Scieszka; *Seven Blind Mice* by
        Ed Young; *Working Cotton,* illustrated by Carol Byard, text by Shirley
        Anne Williams

1994   *Grandfather's Journey* by Allen Say, Houghton
        Honor Books: *Peppe the Lamplighter,* illustrated by Ted Lewin, text by
        Elisa Bartone, Lothrop; *In the Small Small Pond* by Denise Fleming, Holt;
        Raven: A Trickster Tale from the Pacific Northwest by Gerald McDermott,
        Harcourt; *Yo! Yes?* by Chris Raschka, Orchard; *Owen,* by Kevin Henkes,
        Greenwillow

1995   *Smoky Night,* illustrated by David Diaz, text by Eve Bunting, Harcourt
        Honor Books: *John Henry,* illustrated by Jerry Pinkney, text by Julius
        Lester, Dial; *Swamp Angel,* illustrated by Paul Zelinsky, text by Anne
        Isaacs, Dutton; *Time Flies* by Eric Rohmann, Crown

1996   *Officer Buckle and Gloria* by Peggy Rathman, Putnam
        Honor Books: *Alphabet City* by Stephen T. Johnson, Viking; *The Faithful
        Friend,* illustrated by Brian Pinkney, text by Robert D. San Souci, Simon &
        Schuster; *Tops and Bottoms* by Janet Stevens, Harcourt; *Zin! Zin! Zin! A
        Violin,* illustrated by Marjorie Priceman, text by Lloyd Moss, Simon &
        Schuster

1997   *Golem* by David Wisniewski, Clarion
        Honor Books: *Hush! A Thai Lullaby,* illustrated by Holly Meade, text by
        Minfong Ho, Melanie Kroupa, Orchard; *The Graphic Alphabet* by David
        Pelletier, edited by Neal Porter, Orchard; *The Paperboy* by Dav Pilkey,
        Richard Jackson, Orchard; *Starry Messenger* by Peter Sis, Francis Foster
        Books, Farrar, Straus & Giroux

1998   *Rapunzel* by Paul O. Zelinsky, Dutton
Honor Books: *The Gardener*, illustrated by David Small, text by Sarah Stewart, Farrar; *Harlem*, illustrated by Christopher Myers, text by Walter Dean Myers, Scholastic; *There Was an Old Lady Who Swallowed a Fly* by Simms Taback, Viking

1999   *Snowflake Bentley*, illustrated by Mary Azarian, text by Jacqueline Briggs Martin, Houghton
Honor Books: *Duke Ellington: The Piano Prince and the Orchestra*, illustrated by Brian Pinkney, text by Andrea Davis Pinkney, Hyperion; *No, David!* by David Shannon, Scholastic; *Snow* by Uri Shulevitz, Farrar; *Tibet Through the Red Box* by Peter Sis, Frances Foster

2000   *Joseph Had a Little Overcoat* by Simms Taback, Viking
Honor Books: *A Child's Calendar*, illustrated by Trina Schart Hyman, text by John Updike, Holiday House; *Sector 7* by David Wiesner, Clarion; *When Sophie Gets Angry—Really, Really Angry* by Molly Bang, Scholastic; *The Ugly Duckling*, illustrated by Jerry Pinkney, text by Hans Christian Andersen, adapted by Jerry Pinkney, Morrow

2001   *So You Want to Be President?* illustrated by David Small, written by Judith St. George, Philomel
Honor Books: *Casey at the Bat*, illustrated by Christopher Bing, written by Ernest Thayer, Handprint; *Click, Clack, Moo: Cows that Type*, illustrated by Betsy Lewin, written by Doreen Cronin, Simon & Schuster; *Olivia* by Ian Falconer, Atheneum

2002   *The Three Pigs* by David Wiesner, Clarion
Honor Books: *The Dinosaurs of Waterhouse Hawkins*, illustrated by Brian Selznick, written by Barbara Kerley, Scholastic; *Martin's Big Words: The Life of Dr. Martin Luther King, Jr.*, illustrated by Bryan Collier, written by Doreen Rappaport, Jump at the Sun; *The Stray Dog* by Marc Simont, HarperCollins

2003   *My Friend Rabbit* by Eric Rohmann, Roaring Brook Press
Honor Books: *The Spider and the Fly*, illustrated by Tony DiTerlizzi, written by Mary Howitt, Simon & Schuster; *Hondo & Fabian* by Peter McCarty, Holt; *Noah's Ark* by Jerry Pinkney, SeaStar Books

2004   *The Man Who Walked Between the Towers* by Mordicai Gerstein, Roaring Brook Press
Honor Books: *Ella Sarah Gets Dressed* by Margaret Chodos-Irvine, Harcourt; *What Do You Do with a Tail Like This?* illustrated and written by Steve Jenkins and Robin Page, Houghton; *Don't Let the Pigeon Drive the Bus* by Mo Willems, Hyperion

2005   *Kitten's First Full Moon* by Kevin Henkes, Greenwillow
Honor Books: *The Red Book* by Barbara Lehman, Houghton Mifflin Company; *Coming on Home Soon* illustrated by E.B. Lewis, written by Jacqueline Woodson, Putnam; *Knuffle Bunny: A Cautionary Tale*, illustrated and written by Mo Willems, Hyperion

The Canadian Library Awards

This award has been given each year since 1947 by the Canadian Library Association to a distinguished children's book authored by a citizen of Canada. A similar medal has been given annually since 1954 to a significant children's book published in French.

1947   *Starbuck Valley Winter* by Roderick Haig-Brown, Collins

1948   *Kristli's Trees* by Mabel Dunham, Hale

1950   *Franklin of the Arctic* by Richard S. Lambert, McClelland & Stewart

1952   *The Sun Horse* by Catherine Anthony Clark, Macmillan of Canada

1954   *Mgr. de Laval* by Emile S. J. Gervais, Comité des Fondateurs de l'Eglise Canadienne

1956   *Train for Tiger Lily* by Louise Riley, Macmillan of Canada

1957   *Glooskap's Country* by Cyrus Macmillan, Oxford

1958   *Lost in the Barrens* by Farley Mowat, Little, Brown
       Le Chevalier du Roi by Béatrice Clément, Les Editions de l'Atelier

1959   *The Dangerous Cove* by John F. Hayes, Copp Clark
       Un Drôle de Petit Cheval by Hélène Flamme, Editions Léméac

1960   *The Golden Phoenix* by Marius Barbeau and Michael Hornyansky, Walck
       L'Eté Enchanté by Paule Daveluy, Les Editions de l'Atelier

1961   *The St. Lawrence* by William Toye, Oxford
       Plantes Vagabondes by Marcelle Gauvreau, Centre de Psychologie et de Pédagogie

1962   *Les Iles du Roi Maha Maha II* by Claude Aubry, Les Editions du Pélican

1963   *The Incredible Journey* by Sheila Burnford, Little, Brown
       Drôle d'Automne by Paule Daveluy, Les Editions du Pélican

1964   *The Whale People* by Roderick Haig-Brown, William Collins of Canada
       Feerie by Cécile Chabot, Librairie Beauchemin Ltée.

1965   *Tales of Nanabozho* by Dorothy Reid, Oxford
       Le Loup de Noël by Claude Aubry, Centre de Psychologie de Montréal

1966   *Tikta 'Liktak* by James Houston, Kestrel
       Le Chêne des Tempêtes by Andrée Mallet-Hobden, Fides; *The Double Knights* by James McNeal, Walck; *Le Wapiti* by Monique Corriveau, Jeunesse

1967   *Raven's Cry* by Christie Harris, McClelland & Stewart

1968   *The White Archer* by James Houston, Kestrel
       Légendes Indiennes du Canada by Claude Mélançon, Editions du Jour

1969   *And Tomorrow the Stars* by Kay Hill, Dodd

1970   *Sally Go Round the Sun* by Edith Fowke, McClelland & Stewart
       Le Merveilleuse Histoire de la Naissance by Lionel Gendron, Les Editions de l'Homme

1971   *Cartier Discovers the St. Lawrence* by William Toye, Oxford University
       La Surprise de Dame Chenille by Henriette Major, Centre de Psychologie de Montréal

1972   *Mary of Mile 18* by Ann Blades, Tundra

1973   *The Marrow of the World* by Ruth Nichols, Macmillan of Canada
       Le Petit Sapin Qui A Poussé sur une Étoile by Simone Bussières, Presses Laurentiennes

1974   *The Miraculous Hind* by Elizabeth Cleaver, Holt of Canada

1975   *Alligator Pie* by Dennis Lee, Macmillan of Canada
1976   *Jacob Two-Two Meets the Hooded Fang* by Mordecai Richler, Knopf
1977   *Mouse Woman and the Vanished Princesses* by Christie Harris, McClelland & Stewart
1978   *Garbage Delight* by Dennis Lee, Macmillan
1979   *Hold Fast* by Kevin Major, Clarke, Irwin
1980   *River Runners: A Tale of Hardship and Bravery* by James Houston, McClelland & Stewart
1981   *The Violin Maker's Gift* by Donn Kushner, Macmillan of Canada
1982   *The Root Cellar* by Janet Lunn, Lester & Orpen Dennys
1983   *Up to Low* by Brian Doyle, Groundwood
1984   *Sweetgrass* by Jan Hudson, Tree Frog Press
1985   *Mama's Going to Buy a Mockingbird* by Jean Little, Penguin
1986   *Julie* by Cora Taylor, Western
1987   *Shadow in Hawthorn Bay* by Janet Lunn, Scribner's
1988   *A Handful of Time* by Kit Pearson, Viking
1989   *Easy Avenue* by Brian Doyle, Groundwood
1990   *Sky Is Falling* by Kit Pearson, Viking
1991   *Redwork* by Bedard Michael, Lester & Orpen Dennys
1992   *Eating between the Lines* by Kevin Major, Doubleday Canada
1993   *Ticket to Curlew* by Celia Barker Lottridge, Groundwood
1994   *Some of the Kinder Planets* by Tim Wynne-Jones, Groundwood
1995   *Summer of the Mad Monk* by Cora Taylor, Douglas & McIntyre
1996   *The Tiny Kite of Eddie Wing* by Maxine Trottier, Stoddart
1997   *Uncle Ronald* by Brian Doyle, Groundwood
1998   *Silverwing* by Kenneth Oppel, Simon & Schuster
1999   *Stephen Fair* by Tim Wynne-Jones, DK Ink
2000   *Sunwing* by Kenneth Oppel, Simon & Schuster
2001   *Wild Girl and Gran* by Nan Gregory, Red Deer Press
2002   *Orphan at My Door* by Jean Little, Scholastic
2003   *Hana's Suitcase* by Karen Levine, Second Story Press
2004   *Boy O' Boy* by Brian Doyle, Groundwood
2005   *Last Chance Bay* by Anne Laurel Carter, Penguin

The Carnegie Medal

The British Library Association gives this medal each year to the author of a distinguished children's book written in English and first published in the United Kingdom. The award was established in 1937.

1936   *Pigeon Post* by Arthur Ransome, Cape
1937   *The Family from One End Street* by Eve Garnett, Muller
1938   *The Circus Is Coming* by Noel Streatfield, Dent
1939   *Radium Woman* by Eleanor Doorly, Heinemann
1940   *Visitors from London* by Kitty Barne, Dent
1941   *We Couldn't Leave Dinah* by Mary Treadgold, Penguin
1944   *The Wind on the Moon* by Eric Linklater, Macmillan
1946   *The Little White Horse* by Elizabeth Goudge, Brockhampton Press
1947   *Collected Stories for Children* by Walter de la Mare, Faber

1948   *Sea Change* by Richard Armstrong, Dent
1949   *The Story of Your Home* by Agnes Allen, Transatlantic
1950   *The Lark on the Wing* by Elfrida Vipont Foulds, Oxford
1951   *The Wool-Pack* by Cynthia Harnett, Methuen
1952   *The Borrowers* by Mary Norton, Dent
1953   *A Valley Grows Up* by Edward Osmond, Oxford
1954   *Knight Crusader* by Ronald Welch, Oxford
1955   *The Little Bookroom* by Eleanor Farjeon, Oxford
1956   *The Last Battle* by C. S. Lewis, Bodley Head
1957   *A Grass Rope* by William Mayne, Oxford
1958   *Tom's Midnight Garden* by Philippa Pearce, Oxford
1959   *The Lantern Bearers* by Rosemary Sutcliff, Oxford
1960   *The Making of Man* by I. W. Cornwall, Phoenix
1961   *A Stranger at Green Knowe* by Lucy Boston, Faber
1962   *The Twelve and the Genii* by Pauline Clarke, Faber
1963   *Time of Trial* by Hester Burton, Oxford
1964   *Nordy Banks* by Sheena Porter, Oxford
1965   *The Grange at High Force* by Philip Turner, Oxford
1967   *The Owl Service* by Alan Garner, Collins
1968   *The Moon in the Cloud* by Rosemary Harris, Faber
1969   *The Edge of the Cloud* by K. M. Peyton, Oxford
1970   *The God Beneath the Sea* by Leon Garfield and Edward Blishen, Kestrel
1971   *Josh* by Ivan Southall, Angus & Robertson
1972   *Watership Down* by Richard Adams, Rex Collings
1973   *The Ghost of Thomas Kempe* by Penelope Lively, Heinemann
1974   *The Stronghold* by Mollie Hunter, Hamilton
1975   *The Machine-Gunners* by Robert Westall, Macmillan
1976   *Thunder and Lightnings* by Jan Mark, Kestrel
1977   *The Turbulent Term of Tyke Tiler* by Gene Kemp, Faber
1978   *The Exeter Blitz* by David Rees, Hamish Hamilton
1979   *Tulku* by Peter Dickinson, Dutton
1980   *City of Gold* by Peter Dickinson, Gollancz
1981   *The Scarecrows* by Robert Westall, Chatto & Windus
1982   *The Haunting* by Margaret Mahy, Dent
1983   *Handles* by Jan Mark, Kestrel
1984   *The Changeover* by Margaret Mahy, Dent
1985   *Storm* by Kevin Crossley-Holland, Heinemann
1986   *Granny Was a Buffer Girl* by Berlie Doherty, Methuen
1987   *The Ghost Drum* by Susan Price, Faber
1988   *Pack of Lies* by Geraldine McCaughrean, Point
1989   *My War with Goggle Eyes* by Anne Fine, Joy Street Books
1990   *Wolf* by Gillian Cross, Oxford
1991   *Dear Nobody* by Berlie Doherty, Orchard
1992   *The Flour Babies* by Anne Fine, Little, Brown
1993   *Stone Cold* by Robert Swindells, Chivers North American
1994   *Whispers in the Graveyard* by Theresa Breslin, Methuen
1995   *Northern Lights* by Philip Pullman (U.S. title: *The Golden Compass*), Scholastic
1996   *Junk,* Melvin Burgess, Anderson

1998   *Skellig* by David Almond, Hodder
1999   *Postcards from No Man's Land* by Aidan Chambers, Bodley Head
2000   *The Other Side of Truth* by Beverly Naidoo, Puffin
2001   *The Amazing Maurice and His Educated Rodents* by Terry Pratchett, Doubleday
2002   *Ruby Holler* by Sharon Creech, Bloomsbury
2003   *A Gathering Light* by Jennifer Donnelly, Bloomsbury
2004   *Millions* by Frank Cottrell Boyce, Macmillan

Coretta Scott King Award

Established in 1969, this award commemorates the life and work of Martin Luther King Jr. and honors Coretta Scott King "for her courage and determination to continue the work for peace and world brotherhood." It is presented annually at the American Library Association to an African-American author (A) and illustrator (I) whose works "encourage and promote" world unity and peace, and serve as an inspiration to young people in the achievement of their goals. A plaque, honorarium, and an encyclopedia are presented as gifts.

1971   *Black Troubador: Langston Hughes* by Charlemae H. Rollins
1972   *Seventeen Black Artists* by Elton C. Fax
1973   *I Never Had It Made, The Autobiography of Jackie Robinson* by Jackie Robinson, as told to Alfred Duckett
1974   *Ray Charles* by Sharon Bell Mathis (A) and George Ford (I)
1975   *The Legend of Africania* by Eloise Greenfield (A) and Herbert Temple (I)
1976   *Duey's Tale* by Pearl Bailey
1977   *The Story of Stevie Wonder* by James Haskins
1978   *Africa Dream* by Eloise Greenfield (A) and Carole Byard (I)
1979   *Escape to Freedom: A Play About Young Frederick Douglass* by Ossie Davis (A)
        Something on My Mind by Tom Feelings (I)
1980   *The Young Landlords* by Walter Dean Myers (A)
        Cornrows by Carole Byard, (I)
1981   *This Life* by Sidney Poitier (A)
        Beat the Story Drum, Pum-Pum by Ashley Bryan (I)
1982   *Let the Circle Be Unbroken* by Mildred D. Taylor (A)
        My Mama Needs Me by Mildred P. Walter (A) and Pat Cummings (I)
1983   *Black Child* by Peter Magubane (I)
        Sweet Whispers, Brother Rush by Virginia Hamilton
1984   *Everett Anderson's Goodbye* by Lucille Clifton et al. (A) and Ann Grifalconi (I)
1985   *Motown and Didi: A Love Story* by Walter D. Myers
1986   *Patchwork Quilt* by Valerie Flournoy (A) and Jerry Pinkey (I)
        People Could Fly by Virginia Hamilton (A) and Leo and Diane Dillon (I)
1987   *Half a Moon and One Whole Star* by Crescent Dragonwagon (A) and Jerry Pinkney (I)
        Justin and the Best Biscuits in the World by Mildred P. Walter (A) and Catherine Stock (I)

1988   *Friendship* by Mildred D. Taylor (A) and Max Ginsburg (I)
        Mufaro's Beautiful Daughters: An African Tale, edited and illustrated by
        John Steptoe
1989   *Fallen Angels* by Walter D. Myers
        Mirandy and Brother Wind by Patricia C. Mckissack (A) and Jerry
        Pinkney (I)
1990   *Long Hard Journey* by Patricia McKissack and Frederick McKissack (A)
        Nathaniel Talking by Eloise Greenfield and Jan S. Gilchrist (I)
        Black Butterfly, Children's Press
1991   *Aida* by Leontyne Price (A) and Leo and Diane Dillon (I)
        The Road to Memphis by Mildred D. Taylor (A)
1992   *Now Is Your Time: The African American Struggle for Freedom*, Walter D.
        Myers (A)
        Tar Beach by Faith Ringgold
1993   *The Dark Thirty: Southern Tales of the Supernatural* by Patricia
        McKissack (A)
        The Origin of Life on Earth: An African Creation Myth by Kathleen Atkins
        Wilson (I), text by David A. Anderson
1994   *Toning the Sweep* by Angela Johnson (A)
        Soul Looks Back in Wonder by Tom Feelings (I), text by Maya Angelou et al.
1995   *Christmas in the Big House, Christmas in the Quarters* by Patricia and
        Frederick McKissack (A)
        The Creation by James Ransome (I), text by James Weldon Johnson
1996   *Her Stories* by Virginia Hamilton (A) and Leo and Diane Dillon (I)
        The Middle Passage: White Ships, Black Cargo by Tom Feelings (I)
1997   *Slam!* by Walter Dean Myers (A)
        Minty: A Story of Young Harriet Tubman by Jerry Pinkney (I), text by Alan
        Schroeder
1998   *Forged by Fire* by Sharon M. Draper (A)
        In Daddy's Arms I Am Tall: African Americans Celebrating Fathers, illus-
        trated by Javaka Steptoe (I), text by Alan Schroeder
1999   *Heaven* by Angela Johnson (A)
        i see the rhythm, illustrated by Michele Wood (I), text by Toyomi Igus
2000   *Bud, Not Buddy* by Christopher Paul Curtis (A)
        In the Time of the Drums, illustrated by Brian Pinkney (I), text by Kim L.
        Siegelson
2001   *Miracle's Boys* by Jacqueline Woodson (A)
        Uptown by Bryan Collier (I)
2002   *The Land* by Mildred Taylor (A)
        Goin' Someplace Special, illustrated by Jerry Pinkney (I), text by Patricia
        McKissack
2003   *Bronx Masquerde* by Nikki Grimes (A)
        Talkin' about Bessie: The Story of Aviator Elizabeth Coleman, illustrated
        by E. B. Lew (I)
2004   *The First Part Last* by Angela Johnson (A)
        Beautiful Blackbird by Ashley Bryan (I)
2005   *Remember: The Journey to School Integration* by Toni Morrison (A)
        Ellington Was Not a Street, illustrated by Kadir A. Nelson (I), text by
        Ntozake Shange

The Eva L. Gordon Award

Established by the American Nature Study Society to recognize an author of children's science literature.

1964   Millicent Selsam
1965   Edwin Way Teale
1966   Robert M. McClung
1970   Jean Craighead George
1971   Veme Rockcastle
1974   Phyllis Busch
1976   Jeanne Bendick
1977   Nina Schneider and Herman Schneider
1978   George F. Mason; Dorothy Shuttleworth
1979   Ross Hutchins
1980   Glenn O. Blough
1981   Herbert Zim
1982   Peter Pamell
1983   Lawrence Pringle
1984   Seymour Simon
1985   Vicki Cobb
1986   Dorothy Hinshaw Patent
1987   Patricia Lauber
1988   Franklyn Branley
1989   Ada Graham and Frank Graham
1990   Joanna Cole
1991   Jim Arnosky
1992   Byrd Baylor
1993   Augusta Goldin
1994   Eric Carle
1995   Joanna Ryder
1996   David Macaulay
1997   Gail Gibbon
1998   Margery Flackham
1999   Bruce Hiscock

Hans Christian Andersen Award

Every other year IBBY (International Board on Books for Young People) presents the Hans Christian Andersen Award to a living author and illustrator whose complete works have made a lasting contribution to children's literature.

1956   Author: Eleanor Farjeon (Great Britain)
1958   Author: Astrid Lindgren (Sweden)
1960   Author: Erich Klastner (West Germany)
1962   Author: Meindert DeJong (USA)
1964   Author: Rene Guillot (France)
1966   Author: Tove Jansson (Finland)
        Illustrator: Alois Carigiet (Switzerland)
1970   Author: Gianni Rodari (Italy)

Illustrator: Maurice Sendak (USA)
1972   Author: Scott O'Dell (USA)
       Illustrator: Ib Spang Olsen (Denmark)
1974   Author: Maria Gripe (Sweden)
       Illustrator: Faarshid Mesghali (Iran)
1976   Author: Cecil Bodker (Denmark)
       Illustrator: Tatjana Mawrina (USSR)
1978   Author: Paula Fox (USA)
       Illustrator: Otto S. Svend (Denmark)
1980   Author: Bohumil Riha (Czechoslovakia)
       Illustrator: Suekichi Akaba (Japan)
1982   Author: Lygia Bojunga Nunes (Brazil)
       Illustrator: Zbigniew Rychilicki (Poland)
1984   Author: Christine Nostlinger (Austria)
       Illustrator: Mitsumasa Anno (Japan)
1986   Author: Patricia Wrightson (Australia)
       Illustrator: Robert Ingpen (Australia)
1988   Author: Annie M. G. Schmidt (Netherlands)
       Illustrator: Dusan Kallay (Czechoslovakia)
1990   Author: Tormmmod Haugen (Norway)
       Illustrator: Lisbeth Zwerger (Austria)
1992   Author: Virginia Hamilton (USA)
       Illustrator: Kveta Pacovska (Czechoslovakia)
1994   Author: Michio Mado (Japan)
       Illustrator: Jorg Muller (Switzerland)
1996   Author: Uri Orlev (Israel)
       Illustrator: Klaus Ensikat (Germany)
1998   Author: Katherine Paterson (USA)
       Illustrator: Tomi Ungerer (France)
1998   Author: Katherine Paterson (USA)
       Illustrator: Tomi Ungerer (France)
2000   Author: Anna Maria Machado (Brazil)
       Illustrator: Anthony Browne (UK)
2002   Author: Aidan Chambers (UK)
       Illustrator: Quentin Blake (UK)
2004   Author: Martin Waddell (Ireland)
       Illustrator: Max Velthuijs (The Netherlands)

International Reading Association Children's Book Award

Given for the first time in 1975, this award is presented annually for a book published in the preceding year and written by an author "who shows unusual promise in the children's book field." Sponsored by the Institute for Reading Research, the award is administered by the International Reading Association.

1975   *Transport 7-41-R* by T. Degens, Viking
1976   *Dragonwings* by Laurence Yep, Harper
1977   *A String in the Harp* by Nancy Bond, McElderry/Atheneum
1978   *A Summer to Die* by Lois Lowry, Houghton

1979   *Reserved for Mark Anthony Crowder* by Alison Smith, Dutton

1980   *Words by Heart* by Ouida Sebestyen, Atlantic/Little, Brown

1981   *My Own Private Sky* by Delores Beckman, Dutton

1982   *Good Night, Mr. Tom* by Michelle Magorian, Kestrel/Penguin (Great Britain); Harper (U.S.A.)

1983   *The Darkangel* by Meredith Ann Pierce, Atlantic/Little

1984   *Ratha's Creature* by Clare Bell, Atheneum

1985   *Badger on the Barge* by Janni Howker, Greenwillow

1986   *Prairie Songs* by Pam Conrad, illustrated by Daryl S. Zudeck, Harper

1987   *The Line Up Book* by Marisabina Russo, Greenwillow

1988   *Third Story Cat* by Leslie Baker, Little, Brown

1989   *Probably Still Nick Swansen* by Virginia E. Wolff, Henry Holt (Older)
        Rechenka's Eggs by Patricia Polacco, illustrated by Patricia Polacco, Philomel (Younger).

1990   *Children of the River* by Linda Crew, Delacorte (Older)
        No Star Nights by Anna E. Smucker, illustrated by Steve Johnson, Knopf (Younger)

1991   *Is This a House for Hermit Crab?* by Megan McDonald, illustrated by F. D. Schindler, Orchard (Younger)
        Under the Hawthorn Tree by Marita Conlon-McKenna, illustrated by Donald Teskey, Holiday (Older)

1992   *Rescue Josh McGuire* by Ben Mikaelsen, Hyperion (Older)
        Ten Little Rabbits by Virginia Grossman, illustrated by Sylvia Long, Chronicle (Younger)

1993   *Old Turtle*, by Douglas Wood and Cheng-Khee Chee, Pfeifer-Hamilton (Younger)
        Letters from Rifka by Karen Hesse, Henry Holt (Older)

1994   *Sweet Clara and the Freedom Quilt* by Deborah Hopkinson, Henry Holt (Younger)
        Behind the Secret Window by Nelly S. Toll, Dutton (Older)

1995   *The Ledger Book of Thomas Blue Eagle* by Gay Matthaei, Jewel Grutman, and Adam Cvijanovic, Thomasson-Grant (Younger)
        Spite Fences by Trudy Krisher, Bantam (Older)
        Stranded at Plymouth Plantation, 1626 by Gary Bowen, HarperCollins (Informational)

1996   *More About Anything Else* by Marie Bradby and Chris K. Soentpiet, Orchard (Younger)
        The King's Shadow by Elizabeth Alder, Farrar, Straus & Giroux (Older)
        The Case of the Mummified Pigs and Other Mysteries in Nature by Susan E. Quinlan, Boyds Mill (Informational)

1997   *The Fabulous Flying Fandinis* by Ingrid Slyder, Penguin (Younger)
        Don't You Dare Read This, Mrs. Dunphrey by Margaret Peterson Haddix, Simon & Schuster (Older)
        The Brooklyn Bridge, by Elizabeth Mann, Mikaya (Informational)

1998   *Nim and the War Effort* by Milly Lee and Yangsook Choi, Farrar, Straus & Giroux (Younger)
        Moving Mama to Town by Ronder Thomas Young, Orchard (Older)
        Just What the Doctor Ordered: The History of American Medicine by Brandon Marie Miller, Lerner (Informational)

1999   *My Freedom Trip: A Child's Escape From North Korea* by Frances and
       Ginger Park, Boyds Mills Press (Younger)
       Choosing Up Sides by John H. Ritter, Philomel (Older)
       First in the Field: Baseball Hero Jackie Robinson by Derek T. Dingle,
       Hyperion (Informational)

2000   *The Snake Scientist* by Sy Montgomery, Houghton (Younger)
       Molly Bannaky by Alice McGill, Houghton (Younger)
       Bud, Not Buddy by Christopher Paul Curtis, Delacorte (Older)
       Eleanor's Story: An American Girl in Hitler's Germany by Eleanor
       Ramrath Garner, Peachtree (Older)

2001   *Stranger in the Woods* by Carl R. Sams II and Jean Stoick, Carl R. Sams II
       Photography (Younger)
       My Season with Penguins by Sophie Webb, Houghton (Younger)
       Jake's Orphan by Peggy Brooke, Dorling Kindersley (Older)
       Girls Think of Everything by Catherine Thimmesh and Melissa Sweet,
       Houghton (Older)

2002   *Silver Seeds* by Paolilli and Dan Brewer, Viking (Primary–Fiction)
       Aero and Officer Mike by Joan Plummer Russell, Boyds Mills Press
       (Primary–Nonfiction)
       Coolies by Yin, Philomel (Intermediate–Fiction)
       Pearl Harbor Warriors by Dorinda Makanaonalani Nicholson and Larry
       Nicholson, Woodson House (Intermediate–Nonfiction)
       A Step From Heaven by An Na, Front Street (Young Adult–Fiction)
       Meltdown: A Race Against Nuclear Disaster at Three Mile Island by
       Wilborn Hampton, Candlewick (Young Adult–Nonfiction)

2003   *One Leaf Rides the Wind* by Celeste Davidson Mannis, Viking
       (Primary–Fiction)
       The Pot That Juan Built by Nancy Andrews-Goebel, Lee & Low Books
       (Primary–Nonfiction)
       Who Will Tell My Brother? By Marlene Carvell, Hyperion
       (Intermediate–Fiction)
       If the World Were a Village: A Book about the World's People by David J.
       Smith, Kids Can Press (Intermediate–Nonfiction)
       Mississippi Trial, 1955 by Chris Crowe, Phyllis Fogelman Books (Young
       Adult–Fiction)
       Headin' for Better Times: The Arts of the Great Depression by Duane
       Damon, Lerner (Young Adult–Nonfiction)

2004   *Mary Smith* by Andrea U'ren, Farrar, Straus & Giroux (Primary–Fiction)
       Uncle Andy's: A Faabbbulous Visit with Andy Warhol by James Warhola,
       Penguin (Primary–Nonfiction)
       Sahara Special by Esmé Raji Codell, Hyperion (Intermediate–Fiction)
       Carl Sandburg: Adventures of a Poet by Penelope Niven, Harcourt
       (Intermediate–Nonfiction)
       Buddha Boy by Kathe Koja, Farrar, Straus & Giroux (Young
       Adult–Fiction)
       At the End of Words: A Daughter's Memoir by Miriam Stone, Candlewick
       (Young Adult–Nonfiction)

2005   *Miss Bridie Chose a Shovel* by Leslie Conner, illustrated by Mary Azarian,
       Houghton (Primary–Fiction)

Eliza and the Dragonfly by Susie Caldwell Rinehart, illustrated by Anisa Claire Hovemann, Dawn (Primary–Nonfiction)

The Golden Hour by Maiya Williams, Amulet Books (Intermediate–Fiction)

Buildings in Disguise by Joan Marie Arbogast, Boyds Mills Press (Intermediate–Nonfiction)

Emako Blue by Brenda Woods, Putnam (Young Adult–Fiction)

The Burn Journals by Brent Runyon, Knopf (Young Adult–Nonfiction)

The Kate Greenaway Medal

The Kate Greenaway Medal, given annually by the British Library Association, recognizes the outstanding illustration of a children's book first published in the United Kingdom in the preceding year.

1956   *Tim All Alone*, written and illustrated by Edward Ardizzone, Oxford

1957   *Mrs. Easter and the Storks*, written and illustrated by V. H. Drummond, Faber

1958   No award

1959   *Kashtanka and a Bundle of Ballads*, written and illustrated by William Stobbs, Oxford

1960   *Old Winkle and the Seagulls* by Elizabeth Rose, illustrated by Gerald Rose, Faber

1961   *Mrs. Cockle's Cat* by Philippa Pearce, illustrated by Anthony Maitland, Kestrel

1962   *Brian Wildsmith's ABC*, written and illustrated by Brian Wildsmith, Oxford

1963   *Borka*, written and illustrated by John Burningham. Jonathan Cape

1964   *Shakespeare's Theatre*, written and illustrated by C. W. Hodges, Oxford

1965   *Three Poor Tailors*, written and illustrated by Victor Ambrus, Hamilton

1966   *Mother Goose Treasury*, written and illustrated by Raymond Briggs, Hamilton

1967   *Charlie, Charlotte and the Golden Canary*, written and illustrated by Charles Keeping, Oxford

1968   *Dictionary of Chivalry* by Grant Uden, illustrated by Pauline Baynes, Kestrel

1969   *The Quangle-Wangle's Hat* by Edward Lear, illustrated by Helen Oxenbury, Heinemann; *Dragon of an Ordinary Family* by Margaret Mahy, illustrated by Helen Oxenbury, Heinemann

1970   *Mr. Gumpy's Outing*, written and illustrated by John Burningham, Jonathan Cape

1971   *The Kingdom Under the Sea*, written and illustrated by Jan Piénkowski, Jonathan Cape

1972   *The Woodcutter's Duck*, written and illustrated by Krystyna Turska, Hamilton

1973   *Father Christmas*, written and illustrated by Raymond Briggs, Hamilton

1974   *The Wind Blew*, written and illustrated by Pat Hutchins, Bodley Head

1975   *Horses in Battle*, written and illustrated by Victor Ambrus, Oxford
        Mishka, written and illustrated by Victor Ambrus, Oxford

1976   *The Post Office Cat*, written and illustrated by Gail E. Haley, Bodley Head

1977   *Dogger*, written and illustrated by Shirley Hughes, Bodley Head
1978   *Each Peach Pear Plum*, written and illustrated by Janet and Allan Ahlberg, Kestrel
1979   *Haunted House*, written and illustrated by Jan Piénkowski, Dutton
1980   *Mr. Magnolia* by Quentin Blake, Jonathan Cape
1981   *The Highwayman* by Alfred Noyes, illustrated by Charles Keeping, Oxford
1982   *Long Neck and Thunder Foot* (Kestrel) and *Sleeping Beauty and Other Favorite Fairy Tales* (Gollancz), both illustrated by Michael Foreman
1983   *Gorilla* by Anthony Browne, Julia McRae Books
1984   *Hiawatha's Childhood* by Errol LeCain, Faber
1985   *Sir Gawain and the Loathly Lady* by Selina Hastings, illustrated by Juan Wijngaard, Walker
1986   *Snow White in New York* by Fiona French, Oxford
1987   *Shadow in Hawthorn Bay* by Janet Lunn, Scribner's
1988   *Crafty Chameleon* by Mwenye Hadithi, illustrated by Adrienne Kennaway, Hodder & Stoughton
1989   *Can't You Sleep, Little Bear?* by Martin Waddell and Barbara Firth, Walker
1990   *War Boy: A Country Childhood* by Michael Foreman, Pavilion Books
1991   *Whales' Song* by Dyan Sheldon, illustrated by Gary Blythe, Hutchinson
1992   *Jolly Postman* by Janet Ahlberg, illustrated by Janet Ahlberg, Little, Brown
1993   *Zoo* by Anthony Browne, Knopf
1994   *Way Home* by Gregory Rogers, text by Libby Hathorn, Andersen
1995   *The Christmas Miracle of Jonathan Toomey*, illustrated by P. J. Lynch, text by Susan Wojciechowski, Walker
1996   *The Baby Who Wouldn't Go to Bed* by Helen Cooper, Doubleday
1997   *When Jessie Came Across the Sea* by P. J. Lynch, Walker
1998   *Pumpkin Soup* by Helen Cooper, Doubleday
1999   *Alice's Adventures in Wonderland* by Helen Oxenbury, Walker
2000   *I Will Not Ever Never Eat a Tomato* by Lauren Child, Orchard
2001   *Pirate Diary* by Chris Riddell, Walker
2002   *Jethro Byrde—Fairy Child* by Bob Graham, Walker
2003   *Ella's Big Chance* by Shirley Hughes, Bodley Head
2004   *Jonathan Swift's* "Gulliver" by Chris Riddell, Walker

The Laura Ingalls Wilder Award

This award was first given in 1954 and was presented every five years from 1960 to 1980. Beginning in 1980 the award was given every three years; it is now given every two years. The medal is administered by the Association of Library Service to Children of the American Library Association. The award recognizes an author or illustrator whose books, published in the United States, have over a period of years made a substantial contribution to literature for children.

1954   Laura Ingalls Wilder
1960   Clara Ingram Judson
1965   Ruth Sawyer
1970   E. B. White
1975   Beverly Cleary

1980   Theodore Geisel (Dr. Seuss)
1983   Maurice Sendak
1986   Jean Fritz
1989   Elizabeth George Speare
1992   Marcia Brown
1995   Virginia Hamilton
1998   Russell Freedman
2001   Milton Meltzer
2003   Eric Carle
2005   Laurence Yep

The Mildred L. Batchelder Award

This award is given by the American Library Association for the best translation of a work published in a language other than English.

1968   *The Little Man* by Erich Kastner, translated by James Kirkup, illustrated by Rick Schreiter, Knopf
1969   *Don't Take Teddy* by Babbis Friis-Baastad, translated by Lise Somme McKinnon, Scribner's
1970   *Wildcat Under Glass* by Alki Zei, translated by Edward Fenton, Holt
1971   *In the Land of Ur: The Discovery of Ancient Mesopotamia* by Hans Baumann, translated by Stella Humphries, illustrated by Hans Peter Renner, Pantheon
1972   *Friedrich* by Hans Peter Richter, translated by Edite Kroll, Holt
1973   *Pulga* by Siny Rose Van Iterson, translated by Alexander Gode and Alison Gode, Morrow
1974   *Petros' War* by Alki Zei, translated by Edward Fenton, Dutton
1975   *An Old Tale Carved Out of Stone* by Aleksandr M. Linevski, translated by Maria Polushkin, Crown
1976   *The Cat and Mouse Who Shared a House*, written and illustrated by Ruth Hurlimann, translated by Anthea Bell, Walck
1977   *The Leopard* by Cecil Bodker, translated by Gunnar Poulsen, Atheneum
1978   No award
1979   *Konrad* by Christine Nostlinger, translated by Anthea Bell, illustrated by Carol Nicklaus, Watts
         Rabbit Island by Jorg Steiner, translated by Ann Conrad Lammers, illustrated by Jorg Muller, Harcourt
1980   *The Sound of Dragon's Feet* by Alki Zei, translated by Edward Fenton, Dutton
1981   *The Winter When Time Was Frozen* by Els Pelgrom, translated by Raphael Rudnils and Maryka Rudnik, Morrow
1982   *The Battle Horse* by Harry Kullman, translated by George Blecher and Lone Thygesen-Blecher, Bradbury
1983   *Hiroshima no Pika*, written and illustrated by Toshi Maruki, translated by Komine Shoten, Lothrop, Lee & Shepard
1984   *Ronia, the Robber's Daughter* by Astrid Lindgren, translated by Patricia Crampton, Viking
1985   *The Island on Bird Street* by Uri Orlev, translated by Hillel Halkin, Houghton

1986   *Rose Blanche* by Christophe Gallaz and Roberto Innocenti, translated by Martha Coventry and Richard Graglia, illustrated by Roberto Innocenti, Creative Education

1987   *No Hero for the Kaiser* by Rudolf Frank, translated by Patricia Crampton, illustrated by Klaus Steffans, Lothrop, Lee & Shepard

1988   *If You Didn't Have Me* by Ulf Nilsson, illustrated by Eva Eriksson, translated by Lone Thygesen-Blecher and George Blecher, McElderry

1989   *Crutches* by Peter Härtling, translated by Elizabeth D. Crawford, Lothrop, Lee & Shepard

1990   *Buster's World* by Bjarne Reuter, translated by Anthea Bell, Dutton

1991   *A Hand Full of Stars* by Rafik Schami, translated by Rika Lesser, Dutton

1992   *Man from the Other Side* by Uri Orlev, translated by Hillel Halkin, Houghton

1993   No award

1994   *The Apprentice*, by Pilar Molina Llorente, translated by Robin Longshaw, Farrar, Straus & Giroux

1995   *The Boys from St. Petri* by Bjarne Reuter, translated by Anthea Bell

1996   *The Lady with the Hat* by Uri Orlev, translated by Hillel Halkin, Houghton

1997   *The Friends* by Kazumi Yumoto, translated by Cathy Hirano, Farrar, Straus & Giroux

1998   *The Robber and Me* by Josef Holub, edited by Mark Aronson, translated by Elizabeth D. Crawford, Holt

1999   *Thanks to My Mother* by Schoschana Rabinovici, translated by James Skofield, Dial

2000   *The Baboon King* by Anton Quintana, translated by John Nieuwenhuizen, Walker

2001   *Samir and Yonatan* by Daniella Carmi, translated by Yael Lotan, Scholastic

2002   *How I Became an American* by Karin Gündisch, translated by James Skofield, Cricket Books

2003   *The Thief Lord* by Cornelia Funke, translated by Oliver Latsch, Chicken House

2004   *Run, Boy, Run* by Uri Orlev, translated by Hillel Halkin, Walter Lorraine Books

2005   *The Shadows of Ghadames* by Joëlle Stolz, translated by Catherine Temerson, Delacorte

The National Book Award for Young People's Literature

This award, formerly a National Book Award/American Book Award from 1969 to 1983, was added to the National Book Awards in 1996. Presented each year, the Young People's category recognizes outstanding contributions to literature for children and young adults in various genres by writers in the United States.

1996   *Parrot in the Oven: Mi Vida* by Victor Martinez

1997   *Dancing on the Edge* by Han Nolan

1998   *Holes* by Louis Sachar

1999   *When Zachary Beaver Came to Town* by Kimberly Willis Holt

2000   *Homeless Bird* by Gloria Whelan
2001   *True Believer* by Virginia Euwer Wolff
2002   *The House of the Scorpion* by Nancy Farmer
2003   *The Canning Season* by Polly Horvath
2004   *Godless* by Pete Hautman
2005   *The Penderwicks* by Jeanne Birdsall

National Council of Teachers of English Award for Excellence in Poetry for Children

This award is presented by the National Council of Teachers of English to a living American poet in recognition of the poet's aggregate body of work in children's literature. It was given annually until 1982, and now is presented every three years.

1977   David McCord
1978   Aileen Fisher
1979   Karla Kuskin
1980   Myra Cohn Livingston
1981   Eve Merriam
1982   John Ciardi
1985   Lilian Moore
1988   Arnold Adoff
1991   Valerie Worth
1994   Barbara Juster Esbensen
1997   Eloise Greenfield
2000   X. J. Kennedy
2003   Mary Ann Hoberman

The Newbery Medal

Named in honor of John Newbery (1713–1767), the first English publisher of children's books, this medal has been given annually since 1922 by the American Library Association's Association for Library Service to Children. The recipient is recognized as author of the most distinguished book in children's literature published in the United States in the preceding year. The award is limited to citizens or residents of the United States.

1922   *The Story of Mankind* by Hendrik Willem van Loon, Liveright
Honor Books: *The Great Quest* by Charles Hawes, Little, Brown; *Cedric the Forester* by Bernard Marshall, Appleton; *The Old Tobacco Shop* by William Bowen, Macmillan; *The Golden Fleece and the Heroes Who Lived Before Achilles* by Padraic Colum, Macmillan; *Windy Hill* by Cornelia Meigs, Macmillan
1923   *The Voyages of Doctor Dolittle* by Hugh Lofting, Lippincott
1924   *The Dark Frigate* by Charles Hawes, Atlantic/Little, Brown
1925   *Tales from Silver Lands* by Charles Finger, Doubleday

Honor Books: *Nicholas* by Anne Carroll Moore, Putnam; *Dream Coach* by Anne Parrish, Macmillan

1926   *Shen of the Sea* by Arthur Bowie Chrisman, Dutton
        Honor Book: *Voyagers* by Padraic Colum, Macmillan

1927   *Smoky, the Cowhorse* by Will James, Scribner's

1928   *Gayneck, The Story of a Pigeon* by Dhan Gopal Mukerji, Dutton
        Honor Books: *The Wonder Smith and His Son* by Ella Young, Longmans;
        Downright Dencey by Caroline Snedeker, Doubleday

1929   *The Trumpeter of Krakow* by Eric P. Kelly, Macmillan
        Honor Books: *Pigtail of Ah Lee Ben Loo* by John Bennett, Longmans;
        Millions of Cats by Wanda Gág, Coward; *The Boy Who Was* by Grace
        Hallock, Dutton; *Clearing Weather* by Cornelia Meigs, Little, Brown;
        Runaway Papoose by Grace Moon, Doubleday; *Tod of the Fens* by Elinor
        Whitney, Macmillan

1930   *Hitty, Her First Hundred Years* by Rachel Field, Macmillan
        Honor Books: *Daughter of the Seine* by Jeanette Eaton, Harper; *Pran of
        Albania* by Elizabeth Miller, Doubleday; *Jumping-Off Place* by Marian
        Hurd McNeely, Longmans; *Tangle-Coated Horse and Other Tales* by Ella
        Young, Longmans; *Vaino* by Julia Davis Adams, Dutton; *Little Blacknose*
        by Hildegarde Swift, Harcourt

1931   *The Cat Who Went to Heaven* by Elizabeth Coatsworth, Macmillan
        Honor Books: *Floating Island* by Anne Parish, Harper; *The Dark Star
        of Itza* by Alida Malkus, Harcourt; *Queer Person* by Ralph Hubbard,
        Doubleday; *Mountains Are Free* by Julia Davis Adams, Dutton; *Spice and the
        Devil's Cave* by Agnes Hewes, Knopf; *Meggy Macintosh* by Elizabeth Janet
        Gray, Doubleday; *Garram the Hunter* by Herbert Best, Doubleday; *Ood-
        Le-Uk the Wanderer* by Alice Lide and Margaret Johansen, Little, Brown

1932   *Waterless Mountain* by Laura Adams Armer, Longmans
        Honor Books: *The Fairy Circus* by Dorothy P. Lathrop, Macmillan; *Calico
        Bush* by Rachel Field, Macmillan; *Boy of the South Seas* by Eunice
        Tietjens, Coward; *Out of the Flame* by Eloise Lownsbery, Longmans;
        Jane's Island by Marjorie Allee, Houghton; *Truce of the Wolf and Other
        Tales of Old Italy* by Mary Gould Davis, Harcourt

1933   *Young Fu of the Upper Yangtze* by Elizabeth Foreman Lewis, Winston
        Honor Books: *Swift Rivers* by Cornelia Meigs, Little, Brown; *The Railroad
        to Freedom* by Hildegarde Swift, Harcourt; *Children of the Soil* by Nora
        Burglon, Doubleday

1934   *Invincible Louisa* by Cornelia Meigs, Little, Brown
        Honor Books: *The Forgotten Daughter* by Caroline Snedeker, Doubleday;
        Swords of Steel by Elsie Singmaster, Houghton; *ABC Bunny* by Wanda
        Gág, Coward; *Winged Girl of Knossos* by Erik Berry, Appleton; *New Land*
        by Sarah Schmidt, McBride; *Big Tree of Bunlahy* by Padraic Colum,
        Macmillan; *Glory of the Seas* by Agnes Hewes, Knopf; *Apprentice of
        Florence* by Anne Kyle, Houghton

1935   *Dobry* by Monica Shannon, Viking
        Honor Books: *Pageant of Chinese History* by Elizabeth Seeger, Longmans;
        Davy Crockett by Constance Rourke, Harcourt; *Day on Skates* by Hilda
        Van Stockum, Harper

1936   *Caddie Woodlawn* by Carol Brink, Macmillan

Honor Books: *Honk, The Moose* by Phil Strong, Dodd; *The Good Master* by Kate Seredy, Viking; *Young Walter Scott* by Elizabeth Janet Gray, Viking; *All Sail Set* by Armstrong Sperry, Winston

1937   *Roller Skates* by Ruth Sawyer, Viking
Honor Books: *Phoebe Fairchild: Her Book* by Lois Lenski, Stokes; *Whistler's Van* by Idwal Jones, Viking; *Golden Basket* by Ludwig Bemelmans, Viking; *Winterbound* by Margery Bianco, Viking; *Audubon* by Constance Rourke, Harcourt; *The Codfish Musket* by Agnes Hewes, Doubleday

1938   *The White Stag* by Kate Seredy, Viking
Honor Books: *Pecos Bill* by James Cloyd Bowman, Little, Brown; *Bright Island* by Mabel Robinson, Random; *On the Banks of Plum Creek* by Laura Ingalls Wilder, Harper

1939   *Thimble Summer* by Elizabeth Enright, Rinehart
Honor Books: *Nino* by Valenti Angelo, Viking; *Mr. Popper's Penguins* by Richard and Florence Atwater, Little, Brown; *"Hello the Boat!"* by Phyllis Crawford, Holt; *Leader by Destiny: George Washington, Man and Patriot* by Jeanette Eaton, Harcourt; *Penn* by Elizabeth Janet Gray, Viking

1940   *Daniel Boone* by James Daugherty, Viking
Honor Books: *The Singing Tree* by Kate Seredy, Viking; *Runner of the Mountain Tops* by Mabel Robinson, Random; *By the Shores of Silver Lake* by Laura Ingalls Wilder, Harper; *Boy with a Pack* by Stephen W. Meader, Harcourt

1941   *Call It Courage* by Armstrong Sperry, Macmillan
Honor Books: *Blue Willow* by Doris Gates, Viking; *Young Mac of Fort Vancouver* by Mary Jane Carr, Crowell; *The Long Winter* by Laura Ingalls Wilder, Harper; *Nansen* by Anna Gertrude Hall, Viking

1942   *The Matchlock Gun* by Walter D. Edmonds, Dodd
Honor Books: *Little Town on the Prairie* by Laura Ingalls Wilder, Harper; *George Washington's World* by Genevieve Foster, Scribner's; *Indian Captive: The Story of Mary Jemison* by Lois Lenski, Lippincott; *Down Ryton Water* by Eva Roe Gaggin, Viking

1943   *Adam of the Road* by Elizabeth Janet Gray, Viking
Honor Books: *The Middle Moffat* by Eleanor Estes, Harcourt; *Have You Seen Tom Thumb?* by Mabel Leigh Hunt, Lippincott

1944   *Johnny Tremain* by Esther Forbes, Houghton
Honor Books: *These Happy Golden Years* by Laura Ingalls Wilder, Harper; *Fog Magic* by Julia Sauer, Viking; *Rufus M.* by Eleanor Estes, Harcourt; *Mountain Born* by Elizabeth Yates, Coward

1945   *Rabbit Hill* by Robert Lawson, Viking
Honor Books: *The Hundred Dresses* by Eleanor Estes, Harcourt; *The Silver Pencil* by Alice Dalgliesh, Scribner's; *Abraham Lincoln's World* by Genevieve Foster, Scribner's; *Lone Journey: The Life of Roger Williams* by Jeanette Eaton, Harcourt

1946   *Strawberry Girl* by Lois Lenski, Lippincott
Honor Books: *Justin Morgan Had a Horse* by Marguerite Henry, Rand; *The Moved-Outers* by Florence Crannell Means, Houghton; *Bhimsa, The Dancing Bear* by Christine Weston, Scribner's; *New Found World* by Katherine Shippen, Viking

1947   *Miss Hickory* by Carolyn Sherwin Bailey, Viking
Honor Books: *Wonderful Year* by Nancy Barnes, Messner; *Big Tree* by

Mary Buff and Conrad Buff, Viking; *The Heavenly Tenants* by William Maxwell, Harper; *The Avion My Uncle Flew* by Cyrus Fisher, Appleton; *The Hidden Treasure of Glaston* by Eleanore Jewett, Viking

1948   *The Twenty-one Balloons* by William Pène du Bois, Lothrop
Honor Books: *Pancakes-Paris* by Claire Huchet Bishop, Viking; *Li Lun, Lad of Courage* by Carolyn Treffinger, Abingdon; *The Quaint and Curious Quest of Johnny Longfoot* by Catherine Besterman, Bobbs; *The Cow-Tail Switch, and Other West African Stories* by Harold Courlander, Holt; *Misty of Chincoteague* by Marguerite Henry, Rand

1949   *King of the Wind* by Marguerite Henry, Rand
Honor Books: *Seabird by* by Holling C. Holling, Houghton; *Daughter of the Mountains* by Louise Rankin, Viking; *My Father's Dragon* by Ruth S. Gannett, Random; *Story of the Negro* by Arna Bontemps, Knopf

1950   *The Door in the Wall* by Marguerite de Angeli, Doubleday
Honor Books: *Tree of Freedom* by Rebecca Caudill, Viking; *The Blue Cat of Castle Town* by Catherine Coblentz, Longmans; *Kildee House* by Rutherford Montgomery, Doubleday; *George Washington* by Genevieve Foster, Scribner's; *Song of the Pines* by Walter and Marion Havighurst, Winston

1951   *Amos Fortune, Free Man* by Elizabeth Yates, Aladdin
Honor Books: *Better Known as Johnny Appleseed* by Mabel Leigh Hunt, Lippincott; *Gandhi, Fighter without a Sword* by Jeanette Eaton, Morrow; *Abraham Lincoln, Friend of the People* by Clara Ingram Judson, Follett; *The Story of Appleby Capple* by Anne Parrish, Harper

1952   *Ginger Pye* by Eleanor Estes, Harcourt
Honor Books: *Americans Before Columbus* by Elizabeth Baity, Viking; *Minn of the Mississippi* by Holling C. Holling, Houghton; *The Defender* by Nicholas Kalashnikoff, Scribner's; *The Light at Tern Rock* by Julia Sauer, Viking; *The Apple and the Arrow* by Mary Buff and Conrad Buff, Houghton

1953   *Secret of the Andes* by Ann Nolan Clark, Viking
Honor Books: *Charlotte's Web* by E. B. White, Harper; *Moccasin Trail* by Eloise McGraw, Coward; *Red Sails to Capri* by Ann Weil, Viking; *The Bears of Hemlock Mountain* by Alice Dalgliesh, Scribner's; *Birthdays of Freedom*, vol. 1, by Genevieve Foster, Scribner's

1954   *...And Now Miguel* by Joseph Krumgold, Crowell
Honor Books: *All Alone* by Claire Huchet Bishop, Viking; *Shadrach* by Meindert DeJong, Harper; *Hurry Home Candy* by Meindert DeJong, Harper; *Theodore Roosevelt, Fighting Patriot* by Clara Ingram Judson, Follett; *Magic Maize* by Mary and Conrad Buff, Houghton

1955   *The Wheel on the School* by Meindert DeJong, Harper
Honor Books: *The Courage of Sarah Noble* by Alice Dalgliesh, Scribner's; *Banner in the Sky* by James Ullman, Lippincott

1956   *Carry On, Mr. Bowditch* by Jean Lee Latham, Houghton
Honor Books: *The Secret River* by Marjorie Kinnan Rawlings, Scribner's; *The Golden Name Day* by Jennie Lindquist, Harper; *Men, Microscopes, and Living Things* by Katherine Shippen, Viking

1957   *Miracles on Maple Hill* by Virginia Sorensen, Harcourt
Honor Books: *Old Yeller* by Fred Gipson, Harper; *The House of Sixty Fathers* by Meindert DeJong, Harper; *Mr. Justice Holmes* by Clara Ingram Judson, Follett; *The Corn Grows Ripe* by Dorothy Rhoads, Viking; *Black Fox of Lorne* by Marguerite de Angeli, Doubleday

1958   *Rifles for Watie* by Harold Keith, Crowell
Honor Books: *The Horsecatcher* by Mari Sandoz, Westminster; *Gone-Away Lake* by Elizabeth Enright, Harcourt; *The Great Wheel* by Robert Lawson, Viking; *Tom Paine, Freedom's Apostle* by Leo Gurko, Crowell

1959   *The Witch of Blackbird Pond* by Elizabeth George Speare, Houghton
Honor Books: *The Family Under the Bridge* by Natalie S. Carlson, Harper; *Along Came a Dog* by Meindert DeJong, Harper; *Chucaro: Wild Pony of the Pampa* by Francis Kalnay, Harcourt; *The Perilous Road* by William O. Steele, Harcourt

1960   *Onion John* by Joseph Krumgold, Crowell
Honor Books: *My Side of the Mountain* by Jean George, Dutton; *America Is Born* by Gerald W. Johnson, Morrow; *The Gammage Cup* by Carol Kendall, Harcourt

1961   *Island of the Blue Dolphins* by Scott O'Dell, Houghton
Honor Books: *America Moves Forward* by Gerald W. Johnson, Morrow; *Old Ramon* by Jack Schaefer, Houghton; *The Cricket in Times Square* by George Selden, Farrar

1962   *The Bronze Bow* by Elizabeth George Speare, Houghton
Honor Books: *Frontier Living* by Edwin Tunis, World; *The Golden Goblet* by Eloise McGraw, Coward; *Belling the Tiger* by Mary Stolz, Harper

1963   *A Wrinkle in Time* by Madeleine L'Engle, Farrar
Honor Books: *Thistle and Thyme* by Sorche Nic Leodhas, Holt; *Men of Athens* by Olivia Coolidge, Houghton

1964   *It's Like This, Cat* by Emily Cheney Neville, Harper
Honor Books: *Rascal* by Sterling North, Dutton; *The Loner* by Esther Wier, McKay

1965   *Shadow of a Bull* by Maia Wojciechowska, Atheneum
Honor Book: *Across Five Aprils* by Irene Hunt, Follett

1966   *I, Juan de Pareja* by Elizabeth Borten de Trevino, Farrar
Honor Books: *The Black Cauldron* by Lloyd Alexander, Holt; *The Animal Family* by Randall Jarrell, Pantheon; *The Noonday Friends* by Mary Stolz, Harper

1967   *Up a Road Slowly* by Irene Hunt, Follett
Honor Books: *The King's Fifth* by Scott O'Dell, Houghton; *Zlateh the Goat and Other Stories* by Isaac Bashevis Singer, Harper, *The Jazz Man* by Mary H. Weik, Atheneum

1968   *From the Mixed-Up Files of Mrs. Basil E. Frankweiler* by E. L. Konigsburg, Atheneum
Honor Books: *Jennifer, Hecate, Macbeth, William McKinley, and Me, Elizabeth* by E. L. Konigsburg, Atheneum; *The Black Pearl* by Scott O'Dell, Houghton; *The Fearsome Inn* by Isaac Bashevis Singer, Scribner's; *The Egypt Game* by Zilpha Keatley Snyder, Atheneum

1969   *The High King* by Lloyd Alexander, Holt
Honor Books: *To Be a Slave* by Julius Lester, Dial; *When Shlemiel Went to Warsaw and Other Stories* by Isaac Bashevis Singer, Farrar

1970   *Sounder* by William H. Armstrong, Harper
Honor Books: *Our Eddie* by Sulamith Ish-Kishor Pantheon; *The Many Ways of Seeing: An Introduction to the Pleasures of Art* by Janet Gaylord Moore, World; *Journey Outside* by Mary Q. Steele, Viking

1971 *Summer of the Swans* by Betsy Byars, Viking
Honor Books: *Kneeknock Rise* by Natalie Babbitt, Farrar; *Enchantress from the Stars* by Sylvia Louise Engdahl, Atheneum; *Sing Down the Moon* by Scott O'Dell, Houghton

1972 *Mrs. Frisby and the Rats of NIMH* by Robert C. O'Brien, Atheneum
Honor Books: *Incident at Hawk's Hill* by Allan W. Eckert, Little, Brown; *The Planet of Junior Brown* by Virginia Hamilton, Macmillan; *The Tombs of Atuan* by Ursula K. Le Guin, Atheneum; *Annie and the Old One* by Miska Miles, Atlantic/Little, Brown; *The Headless Cupid* by Zilpha Keatley Snyder, Atheneum

1973 *Julie of the Wolves* by Jean George, Harper
Honor Books: *Frog and Toad Together* by Arnold Lobel, Harper, *The Upstairs Room* by Johanna Reiss, Crowell; *The Witches of Worm* by Zilpha Keatley Snyder, Atheneum

1974 *The Slave Dancer* by Paula Fox, Bradbury
Honor Book: *The Dark Is Rising* by Susan Cooper, Atheneum/McElderry

1975 *M. C. Higgins, the Great* by Virginia Hamilton, Macmillan
Honor Books: *Figgs & Phantoms* by Ellen Raskin, Dutton; *My Brother Sam Is Dead* by James Lincoln Collier and Christopher Collier, Four Winds; *The Perilous Guard* by Elizabeth Marie Pope, Houghton; *Philip Hall Likes Me, I Reckon Maybe* by Bette Greene, Dial

1976 *The Grey King* by Susan Cooper, Atheneum/McElderry
Honor Books: *The Hundred Penny Box* by Sharon Bell Mathis, Viking; *Dragonwings* by Laurence Yep, Harper

1977 *Roll of Thunder, Hear My Cry* by Mildred D. Taylor, Dial
Honor Books: *Abel's Island* by William Steig, Farrar; *A String in the Harp* by Nancy Bond, Atheneum/McElderry

1978 *Bridge to Terabithia* by Katherine Paterson, Crowell
Honor Books: *Anpao: An American Indian Odyssey* by Jamake Highwater, Lippincott; *Ramona and Her Father* by Beverly Cleary, Morrow

1979 *The Westing Game* by Ellen Raskin, Dutton
Honor Book: *The Great Gilly Hopkins* by Katherine Paterson, Crowell

1980 *A Gathering of Days: A New England Girl's Journal, 1830–32* by Joan Blos, Scribner's
Honor Book: *The Road from Home: The Story of an Armenian Girl* by David Kherdian, Greenwillow

1981 *Jacob Have I Loved* by Katherine Paterson, Crowell
Honor Books: *The Fledging* by Jane Langton, Harper; *A Ring of Endless Light* by Madeleine L'Engle, Farrar

1982 *A Visit to William Blake's Inn: Poems for Innocent and Experienced Travelers* by Nancy Willard, Harcourt
Honor Books: *Ramona Quimby, Age 8* by Beverly Cleary, Morrow; *Upon the Head of a Goat* by Aranka Siegal, Farrar

1983 *Dicey's Song* by Cynthia Voigt, Atheneum
Honor Books: *The Blue Sword* by Robin McKinley, Greenwillow; *Dr. De Soto* by William Steig, Farrar; *Graven Images* by Paul Fleischman, Harper; *Homesick: My Own Story* by Jean Fritz, Putnam; *Sweet Whispers, Brother Rush* by Virginia Hamilton, Philomel

1984 *Dear Mr. Henshaw* by Beverly Cleary, Morrow
Honor Books: *The Sign of the Beaver* by Elizabeth George Speare, Houghton; *A Solitary Blue* by Cynthia Voigt, Atheneum; *Sugaring Time* by Kathryn Lasky, Macmillan; *The Wish Giver* by Bill Brittain, Harper

1985 *The Hero and the Crown* by Robin McKinley, Greenwillow
Honor Books: *Like Jake and Me* by Mavis Jukes, Knopf; *The Moves Make the Man* by Bruce Brooks, Harper; *One-Eyed Cat* by Paula Fox, Bradbury

1986 *Sarah, Plain and Tall* by Patricia MacLachlan, Harper
Honor Books: *Commodore Perry in the Land of the Shogun* by Rhoda Blumberg, Lothrop; *Dogsong* by Gary Paulsen, Bradbury

1987 *The Whipping Boy* by Sid Fleischman, Greenwillow
Honor Books: *On My Honor* by Marion Dane Bauer, Clarion; *Volcano: The Eruption and Healing of Mount St. Helens* by Patricia Lauber, Bradbury; *A Fine White Dust* by Cynthia Rylant, Bradbury

1988 *Lincoln: A Photobiography* by Russell Freedman, Clarion/Houghton
Honor Books: *After the Rain* by Norma Fox Mazer, Morrow; *Hatchet* by Gary Paulsen, Bradbury

1989 *Joyful Noise: Poems for Two Voices* by Paul Fleischman, Harper
Honor Books: *In the Beginning: Creation Stories from Around the World* by Virginia Hamilton, Harcourt; *Scorpions* by Walter Dean Myers, Harper

1990 *Number the Stars* by Lois Lowry, Houghton
Honor Books: *Afternoon of the Elves* by Janet Lisle, Orchard Books; *Shabanu, Daughter of the Wind* by Suzanne Staples, Knopf; *Winter Room* by Gary Paulsen, Orchard

1991 *Maniac Magee* by Jerry Spinelli, Little, Brown
True Confessions of Charlotte Doyle by Avi, Orchard

1992 *Shiloh* by Phyllis Reynolds, Atheneum
Honor Books: *Nothing But the Truth* by Avi, Orchard; *The Wright Brothers* by Russell Freedman, Holiday House

1993 *Missing May* by Cynthia Rylant, Orchard
Honor Books: *What Hearts* by Bruce Brooks, HarperCollins; *The Dark-Thirty: Southern Tales of the Supernatural* by Patricia McKissack, Knopf; *Somewhere in Darkness* by William Dean Myers, Scholastic

1994 *The Giver* by Lois Lowry, Houghton
Honor Books: *Crazy Lady!* by Jane Leslie Conly, HarperCollins; *Dragon's Gate* by Laurence Yep, Harper Trophy; *Eleanor Roosevelt* by Russell Freedman, Clarion

1995 *Walk Two Moons* by Sharon Creech, HarperCollins
Honor Books: *Catherine, Called Birdy* by Karen Cushman, Clarion; *The Ear, the Eye, and the Arm* by Nancy Farmer, Orchard

1996 *The Midwife's Apprentice* by Karen Cushman, Clarion
Honor Books: *What Jamie Saw* by Carolyn Coman, Front Street; *The Watsons Go to Birmingham–1963* by Christopher Paul Curtis, Delacorte

1997 *The View from Saturday* by E. L. Konigsburg, Atheneum
Honor Books: *A Girl Named Disaster* by Nancy Farmer, Orchard; *Moorchild* by Eloise McGraw, McElderry; *The Thief* by Megan Whalen Turner, Greenwillow; *Belle Prater's Boy* by Ruth White, Farrar, Straus & Giroux

1998 *Out of the Dust* by Karen Hesse, Scholastic
Honor Books: *Ella Enchanted* by Gail Carson Levine, HarperCollins;

Lily's Crossing by Patricia Reilly Giff, Delacorte; *Wringer* by Jerry Spinelli, HarperCollins

1999 *Holes* by Louis Sachar, Frances Foster
Honor Book: *A Long Way from Chicago* by Richard Peck, Dial

2000 *Bud, Not Buddy* by Christopher Paul Curtis, Delacorte
Honor Books: *Getting Near to Baby* by Audrey Couloumbis, Putnam; *Our Only May Amelia* by Jennifer L. Holm, HarperCollins; *26 Fairmount Avenue* by Tomie dePaola, Putnam

2001 *A Year Down Yonder* by Richard Peck, Dial
Honor Books: *Hope Was Here* by Joan Bauer, Putnam; *Because of Winn-Dixie* by Kate DiCamillo, Candlewick; *Joey Pigza Loses Control* by Jack Gantos, Farrar, Straus & Giroux; *The Wanderer* by Sharon Creech, HarperCollins

2002 *A Single Shard* by Linda Sue Park, Houghton
Honor Books: *Everything on a Waffle* by Polly Horvath, Farrar, Straus & Giroux; *Carver: A Life In Poems* by Marilyn Nelson, Front Street

2003 *Crispin: The Cross of Lead* by Avi, Hyperion
Honor Books: *The House of the Scorpion* by Nancy Farmer, Atheneum; *Pictures of Hollis Woods* by Patricia Reilly Giff, Random House; *Hoot* by Carl Hiaasen, Knopf; *A Corner of The Universe* by Ann M. Martin, Scholastic; *Surviving the Applewhites* by Stephanie S. Tolan, HarperCollins

2004 *The Tale of Despereaux: Being the Story of a Mouse, a Princess, Some Soup, and a Spool of Thread* by Kate DiCamillo, illustrated by Timothy Basil Ering, Candlewick
Honor Books: *Olive's Ocean* by Kevin Henkes, Greenwillow; *An American Plague: The True and Terrifying Story of the Yellow Fever Epidemic of 1793* by Jim Murphy, Clarion

2005 *Kira-Kira* by Cynthia Kadohata, Atheneum
Honor Books: *Al Capone Does My Shirts* by Gennifer Choldenko, Putnam; *The Voice That Challenged a Nation: Marian Anderson and the Struggle for Equal Rights* by Russell Freedman, Houghton; *Lizzie Bright and the Buckminster Boy* by Gary D. Schmidt, Houghton

The Phoenix Award

The Phoenix Award is given by the Children's Literature Association to a book published twenty years earlier that did not receive any major award.

1985 *Mark of the Horse Lord* by Rosemary Sutcliff, Walck
1986 *Queenie Peavy* by Robert Burch, Viking
1987 *Smith* by Leon Garfield, Constable
1988 *The Rider and His Horse* by Eric Christian Haugaard, Houghton
1989 *The Night Watchman* by Helen Cresswell, Macmillan
1990 *Enchantress from the Stars* by Sylvia Louise Engdahl, Atheneum
1991 *A Long Way from Verona* by Jane Gardam, Macmillan
1992 *A Sound of Chariots* by Mollie Hunter, Harper
1993 *Carrie's War* by Nina Bawden, Harper; Honor Book: *A Proud Taste for Scarlet and Miniver* by E. L. Konigsberg, Atheneum

1994   *Of Nightingales That Weep* by Katherine Paterson, Crowell
Honor Books: *My Brother Sam Is Dead* by James Lincoln Collier and Christopher Collier, Four Winds; *Listen for the Fig Tree* by Sharon Bell Mathis, Viking

1995   *Dragonwings* by Laurence Yep, Harper & Row
Honor Book: *Tuck Everlasting* by Natalie Babbit, Farrar

1996   *The Stone Book* by Alan Garner, Collins
Honor Book: *Abel's Island* by William Steig, Farrar

1997   *I Am the Cheese* by Robert Cormier, Pantheon

1998   *A Chance Child* by Jill Paton Walsh, Macmillan
Honor Books: *Devil in Vienna* by Doris Orgel, Dial; *Beauty* by Robin McKinley, Harper & Row

1999   *Throwing Shadows* by E. L. Konigsburg, Atheneum
Honor Book: *Beauty* by Robin McKinley, HarperCollins

2000   *Keeper of the Isis Light* by Monica Hughes, Atheneum
Honor Book: *The Fledgling* by Jane Langton, HarperCollins

2001   *The Seventh Raven* by Peter Dickinson, Gollancz
Honor Book: *The Night Journey* by Kathryn Lasky, Warner

2002   *A Formal Feeling* by Zibby Oneal, Fawcett
Honor Book: *Story for a Black Night* by Clayton Bess, Parnassus

2003   *The Long Night Watch* by Ivan Southall, Methuen
Honor Book: *A Solitary Blue* by Cynthia Voigt, Atheneum

2004   *White Peak Farm* by Berlie Doherty, Methuen
Honor Book: *Angel Square* by Brian Doyle, Douglas & McIntyre

2005   *The Catalogue of the Universe* by Margaret Mahy, McElderry
Honor Book: *Fire and Hemlock* by Diana Wynne Jones, Morrow

The Scott O'Dell Award for Historical Fiction

The award was established in 1981 by Scott O'Dell and is administered by the advisory committee of the Bulletin of the Center for Children's Books. The book must be historical fiction, have unusual literary merit, be written by a citizen of the United States, and be set in the New World. It must have been published in the previous year by a U.S. publisher and must be written for children or young adults. The award is not given every year.

1984   *The Sign of the Beaver* by Elizabeth George Speare, Houghton
1985   *The Fighting Ground* by Avi [Wortis], Harper & Row
1986   *Sarah, Plain and Tall* by Patricia MacLachlan, Harper & Row
1987   *Streams to the River* by Scott O'Dell, Houghton
1988   *Charlie Skedaddle* by Patricia Beatty, Morrow
1989   *Honorable Prison* by Lyll B. De Jenkins, Lodestar
1990   *Shades of Gray* by Carolyn Reeder, Macmillan
1991   *Time of Troubles* by Pieter Van Raven, Scribner's
1992   *Stepping on the Cracks* by Mary D. Hahn, Clarion Books
1994   *Bull Run* by Paul Fleischman, HarperCollins

1995   *Under the Blood-Red Sun* by Graham Salisbury, Delacorte
1996   *The Bomb* by Theodore Taylor, Harcourt
1997   *Jip: His Story* by Katherine Paterson, Lodestaer
1999   *Forty Acres and Maybe a Mule* by Harriette Robinet, Atheneum
2000   *Two Suns in the Sky* by Miriam Bat-Ami, Front Street
2001   *The Art of Keeping Cool* by Janet Taylor Lisle, Atheneum
2002   *The Land* by Mildred Taylor, Fogelman
2003   *Trouble Don't Last* by Shelley Pearsall, Knopf
2004   *A River Between Us* by Richard Peck, Dial
2005   *Worth* by A. LaFaye, Simon & Schuster

The Orbis Pictus Award for Outstanding Nonfiction

This award, established in 1990 by the National Council of Teachers of English (NCTE) to recognize excellence in nonfiction writing, commemorates *Orbis Pictus* (1657), considered the first informational book written for children.

1990   *The Great Little Madison* by Jean Fritz; Honor Books: *The Great American Gold Rush* by Rhoda Blumberg; *The News About Dinosaurs* by Patricia Lauber

1991   *Franklin Delano Roosevelt* by Russell Freedman; Honor Books: *Seeing Earth from Space* by Patricia Lauber; *Arctic Memories* by Normee Ekoomiak

1992   *Flight: The Journey of Charles Lindbergh* by Robert Burleigh; Honor Books: *Now Is Your Time! The African-American Struggle for Freedom* by Walter Dean Myers; *Prairie Vision: The Life and Times of Solomon Butcher* by Pam Conrad

1993   *Children of the Dust Bowl: The True Story of the School at Weedpatch Camp* by Jerry Stanley; Honor Books: *Talking to Artists* by Pat Cummings; *Come Back, Salmon* by Molly Cone

1994   *Across America on an Emigrant Train* by Jim Murphy; Honor Books: *To the Top of the World: Adventures with Arctic Wolves* by Jim Brandenburg; *Making Sense: Animal Perception and Communication* by Bruce Brooks

1995   *Safari Beneath the Sea: The Wonder World of the North Pacific Coast* by Diane Swanson; Honor Book: *Wildlife Rescue: The Work of Dr. Kathleen Ramsay* by Jennifer Owings Dewey

1996   *The Great Fire* by Jim Murphy; Honor Books: *Dolphin Man: Exploring the World of Dolphins* by Laurence Pringle; *Rosie the Riveter: Women Working on the Home Front in World War II* by Penny Colman

1997   *Leonardi da Vinci* by Diane Stanley; Honor Books: *Full Steam Ahead: The Race to Build a Transcontinental Railroad* by Rhoda Blumberg; *The Life and Death of Crazy Horse* by Russell Freedman; *One World, Many Religions: The Ways We Worship* by Mary Pope Osborne

1998   *An Extraordinary Life: The Story of a Monarch Butterfly* by Laurence Pringle. Honor Books: *A Drop of Water: A Book of Science and Wonder* by Walter Wick; *A Tree Is Growing* by Arthur Doros; *Charles A. Lindbergh: A Human Hero* by James Cross Giblin; *Kennedy Assassinated! The World*

Mourns: A Reporter's Story by Wilborn Hampton; *The Tragic Fate of the California Indians from the Gold Rush* by Jerry Stanley

1999   *Shipwreck at the Bottom of the World* by Jennifer Armstrong. Honor Books: *Black Whiteness: Admiral Byrd Alone in the Antarctic* by Robert Burleigh; *Fossil Fuel: The Rivalry of the First American Dinosaur Hunters* by Thom Holmes; *Hottest, Coldest, Highest, Deepest* by Steve Jenkins; *No Pretty Pictures: A Child of War* by Anita Lobel

2000   *Through My Eyes* by Ruby Bridges and Margo Lundell. Honor Books: *At Her Majesty's Request: An African Princess in Victorian England* by Walter Dean Myers; *Clara Schumann: Piano Virtuoso* by Susanna Reich; *Mapping the World* by Sylvia A. Johnson; *The Snake Scientist* by Sy Montgomery and Nic Bishop; *The Top of the World: Climbing Mount Everest* by Steve Jenkins

2001   *Hurry Freedom: African Americans in Gold Rush California* by Jerry Stanley. Honor Books: *The Amazing Life of Benjamin Franklin* by James Cross Giblin and Michael Dooling; *America's Champion Swimmer: Gertrude Ederle* by David A. Adler and Terry Widener; *Michelangelo* by Diane Stanley; *Osceola: Memories of a Sharecropper's Daughter* by Alan B. Govenar and Shane W. Evans; *Wild & Swampy* by Jim Arnosky

2002   *Black Potatoes: The Story of the Great Irish Famine, 1845–1850* by Susan Campbell Bartoletti. Honor Books: *The Cod's Tale* by Mark Kurlansky, illustrated by S. D. Schindler; *The Dinosaurs of Waterhouse Hawkins: An Illuminating History of Mr. Waterhouse Hawkins, Artist and Lecturer* by Barbara Kerley, illustrated by Brian Selznick; *Martin's Big Words: The Life of Martin Luther King, Jr.* by Doreen Rappaport, illustrated by Bryan Collier

2003   *When Marian Sang: The True Recital of Marian Anderson: The Voice of a Century* by Pam Muñoz Ryan, illustrated by Brian Selznick. Honor Books: *Confucius: The Golden Rule* by Russell Freedman, illustrated by Frederick Clement; *Emperor's Silent Army: Terracotta Warriors of Ancient China* by Jane O'Connor; *Phineas Gage: A Gruesome but True Story about Brain Science* by John Fleischman; *Tenement: Immigrant Life on the Lower East Side* by Raymond Bial; *The Fly: The Story of the Wright Brothers* by Wendie C. Old, illustrated by Robert Andrew Parker

2004   *An American Plague: The True and Terrifying Story of the Yellow Fever Epidemic of 1793* by Jim Murphy. Honor Books: *Empire State Building: When New York Reached for the Skies* by Elizabeth Mann, illustrated by Alan Witschonke; *In Defense of Liberty: The Story of America's Bill of Rights* by Russell Freedman; *Leonardo; Beautiful Dreamer* by Robert Byrd; *The Man Who Made Time Travel* by Kathryn Lasky, illustrated by Kevin Hawkes; *Shutting Out the Sky: Life in the Tenements of New York 1880–1924* by Deborah Hopkinson

2005   *York's Adventures with Lewis and Clark: An African-American's Part in the Great Expedition* by Rhoda Blumberg. Honor Books: *Actual Size* by Steve Jenkins; *The Race to Save the Lord God Bird* by Phillip Hoose; *Secrets of the Sphinx* by James Cross Biblin, illustrated by Bagram Ibatoulline; *Seurat and La Grande Jatte: Connecting the Dots* by Robert Burleigh; *The Voice That Challenged a Nation: Marion Anderson and the Struggle for Equal Rights* by Russell Freedman

Selected Children's Magazines

American Girl. Pleasant Company, Box 998, Middleton, WI 53562

Boy's Life (boys 8 to 15). Boy Scouts of America, P. O. Box 15279, Irving, TX 75015

Calliope (world history). Cobblestone Publishing Co., 30 Grove Street, Peterborough, NH 03458

Chickadee (preschoolers). Owlkids, 10 Lower Spadina Avenue, Suite 400, Toronto, Ontario, Canada, M5V 2Z2

Cobblestone (history). Cobblestone Publishing Co., 30 Grove Street, Peterborough, NH 03458

Cousteau Kids (underwater life). Cousteau Society, Membership Department, 710 Settlers Landing Road, Hampton, VA 23669.

Cricket. Cobblestone Publishing Co., 30 Grove Street, Peterborough, NH 03458

Dolphin Log (underwater life). Cousteau Society, Inc., 8440 Santa Monica Blvd., Los Angeles, CA 90069

Dragon Fly. National Science Teachers Association, American Association for the Advancement of Science, 1840 Wilson Boulevard, Arlington, VA 22201

Faces (anthropology and natural history). Cobblestone Publishing Co., 30 Grove Street, Peterborough, NH 46206

Footsteps (African American heritage). Cobblestone Publishing Co., 30 Grove Street, Peterborough, NH 03458.

Highlights for Children. P. O. Box 269, Columbus, OH 43272

Hopscotch (girls 6 to 12) P. O. Box 1292, Saratoga Springs, NY 12866

Ladybug. Cobblestone Publishing Co., 30 Grove Street, Peterborough, NH 03458

National Geographic Kids. P.O. Box 64066, Tampa, FL 33664

New Moon. New Moon Publishing Company, 34 E. Superior Street, Suite 200, Duluth, MN 55802

Odyssey (science). Cobblestone Publishing Co., 30 Grove Street, Peterborough, NH 03458

Owl (science and nature). Owlkids, 10 Lower Spadina Avenue, Suite 400, Toronto, Ontario, Canada M5V 2Z2

Ranger Rick (animals and environment). National Wildlife Federation, 11100 Wildlife Center Drive, Reston, VA 20190

Skipping Stones (international multicultural). P.O. Box 3939, Eugene, OR 97403

Spider (literature and art). Cobblestone Publishing Co., 30 Grove Street, Peterborough, NH 03458

Sports Illustrated for Kids. P.O. Box 61990, Tampa, FL 33661

3-2-1/Contact (science, natural history, technology). Children's Television Workshop, 1 Lincoln Plaza, New York, NY 10023

Wonder Science. American Chemical Society, 1155 Sixteenth Street NW, Washington, DC 20036

Your Big Backyard (nature). National Wildlife Federation, 11100 Wildlife Center Drive, Reston, VA 20190

Zillions. Consumer Union, 101 Truman Avenue, Yonkers, NY 10703

Selected Reviewing Media for Children's Books

Appraisal (science books)
ALA (American Library Association)
Booklist
The ALAN Review
Bulletin of the Center for Children's Books
Children's Catalog
Children's Literature Assembly Bulletin (NCTE)
The Horn Book Magazine
Kirkus Reviews
Language Arts
Library Journal
Library Talk
The New Advocate
Parents' Choice
Publishers Weekly
Quarterly of the Children's Literature Association
Reading Teacher
School Library Journal
Science Books and Films
VOYA—Voice of Youth Advocates
Wilson Library Journal

Selected Websites about Children's Literature

American Library Association
www.ala.org/alsc/awards.html

Association for Library Service for Children
www.ala.org/ala.alsc/

Canadian Library Association Book of the Year for Children Award
www.cla.ca/awards/boyc.htm

Children's Book Council
www.adelaide.sa.gov.au/children'slibrary/awardlist.html

Children's Library Association
www.cla.ca/awards/boycwinners.html

The Children's Literature Association
ebbs.english.vt.edu/chla/Phoenix.html

The Children's Literature Web Guide
www.ucalgary.ca/-dkbrown

Children's Picture Book Database
www.lib.muohio.edu/pictbks/

Database of Award-Winning Children's Literature
www.dawcl.com

International Board on Books for Young People
www.ibby.org/

International Children's Digital Library
www.icdlbooks.org

International Reading Association
www.reading.org

Kay Vandergrift's Children's Literature Page
www.scils.rutgers.edu/~kvander/ChildrenLit/index.html

Kay Vandergrift's Social History of Children's Literature
www.scils.rutgers.edu/~kvander/HistoryofChildLit/index.html

The Library Association
la-hq.org.uk/directory/medals_awards/medals_pastcar.html

National Book Award for Young People's Literature
www.geocities.com/adbooks./nba.html

National Book Award Winners
www.nationalbook.org

National Council for the Social Studies
www.ncss.org

National Council of Teachers of English (NCTE)
www.ncte.org/elem/awards

National Science Teachers Association
www.nsta.org

Glossary of Literary Terms

Allegory a literary work in which characters and actions represent abstractions

Alliteration repetition of initial consonant sound

Allusion indirect reference to something or someone outside the literary work

Antagonist force in conflict with protagonist; usually designated as self, another person, society, nature

Anthropomorphism the giving of human qualities to animals or objects

Assonance repetition of vowel sound in phrase

Backdrop setting generalized or relatively unimportant setting

Ballad verse narrative of love, courage, the supernatural; may be of folk origin

Biography the history of the life of an individual

cadence rhythmic flow in prose

Character human being, real or personified animal or object taking a role in literature

Character development filling out a variety of character traits to provide the complexity of a human being

Chronological order events related in the order of their happening

Classic literary work that lives to be read and reread

Cliché overused term that has lost meaning

Cliff-hanger unresolved suspense that concludes a chapter

Climax action that precipitates resolution of conflict

Closed ending conclusion leaving no plot questions unanswered

Coincidence chance concurrence of events

Complication early action; part of rising plot

Concept an idea around which a work may be written

Condescension an attitude or tone that underestimates the reader

Conflict struggle between protagonist and opposing force

Connotation associative or emotional meaning of a word

Consonance repetition of consonant sound in phrase

Cumulative tale a story, often folk in origin, that continually repeats a series, then adds a new item

Denotation explicit or dictionary meaning

Denouement final or closing action following the climax

Diction choice of words or wording

Didacticism in literature, an instructive or moralistic lesson often at the expense of entertainment

Distanced tone an attitude of objectivity through which a story is told

Dramatic point of view *see* objective or dramatic point of view

Dynamic character one who changes in the course of the story

Echo words repeated in familiar pattern

End rhyme rhyming words at the ends of poetic lines

Epic long narrative poem about a heroic figure whose actions reveal the values of the culture

Episodic plot plot with independent, short-storylike chapters linked by characters or theme more than by action

Explicit theme theme stated clearly in the story

Exposition presentation of essential information needed for understanding the action

Fable brief story, usually with animal characters, that states a didactic theme or moral

Falling action final or closing action following climax; denouement

Fantasy story about the nonexistent or unreal in which action may depend on magic or the supernatural

Figurative language devices making comparisons, saying one thing in terms of another

First-person point of view "I" narration in which a person's experiences, thoughts, and feelings are told by himself or herself

Flashback return to event that occurred before present scene; retrospect

Flat character one that is little developed

Foil a character whose contrasting traits point up those of a central character

Folk epic long narrative poem passed down by word of mouth, often about a hero

Folk rhyme rhymes passed down by word of mouth

Folktale story passed down by word of mouth

Foreshadowing hints of what is to come

Formula fiction fiction with a hackneyed or repetitive sequence of events

Frame framework in which a story is set, frequently noted at beginning and end

Genre a kind or type of literature that has a common set of characteristics

High fantasy a type of fantasy characterized by conflict between good and evil

Hyperbole exaggeration or overstatement

Imagery verbal appeals to the senses

Implicit theme theme implied from the story's context

Inevitability sense that it had to happen; in literature, a sense that the outcome was necessary and inescapable

Integral setting essential and specific setting that influences character, plot, and theme

Internal rhymes rhymes in a line that are after first and before last words

Irony recognition of reality different from what it truly is

Legend a traditional narrative of a people, often with some basis in historical truth

Limerick five-line humorous verse with strict traditional rhythm and rhyme pattern

Limited omniscient point of view third-person narration in which story is seen through the mind(s) of one or a few characters

Lyric poem songlike poem; compact expression of feeling

Metaphor implied comparison

Meter somewhat regular rhythm pattern of stressed and unstressed syllables in a line of poetry

Motif recurring element in literary work, often found in traditional literature

Myth story originating in folk beliefs and showing supernatural forces operating

Narrative order sequence in which events are recounted

Narrative poem poem that tells a story

Objective or dramatic point of view third-person narration in which actions and speeches are recorded without interpretation

Omniscient point of view an all-knowing writer tells the story in third person

Onomatopoeia words that sound like their meanings, such as *meow, moo*

Open ending final outcome of conflict unknown

Parody imitation of known form for comic effect

Personification giving human traits to nonhumans or objects

Phonetic intensive use of sound to enhance meaning

Picture book a book that relies on pictures to enlarge or illuminate the text; the pictures may provide a correlative story of their own

Plot sequence of events involving character in conflict

Poetry distilled and imaginative expression of feeling

Point of view the mind(s) through which the reader sees the story

Pourquoi tales that respond to the question "why?"

Primary theme major underlying and unifying truth of a story

Progressive plot plot with central climax

Protagonist central character in the conflict

Pun humorous use of a word with several meanings

Realism story based on the possible, though not necessarily probable

Resolution falling action following climax

Rhyme repetition of identical or similar stressed sound or sounds

Rhythm recurring flow of strong and weak beats

Rising action exposition and complications that lead to the climax

Romance story with scenes and incidents remote from ordinary life

Romantic novel story focuses on boy-girl relationships

Round character a fully developed or three-dimensional character

Science fiction story that relies on invention or extension of nature's laws, not on the supernatural or magical

Secondary theme less important or minor theme of a story

Sensationalism focus on the thrilling or startling

Sentiment emotion or feeling

Sentimentality overuse of sentiment; false arousal of feelings

Setting the time and place in which the action occurs

Simile stated comparison, usually using *like* or *as*

Sound effect any device of sound that affects meaning

Static character one who does not change in the course of the story

Stereotype character possessing expected traits of a group rather than being an individual

Stock character flat character with very little development; found in numerous stories, such as folktales

Style mode of expression

Suspense state of uncertainty that keeps the reader reading

Symbol person, object, situation, or action operating on two levels of meaning—literal and figurative or suggestive

Synesthesia simultaneous appeal to several senses

Theme statement giving the underlying truth about people, society, or the human condition, either explicitly or implicitly

Tone writer's attitude toward his or her subject and readers

Touchstone example of excellence referred to for comparison

Understatement reverse exaggeration or playing down

Verse here used to denote rhyming metrical structure with less emotional intensity than poetry

Vicarious experience experience available to readers through reading about it rather than living it

Wordless picture book a book that has no written narrative but tells a story with pictures alone

Credits

Art Credits

p. 2: Illustration copyright © 1952 by Garth Williams Renewed © 1980 by Garth Williams.

p. 12: Illustration from *Wild Robert* by Diana Wynne-Jones; illustrated by Mark Zug. Reprinted by permission of HarperCollins Publishers.

p. 38: Illustration from *The Three Pigs* by David Wiesner. Copyright © 2001 by David Wiesner. Reprinted by permission of Clarion Books/Houghton Mifflin Company. All rights reserved.

p. 74: Illustration from *In the Time of the Drums* by Kim L. Siegelson; illustrated by Brian Pinkney. Jacket painting © 1999 by Brian Pinkney. Reprinted by permission of Hyperion Books for Children.

p. 98: Illustration from *Salsa Stories* by Lulu Delacre. Copyright © 2000 by Lulu Delacre. Reprinted by permission of Scholastic Inc.

p. 130: Illustration reprinted with the permission of Aladdin Paperbacks, an imprint of Simon & Schuster Children's Publishing Division from *The Landry News* by Andrew Clements, illustrated by Brian Selznick (New York, 2000).

p. 148: Illustration copyright © 1995 by Vera Rosenberry from *Binya's Blue Umbrella* by Ruskin Bond. Reprinted by permission of Boyds Mills Press, Inc.

p. 168: Illustration from *The Jamie and Angus Stories* by Anne Fine; illustrated by Penny Dale. Text copyright © 2002 by Anne Fine. Illustrations copyright © by Penny Dale. Reprinted by permission of the publisher Candlewick Press, Inc., Cambridge, MA, on behalf of Walker Books Ltd., London.

p. 188: Illustration from *Bandit's Moon* by Sid Fleischman. Illustrations copyright © 1998 by Joseph A. Smith.

p. 210: Illustration from *Toad Triumphant* by William Horwood; illustrated by Patrick Benson. Copyright © 1998 by the author and reprinted by permission of St. Martin's Press, LLC.

p. 238: Illustration from *A Hippopotamusn't and Other Animal Stories* by J. Patrick Lewis; pictures by Victoria Chess. Copyright © 1990 by Victoria Chess for pictures. Used by permission of Dial Books for Young Readers, a division of Penguin Young Readers Group, a member of Penguin Group (USA) Inc., 345 Hudson Street, New York, NY 10014. All rights reserved.

p. 270: Illustration copyright © 2000 by David Small, illustrations, from *So You Want to Be President?* by Judith St. George, illustrated by David Small. Used by permission of Philomel Books, an imprint of Penguin Putnam Books for Young Readers, a division of Penguin Putnam Inc.

p. 286: Illustration from *Black Potatoes: The Story of the Great Irish Famine, 1845–1850* by Susan Campbell Bartoletti (Boston: Houghton Mifflin, 2001).

Literary Credits

Poetry

Adoff, Arnold. "Let the Biter Beware" from *Chocolate Dreams* by Arnold Adoff. Text copyright © 1989 by Arnold Adoff. Reprinted by permission of HarperCollins Publishers.

Aldis, Dorothy. "Fourth of July Night" from *Hop, Skip and Jump!* by Dorothy Aldis, copyright © 1934, renewed copyright © 1961 by Dorothy Aldis. Reprinted by permission of G. P. Putnam's Sons, a division of Penguin Putnam Books for Young Readers Group, a Member of Penguin Group (USA) Inc., 345 Hudson Street, New York, NY 10014. All rights reserved.

Behn, Harry. "Circles" from *The Little Hill* Poems & Pictures by Harry Behn. Copyright © 1949 Harry Behn. Renewed © 1977 by Alice L. Behn. Reprinted by permission of Marian Reiner.

Brown, Abbie Farwell. "A Music Box" from *Pinafore Palace* by Abbie Brown Farwell, edited by Kate Douglas Wiggin and Nora Archibald Smith.

Carroll, Lewis. "Jabberwocky" reprinted by permission of Simon & Schuster Books for Young Readers, an imprint of Simon & Schuster Children's Publishing Division, from *Alice's Adventures in Wonderland* by Lewis Carroll (New York, 1963).

Cullen, Countee. "Incident" reprinted by permission of GRM Associates, Inc.; agents for the Estate of Ida M. Cullen. From the book *Color* by Countee Cullen. Copyright © 1925 by Harper & Brothers; copyright renewed 1953 by Ida M. Cullen.

Dickinson, Emily. "The Moon Was but a Chin of Gold" reprinted by permission of the publishers and the Trustees of Amherst College from *The Poems of Emily Dickinson*, Thomas H. Johnson, ed. (Cambridge, MA: The Belknap Press of Harvard University Press, copyright © 1951, 1955, 1979, 1983 by the President and Fellows of Harvard College).

Dickinson, Emily. "There is no Frigate like a Book" reprinted by permission of the publishers and the Trustees of Amherst College from *The Poems of Emily Dickinson*, Thomas H. Johnson, ed. (Cambridge, MA: The Belknap Press of Harvard University Press, copyright © 1951, 1955, 1979, 1983 by the President and Fellows of Harvard College).

Fisher, Aileen. "At Night" from *Out in the Dark and Daylight* by Aileen Fisher. Copyright © 1980 by Aileen Fisher. Reprinted by permission of Marian Reiner on behalf of the Boulder Public Library Foundation, Inc.

Florian, Douglas. "The Wind" from *Autumnblings: Poems and Paintings* by Douglas Florian. Copyright © 2003 by Douglas Florian. Reprinted by permission of HarperCollins Publishers.

Francis, Robert. "The Base Stealer" from *Collected Poems, 1936–1976*. Copyright © 1976 by Robert Francis and reprinted by permission of Wesleyan University Press.

George, Kristine O'Connell. "New Friends Talking" and "Passing Notes" from *Swimming Upstream: Middle Grade Poems* by Kristen O'Connell George. Text copyright © 2002 by Kristen O'Connell George. Reprinted by permission of Clarion Books, an imprint of Houghton Mifflin Company. All rights reserved.

Giovanni, Nikki. "the drum" from *Spin a Soft Black Song* by Nikki Giovanni. Copyright © 1971, 1985 by Nikki Giovanni. Reprinted by permission of Hill and Wang, a division of Farrar, Straus and Giroux, LLC.

Grimes, Nikki. "His Name Jessie" from *What is Goodbye?* by Nikki Grimes. Illustrated by Raul Colon. Text copyright © 2004 by Nikki Grimes. Illustrations copyright © 2004 by Raul Colon. Reprinted by permission of Hyperion Books for Children.

Hall, Jim. "White Trash" reprinted from *False Statements* by permission of Carnegie Mellon University Press. Copyright © 1986 by Jim Hall.

Hughes, Langston. "Dream Deferred" from *The Collected Poems of Langston Hughes* by Langston Hughes. Copyright © 1994 by The Estate of Langston Hughes. Reprinted by permission of Alfred A. Knopf, a division of Random House, Inc. and Harold Ober Associates.

Hughes, Langston. "I Loved My Friend" from *The Collected Poems of Langston Hughes* by Langston Hughes. Copyright © 1994 by The Estate of Langston Hughes. Reprinted by permission of Alfred A. Knopf, a division of Random House, Inc. and Harold Ober Associates.

Hunt, Evelyn Tooley. "Mama Is a Sunrise" from *The Lyric* by Evelyn Tooley Hunt.

Kennedy, X. J. "A Choosy Wolf." Copyright © 1979 by X. J. Kennedy. First appeared in *The Phantom Ice Cream Man: More Nonsense Verse,* published by Atheneum. Reprinted by permission of Curtis Brown, Ltd.

Livingston, Myra Cohn. "74th Street" from *The Malibu and Other Poems* by Myra Cohn Livingston. Copyright © 1972 by Myra Cohn Livingston. Reprinted by permission of Marian Reiner.

Livingston, Myra Cohn. "Whispers" from *Whispers and Other Poems* by Myra Cohn Livingston. Copyright © 1958, 1986 by Myra Cohn Livingston. Reprinted by permission of Marian Reiner.

Moore, Lilian. "Bike Ride," from *Think of Shadows* by Lilian Moore. Copyright © 1975, 1980 by Lilian Moore. Reprinted by permission of Marian Reiner.

Nash, Ogden. "Obvious Reflections" from *The Face Is Familiar* by Ogden Nash. Copyright © 1940 by Ogden Nash, renewed. Reprinted by permission of Curtis Brown, Ltd.

Nelson, Marilyn. "The Last Rose of Summer" from *Carver: A Life in Poems* by Marilyn Nelson (Front Street, 2001). Reprinted by permission of Boyds Mills Press.

Prelutsky, Jack. "I Wave Good-bye When Butter Flies" from *Something Big Has Been Here* by Jack Prelutsky. Text copyright © 1990 by Jack Prelutsky. Reprinted by permission of HarperCollins Publishers.

Richards, Laura E. "The Owl and the Eel and the Warming Pan" from *Tirra Lirra* by Laura E. Richards. Copyright © 1930, 1932 by Laura E. Richards; copyright © renewed 1960 by Hamilton Richards. Reprinted by permission of Little, Brown and Co., Inc.

Sandburg, Carl. "Lost" from *Chicago Poems* by Carl Sandburg. Copyright © 1916 by Holt, Rinehart and Winston, and renewed © 1944 by Carl Sandburg. Reprinted by permission of Harcourt, Inc.

Stevenson, Robert Lewis. "The Swing" reprinted by permission of Simon & Schuster Books for Young Readers, an imprint of Simon & Schuster Children's Publishing Division from *A Child's Garden of Verses* by Robert Lewis Stevenson, illustrated by Tasha Tudor (New York, 1999).

Updike, John. "October." Copyright © 1965 by John Updike. All rights reserved. Reprinted from *A Child's Calendar* by permission of Holiday House, Inc.

Williams, William Carlos. "The Winds" from *Collected Poems: 1909–1939,* Volume I, by William Carlos Williams. Copyright © 1938 by New Directions Publishing Corp. Reprinted by permission of New Directions Publishing Corp.

Text

Bridges, Ruby. Excerpt from *Through My Eyes* by Ruby Bridges (New York: Scholastic 1999).

Choldenko, Gennifer. Excerpt from *Al Capone Does My Shirts* by Gennifer Choldenko (New York: G. P. Putnam's Sons, 2004).

DiCamillo, Kate. Excerpt from *Because of Winn-Dixie* by Kate DiCamillo (Cambridge, MA: Candlewick Press, 2000).

DiCamillo, Kate. Excerpt from *The Tale of Despereaux* by Kate DiCamillo (Cambridge, MA: Candlewick Press, 2003).

Freedman, Russell. Excerpt from *The Voice that Challenged a Nation: Marian Anderson and the Struggle for Equal Rights* by Russell Freedman (New York: Houghton Mifflin, 2004).

Gantos, Jack. Excerpt from *Joey Pigza Swallowed the Key* by Jack Gantos. Copyright © 1998 by Jack Gantos. Reprinted by permission of Farrar, Straus and Giroux, LLC.

Snicket, Lemony. Excerpt from *The Ersatz Elevator* by Lemony Snicket. Text copyright © 2001 by Lemony Snicket. Reprinted by permission of HarperCollins Children's Books, a division of HarperCollins Publishers.

Stanley, Diane. Excerpt from *Joan of Arc* by Diane Stanley (New York: William Morrow and Company, Inc., 1998).

Stewart, David. Excerpt from "The limerick is furtive and mean" by David Stewart in *Smithsonian,* September 2002.

Taylor, Mildred D. Excerpt from *The Land* by Mildred D. Taylor. Copyright © 2001 by Mildred D. Taylor. Used by permission of Dial Books for Young Readers, a division of Penguin Young Readers Group, a member of Penguin Group (USA) Inc., 345 Hudson Street, New York, NY 10014. All rights reserved.

Tolan, Stephanie. Excerpt from *Surviving the Applewhites* by Stephanie Tolan. Copyright © 2002 by Stephanie S. Tolan. Reprinted by permission of HarperCollins Publishers.

Whelan, Gloria. Excerpt from *Homeless Bird* by Gloria Whelan (New York: HarperCollins Children's Books, 2000).

White, E. B. Excerpts from *Charlotte's Web* by E. B. White. Copyright © 1952 by E. B. White. Text copyright renewed 1980 by E. B. White. Reprinted by permission of HarperCollins Publishers.

Wolff, Virginia Euwer. *True Believer* by Virginia Euwer Wolff. Excerpt reprinted by permission of Atheneum Books for Young Readers, an imprint of Simon & Schuster Children's Publishing Division from *True Believer* by Virginia Euwer Wolff. Copyright © 2001 by Virginia Euwer Wolff.

Woodson, Jacqueline. Excerpt from *Miracle's Boys* by Jacqueline Woodson (New York: G. P. Putnam's Sons, 2000).

Index